H

MW00474947

Hockey's Wildest Season

The Changing of the Guard in the NHL, 1969–1970

JOHN G. ROBERTSON

McFarland & Company, Inc., Publishers

Jefferson, North Carolina

LIBRARY OF CONGRESS CATALOGUING-IN-PUBLICATION DATA

Names: Robertson, John G., 1964– author.
Title: Hockey's wildest season : the changing of the guard
in the NHL, 1969–1970 / John G. Robertson.
Description: Jefferson, North Carolina : McFarland & Company, Inc.,
Publishers, 2021 | Includes bibliographical references and index.
Identifiers: LCCN 2021003338 | ISBN 9781476680705 (paperback : acid free paper) ∞
ISBN 9781476641256 (ebook)
Subjects: LCSH: Hockey—United States—History. | Hockey—
Canada—History. | National Hockey League—History.
Classification: LCC GV | DDC 796.962/64—dc23
LC record available at https://lccn.loc.gov/2021003338

BRITISH LIBRARY CATALOGUING DATA ARE AVAILABLE

ISBN (print) 978-1-4766-8070-5
ISBN (ebook) 978-1-4766-4125-6

Front cover: Boston Bruins defenseman Bobby Orr scoring
the Stanley Cup–winning goal in overtime against
the St. Louis Blues on May 10, 1970

Printed in the United States of America

McFarland & Company, Inc., Publishers
Box 611, Jefferson, North Carolina 28640
www.mcfarlandpub.com

First and foremost, this book is dedicated to those aging hockey fans who remember the excitement provided by the National Hockey League at the end of the 1960s and the beginning of the 1970s—and to those fans who were born sometime afterward but wish they had been around to see it. It certainly was a fun era to follow the sport.

Secondly, the book is also dedicated to the coaches, players, officials, and peripheral figures from the 1969–70 NHL season who passed away between January 2018 and January 2021—the timespan when this book was being researched, written and edited. They include George Armstrong, André Boudrias, Arnie Brown, Danny Grant, Ted Green, Bruce Hood, Harry Howell, Red Kelly, Ted Lindsay, Ab McDonald, John McKenzie, Stan Mikita, Jim Neilson, Bob Nevin, Dean Prentice, Ken Schinkel, Eddie Shack and Red Sullivan. There are likely more hockey figures mentioned in the pages of this book whose recent deaths escaped my notice. Their omissions are, of course, accidental. May they all rest in peace.

Acknowledgments

For helping make this book come to fruition, special thanks go to...

- Steve Currier who provided me with a bonanza of newspaper articles and other information about the woebegone Oakland/California Seals franchise.
- Alicia Juillet who kindly provided me with photos of the 1969–70 Detroit Red Wings.
- Taryn Daneman of the National Hockey League's Office of Officials for providing photographs of John Ashley and Bruce Hood.
- Carl Madden for his sharp-eyed proofreading efforts and his plentiful helpful suggestions.
- Christopher Sykes for his technical assistance.
- The passionate hockey fans who maintain and constantly update the excellent websites hockey-reference.com and hockeydb.com. They truly provide a gold mine of information and statistics for researchers—and everyone else who cares about the history of the sport and the accuracy of its statistics.
- The hockey history buffs who posted snippets of game videos from the 1969–70 NHL season on YouTube. Nothing beats being able to view actual footage from these contests.
- The people who maintain the Google Newspaper Archive website. It is a great repository of prime-source research material.
- My niece, Laura Neal, who provided me with detailed chiropractic information about Terry Sawchuk's uncommon spinal condition.

Table of Contents

Acknowledgments   vi

Notes on Names, Spellings and Terms   xi

Preface: Childhood Memories   1

PART I: THE NHL BEFORE 1969–70

1. What a Difference a Decade Makes!   6
2. The Original Six Era: Big Three, Little Three   9
3. From Six Teams to 12: The NHL Doubles Down   12
4. The Mild, Mild West: Not Separate but Not Equal   20

PART II: THE 1969–70 NHL SEASON

5. Mayhem in Ottawa: The Wayne Maki–Ted Green Incident   34
6. The Old Boys' Club: The NHL's Geezer Goaltenders   42
7. How Mick Jagger Nearly Caused an NHL Forfeit   53
8. Organic Matter: The East Dominates the All-Star Game   56
9. A Cool Wedding Quashed   61
10. "Boston's Mighty Orr" Leads the Bruins   63
11. The New York Rangers: Revamped and Dangerous   72
12. Chicago Black Hawks Rising … with Shutouts   80
13. The Suddenly Soaring Detroit Red Wings   86
14. Montreal Canadiens: Unknowingly on Thin Ice   91
15. Toronto Maple Leafs: Treading Water   97
16. St. Louis Blues: The Biggest of the Small Fish   101
17. Pittsburgh Penguins: Improving and Anonymous   103

18. Minnesota North Stars: Drawn and Quartered   106
19. Oakland Seals: Struggling to Be Relevant   110
20. The Kings: Losing and Loathing in Los Angeles   116
21. Philadelphia Flyers: 24 Ties … But Still One Short   119
22. The Plummeting New Yorkers   124
23. It Happened One Night: The Rangers' Long Bus Ride   126
24. Surging Popularity: The Numbers Speak for Themselves   129
25. Saturday, April 4: Clearly Clarifying Nothing   131
26. Sunday, April 5 (A): Theater of the Absurd   135
27. Sunday, April 5 (B): Five Empty-Net Goals   145

PART III: THE ALL-AMERICAN 1970
STANLEY CUP PLAYOFFS

28. The Stanley Cup … Canada's Trophy?   154
29. The Quarterfinals: Blowouts, Brawls and a Bounty   158
30. Boston–Chicago Semifinal: A Surprising Sweep   175
31. St. Louis–Pittsburgh Semifinal: The Blues Are Tested   182

PART IV: THE FINALS—FROM
SHADOW TREATMENT TO CLASSIC FINISH

32. Game #1: Plante Goes Down; Bruins Go Up   190
33. Game #2: Another Half Dozen Goals   197
34. Game #3: "We Are Looking Forward to Sunday"   200
35. "First Annual Bobby Orr Awards Luncheon"   204
36. Anticipation   206
37. Game #4: "And What Could Be Better Than That?"   208
38. A Photo for the Ages   216

PART V: DENOUEMENT

39. Celebrations   222
40. Michel Brière: An Athlete Dying Young   224
41. An Unexpected Resignation   229
42. The Strange Death of Terry Sawchuk   232

43. Social Notice: Say, Who's That Fellow Dating Bernie Geoffrion's Daughter? 236
44. The NHL's Tiebreaker and Divisional Realignment 237
45. The Cup, the Bruins and the Rest of the Original Six 241
46. The 1967 Expansion Teams 246

Aftermath: Miscellany 256
Chapter Notes 259
References 269
Index 271

Notes on Names,
Spellings and Terms

- The nickname of Chicago's NHL franchise is spelled as one word: "Blackhawks." However, from the club's inception in 1926 to 1986, the most common version used in newspapers and other print media was two words: "Black Hawks." Since this book largely deals with the 1969–70 NHL season, I have decided to be faithful to the frequent spelling of the day and use the two-word version. (In 1986, it was discovered that the one-word spelling was accurate as per the original documents from the NHL which granted the Chicago franchise. Therefore, every two-word spelling of the name for 60 years had been technically incorrect.)

- The Seals franchise—which remarkably had four different names at varying times during its shaky nine years in California—was officially called the Oakland Seals in 1969–70. That is how I refer to the team throughout this book when referring to that specific season.

- During the two-division era of the NHL from 1967–68 to 1973–74, the names of those divisions were East and West—not Eastern and Western—although the latter pair did frequently appear in adjective form in print media. The NHL's official website (NHL.com) confirms East and West as the official names of the divisions in 1969–70, so those are the terms I have used throughout this book.

- Over the NHL's history, there seems to have been no agreement regarding whether the last playoff series of the season is the Stanley Cup "final" (singular) or "finals" (plural). The terms were used interchangeably. My preference is the plural—after all, there is more than one game played in the championship round. Today the NHL oddly prefers the singular, but in 1970 there was no particularly dominant term. Thus, you will see both terms used frequently in this book. They mean exactly the same thing.

- I have done my best to properly include the correct accents on French-Canadian players' names. This was seldom done in anglophone newspapers in 1970. Even today, very few English-language hockey reports in the print media bother to apply accents—which is a shame because accents certainly assist in correct pronunciation. Jimmy Lennon, boxing's golden-voiced ring announcer, was once asked why he took such extreme care to pronounce the names of every boxer correctly—even the most obscure journeyman pugilists. Lennon replied, "Every man is entitled to the dignity of his own name." I concur. Accordingly, I have included the correct accents on players' and officials' first and last names in the cases of Claude Béchard, Jean Béliveau, André Boudrias, Michel Brière, Jacques Laperrière, Réal Lemieux, Jean Paul Parisé, and others. If I have omitted an accent from anyone's name—and I probably have—it is an unfortunate oversight.

- I have, however, deliberately used the anglicized spelling of Montreal; that is, I have excluded the acute accent over the letter E that appears in the French spelling (Montréal). No disrespect is intended. Anglophones and francophones pronounce the city's name quite differently. In this case I have stayed true to the English-language research materials that were almost exclusively consulted for this project.

Preface:
Childhood Memories

"Don't you wish you could take a single childhood memory and blow it up into a bubble and live inside it forever?"
—Sarah Addison Allen

Vague childhood memories can be powerful but inaccurate forces; they are often responsible for one's perceptions of the past. With the passage of several decades, a person may rightfully wonder whether some distant event really occurred or if it were the byproduct of some confusing cerebral trick.

I cannot remember a time when I was not a hockey fan. Although I began collecting 10-cent wax packets of O-Pee-Chee hockey cards at the tender age of three because seemingly every boy on my block in Galt, Ontario, was engaged in the hobby, my first memories of watching the National Hockey League are from the 1969–70 season just after my sixth birthday. *Hockey Night in Canada* was (and is) something of a Canadian institution on Saturday nights, but the earliest games that have stuck in my mind all these years later are not *HNIC* telecasts. Instead they are the Sunday afternoon NHL encounters that were broadcasted on American television at that time. They were the *NHL Game of the Week* contests that aired on the Columbia Broadcasting System. Living close to the American border—as most Canadians do—I could watch them on the CBS affiliate from Buffalo, New York. In 1970, that particular station was known as WBEN-TV. Dan Kelly—arguably the top play-by-play announcer in hockey history—provided the captivating commentary for most of those games.

The afternoon starting times—mandated by CBS, of course—certainly made those games more accessible and viewer-friendly to someone my age who had an early bedtime. Half a century after the fact I faintly recall watching a Toronto-Boston game that winter in the family living room on

1

our black-and-white TV set, a contest that featured a bevy of goals. (In researching this book, I found a 7–6 Boston win over Toronto on Sunday afternoon, February 1, 1970, that was played at Boston Garden, confirming my memory was indeed accurate. "Bruins shade Leafs in 7–6 free-for-all" declared a headline in the next day's *Montreal Gazette*. To my great delight, portions of the original CBS broadcast of this game have been preserved and posted on YouTube by a kind, hockey-history-loving soul!) The next game I distinctly remember watching on that same television set was the farcical match on Sunday, April 5, 1970, between the Detroit Red Wings and the New York Rangers from Madison Square Garden. I am reasonably certain the NHL would prefer its knowledgeable fans completely forget about that sham.

In 1970 I knew as much about hockey as any six-year-old Canadian boy did, but I certainly saw some peculiar things on the TV screen and heard others just as weird on the radio on that spring Sunday that absolutely flummoxed me: Why were the New York Rangers pulling their goalie for a sixth attacker in a game they were already leading by six goals? Why were the Montreal Canadiens seemingly unconcerned that the Chicago Black Hawks were scoring a plethora of empty-net goals on them? "It's complicated," I was told by the adults in the room (who themselves were desperately trying to figure out the NHL's tie-breaking rules and the all-important arithmetic guiding this truly odd behavior).

Indeed, the situations definitely were complicated, far beyond the comprehension of this kindergarten pupil regardless of how closely I followed the sport. A half dozen years later, when I began developing a love for sports history, I decided to read as much as I could about that Sunday's key NHL games to make sure I had not imagined all the irregular chaos. The proof was there. It was real … and wild … and crazy … and unprecedented. As bizarre as those final regular-season games from the 1969–70 regular season were, they certainly kindled my interest in how that NHL season would eventually conclude. They compelled me to watch as many Stanley Cup playoff games that spring as my early curfews would allow. I was hooked.

It was a bizarre campaign indeed, that 1969–70 NHL season. The final weekend of the regular season and the subsequent Stanley Cup playoffs were merely the two-pronged climax of a thoroughly wild and captivating NHL season that began in the preseason with a near fatality in one of hockey's ugliest incidents and ended in one of the sport's most iconic moments. Between the horrifying start to the season and the fabulous finish there were several captivating and compelling developments. They include these gems:

- A modest, youthful Boston defenseman won the league's scoring title—an utterly unheard-of accomplishment. Moreover, he did it quite comfortably. In the process, he became the NHL's most talked-about star and the face of the sport.
- A discarded rookie goalie from the Montreal Canadiens became a tremendous phenom in Chicago, setting a remarkable modern-era record for shutouts in a season. His brother was his greatest nemesis.
- Another Montreal goaltender—one of the NHL's most popular players—angrily retired from the Habs in January, but shortly thereafter was coaxed into joining the unfashionable Minnesota North Stars. He led his new teammates to a surprise playoff berth.
- A hugely popular British musical group very nearly caused an NHL game in Los Angeles to be forfeited.
- Three veteran Detroit teammates—with a combined age of 111— gelled to become the most effective line in the NHL.
- That same Detroit team curiously fired its coach after just two games—despite the Red Wings having a perfect record at the time.
- The annual NHL All-Star Game featured a weird controversy about, of all things, the organist at the St. Louis Arena.
- The Philadelphia Flyers spectacularly and inexplicably collapsed in the waning weeks of the season, frittering away what seemed to be a certain playoff berth.
- The New York Rangers, front-runners for most of the season, surprisingly fell apart in March and nearly matched the Flyers' dubious cave-in. Their season was salvaged only by an absurd victory on the final Sunday of the regular season.

The NHL was turned upside-down in 1969–70. The former have-nots from the Original Six era became the league's new dominant teams while the usual standard bearers faltered into insignificance. (As it turned out, the three most successful teams in NHL history failed to win a single play-off game in 1970.) It was also a time when the NHL's six expansion teams from 1967 were struggling—not very successfully—to be accepted as equals with their established counterparts. That lofty pursuit was still a few years away from happening.

In 1969–70, the 12 NHL teams combined to score 2,649 goals in 456 regular-season games and another 206 goals in 34 Stanley Cup playoff matches. Along the meandering way there were the usual amounts of sur-prises (both good and bad), controversies, amusing anecdotes, feel-good stories, emerging stars, fading veterans, and struggling teams one sees during every hockey season. Not long after the season ended, a couple of noteworthy tragedies occurred too.

So let's turn back the calendar—more than 50 calendars, actually—to the autumn of 1969, to the fun, fascinating, free-wheeling, 12-team NHL, and examine the circuit's 53rd season—the wildest campaign in its colorful history.

PART I

The NHL Before 1969–70

1

What a Difference a Decade Makes!

"Hello, Canada and hockey fans in the United States and
Newfoundland..."
—the usual phrase with which Foster Hewitt
of *Hockey Night in Canada* began his
pre–1949 radio broadcasts

It is the evening of Thursday, April 14, 1960. The scoreboard clock at
Toronto's Maple Leaf Gardens—one of Canada's two hockey cathedrals—
has wound down to zero. The gentle sound of bells wafts over the generally sullen crowd in the building; Maple Leaf Gardens doesn't have a coarse
buzzer to signal when a period has concluded. Tonight's game is over.
Jacques Plante, the visiting team's flaky but exquisite goaltender, removes
his protective mask and jumps for joy in his goal crease. Moments later
he is engulfed by happy, rambunctious teammates in their road white uniforms who swarm off the bench to celebrate.

There had been little drama on the ice this night. The fabulous Montreal Canadiens decisively beat the hometown Toronto Maple Leafs,
4–0—sweeping the gallant but overmatched challengers in four straight
games—to capture an unprecedented *fifth successive Stanley Cup*. Only
the Montreal players seem genuinely surprised by their success. "This was
an easy game for the Canadiens,"[1] opined Austin (Dink) Carroll, a longtime *Montreal Gazette* sports reporter in his report the following day. Most
everyone concurs.

The entire series really was no contest. The Canadiens outscored
the Maple Leafs by an aggregate tally of 15–5 in the four contests of the
1960 Stanley Cup finals. Toronto did not score more than two goals in any
game. This particular championship was the most impressive in the Canadiens' string of five: Montreal romped through both rounds of the playoffs without losing a single game, equaling the 1952 Detroit Red Wings' feat
under that same playoff format. Les Habitants—"the Habs" in abbreviated

6

English—are seemingly invincible. They have the best coach, the best goalie, the best forward and the best defenseman in the NHL. One page in the next day's *Gazette* contained a quarter-page cartoon by John Collins. It featured coach Hector (Toe) Blake, the Stanley Cup, and a large "5." The caption said, "Les Canadiens sont là!" ("The Canadiens are there!") Similarly, another quarter of that same broadsheet page was occupied by a congratulatory ad from Molson Breweries—the team's major sponsor. Individual head photos of every Hab on the roster bedecked an enormous numeral five. "Congratulations, Canadiens. Five in a row," was the succinct message. It had obviously been created well in advance for the inevitable occasion.

It was also legendary Montreal star Maurice (Rocket) Richard's final NHL game. Richard, age 38, did not score one of Montreal's four goals, but he did notch his 82nd career Stanley Cup goal in Game #3 two nights earlier. After Game #4 he bluntly stated, "I just can't keep up the pace anymore. Some of the younger fellows on the team can skate all night. I can't."[2]

Excluding nostalgic value, Richard's imminent retirement from hockey was almost a non-issue for the mighty Canadiens. He was hardly needed at this stage in his illustrious career. There was plenty of young, fresh talent in the Montreal lineup to replace the aging superstar. That always seemed to be the case in Montreal.

Why should the Habs worry for even a moment about their future? In every single NHL season since 1950–51, Montreal has participated in the Stanley Cup finals. That makes *ten successive trips to the championship round* for the

Montreal superstar Maurice (Rocket) Richard is pictured here circa 1954. He was a substantial factor in the Canadiens' dynasty during the late 1950s (courtesy Library and Archives Canada; MIKAN inventory #3612870).

vaunted Habs. They are to the National Hockey League what the New York Yankees are to Major League Baseball—even more so. During the 1950s, an autumn without the Yankees in World Series is almost as strange as a spring without the Montreal Canadiens vying for the Stanley Cup. A few years later, in narrating a re-released version the NHL's official highlight film of the 1960 Stanley Cup playoffs, Brian McFarlane of *Hockey Night in Canada* unequivocally states this about the 1959–60 version of the Habs: "Most fans agree this is the finest team ever assembled." The fact that the Maple Leafs were clearly the second-best club in the six-team NHL in 1959–60 and still were no match for the Canadiens only reinforces the champions' dominance over the entire league.

The Stanley Cup had again been won by a Canadian-based NHL team. Such a familiar trend, it seemed, could go on indefinitely.

Fast forward ten years: The 1970 Stanley Cup playoffs feature teams from Pennsylvania, Missouri, Minnesota, and California. The Chicago Black Hawks, Boston Bruins, Detroit Red Wings and New York Rangers add a ring of familiarity to the tournament. Yet the teams that are *absent* from the NHL's annual postseason shindig include the illustrious Montreal Canadiens and Toronto Maple Leafs. Those two decorated franchises had combined to win all but six Stanley Cups since 1942. How could that have possibly occurred?

Times were changing as the turbulent 1960s came to an end. The National Hockey League was changing too.

2

The Original Six Era
Big Three, Little Three

"The season of 1942–43 was the start of an upsurge for the Montreal Canadiens that was to make them one of the flashiest and most powerful teams in the NHL."[1]
—hockey historian Brian McFarlane

"The [Original Six] NHL was comprised of the 100 finest players in the world and the fans knew who we were. They could identify us. They knew we belonged. A game was an event. It was special theater."[2]
—Eric Nesterenko, NHL player
from 1951 to 1972

It was the era of Toe, Punch, the Big M, Boom Boom, the Rocket … and the Pocket Rocket too. It was the era of the Golden Jet, Moose, Chico, Woody, Chief, Cowboy, the Production Line, Bronco, the Punch Line, Mr. Hockey, Pie, and the Uke Line. It was also the era of fearless bare-faced goalies named Turk, Mr. Goalie, Jake the Snake, Gump, Apple Cheeks, Steady Eddie, and Sugar Jim. It was the "Original Six" era of the National Hockey League.

Hockey fans and historians romantically tend to look back at the misnamed Original Six period of the NHL with rose-colored glasses. Many of the sport's followers fondly think the 25 seasons it encompassed from 1942–43 to 1966–67 were the greatest period in the sport's history. It certainly was—if you were a fan of the Montreal Canadiens, Toronto Maple Leafs or Detroit Red Wings. On the other hand, if you supported the Boston Bruins, Chicago Black Hawks or New York Rangers, it was basically the Dark Ages of hockey. One telling statistic says it all: Of the 25 Stanley Cups awarded in those seasons, 24 of them were won by Montreal, Toronto and Detroit. It was not just a quirky anomaly; there were good reasons why those three teams dominated while the other three clubs struggled to merely be competitive.

Iconic Original Six hockey: Maurice Richard scores one of his 544 career goals (courtesy Library and Archives Canada; MIKAN inventory #4951617).

For many years the NHL had a rule that gave the Montreal Canadiens first crack at Quebec-based players. It was originally put in place during the 1930s and 1940s. It was later brought back in 1963 with the debut of the amateur draft. The league also adopted territorial rules for recruitment. Each team had a 50-mile radius from which it had the first chance to sign amateur players—so long as they had not already committed to any other NHL team. The 50-mile rule wasn't just for Montreal—other teams were granted the same territorial rights too. But because so many of the Habs' best players ended up being French Canadian—hardly a huge surprise— most fans misremember the rule only as only applying to Montreal. Of course, Toronto also enjoyed a similar privilege, being able to secure players who lived within 50 miles of Maple Leaf Gardens. Detroit, too, because of geography, was able to tap into a rich vein of amateur Canadian hockey talent.

Still, the point is often overlooked that the territorial rule only applied to players who were not already signed by another team. Once a player agreed to an NHL sponsorship-level contract, the NHL club could assign him to one of its junior squads. Any team could persuade a youngster to sign a commitment card when he came of age, but the Habs and Leafs generally knew where the raw talent lay. Montreal was especially adept at recruiting players for their vast farm system. Hardly any prospects in Quebec eluded the clutches of the Montreal Canadiens. (Rod Gilbert and Jean Ratelle were two very noteworthy exceptions who were signed by the New York Rangers. Marcel Pronovost and Pit Martin were other French-Canadians who opted to sign with teams other than the Habs.)

It was an era when nearly 100 percent of NHL players were born in or at least raised in Canada. (At one point in the early 1960s, Tommy Williams was the only American player firmly established in the NHL. He was born in Duluth, Minnesota.) The league's territorial rules meant that Boston, Chicago, and especially New York were left with much slimmer pickings than Toronto, Montreal or Detroit. Those clubs generally relied upon acquiring players who lived outside the protected areas of the Habs, Leafs and Red Wings or those athletes who had somehow been overlooked by them. The Maple Leafs and Canadiens also benefited from something that could not be measured—being the two Canadian-based teams featured every week on *Hockey Night in Canada*. Few Canadian boys in that era grew up rooting for non–Canadian NHL teams. If a promising Canadian youngster had the opportunity, he typically signed a commitment card with either Montreal or Toronto, naturally. The results were predictable.

Perhaps an even more telling statistic than the lack of diversity among the Stanley Cup winners during the Original Six era is the consistency regarding the most inept NHL clubs—the teams that failed to qualify for the Stanley Cup playoffs—over that same time. From the 1942–43 season through the 1966–67 campaign, the three teams that most commonly watched the playoffs from the sidelines were the New York Rangers (18 times), Chicago Black Hawks (13 times), and Boston Bruins (11 times). Toronto was absent from the postseason just four times in that same era. Detroit missed the playoffs only three times. Montreal failed but once. In no season during the 25 years of Original Six era did two of the NHL's three dominant teams not qualify for the Stanley Cup playoffs simultaneously. In every season Montreal, Toronto or Detroit was in the Stanley Cup final. Only three finals featured matchups between two American-based clubs.

Numbers do not lie: The Original Six era of the NHL was indisputably comprised of three routinely dominant teams and three have-not clubs that struggled to achieve mediocrity. The post–1967 expansion era would forever change that aspect of the NHL within a few years.

From Six Teams to 12
The NHL Doubles Down

"With stability achieved under the Original Six, President Clarence Campbell wanted to double the size of the [National Hockey] League by adding a second division, mainly to reap the financial rewards found in TV licensing deals that had become primary economic drivers for other sporting leagues."[1]

—Montreal Canadiens historian
Andrew Zadarnowski

The 1967–68 NHL season was perhaps the most pivotal in its history. It established a clear line between the old and the new. Hockey was abruptly casting off its past and entering a modern, rollicking era.

With the demise of the lowly and unfashionable Brooklyn Americans after the 1941–42 NHL season, for the next 25 seasons the NHL operated as a tight-knit, six-team organization with its member clubs firmly established in Boston, Chicago, Detroit, Montreal, New York City and Toronto. By the 1966–67 campaign, the final season of the NHL's misnamed "Original Six" era, each team played every other team 14 times in the regular season—seven times at home and seven times on the road. (Thus, if a playoff series went seven games, it was possible for two teams to meet 21 times in a single NHL season. It happened frequently.) The league's games were contested in stately, imposing, concrete arenas whose names exuded hockey tradition: Boston Garden, Chicago Stadium, Olympia Stadium, Montreal Forum, Madison Square Garden, and Maple Leaf Gardens. Overnight passenger railroad service to every NHL city was sufficient to cover all the league's compact travel needs. Four of the six teams qualified for the Stanley Cup playoffs each spring. Both semifinals and the Cup finals were always best-of-seven affairs. Win eight playoff games and you win the Stanley Cup. It was all so comfortingly familiar to hockey fans on both side of the border. Why shouldn't it last forever?

In the early 1950s there was some scuttlebutt about Cleveland being granted an NHL franchise as the city had a good track record of supporting the Barons, its minor league team, but nothing came of it. Chicago opted to play a select few home games in St. Louis and St. Paul to test the waters of westward hockey expansion. Again, it amounted to little more than an occasional curiosity.

But times were changing. Cross-country air travel was greatly reducing the time required to traverse the continent. By the start of the 1960s, there really were no logistical or geographical reasons why there should not be NHL teams located west of the Mississippi River. Major League Baseball had proven that point in the late 1950s. Some esteemed sports writers believed that NHL expansion was long overdue. Jim Murray of the *Los Angeles Times* was one such scribe. He wrote,

> The National Hockey League makes a mockery of its title by restricting its franchises to six teams. Other big-money sports are expanding … but hockey likes it there in the back of the cave. Any businessman will tell you that in a dynamic economy you either grow or perish. Baseball had to be dragged kicking and screaming out of its rut. Football groped its way on the end of a short rope. Hockey just can't sit there forever, braiding buggy whips.[2]

However, it was not until 1965 that the NHL began seriously studying the idea of expanding beyond its traditional markets. By that time, the league realized it would not reap anywhere near the lucrative TV money of the other major North American team sports unless there was more than just a handful of teams in the NHL family. There was also some external pressure. The minor professional Western Hockey League was threatening to declare itself a major league and make a legal challenge to play for the Stanley Cup. Expansion was both sensible and necessary for the long-term future of the NHL. A $3.6-million television deal with CBS was also an undeniable incentive for the league to put more NHL teams in major American markets.

On February 9, 1966, for the princely price of $2 million apiece, the NHL announced that six expansion franchises would enter the league in 1967–68, dramatically doubling its size—and changing it forever. The new clubs were the Los Angeles Kings, Minnesota North Stars, Philadelphia Flyers, Pittsburgh Penguins, St. Louis Blues and Oakland Seals. [Author's note: When the Seals began play in 1967–68, they were called the "California Seals." Crooner Bing Crosby was part of its ownership group! Their name was changed to the "Oakland Seals" within a month. By the 1970–71 season they were very briefly called the "Bay Area Seals" and shortly thereafter the "California Golden Seals." In their rocky nine-year history, the unfashionable Seals never led the NHL in anything other than losses and name changes.] Applications from Cleveland, Louisville, Baltimore, Buffalo and

Vancouver were all examined and rejected. The quaint and cozy six-team NHL passed into beloved nostalgia, a development that was thoroughly mourned by hockey purists.

News of the NHL's six chosen cities did not sit particularly well with Canada's federal government. Prime Minister Lester Pearson, an avid sports fan, was irate and incredulous when Vancouver was excluded—especially since the city had been deemed an "acceptable" candidate for a new franchise when the NHL's expansion process began in 1965. Pearson haughtily declared, "The NHL's decision to expand only in the United States impinges on the sacred principles of all Canadians."[3] He was not alone in his disgust. Former Toronto Maple Leafs owner Conn Smythe said it was "disgraceful" that Vancouver had been denied an expansion team. (Calmer heads blamed Vancouver's exclusion on the indisputable fact that a proposal to build a modern arena—at taxpayers' expense—had been defeated by Vancouverites in a municipal referendum.) Interestingly, it was rumored that the Toronto Maple Leafs and Montreal Canadiens combined to thwart Vancouver's application because they were not especially keen in having a third Canadian team share in the lucrative television money the Canadian Broadcasting Corporation generated for them with its wildly popular *Hockey Night in Canada* telecasts. It was also widely believed that the Maple Leafs quashed the Buffalo application, not wanting another NHL franchise just a 90-minute drive away, albeit across an international border.

Three of the chosen cities (St. Louis, Pittsburgh and Philadelphia) previously had NHL teams in the 1920s and 1930s when the league attempted its first major foray into the United States. The Pittsburgh Pirates entered the league in 1925–26; they joined the Boston Bruins and New York

Lester Pearson, Canada's prime minister from 1963 to 1968, was a highly vocal critic of the 1967 expansion when Vancouver was not among the six cities granted an NHL franchise. The Vancouver Canucks would eventually join the NHL in 1970 (courtesy Library and Archives Canada; MIKAN inventory #4951614).

Americans as the league's third American entry. The Pirates played their home games at Duquesne Gardens—an inadequate wooden building that could accommodate fewer than 5,700 fans, including standees. (If the city's fire code was ignored, sometimes as many as 8,000 fans could squeeze into the arena.) Still, the team never attracted much of a following in their five seasons in Pittsburgh and only enjoyed mediocre results. They qualified for the Stanley Cup playoffs in 1926 and 1928. Each time they were eliminated in the first round by the eventual Cup champions. The Pirates were mired in about $400,000 debt by the end of their forgettable five-season run in Pittsburgh. In their last NHL season, 1929–30, the Pirates suffered through a calamitous campaign, winning just five of 44 games.

One of the team's co-owners was former world lightweight boxing champion Benny Leonard. He shifted operations to Philadelphia for the 1930–31 season where the team was known as the Quakers. It was Leonard's intention to move the Quakers back to Pittsburgh once a new, more spacious arena was constructed. That did not happen until Pittsburgh's Civic Arena opened in 1961. The Quakers were a disaster at the box office and in the standings. Playing at the Philadelphia Arena—a structure that could only hold approximately 5,500 spectators—the Quakers started the season with two straight shutout losses. After 21 games Philadelphia had a dismal record of 1-19-1. Finishing their lone NHL season with a pitiful 4–36–4 record, the team reputedly lost another $100,000—a staggering sum at the time. The Quakers ceased operation shortly thereafter. They did not exactly fold, however. For the next five seasons, a team representative dutifully attended the annual NHL governors' meetings to announce that Philadelphia would not have a team competing in the upcoming season. The NHL ended the silly charade by formally dissolving the Pittsburgh/Philadelphia franchise on May 7, 1936. Mourners were few.

St. Louis' NHL history before 1967 was similar to Philadelphia's: brief and utterly forgettable. It consisted of just one season—1934–35—after the original Ottawa Senators sought greener pastures in Missouri. The transplanted Senators were rechristened the St. Louis Eagles. Playing out of the huge St. Louis Arena—the second largest indoor facility in the United States at the time with its capacity to hold more than 14,000 spectators—the Eagles did not give their fans very much to cheer about. Their record was a lackluster 11–31–6, placing them at the bottom of the Canadian Division standings. The Eagles ceased operations not long after their final game concluded on March 19, 1935. (Hall-of-Famer Syd Howe holds the unique distinction of having played for both the St. Louis Eagles and Philadelphia Quakers!) Thus, if the hockey fans of St. Louis, Pittsburgh and Philadelphia remembered their old teams at all, there were few fond memories connected to them.

With the six new franchises awarded, a special NHL expansion draft was conducted at the Queen Elizabeth Hotel in Montreal on Tuesday, June 6, 1967. This was less than 24 hours after the Six-Day War began, so the conflict between Israel and Egypt was getting far more press attention than the destinies of 120 hockey players. The draft's purpose was to stock the new teams with professional players in an orderly and fair manner. "The conditions laid down for the fulfillment of franchises have been met,"[4] announced NHL president Clarence Campbell on June 5, who would personally supervise the draft. That statement was not just polite fluff. For a moment it looked like the Philadelphia Flyers might lose their franchise due to a technical glitch far beyond their control. A power failure in New Jersey and some parts of Pennsylvania was preventing the ownership group of the Flyers from providing telegraphed proof that their $2 million franchise fee had been properly transferred to the NHL. "I was sweating it out," said a relieved and happy Bill Putnam, the Flyers' president. "The Fidelity Bank [of Philadelphia] finally managed to get through by using New York Telephone tie lines to contact the Royal Bank [in Montreal] to authorize payment."[5]

The expansion draft was an absolute necessity because virtually every active professional hockey player of repute in North America was already under contract with one of the six existing franchises or some minor professional team. The six NHL expansion teams had to get players from somewhere. Some noteworthy veterans who were unprotected muddied the waters by stating they would rather hang up their skates than play for one of the six new teams. Thus, each expansion club risked having a drafted player retire from hockey than join a nascent squad. Ex-Hab superstar Bernie (Boom Boom) Geoffrion, who, at 36, was concluding an outstanding Hall-of-Fame career with the New York Rangers, was the most vocal of the dissenters. In 1964, Geoffrion had angrily walked out on the Montreal Canadiens when he was not named the team's captain, so no one figured he was bluffing about refusing to be drafted by an NHL expansion team. Accordingly, none dared draft the petulant Boom Boom. Geoffrion's attitude was the exception rather than the norm, however. Most players realistically viewed expansion as a welcome way of breaking into the NHL for the first time or extending their dwindling careers for another year or two.

Sam Pollock, the esteemed general manager of the Montreal Canadiens, was largely responsible for creating the rules for the 1967 expansion draft. Here were the basic regulations he devised for the event:

• The six existing teams each created a list of designated players who *could not* be selected in the draft. Each team's "protected list" included one goaltender and 11 other players.

- Each of the six new teams selected, one at a time, 20 unprotected players (two of which were goaltenders) from the Original Six clubs. A lottery determined the order in which each expansion team drafted a player.
- Goaltenders, two per team, would be selected in the first two rounds. The subsequent 18 rounds were for non-goalies only.
- Junior players could not be drafted, nor could anyone who was playing professionally but still young enough to be in the junior ranks. In effect, this exempted any player born on or after June 1, 1946, from the expansion draft. (Boston's 19-year-old rookie sensation Bobby Orr was the most prominent example.) Furthermore, any players who had contracts dated before June 1, 1966, with two minor professional outfits—the Western Hockey League and Central Professional Hockey League—were also deemed untouchable.
- With slight variations, as soon as an existing team lost a player to the draft, that team could add another player to its protected list. Thus, some players were initially eligible to be drafted but were later protected by their existing teams.
- The expansion teams were under time constraints to make their selections: After a player was drafted, the next team in the draft order had just three minutes to decide on its pick. A team losing a player to the draft was also allotted just three minutes to add another name to its list of protected players.

The quality of the players who were drafted was questionable. Some hockey writers disparagingly referred to the entire expansion draft as a "rummage sale." Still, some noteworthy players were gobbled up by new teams. Among them was 37-year-old Terry Sawchuk—arguably the greatest goaltender in NHL history. He had been on the Toronto Maple Leafs' roster in 1966–67 and had played a significant role in their Stanley Cup triumph that spring. The Los Angeles Kings used the first overall pick to claim Sawchuk who had been injury-plagued in recent years and was clearly on the downside of his terrific career. (Sawchuk told reporters that he was pondering retirement but that he would consider whatever offer was presented to him by the Kings.) Glenn Hall, nicknamed "Mr. Goalie," another veteran but aging netminder, was chosen by St. Louis as the third pick. The Philadelphia Flyers had the second selection. They went with youth, snaring the very promising Bernie Parent from the Boston Bruins. Later in the draft, Boston lost another young goaltender to the Flyers: Doug Favell.

Post-draft trades occurred too. The Rangers, unhappy about losing 22-year-old defenseman Rod Seiling to St. Louis in the draft, promptly dealt a pair of established players (Gary Sabourin and Bob Plager) along with two amateurs in their system (Tim Ecclestone and Bob Kannegiesser) to the Blues to get Seiling back.

The pickings seemed much slimmer once the draft of the non-goaltenders began. A forward, the very capable Dave Balon of the Montreal Canadiens, was selected first by the Minnesota North Stars. The expansion teams overlooked quite a few players who, in retrospect, would have been high quality acquisitions: Serge Savard, Jacques Lemaire, and Wayne Cashman were among the players who were initially exposed to the draft but later added to their teams' respective protected lists after team-mates had been selected. The whole process took about five hours to complete. Pat Curran of the *Montreal Gazette* was impressed by how smoothly the draft moved along, declaring it "ran off with unexpected ease."[6]

There was a comical moment to inject some levity to the serious business of determining the personnel for the six new NHL teams. It involved California's general manager, Rudy Pilous, who had coached the Chicago Black Hawks to the Stanley Cup in 1961. The fun-loving Pilous was rumored to be intensely negotiating with the stubborn Bernie (Boom Boom) Geoffrion in the vain hope of getting him to agree to play for an expansion team. When it came time to announce his team's 15th-round draft pick, Pilous evoked a huge laugh: With overly dramatic flair he said the Seals were selecting "Boom Boom"—Alain (Boom Boom) Caron, a journeyman forward from Chicago's farm system!

Unfortunately for Pilous, he would be dismissed by the Seals before they had played a single game. He moved on, taking a position with the Denver Spurs of the Western Hockey League. Bert Olmstead, a martinet if there ever was one, was the Seals' coach and general manager by the time the first puck was dropped in the 1967–68 season. A multiple Stanley Cup winner with both Toronto and Montreal as a player who possessed only average talent but a fanatical work ethic, Olmstead could not tolerate anyone who did not put forth total effort 100 percent of the time. Curt and impatient with the media, and brutally harsh with his players, Olmstead may have been the most reviled coach in NHL history. At one of his typical grueling two-hour practices, Olmstead so overworked Pat Hicke, an asthmatic, that he collapsed on the ice and nearly died. When Olmstead did reluctantly speak to the press, he did not hesitate to shame his own players. In one blistering tirade, Olmstead declared, "If I were a [Seals] player, I don't even know if I'd want to be associated with this bunch. I'd be tossing a few of them out of that dressing room on their cans. They have no pride."[7] Seals historian Steve Currier noted with much understatement, "Olmstead was not a people person."[8] Olmstead lasted just one turbulent season in Oakland.

Al Abrams, the sports editor of the *Pittsburgh Post-Gazette*, was both amazed and bemused by the level of interest that the expansion draft created among diehard hockey fans who gathered in Montreal to witness it. He wrote,

"There are some hockey nuts," said a man of cast experience in sports, "who think the drafting of 20 players each by the six new National Hockey League teams is more newsworthy than the war that just broke out in the Middle East yesterday or what has been going on in Vietnam for years."

From past experience with the breed of hockey fan I have met in Pittsburgh and in close observation here the past couple of days during the annual meeting of the NHL, a man would have to be nuts to argue the point. Let us say the [person] who follows a hobby, such as hockey or any other sport for that matter, is far happier than the person who broods over the sorry state of world affairs. Think what you will of him; he or she has no worries in that direction. Perhaps they're better off.[9]

Overall, it was believed that Philadelphia and Oakland fared the best in the draft. (Oakland already had an edge on the other five expansion teams because they retained the services of 12 players who had played for the minor-league California Seals the previous season. Accordingly, *The Hockey News* picked the Seals to finish atop the West Division in 1967– 68.) Boston was generally perceived to have lost the most talent from their stockpile of players. On the other hand, Montreal was thought to have escaped from the process with only minimal losses.

Now all that remained to be determined was whether or not the six new NHL clubs would be competitive in 1967–68.

4

The Mild, Mild West
Not Separate but Not Equal

"I was disgusted with expansion. I always maintained it
should have been done by bringing in two new teams at
a time. Let those two build a strong foundation, and then
after a few years, reach for two more teams. It is impossible
to find all at once six teams with owners who have a great
deal of money, who are dedicated to hockey, and who live
in the city where the team plays. Six men like that just don't
exist."
—74-year-old Conn Smythe, former owner of
the Toronto Maple Leafs, in an interview with
the *Canadian Magazine* newspaper supplement
prior to the start of the 1969–70 NHL season

Although NHL expansion in general was belittled by many hockey
traditionalists, it was undoubtedly a boon to many fringe players who were
languishing in the minor pro leagues with little hope of advancing to the
six-team NHL. Of course, a twofold increase in the league's teams doubled
job opportunities at hockey's top level. One such player was Bill Masterton,
a Winnipeg native who had been the star player on the University of Denver Pioneers—a team that won the 1961 NCAA championship.

Masterton signed a pro contract with the Montreal Canadiens organization. He was assigned to the Hull-Ottawa Canadiens of the Eastern
Professional Hockey League. There was little chance he would crack the
powerful Habs lineup, however, so he returned to school and got a master's degree. He was reinstated as an amateur, acquired American citizen-
ship, and represented the United States at the IIHF world championship
tournament in Vienna in 1967. Masterton, his wife, and their two adopted
children were happily living in Minneapolis where he was employed by the
Honeywell Corporation. (His work was part of NASA's Apollo space program.) However, with the NHL expanding into Minnesota, the 29-year-old

Masterton was approached out of the blue by North Stars coach Wren Blair about giving pro hockey another try with his hometown NHL team. Blair had scouted Masterton for the Canadiens and secured Masterton's rights for the North Stars. Masterton notably became the first player to sign an NHL contract for Minnesota.

On October 11, 1967, Masterton earned himself a place in North Stars history by scoring the team's first regular-season goal in a game versus St. Louis. Carol Masterton would recall that it was a "dream come true" for her husband. "He always wanted a shot in the NHL," she noted. "Expansion was a wonderful thing for guys like him."[1] Thirty-eight games into the 1967–68 season, Masterton had notched four goals and eight assists for the North Stars. Life was good.

Things took a sudden, tragic turn for Masterton on Saturday, January 13, 1968, in a game at the Met Center in Minneapolis—the North Stars' modern new arena. The evening before Super Bowl II, the North Stars were hosting the Oakland Seals. The Minneapolis ABC affiliate recorded fragments of the game (which were discovered in its archives in 2018), but there is no known footage of the disturbing incident. Nevertheless, this much is known: Late in the first period, Masterton rushed the puck at full speed toward the Oakland zone. A moment after Masterton made a pass to teammate Wayne Connelly, two Seals—Ron Harris and Larry Cahan—simultaneously and solidly hit him. Some witnesses believed Masterton had been knocked senseless before he hit the ice. "He was out of things before he even fell,"[2] insisted coach Wren Blair. Referee Wally Harris (no relation to Ron), who was in his second season as an NHL official, always insisted the hit delivered on Masterton was hard but completely legal and quite ordinary.

[Author's note: An investigative report by the *Toronto Star* in 2011 put forth compelling evidence that Masterton was displaying symptoms of an untreated concussion he had incurred from his head being slammed into the glass in an earlier game. By examining the autopsy and medical records from 1968, neurosurgeon Dr. Charles Tator concluded that Masterton's death resulted from "second-impact syndrome" which pointed to existing cerebral damage.]

Masterton, like the vast majority of NHL players in 1968, did not wear a helmet. He crashed backwards to the ice, violently striking his head on the playing surface. The sound was audible to the players on the North Stars' bench. Masterton was obviously seriously injured. Blood was pouring from his ears, nose and mouth. Masterton regained consciousness briefly and mumbled, "Never again … never again…"[3] before passing out. He was rushed to Fairview-Southdale Hospital in nearby Edina, Minnesota. After a short delay, the North Stars–Seals game continued as if nothing had happened. The contest ended in a 2–2 tie.

Carol Masterton had attended the game at the Met Center and witnessed the awful incident. She believed it was a highly tragic freak occurrence; she never blamed anyone or held any animus towards either Cahan or Harris. Masterton's parents were listening to a radio broadcast of the game 400 miles away in Winnipeg. They instinctively knew their son's injury was life-threatening and immediately headed for Minnesota to be with him.

Masterton's prognosis was not promising in the slightest. Three physicians and two neurosurgeons consulted. Together they deemed surgery too risky. Thus, there was no hope of Masterton surviving. (Masterton's teammates were playing in Boston the following night and were informed of the grim situation between periods. The North Stars lost that game badly, 9–2.) He was removed from life support and died at 1:55 a.m. on Monday, January 16—about 30 hours after suffering the head injury. His wife, young children, and parents were gathered at his bedside when death arrived. To date, Masterton is the only NHL player to suffer a fatal injury during a game.

Masterton, like all NHL players, was covered by a blanket insurance policy held by the players' pension fund. His estate received $50,000 in life insurance and an additional $10,000 accidental-death benefit. A day after Masterton died, the NHL All-Star Game was played in Toronto—the first time it had ever been played in midseason. A minute of silence for Masterton was observed in the pregame ceremonies.

"Masterton's Tragic Death Raises Helmet Question," trumpeted a somber headline in the January 16 edition of the *Montreal Gazette*. Although the Masterton fatality was a clear example as to why hockey helmets ought to be worn, the macho mindset of NHLers in 1968—and hockey players of all ages, for that matter—meant that not many of them would be rushing to wear one. "It all goes back to when you're learning to play hockey as a kid," acknowledged North Stars president Walter Bush, Jr., in an Associated Press story. "If you're not wearing a helmet then, you're not likely to wear one as a pro."[4] Indeed, the *Gazette* story noted, "Only a small number of the players in the league wear helmets."[5]

In a Canadian Press story, Chicago Black Hawks superstar Bobby Hull was forthright in his opinions on the contentious topic when asked for his two cents' worth at the All-Star Game. "The reason [the players] don't wear helmets is vanity, that's all," he claimed. "Players who are wearing them now cannot be regarded as sissies. Sissies? I think by the time a player reaches the NHL he doesn't have to prove that he's a man. After this [tragedy], I'm going to take a careful look at the possibility of wearing a helmet."[6]

"The use of helmets is optional," Wren Blair tersely and correctly told the press. "Masterton chose not to [wear one]."[7] The North Stars were typical of every professional hockey team in North America in 1968. Only one regular on the team's roster wore a helmet: André Boudrias. He said he wore his because of his small stature; he was only 5'7½". Boudrias was fearful about getting clipped on the head by taller players' high sticks. "I don't feel [helmets] should be mandatory,"[8] echoed Pittsburgh coach Red Sullivan. Philadelphia Flyers coach Keith Allen conceded in a television interview that in the wake of Masterton's death, some of his players were at least considering wearing helmets.

Coincidentally, Masterton's death occurred on the same day as the death of Douglas Boe, a Princeton University football player who succumbed six months after suffering a brain hemorrhage during a team scrimmage. This unusual confluence of tragedies prompted Al Abrams of the *Pittsburgh Post-Gazette* to ponder whether hockey or football was the more dangerous sport. He sought out Dick Mattiussi of the Penguins for his opinion. Mattiussi told Abrams he would not play football for any price. Meanwhile two members of the NFL's Pittsburgh Steelers—Mike Clark and Dick Compton—were equally adamant about not wanting any part of hockey.

Larry Cahan played 13 seasons in the NHL and, later, another two in the World Hockey Association. He died at age 58 in 1992. His career, though long, was not especially spectacular. Cahan is largely remembered for being one of the two Oakland Seals who delivered the fatal body check on Bill Masterton on January 13, 1968. Cahan's counterpart, Ron Harris, now in his late seventies, has always had difficulty accepting his role in the Masterton tragedy. He played in the NHL until 1976. The ex–Seal has seldom publicly discussed the matter. (Harris declined to be interviewed by The Sports Network in Canada in 2008 on the 40th anniversary of the incident.) There is only one known interview where Harris addressed it: In 2003—some 35 years after Masterton's death—Harris solemnly told the *St. Paul Pioneer Press*, "It bothers you the rest of your life. [The hit] wasn't dirty and it wasn't meant to happen that way. Still, it's very hard because I made the play. It's always in the back of my mind."[9]

As a tribute to the fallen player, the Bill Masterton Memorial Trophy was established by the NHL. It is awarded annually, under the trusteeship of the Professional Hockey Writers' Association, to the NHL player "who best exemplifies the qualities of perseverance, sportsmanship, and dedication to hockey." The University of Denver honored alumnus Masterton too, naming its annual MVP award after him. The North Stars retired Masterton's jersey #19. (After the North Stars' franchise was shifted to Texas in 1993, the Dallas Stars respectfully continued to make the number unavailable.)

Not too surprisingly, the now 12-team NHL became a two-division league for 1967–68. It was somewhat reminiscent of the era that stretched from 1926–27 to 1937–38 when the 10-team (and later eight-team) NHL was split into an American Division and a Canadian Division. (Ironically, for the sake of balance, the New York Americans were in the Canadian Division. Some newspapers balked at the inaccurate name and instead labeled it the "International Division.") However, in a curious decision that would have a profound effect on the NHL for several years, the six established teams made up what was called the East Division even though there was no geographical truth whatsoever in the name. The six expansion franchises were placed in the West Division. This seemed grossly unfair because, on paper, the West Division teams would be decidedly weaker than those in the East Division—but would be rewarded with four teams qualifying for the Stanley Cup playoffs, one of which would gain a precious berth in the final. However, the NHL figured the new teams would reap great publicity and benefits from playoff appearances. Such notoriety could only be good for the NHL in the long run, according to the prevailing wisdom from league headquarters.

There were, of course, growing pains and unexpected troubles for the expansion teams. Although they were among the frontrunners battling for first place in the West Division, no team experienced more peripheral bad luck than the Philadelphia Flyers. Hockey journalist Dick Beddoes wrote, "The history of sports is dotted with examples of front-running teams having the roof cave in on them, figuratively speaking, but the Flyers may have been the first to have one literally blow away from them."[10]

The Toronto hockey scribe was referring to a pair of unfortunate incidents that twice rendered the Flyers' gaudy new $12-million Philadelphia Spectrum unplayable. (Beddoes claimed the arena resembled "a huge brick and glass sardine can."[11]) In late February, strong winds blew off a portion of the Spectrum's roof, leaving a very noticeable hole. The damage was swiftly repaired, but on March 1 it happened again but with even greater damage. Ironically, during the application process for an expansion team, team owners Jerry Wolman and William Putman optimistically issued the follow statement to the press: "We think the promise of building a new arena considerably helped our cause."[12]

Philadelphia mayor Harold J. Tate decreed public safety was at risk and summarily declared the Spectrum closed until the problems with the roof could be permanently resolved. It took Philadelphia's municipal government 19 days to decide whether to make the necessary repairs or close the new facility indefinitely. The former option prevailed. (A rumor circulated in Philadelphia that if the Spectrum was to be shut down, the NHL would move the city's new hockey franchise elsewhere.) Thus, the Flyers were forced to take their show on the road to conclude the regular season. Not one Flyer game was played in Philadelphia during March 1968; the Flyers' home games that month were abruptly shifted to other cities.

"For 31 days," Beddoes wrote, "these nomads of the NHL were buffeted about like a rowboat in a typhoon, living out of suitcases away from their families and the friendly faces of Philly fans."[13] Lou Angotti, the Flyers' feisty 30-year-old captain, said the temporary lack of a home constantly impacted the team in adverse ways. "It just hasn't been worrying about [trying to finish the season in] first place," he said, "but also worrying and wondering where our next few games would be played. If you don't think that affects a team, you're crazy."[14] Nevertheless, Angotti believed the shared ordeal became a cohesive agent in creating team camaraderie. "I know there are going to be ups and downs for as long as we're playing hockey. But when you take everything into consideration, anything that happens after this will have to rank second to the things that happened this year."[15]

On March 3, Madison Square Garden hosted an Oakland–Philadelphia game where the New York City crowd overwhelmingly cheered for the underdog Seals. "We won't go back there unless it's for the Stanley Cup finals,"[16] grumbled Flyers general manager Bud Poile who somehow expected New York sports fans to uncharacteristically embrace a Philadelphia team. The game ended in a hard-fought 1–1 tie. Four days later the Flyers received a decidedly different reception in Toronto where a Bruins–Flyers game was relocated. The locals rooted heartily for the Flyers because of their general hatred for divisional rival Boston. It did not help; Boston prevailed 2–1. The Maple Leafs, however, unsympathetically snatched an exorbitant 50 percent of the gate for the one-night rental of Maple Leaf Gardens. (Beddoes sarcastically described the Maple Leafs' actions as "magnanimous."[17])

One fleecing at the hands of the greedy Leafs was enough for the Flyers' management. Other Philadelphia home games were transferred to Quebec City—a municipality that had last witnessed NHL hockey way back in 1920 in the days of the mostly forgotten Quebec Bulldogs and high-scoring Joe Malone. (The Bulldogs—sometimes called the Athletics by journalists of the day—played one miserable NHL season, finishing in the basement with a 4–20 record.) The folks there were quite happy to host the wandering Flyers for five home dates at Le Colisée, especially since the minor league Quebec Aces were now a Philadelphia farm team. They also provided lots of vocal support which did not go unnoticed by the Flyer players. "If we have to play away from Philly, this is the best place to play," opined Joe Watson. "The guys who played here in Quebec in past years gave it that little bit extra."[18] Although it was estimated that the Flyers—who were routinely drawing full houses to their games before the structural problems with the Spectrum began—lost about $400,000 in gate receipts by having to play their March home games away from Philadelphia, everything worked out well for the team in the end. "To their everlasting credit, the

Flyers managed to finish first in the West Division,"[19] Beddoes duly noted. That was true. The Flyers were the first winners of the Clarence S. Campbell Bowl, awarded to the team that finished the regular season in first place in the West Division. Philadelphia copped top honors in the West with just 73 points—one game below .500. (That mark would not have qualified the Flyers for the postseason had they been in the NHL's far tougher East Division.) The Spectrum was back to being operational just in time for the Flyers' first quarterfinal playoff game versus St. Louis. Alas, perhaps the nomadic Flyers were better suited not to return to their unfamiliar home arena. They were upended by the Blues in seven games. St. Louis won two of the four contests played at the Spectrum—including Game #7.

Philadelphia, despite its obvious arena issues, seemed to be the best supported of the new teams, with third-place St. Louis a strong second. Surprisingly, the Los Angeles Kings failed to draw as well as expected. After beginning the season with home games at the Long Beach Arena, the Kings moved into the posh Los Angeles Forum midway through the 1967–68 campaign. It opened on December 30, 1967, to great acclaim. The Kings' owner, 55-year-old Jack Kent Cooke—once described as "the handsomest millionaire in Canada"—began referring to the new venue as the Fabulous Forum. The nickname stuck. He was underwhelmed by the disappointing fan support for his Kings—a team that came within a point of finishing atop the West Division. Cooke was informed there were some 300,000 expatriate Canadians living within a three-hour drive of Los Angeles. Few of them ever bought tickets to see the Kings play in their new digs, however. In a comment that was well circulated above the 49th parallel, Cooke once quipped, "Now I know why they left Canada: They hate hockey!"[20]

It took a while for sports fans in Pittsburgh to embrace their new professional hockey team too. It was heavily stocked with ex–New York Rangers and members of the old Pittsburgh Hornets, the longtime minor league team that had been displaced by the arrival of the Penguins. Only 9,307 fans—far short of the Civic Arena's 12,500 capacity in 1967—turned out for the Penguins' inaugural home opener on Wednesday, October 11. The Montreal Canadiens, who were not accustomed to playing before any empty seats anywhere, were the visitors. The Habs prevailed, 2–1. The ticketholders witnessed a milestone goal: Jean Béliveau's second-period game-winner was also his 400th career tally. Jimmy Jordan wrote in the next day's *Pittsburgh Post-Gazette*, "Pittsburgh's Penguins couldn't quite cope with the speed and the sharper passing of Montreal's Canadiens last night, and they lost a 2–1 decision as major league hockey returned to Pittsburgh after an absence of 37 seasons." The optimistic Jordan noted, "But the Penguins did show the Canadiens … and the fans that they won't be patsies for anybody this season, whether it's an established club or one of the new expansion teams."[21] Interestingly, the *Post-Gazette* devoted considerably more space in its sports section to Game #6 of the 1967 World Series (featuring the Boston Red Sox and St. Louis Cardinals) than to the hometown Penguins' historic NHL debut.

Montreal journalists also praised the pluck of the Penguins. "Interlocking games won't be mere picnics this new expansion season, not against Pittsburgh anyway," wrote Pat Curran in the *Montreal Gazette.* "The Penguins earned a moral victory in losing to the Habs only 2–1 last night. The hard-working Penguins gave them a battle all the way." Curran commented on the attendance thusly: "The crowd was somewhat disappointing. The Penguins had hoped for at least 10,000 in the 12,500-seat arena, built at a cost of $22 million six years ago, and never filled by the Hornets of the American [Hockey] League." Curran chose to reinforce the positive, though. "Last night's count was still the best ever for a weeknight game here."[22]

That same night—October 11—saw the debut of four other expansion teams. The soon-to-be Oakland Seals thumped the Philadelphia Flyers 5–1 while the St. Louis Blues rallied for a late goal to earn a 2–2 tie at home versus the Minnesota North Stars.

In that first post-expansion NHL season, inter-divisional play was sporadic. Each team's regular-season schedule was increased from 70 to 74 games. Teams played their five divisional rivals 10 times each and the six teams in the other division just four times apiece. A new playoff format was also devised, of course. One team from each division would advance to the Stanley Cup finals, thus ensuring one of the new six teams would be represented in the postseason's championship round. This was a highly contentious issue among longtime fans. Critics reiterated that the system devalued the Cup finals as it was widely assumed the West Division teams were not yet on par in overall skill level with their counterparts in the East. As it turned out, those critics were absolutely correct—at least as far as the Stanley Cup finals of 1968, 1969 and 1970 conclusively proved.

The inter-divisional games during the regular season were generally competitive, however. The Boston Bruins, who finished third in the East Division, compiled a positive but less than overwhelming 14–9–1 record in their 24 games versus the six expansion teams during 1967–68. The East Division champions, the Montreal Canadiens, fared better: They went 16–5–3 that first season against the weaker squads from the West. Fourth-place Chicago did almost as well against the NHL's newcomers, amassing a 15–4–5 mark. The ascending New York Rangers, who finished the season strongly in second place, were the best of the Original Six crowd versus the newbies. The Rangers bested the six expansion outfits by a tune of 17–4–3. Embarrassingly, the defending Stanley Cup champion Toronto

Maple Leafs (who would finish in fifth place in the East and miss the play-offs) ended up with a dismal 10–11–3 record against the West Division clubs. Even the once-proud Detroit Red Wings, who finished 10 points in arrears of Toronto in the East Division's cellar, managed to go 14–7–3 against the West. Thus, the six clubs in East compiled an overall record of 86–40–18 versus the expansion clubs in 1967–68. That translated to a cumulative winning percentage of .660.

The Montreal Canadiens and St. Louis Blues advanced to the 1968 Cup finals. St. Louis being competitive at all was a major surprise considering their rather inauspicious start. Their application for an NHL expansion franchise seemed very weak. Yet, for geographical reasons, the city was granted a "conditional franchise" after their bid was accepted despite many flaws. They had initially defaulted on the payment to the NHL and had no actual representation at the league meeting where their bid was curiously finalized. Baltimore would be granted a franchise instead of St. Louis if the Blues did not get their house in order swiftly. Under financier Sidney Salomon they did.

To increase the West Division's chances, the NHL generously arranged for the Cup final series to open in St. Louis, thus giving the Blues four of the finals' seven potential home dates. The Blues played in the same facility that the woebegone St. Louis Eagles had in 1934–35: The cavernous and old St. Louis Arena. It was a raucous, electric venue for Games #1 and #2, with the arena's organist, Norm Kramer, frequently belting out "When the Saints Go Marching In." The hoopla did not faze the veteran Habs, however. Montreal prevailed in four straight games, albeit by close scores of 3–2, 1–0, 4–3, and 3–2. The first and third games of the championship series both required overtime to determine a winner. Game #2's only goal was a shorthanded tally by defenseman Serge Savard in the third period.

Interestingly, despite each game being decided by a single goal, in only one period of the series did the Blues outscore the Canadiens—and it took them until the second period of Game #4 to do it. "Even though the Missourians bowed in four straight games to Les Habitants," wrote Dick Beddoes, "they played with the same great desire that had brought them from last place to West Division playoff champions. Twice they had to be taken to overtime before they were vanquished." Seemingly as an afterthought, Beddoes added, "Anyone who had suggested in October than an East-West final might be competitive was accorded more than a raised eyebrow."[23]

Pat Curran of the *Montreal Gazette* pinpointed why all four of the Cup final games were tight affairs. He wrote, "Glenn Hall, whose tremendous netminding was a key factor in the Blues' earlier series triumphs over Philadelphia and Minnesota, was mainly responsible for keeping the Blues close in the contest with the Canadiens."[24] Accordingly, Hall, who was the NHL's rookie of the year in 1955–56, was awarded the Conn Smythe Trophy as playoff MVP for 1968. Oddly, Hall had to wait until two days after the Cup finals ended to be notified that he was the recipient. That head-scratching policy was something new.

The 1968 award was not without controversy: It came as a shock to many Montreal supporters, including coach Toe Blake, who fully expected his number-one goalie, Lorne (Gump) Worsley to collect the MVP hardware. Like Hall, Worsley had been superb in the playoffs. He had only allowed 22 goals and was undefeated in the 12 playoff games he started. (Montreal's only playoff loss in 1968 was a 2–1 setback to Chicago in Game #4 of the Eastern final; Rogie Vachon started in net that night for the Habs.) "Who could have played better?" asked Blake. "After all we won the Cup, so Gump should be the logical choice. Surely they're not going to give the trophy to a loser like when Roger Crozier got it two years ago."[25] [Author's note: In 1966, in the Conn Smythe Trophy's second year of existence, Detroit goaltender Roger Crozier won the award despite Montreal defeating Detroit in the Cup finals. After Glenn Hall in 1968, the next player from a losing team to be named playoff MVP was Reggie Leach of the Philadelphia Flyers in 1976, a sniper who scored a record 19 goals in a single postseason. Again, it came in a year where Montreal won the Stanley Cup. Since 1976, only two members from losing teams have won the prestigious Conn Smythe Trophy. Both were goaltenders: Ron Hextall and J.S. Giguere.]

Overall, expansion was considered a success. In the 1968 version his book *The Lively World of Hockey*, hockey historian Brian McFarlane painted an overly rosy picture of the first 12-team NHL season. "Expansion dumbfounded the skeptics," he wrote. "The new teams were not pushovers for the Eastern Division, their gate receipts soared, and the fans in the new cities displayed an unexpected mixture of enthusiasm and sophistication in their rooting."[26] In reality, three of the six expansion teams (Oakland, Pittsburgh and Los Angeles) struggled at the gate. The Seals lost an estimated $1 million in their inaugural season.

Despite the final playoff series lasting just the minimum of four games, its competitiveness was a significant factor in increasing the amount of inter-divisional play. For the regular season in 1968–69, each team's games against divisional opponents were reduced from 10 to eight, while the inter-divisional games were increased from four to six. The arithmetic meant the total number of regular-season games played by each NHL team in 1968–69 marginally rose from 74 to 76. "We decided to increase the schedule in order to minimize the distinction between the East and West divisions and equalize the transportation,"[27] explained NHL president Clarence Campbell.

Little had changed from the previous season. In 1968–69, the NHL's Eastern clubs were again the class of the league. In fact, all six teams in the East finished with records over .500. In contrast, only St. Louis could boast that achievement in the West. Thus, Chicago, the last-place club in the East would have finished second had they been in the woeful West. Despite Clarence Campbell's best efforts, there was undeniably a distinction between the NHL's two divisions—and every scholarly NHL fan recognized it.

Montreal's most serious challengers were now the rapidly improving Boston Bruins who impressively accrued 100 points in the regular season only to finish second to Montreal's 103. Boston won their first playoff series in 11 years—a total demolition of Toronto—to advance to the championship series of the Eastern Division. To anyone who followed the NHL seriously, the glamorous Montreal–Boston semifinal was the de facto Stanley Cup final. Some veteran journalists went as far as to brazenly call it "the real final" in their game reports, a trend probably not appreciated by Clarence Campbell and the other apostles of expansion. Whichever team emerged from the East was generally expected to blow away the Western rep in the actual Cup final. The Canadiens triumphed over the Bruins in six thrilling games—three of which were decided by overtime. Game #6 required two overtimes before the Habs prevailed on Jean Béliveau's only career overtime goal in a game that the Bruins were unlucky to lose. Tom Fitzgerald, a veteran *Boston Globe* hockey writer, consoled the city's disappointed hockey fans. He opined, "The present may belong to the Canadiens. The future definitely belongs to the Bruins."[28] Fitzgerald further declared that Boston and Montreal were clearly the two best hockey teams in the world "barring dissent from Moscow."[29] A return matchup in the Stanley Cup final between St. Louis and Montreal definitely was perceived to be an anticlimactic engagement.

Although the Blues had swept their two divisional playoff series versus Philadelphia and Los Angeles to gain terrific momentum entering the 1969 Stanley Cup finals, in their six regular-season meetings versus the Habs, the Canadiens were clearly the superior team. Montreal had beaten the Blues five times; the remaining game had ended in a tie. Montreal continued its dominance over the overmatched Blues with a tedious and utterly predictable four-game sweep to win the Stanley Cup—their fourth in five years. As was the case in 1968, Montreal only had to overcome a St. Louis lead in Game #4. This time the scores were 3–1, 3–1, 4–0, and 2–1. Only the fourth game was truly competitive. The Habs had now played St. Louis 17 times in succession without losing. In summarizing the Cup finals, an Associated Press correspondent bluntly declared, "For the first three games in the series, Montreal had been in total control with the Blues rarely posing a threat."[30] With Montreal outscoring St. Louis by a decisive 12–3 aggregate over the four games, it was clear the 1967 expansion teams still had a long way to go to catch up to the talent level possessed by the Original Six clubs. Instead of it narrowing, the gap in talent between the NHL's East and West divisions—the old guard and the 1967 upstarts—only seemed to be widening.

PART II

The 1969–70 NHL Season

5

Mayhem in Ottawa

The Wayne Maki–Ted Green Incident

"Ted Green was one of the most feared of the National Hockey League gladiators. Superbly confident in his ability to control and pass the puck, Green made his opponents pay a physical price for entering his space on the rink. Green was never afraid on the ice, and he often aggressively provoked fights as the team's enforcer. A modest man off the ice, when he suited up for a game Green was a wicked terror to be feared. His club and his fans expected him to play that role. Age 29 at the time of the incident, Green was at the top of his game."[1]

—Law professor Roger I. Abrams in an article for the *Huffington Post* on the fortieth anniversary of the Wayne Maki–Ted Green affair

On Sunday, September 21, 1969, the Boston Bruins played the St. Louis Blues in an NHL preseason game in Ottawa. A sellout crowd of about 10,000 fans attended the contest at the Ottawa Civic Center. It pitted the ascending Bruins against the team that had represented the NHL's West Division in the Stanley Cup final the previous two springs. The Bruins were undermanned that weekend, however, with several top players out with injuries or illnesses. Bobby Orr, for one, was battling a cold. He would play, however. Orr knew that many fans had bought tickets specifically to see him in action. Boston's John McKenzie was absent due to a contract dispute with his club. The game was being televised in Boston on WSBK-TV. In one of the most infamous incidents in NHL history, things got very nasty between Boston's Ted Green and St. Louis' Wayne Maki.

The Bruins did not formally have a captain on their roster when the 1969–70 preseason began, but the 29-year-old Green, a defenseman—whose nickname was Terrible Ted—was the de facto leader in the Boston dressing room and wore an "A" on his jersey as an assistant captain. The

34

Montreal Gazette referred to Green as the Bruins' "traffic cop because of his toughness in eight seasons [with Boston]." On the other hand, Maki was something of a journeyman player. Apart from playing 49 games for the Chicago Black Hawks in 1967–68, Maki had spent most of his pro career in the minor leagues with the St. Louis Braves and the Dallas Black Hawks. In 2009, Roger I. Abrams, a legal expert, wrote, "At age 24, the Sault Sainte Marie, Ontario native was yet to make his mark in the National Hockey League. The 1969 preseason was his opportunity to demonstrate his game-playing abilities."[2]

The Bruins were not the only undermanned NHL group that day—so were the NHL officials. Several veteran referees and linesmen were refusing to accept preseason game assignments as part of an ongoing labor disagreement. (Among other things, the men in the conspicuous zebra-striped jerseys wanted guaranteed salaries and the league to pay 100 percent of their pension contributions. They walked out of their training camp in Brantford, Ontario, to make their point.) To make up for their absence, some noteworthy amateur and low-level pro officials were hastily assigned to work the slate of NHL exhibition games.

Refereeing the game in Ottawa on September 21 was Ken Bodendistel of Guelph, Ontario. In effect this game was something of an audition for him to try to make the NHL. Whether or not Bodendistel's inexperience with the intensity and roughness of NHL-caliber hockey played a role in what happened that day at the Ottawa Civic Center is subject to debate. Boston's Derek Sanderson certainly thought so. In his autobiography, Sanderson noted,

> There was an American Hockey League referee, Ken Bodendistel, and he was hesitant to get between the two of them [Green and Maki]. An NHL official would have waded right in, because players know that if you ever hit a referee, you're finished.[3]

Bodendistel never was promoted to the NHL in a full-time capacity, but he did capably serve as the supervisor of officials for the Ontario Hockey League for four decades. Perhaps it was not entirely a coincidence that one day after the infamous Bruins-Blues game in Ottawa, the NHL reached an agreement with their striking officials.

The Bruins had played another preseason contest at the Montreal Forum the night before which had degenerated into a fight-filled game. Sunday's game would take the violence a step further. According to the Canadian Press story that ran in the following day's newspapers, "Veteran defenseman Ted Green was taken to hospital in Ottawa for surgery on Sunday night after he was hit on the head in a stick-swinging duel with Wayne Maki of the St. Louis Blues."[4]

To this day, the precise details are a bit sketchy as to what exactly the catalysts were that caused the infamous stick-swinging incident. Witnesses give varying accounts. No films or videotape of the incident are known to exist; still photos are the only visual record that survive. Oddly enough, the most telling photo was snapped not by a professional photojournalist, but by a 12-year-old spectator who happened to bring his camera to the game.

Green (wearing #6) and Maki (wearing #14) encountered each other in the Boston zone about 13 minutes into the first period as both men pursued a loose puck into a corner. Neither player was wearing a helmet—quite typical for 1969. In the corner, Green pushed Maki to the ice, an action that prompted referee Bodendistel to call a delayed penalty on the Bruins. From his knees, Maki may have speared Green in the chest, the stomach, or in the genitals. (On the fortieth anniversary of the incident, the *Huffington Post* stated it was the latter and called Maki's retaliation "perhaps the most egregious act that can be committed on the ice, and a clear violation of the unwritten code and [the written rules] of hockey.")[5]

Green, in response, elevated his stick and caught Maki on the head or the arm with it, knocking him down a second time. Or perhaps Green swung his stick at Maki and missed him altogether. Be that as it may, Maki then retaliated. Green was skating away from Maki and was utterly oblivious about what was about to happen to him. Maki maliciously whacked Green over the head with his stick, striking him solidly with the hardest part—the point where the blade meets the shaft.

Green dropped to the ice with a thud and laid in a grotesque position as if he had been poleaxed—which was basically the case. The right side of his head had been partially crushed in. The left side of his body was temporarily paralyzed. (*Sport* magazine later ran a horrifying photograph of Green that showed the fallen Bruin lying on the ice with blood hemorrhaging from his skull. The *Calgary Herald* ran a much more benign photo of Green on one knee trying to regain his feet. It was shot from an angle that only showed the left side of Green's skull.) Green began to twitch and fell into unconsciousness. When he awoke at an Ottawa hospital, he was lucid enough to request a priest to administer last rites to him.

Years later, Dan Kelly, the smoothly superb broadcaster for the St. Louis Blues, described the incident as "one of the most horrifying, most violent exchanges I've ever seen in hockey. I could see right away that Green was badly hurt," Kelly vividly recalled. "When he tried to get up, his face was contorted, and his legs began to buckle under him. It was dreadful. I almost became physically ill watching him struggle because I knew this was very, very serious."[6]

Predictably both benches emptied. Bobby Orr pursued Maki and cross-checked him once to the ice. That was the extent of the Bruins' attempt at frontier justice. Orr was booed during the remainder of the volatile game. Both Maki and Green received match penalties. In the second period, Boston's Phil Esposito would himself receive a match penalty for manhandling referee Bodendistel after he called a penalty on the Bruin. An unnamed Canadian Press correspondent wrote, "Esposito skated to his bench, put is head in his hands, and appeared under heavy strain after the incident."[7] The final result was a 5–1 win for St. Louis, but few hockey fans were talking about which team won or lost the meaningless game. The Green–Maki incident dominated the proverbial water-cooler chatter across Canada and wherever hockey was closely followed in the United States.

Green eventually required three brain operations and had a steel plate inserted into his skull to save his life. Two days after the incident, Boston's team physician, Dr. Ashby Moncur, reported that Green was in satisfactory condition and had a "reasonable chance" to regain his health. He was expected to remain hospitalized for two weeks. Moncur even expressed optimism that Green might be able to return to the Bruins' roster towards the end of the 1969–70 season—provided he wore a protective helmet.

Apart from Boston and St. Louis, the Green–Maki incident was not especially newsworthy in the most parts of the United States. However, a brief story about the incident appeared in the *Pittsburgh Post-Gazette* on September 23 that focused on the tough stance the NHL's officials would now take to curb malicious stickwork. Referee-in-chief Scotty Morrison stated that henceforth the rules would be enforced "with an iron hand." Morrison said if any player swung his stick at another player's head, a match penalty would be assessed—"even if the players are ten feet apart."[8]

Boston general manager Milt Schmidt was so horrified by Green's injury and the general goings-on in Ottawa that he purchased two dozen helmets for the Bruins—without consulting with or even notifying the players. Nevertheless, the helmets were distributed to the surprised Bruins. Schmidt ordered them to be worn at the team's next practice. When Schmidt arrived partway through the workout, he saw that no players were wearing them. Schmidt angrily interrupted the practice and told the Bruins that anyone who did not immediately put on a helmet could get off the ice. After a few awkward moments of silence and indecision, Bobby Orr began heading back to the dressing room. Other Bruins began to follow him. It was a defiant, unified response that Schmidt had not anticipated. Schmidt knew he was beaten and did not pursue the matter any further. The helmets were put into storage, never to be seen again. The Bruins had an ally in NHL president Clarence Campbell on the helmet issue. He was not at all interested in making them mandatory equipment. His objection was based on a commonly held belief that helmets would make players careless and would have, in Campbell's words, a "reverse effect" in overall safety.

Nevertheless, Campbell would have to sort things out to minimize the public-relations damage from the disturbing incident in Ottawa. Hal Walker, the sports editor of the *Calgary Herald*, did not want to be in Campbell's shoes. "Nobody will envy Campbell," he wrote in the September 23 edition of his daily column, "particularly when the health, and ultimately the career of a valuable hockey player is at stake. But this is part of his office, a distasteful portion to be sure, but no more onerous than when [in 1948] he had to suspend Don Gallinger and Billy Taylor of the Boston Bruins for life for allegedly betting on games; and no more worrisome than when Jimmy Orlando of the Detroit Red Wings and Gaye Stewart of the Toronto Maple Leafs engaged in a vicious blood-letting with their sticks in Maple Leaf Gardens in the 1940s."[9]

Walker cited an example of how unchecked violence on the playing field had virtually killed a once-popular summer sport in Canada. "The same witless incidents," Walker noted, "destroyed interest in Canada's real national game—field lacrosse—many years ago. People abhorred the violence and showed their displeasure by staying away from the parks. Lacrosse died, first at the box office, then on the field."[10]

Both players were fined by Campbell. Maki was also suspended for 30 games. Green received a lesser 13-game suspension—if and when he ever returned to the NHL. Both men were fined $300 for the altercation—which seemed pitifully small even by the standards of 1969, yet the NHL brass called the monetary penalties "the stiffest in league annals."

Exactly two months elapsed before the Ottawa Police Department decided, on November 21, that there was sufficient evidence to file criminal assault charges against both Green and Maki. (Officially, the charge leveled against each man was "assault occasioning bodily harm.") It marked the first time in the 52-year history of the NHL that a police department had investigated an on-ice incident with the intent of pursuing criminal charges against players. No other professional sports league in North America had a similar stigma attached to it. A conviction carried a possible two-year jail term.

Maki's older brother Ronald (better known by his nickname "Chico") was also an NHL player at the time. Chico had a far more substantial NHL career than Wayne, playing 15 seasons as a right winger for the Chicago Black Hawks from 1961 to 1976. In a 2012 interview, three years before he died, Chico Maki discussed his younger sibling's notorious clash with Ted Green.

"There is a photo that shows he [Wayne] was hit first. Ask the players who were sitting right next to Wayne. They saw what happened," Chico insisted. "Green wasn't an angel. He was a mean SOB. Don't let anyone tell you any different."[11]

Wayne, five years younger than Chico, talked to his older brother about the incident just once. They jointly agreed not to say anything further about it to hockey reporters or other members of the media.

On November 22, one day after Green and Maki were each charged with assault, longtime NHL president Clarence Campbell appeared on *Weekend*, a Canadian Broadcasting Corporation (CBC) television program, to discuss the September 21 incident in Ottawa. It aired across Canada immediately after the network's regular NHL broadcasts that Saturday night. Bob McDevitt of *Hockey Night in Canada* interviewed the 64-year-old Campbell, himself a former a former NHL referee. Campbell was only the third president in the league's history; he had held this position since 1946 and had basically ruled the league as an autocrat since assuming the position. Campbell left little doubt that he strongly resented outsiders getting too deeply involved in what he deemed to be an internal NHL matter. The imperious Campbell further unashamedly confirmed that his office was being less than totally cooperative with the official police investigation into the Maki–Green incident. Here is part of that *Weekend* interview:

> McDEVITT: Mr. Campbell, I understand that the Ottawa Police asked you to turn over to them the information you gathered in your investigation of the Green–Maki stick-swinging affair—and you refused. Why?
>
> CAMPBELL: Well, basically, it's confidential information collected for our purposes. There were no warnings given to anyone. It would have been quite improper—even by police standards—to disclose something that was delivered to us without the normal statutory warnings.
>
> McDEVITT: I'm surprised that it took the police two months to finally get the charges laid. Were you surprised too that it took that long?
>
> CAMPBELL: Well, I'm surprised it took any time at all, really, because this is a bit of a shock to us. I want to make it perfectly clear: There has never been a time when the National Hockey League has challenged the primacy of the responsibilities of civil authority in all situations, including hockey games—or any other cases where there are assaults of any kind that take place. The nature of sports—bodily contact sports—of course, involves assaults of all kinds—some of greater and some of lesser degrees of violence. But for the past fifty years, as far as I know, the National Hockey League has not been exposed to a criminal charge.
>
> McDEVITT: Because of the great outcry following the Green–Maki affair, don't you feel the NHL should really put much stronger legislation in the books to prevent things from happening, such as this?
>
> CAMPBELL: No, I don't think the response to that type of pressure is any good at all. I think you have to react intelligently to the situation as you see it—and I think we're more competent to judge what the situation is than anyone else. And we will certainly do it because our very existence depends on it.
>
> McDEVITT: But surely you don't want the police stepping into the NHL's affairs…
>
> CAMPBELL: No, we do not. Let me say this: I think it would be completely absurd if they decide that's what they want to do.[12]

However, there were some dissenters among NHL owners—men who thought the league's rules and penalties for stick-swinging needed to be made considerably harsher than they presently were. Sixty-six-year-old Harold Ballard, a part owner of the Toronto Maple Leafs in 1969, was one such individual. In a United Press International story that ran in the September 23 *Montreal Gazette*, Ballard proposed stiff measures to combat the problem. "If you hit a person on the street and put him out of business, it's considered a serious offense," Ballard stated. "If you almost kill somebody on the ice by hitting him on the head, it's just as serious."[13] Ballard said he would introduce a motion at the next league meeting that would expel stick-swingers from the NHL. Gordon Juckes, an executive with the Canadian Amateur Hockey Association, was fearful that violent incidents in the NHL would trickle down to youth hockey. "Parents are keeping their children out of hockey because of the injury danger," he declared. "They will accept the fact that their son might be injured during the natural course of the game, but not the fact that he could be clubbed during a fight."[14]

Both Maki and Green were both eventually acquitted of the criminal charges. Two justices of the Ontario Provincial Court listened to the arguments. Maki's assault on Green was interestingly ruled to have been an act of self-defense; Green's assault on Maki was ruled to be typical of the contact that hockey players tacitly but routinely consent to accepting by playing the sport.

Maki was suspended for most of the 1969–70 season; he played in only 16 NHL games for St. Louis plus 39 others with the Buffalo Bisons of the American Hockey League. Green, to no one's great surprise, did not return to the ice that season. Nevertheless, after Boston won the Stanley Cup on May 10, his Bruin teammates voted him a full share of the team's playoff money. Green's name also was inscribed on the Cup when the criteria for such an honor was more arbitrary than it is today. Green returned the following year and played professional hockey in both the NHL and World Hockey Association until retiring at age 39 in 1979. From the moment he returned to the game after his near-death experience on September 21, 1969, Green always donned a hockey helmet during games—but he hated wearing it. Green would eventually have his name inscribed on the Stanley Cup seven times: twice as a player for Boston, and five times as an assistant or co-coach with the Edmonton Oilers.

Maki became something of a hockey pariah; he was dealt to the expansion Vancouver Canucks before the team's inaugural 1970–71 season. Despite being offered the opportunity to sit out any games versus Boston, Maki refused to do so—and was regularly roughed up by the vengeful Bruins.

Maki played about two and a half seasons in Vancouver. He was forced to retire from hockey in December 1972 after being diagnosed with advanced brain cancer. It had initially gone undetected by the team's doctor despite Maki complaining about terrible headaches for weeks. According to Chico Maki, Wayne was given just six months to live, but he extended it to 17 months. He died on May 12, 1974. Maki was never an NHL superstar; he scored precisely 50 goals for Vancouver in his two-plus seasons with the Canucks. Nevertheless, largely because of the circumstances of his death, the club retired Maki's number 11. (It was callously "unretired" from 1997 to 2000 when high-profile free agent Mark Messier joined Vancouver. Messier insisted he be allowed to don his traditional jersey number 11. The Canucks acquiesced in a spineless capitulation that greatly displeased the Maki family.)

At the time of his death in 1974, Wayne Maki was 29 years, five months, and 22 days old. At the time Ted Green suffered his major head injury in Ottawa, Green was 29 years, five months, and 29 days old.

Green died after a long illness at age 79 on October 8, 2019—50 years and 17 days after the infamous 1969–70 preseason game in Ottawa. Curiously, most of his obituaries only barely mentioned the stick-swinging incident that had caused such alarm throughout hockey in 1969. However, one featured this old quote from Bobby Orr: "Who was the toughest guy I ever faced? Ted Green … in practice."[15]

6

The Old Boys' Club
The NHL's Geezer Goaltenders

"How would you like it if at your job, every time you made the slightest mistake, a little red light went on over your head and 18,000 people stood up and screamed at you?"[1]
—Jacques Plante

"It's the only way I can support my family. If I could do it another way, I wouldn't be playing goal."[2]
—Glenn Hall

For the most part, professional hockey is a young man's sport. To play at the game's highest level, one must be in prime physical condition and have the energy of youth as an ally. Seldom does a player advance beyond his 35th birthday and still have a job in the NHL. That was true in the 1969–70 season too.

However, there were notable exceptions to this trend. Most prominent was the NHL's goaltending fraternity. It had four distinguished members who were all born before 1930: Jacques Plante, Gump Worsley, Johnny Bower and Terry Sawchuk. A few other goalies in the league, such as Glenn Hall, Marv Edwards, Charlie Hodge, Les Binkley and Eddie Johnston, were all at least 34 years old and still competing when the 1969–70 season concluded. Exuberant youth and the laws of physiology were apparently no match for battle-hardened experience when it came to an NHL team's last line of defense. All four of the quadragenarians were established NHL icons by 1969.

"There are good goalies and there are great goalies. There are also important goalies. He was an important goalie,"[3] noted Ken Dryden in a documentary about Jacques Plante. That is an accurate statement on a number of levels.

Plante was born on January 17, 1929, in a farmhouse near Mont Carmel, Quebec. He was the oldest of 11 children in an impoverished family.

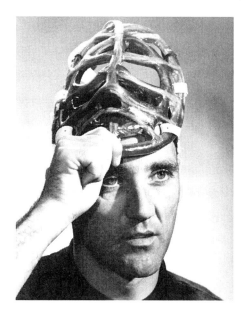

The first NHL goalie to routinely wear a mask, Jacques Plante superbly backstopped the Montreal Canadiens during their streak of five consecutive Stanley Cups in the late 1950s. This photograph is from 1960 when his mask was a novelty item (courtesy Library and Archives Canada; MIKAN inventory #3194972).

He began playing hockey at age three on cold, outdoor rinks. By age seven he had found his position: goaltender. Asthma kept him from playing any other position. Plante was slightly taller than the average netminder. In his early teens he became well known locally for his obvious skills. By age 15, Plante was so much in demand that he was playing goal for four different amateur teams simultaneously.

Plante was perceived as a free-thinking, quirky individual even as a youngster. His choice of headgear certainly perpetuated that notion. Plante kept his head warm by wearing tuques that he knitted himself. (His mother had taught him that skill as a way of saving precious pennies.) "He was good. He was fast. He never dropped any stitches," one of his sisters, Thérèse, proudly recalled. Only when he joined the fashionable Montreal Canadiens in 1953, as a replacement for the injured Gerry McNeil, did Plante not wear one of his homemade tuques while playing. Habs coach Dick Irvin would not permit it, saying it looked undignified.

By the 1954–55 season, Plante was the Canadiens' regular goaltender. He proceeded to win six Stanley Cups as a member of the Habs, seven Vezina Trophies as the league's best goaltender, and the Hart Trophy in 1962 as the NHL's MVP. Anglophone sports journalists frequently called Plante "Jake the Snake"—a nickname Plante disliked.

Plante became noteworthy as hockey's first "mobile" goaltender, something he started long before he got to the NHL. He would venture far from his net to chase down pucks and pass them to his defensemen before opponents got to them first. (Plante admitted it was a bit of a necessity because sometimes his defensemen were not especially swift afoot.) His wandering ways were initially considered reckless and foolhardy—and very occasionally did result in costly blunders. But overall, Plante's strategy was sound. Within a short time, being a good skater and a capable puck handler became part of every goalie's skill set. Plante was also acrobatic and fearless in net, seemingly undisturbed by the congestion of opposing players who tried to block his vision of incoming shots. The dominant Montreal teams of the late 1950s surely would not have been quite so good without Plante being their reliable backstop.

On Sunday, March 18, 1956, the Canadiens defeated the New York Rangers 3–1 at Madison Square Garden in the regular-season finale. As soon as the game ended, Plante—who clinched the Vezina Trophy that night—hurried over to CBS studios to appear live as a challenger on the popular panel show *What's My Line?* (Bennett Cerf deduced that Plante was a member of the Montreal Canadiens and took a wild guess that he was the team's goalie.) Being a stereotypically polite Canadian, Plante did not correct host John Daly who repeatedly mispronounced his surname as "plant" rather than "plawnt" throughout the segment. Daly also mispronounced "Vezina." Viewers north of the border—and hockey fans in general—must have cringed.

The incident Plante is most remembered for occurred on the evening of November 1, 1959, also at Madison Square Garden. About three minutes into the first period, New York's Andy Bathgate's backhand shot smacked Plante squarely in the face, leaving him bloodied. As had happened in countless hockey games before that historic Sunday night, Plante was taken to the arena's infirmary, patched up, and expected to continue the game. Plante, however, threw a curveball to coach Hector (Toe) Blake: He declared he would not return to the game without the strange protective mask he had been wearing during practices. Even NHL teams did not carry a spare goaltender in those days. (Often home teams provided an emergency replacement goaltender who sat in the stands, but that option was seldom chosen.) With Plante having all the leverage, Blake reluctantly concurred. Montreal won the game 3–1. The mask did not seem to impede Plante's vision at all. He was nine and a half minutes away from recording a shutout before the Rangers' Camille Henry finally beat him for New York's lone goal by knocking home a rebound.

The next day's *Montreal Gazette* reported, "Plante played despite a painful facial wound that required seven stitches to close. The tall netminder stopped a shot with his face and he had to be helped off the ice, his blood leaving a red path on the ice. After a doctor had patched up his face— the injury was described as cuts on the left side of his nose and upper lip— Plante came out wearing a flesh-colored helmet [sic] with slits for his eyes and mouth."[4]

Blake was still opposed to the mask and Plante agreed to keep wearing it only until his face had healed. Montreal was riding a huge unbeaten streak at the time, so Blake had very little to complain about. Plante played one final game without his mask, versus Detroit, on March 8, 1960—which the Canadiens lost 3–0. He wore the mask from that point onward. Many other goalies followed his lead. Within a decade it was unusual to see an NHL goaltender without a mask.

Plante and Blake butted heads over other issues too. Blake accused Plante of "indifferent play" in 1962–63. In June 1963, as part of a seven-player deal, Blake traded him to the New York Rangers where he played two more seasons. (One player the Canadiens got in return was goaltender Gump Worsley!) Plante retired in 1965 and did public-relations work for Molson Breweries for a while. However, he was lured back into hockey when NHL expansion came. He played one exhibition game for the Oakland Seals in September 1967. By the 1969–70 season, the 41-year-old Plante was plying his trade with the St. Louis Blues. In Game #1 of the Stanley Cup finals his mask would be a newsworthy item again.

Some knowledgeable hockey people maintain that Jacques Plante was the best NHL goaltender to ever don the pads. Journalist Red Fisher, who eloquently covered the Canadiens for 57 years, was one. In a documentary about Plante produced for History Television in Canada, Fisher said, "Will I see a goaltender who will play better than Plante did? I have my doubts. I really do."[5]

Lorne (Gump) Worsley was born on May 14, 1929. He acquired the curious nickname early in life when a childhood friend claimed his hair resembled that of Andy Gump, a character from the Sidney Smith comic strip *The Gumps*. The odd moniker stuck. Worsley was an excellent amateur soccer player, as was his father. On a few occasions he competed on teams that played exhibition matches versus touring English professional clubs. Worsley was an even better hockey goaltender, however.

Perhaps the most endearing aspect about Worsley was, at 5'7" and 180 pounds, he did not look at all like a professional athlete. *Hockey Night in Canada's* Brian McFarlane recalled, "Gump was everybody's favorite. Just looking at him in the net, you had to kind of smile and say, 'I hope this guy does well.' The little pug nose … the aggressive approach he took in sticking his chin into everything … the way he played was really entertaining."[6]

Despite being born and raised in Montreal, Worsley grew up as a New York Rangers fan in the prewar era when that team was a perennial Stanley Cup contender. His favorite player was goaltender Dave Kerr. He would eventually inherit Kerr's position with the team he followed as a youth—but by then the Rangers were nowhere near the top of the NHL.

In his first three seasons in the minor professional ranks, the chunky 5'7" Worsley was named to the all-star team each season. In 1952–53 the New York Rangers elevated him to the NHL. Despite playing on a weak team in the Big Apple, Worsley won the Calder Trophy as the league's Rookie of the Year. When Worsley demanded a $500 pay raise, the Rangers steadfastly refused and promptly shipped him back to the minor-league Vancouver Canucks. Worsley won the Western Hockey League's MVP award in 1953–54.

By 1954 Worsley was back in the NHL to stay, but the Rangers were frequently little more than a mediocre team throughout the rest of the 1950s. They never won a playoff series in the nine seasons Worsley played in New York. When a New York hockey writer once casually asked him which NHL team gave him the hardest time, Worsley immediately replied, "It's the Rangers."[7] One telling stat says plenty about the quality of teammates Worsley played with for much of his career: He was the first NHL goalie to both win 300 games and lose 300 games.

Keenly aware that hockey goalies had a reputation for being oddballs, Worsley concurred with the general perception. He stated, "Being a goaltender is not a job that would interest any normal, straight-thinking human."[8]

After the 1962–63 season, Worsley moved up considerably in the hockey world when he was dealt to the Montreal Canadiens. (In all likelihood Worsley was traded because he was heavily involved in trying to organize a players' union at the time.) He enjoyed considerable success with Montreal, winning Stanley Cups in 1965, 1966, 1968 and 1969. However, Worsley was used sparingly during the first three months of the 1969–70 season, appearing in just six games, as coach Claude Ruel looked toward the future; Ruel favored the much younger Rogie Vachon and Phil Myre as the Montreal netminders.

Late in 1969, the 40-year-old Worsley, "feeling he had not been given a fair shake," refused demotion to the minors and opted to retire instead, according to the January 2, 1970, edition of *Montreal Gazette*. When Minnesota acquired his rights from Montreal, Worsley quickly reversed his decision on retirement and helped lead the North Stars into the playoffs. His key contribution was starring in Minnesota's important 1–0 victory over Philadelphia on April 4—the second-last day of the regular season. That result put the North Stars over the hump in the West Division and guaranteed them a surprise playoff berth.

One major reason why Worsley was willing to play for the struggling North Stars was geography. Worsley had a fear of flying that he never truly did overcome. When he found out that the North Stars spent fewer hours in the sky than any of the other 11 NHL teams, Worsley agreed to join them. He ended up staying an additional four seasons. Worsley finally retired at the end of the 1973–74 season at the age of 45. Remarkably he never donned a mask during his lengthy career—despite once being knocked unconscious by a Bobby Hull slapshot. "Anyone who wears a mask is scared," he noted, along with "My face is my mask."[9]

Two Canadian rock bands each recorded tribute songs about Worsley decades after he retired from hockey: Huevos Rancheros ("Gump Worsley's Lament") and The Weakerthans ("Elegy for Gump Worsley"). Another Canadian band, Sons of Freedom, named their second album *Gump* after the famous barefaced goaltender.

Johnny Bower, Toronto's ageless goaltender, was approaching the end of the line in 1969–70. He played just one game that season—a loss versus the Montreal Canadiens. Bower officially retired in March 1970 (courtesy Library and Archives Canada; MIKAN inventory #3604625).

Toronto's Johnny Bower was the personification of resilience. He spent 11 long seasons playing minor pro hockey in Cleveland and Providence before being called up to fill one of the extremely scarce NHL goaltending positions on a lasting, full-time basis. Bower spent so much time toiling in the minors that he still holds the American Hockey League record for career wins by a goalie: 240.

Even today no one is quite sure how old Bower was when he finally arrived in the NHL—and he was not about to clarify matters regardless of how often he was asked to do so. (The birth year most often quoted for Bower was 1924, yet he managed to enlist in the wartime Canadian Army in 1940. He served for three years before being discharged for having rheumatoid arthritis in his hands.) Bower wasn't even the surname that appeared on his birth certificate. He was born John William Kiszkan. He began using his mother's surname informally when his parents divorced. He changed it to Bower legally when sportswriters kept bungling the spelling of Kiszkan.

Bower played the entire 70-game NHL schedule for the 1953–54 New York Rangers and posted a mediocre 29–31–10 record, but he recorded a laudable 2.60 goals-against average. Nevertheless, Bower was sent back down the pro hockey ladder to the minor-league Vancouver Canucks the following season. When Bower finally made it back to the NHL with the 1958–59 Toronto Maple Leafs, he was an aged newcomer. Yet he remarkably stayed with Toronto for 12 seasons through the 1969–70 campaign as their premier goaltender.

Somewhere along the line Bower acquired the nickname "The China Wall." It was a reference to the Great Wall of China—not an allusion to Bower's ancestry. His father was Ukrainian. Bower played his whole career without a mask—and was philosophical about his decision. "I just made up my mind that I was going to lose my teeth and have my face cut to pieces,"[10] he once admitted.

Bower developed and mastered a skill that is used by hockey goaltenders of all levels to this day: the poke check. Whenever a puck-carrying opponent moved within Bower's reach, he would take the initiative and attempt to strip him of the puck—by poking at it—before a shot could be taken. Such a maneuver required both skill and excellent timing. Nobody did it better than the man who created it. Bower was the Leafs' star netminder during their last stretch of NHL dominance in the early 1960s. He was on Toronto's Stanley Cup winners in 1962, 1963, 1964 and 1967. Beginning in 1964–65, Bower shared the team's goaltending labors with another all-time great: Terry Sawchuk. That was about the time when the NHL began to require each team carry two netminders. Bower frankly admitted years later, "I wasn't all that glad to see the two-goalie system come in. I wanted to play as many games as I could."[11]

A popular, good-natured figure on and off the ice, in 1965 Bower even recorded a holiday song (accompanied by his 11-year-old son and some neighborhood children dubbed The Rinky Dinks) titled "Honky the Christmas Goose." It did not exactly knock the Beatles out of the Top Ten, but it became a minor hit in Canada, ascending to the #29 spot on the pop chart. As for Bower's singing skills … he was a terrific goaltender! There is a YouTube clip of Bower lip-synching the song at a 2007 charity event. He was 83 (or thereabouts) at the time.

As Bower aged and was still a formidable goaltender, some fans and writers attributed Bower's longevity in the NHL to luck. Teammate Dave Keon scoffed at that idea. "You know what luck is in Bower's case?" he asked. "That's when a lot of preparedness and a little good fortune meet."[12]

However, even the ageless Bower could not escape the ravages of time. He was callously booed off the ice at Maple Leaf Gardens on March 8, 1969, after he allowed a soft third-period goal to Philadelphia's Dick Sarrazin that cost Toronto a victory. He did not play the rest of the regular season and only appeared in one game during the 1969 playoffs. During the 1969–70 season, beset by injuries, Bower played just one game, on December 10, 1969. Bower was age 45 (perhaps). The Maple Leafs lost to Montreal by a 6–3 score. Just before New Year's Day, the Leafs announced Bower had ligament injuries and would be out of their lineup indefinitely. He never returned to the ice. Bower formally announced his retirement from hockey in March 1970. He was honored widely in Canada during his later years. A street in Toronto is named after him. The Royal Canadian Mint put Bower's image on a non-circulating coin set featuring four Maple Leaf greats. He has a star of Canada's Walk of Fame. Bower was inducted into the Hockey Hall of Fame in 1976.

Terrance (Terry) Gordon Sawchuk was born in Winnipeg on December 28, 1929. As a teenager he was arguably the best goaltender in Canada's vast junior hockey ranks, starring for the Galt (ON) Red Wings. He quickly advanced upward through Detroit's minor pro ranks earning rave reviews and MVP awards at every stop. Sawchuk appeared in a handful of games with Detroit in January 1950 in the place of the injured Harry Lumley. However, the Red Wings were so impressed with what they saw from the young netminder that they traded the very capable Lumley to Chicago, making Sawchuk their netminder in an era when NHL teams routinely carried just one goalie on their rosters. NHL goaltenders were expected to play every minute of every game—without exception.

Sawchuk was deceptively large. He did not look like he weighed 180 pounds because he often played in an extreme crouch. He found that he could better see screen shots by doing so, and, as an added bonus, Sawchuk felt he had better balance and mobility. Of course, Sawchuk also put his unguarded face into the firing line too.

Terry Sawchuk's glory years were mostly with the Detroit Red Wings. He finished his illustrious career in 1969–70 guarding the pipes for the New York Rangers. Sawchuk, who recorded 103 shutouts, is regarded by many hockey experts as the greatest of all NHL goalies (courtesy Library and Archives Canada; MIKAN inventory #3591528).

Sawchuk, sporting a crew cut which would become something akin to his trademark, won the Calder Trophy as the NHL's rookie of the year for 1950–51, but he first truly came to prominence as a 22 year old in the 1952 Stanley Cup playoffs. That year the Red Wings were nearly invincible, notching 100 points in the 70-game schedule. The Wings won all eight of their playoff games in easily sweeping aside both Toronto and Montreal. Sawchuk recorded four shutouts and allowed just five goals in those eight games to compile a minuscule 0.63 goals-against average in the postseason. He allowed no goals whatsoever on home ice during the entire 1952 Stanley Cup playoffs. All told, Sawchuk won four Vezina Trophies as the NHL's top goaltender. He also won four Stanley Cups: three with Detroit and one with Toronto. "You couldn't put a pea by him," recalled Detroit's Alex Delvecchio. "When he wanted to play hockey, nobody was better than Terry."[13] Another teammate, Ted Lindsay, had this description of Sawchuk: "You could throw a handful of rice at him and he'd catch every grain."[14]

Goaltending was a dangerous profession in the days before protective face masks were worn. Sawchuk estimated that his face required 400 stitches to patch up the damage from pucks that smashed into it. (*Life* magazine once published a doctored but scary-looking photograph of how Sawchuk would appear if he really had 400 stitches on his face simultaneously. There was not enough room for them all.) Because he played out of his extreme crouch, Sawchuk also permanently damaged his back and walked with a noticeable stoop. Sawchuk was diagnosed with ruptured discs in his back and an obscure medical condition called kyphosis—an abnormal forward curvature of the spine. It was a painful affliction that made it impossible for Sawchuk to sleep comfortably for more than two hours at a time.

Sawchuk's medical procedures were varied and lengthy. His records show he had three operations to remove bone chips from his elbow. Sawchuk was also treated for a collapsed lung and severed tendons in his hand. Furthermore, Sawchuk was extremely self-critical, prone to depression, and constantly worried that he was not playing up to the high expectations always put upon him by fans and teammates.

Despite backstopping the Red Wings to the 1954–55 Stanley Cup, the moody 25-year-old Sawchuk was dealt to the Boston Bruins in a nine-player transaction two months later. (Detroit had a promising newcomer named Glenn Hall waiting for a chance to be an NHL goaltender.) It was not a happy fit for Sawchuk. In 1957, on the verge of a nervous breakdown, he retired from hockey. The Boston media labeled him as a quitter. The Bruins traded his rights back to Detroit in July. Sawchuk quickly un-retired. He spent another seven years with the Red Wings before being picked up on waivers by the Toronto Maple Leafs in 1964. Although he was clearly playing on borrowed time, in 1967 Sawchuk was acquired by the Los Angeles Kings in the NHL expansion draft. He was reacquired by the Red Wings for a third stint and finally by the New York Rangers where his career ended in 1970. On February 1, 1970, in a home game versus Pittsburgh, the 40-year-old Sawchuk recorded his 103rd and final NHL shutout.

Sawchuk battled demons off the ice. Alcohol often got the better of him. It made him an abusive spouse. His wife, Patricia Ann Bowman Morey, whom he married in 1953 after a whirlwind courtship, finally divorced him in 1969 after enduring 16 rough years of domestic mistreatment. Together they had seven children. Sawchuk was also a philanderer. While a member of the Stanley Cup champions Toronto Maple Leafs in 1967, he fathered a child out of wedlock. Such behavior away from the rink made Sawchuk expendable despite his superb goaltending skills. The 1969–70 season would be Sawchuk's swansong.

7

How Mick Jagger Nearly
Caused an NHL Forfeit

On November 4, 1969, the New York Rangers were about to embark on a three-game road trip with stops in Chicago, Oakland, and Los Angeles. The latter two games would be played on consecutive Friday and Saturday nights. At least that was what the NHL's official schedule said. Purely by chance, an employee of the Rangers named Thomas Barwell discovered a tidbit of information that had eluded Rangers general manager Emile Francis—and the NHL in general.

Barwell happened to read an entertainment press release from Los Angeles saying that the Rolling Stones, the famous British rock band, would be performing *twice* at the Inglewood Forum—the home of the Los Angeles Kings—on November 8. One of the concert times directly coincided with the Rangers–Kings game on that Saturday night. Apparently, the hockey game's time had been moved ahead six hours from an 8 p.m. start to 2 p.m. start to accommodate the two 75-minute concerts by the Stones, plus warm-up acts featuring Janis Joplin and Tina Turner.

Barwell told Francis what he had read about the time switch. This was news to him. Francis quickly telephoned NHL president Clarence Campbell to inquire about the new game time in Los Angeles for Saturday. Francis' call was also a revelation to Campbell; this was the first he had heard about any change in the game's starting time. He was grateful for the information and promptly contacted the Kings' owner Jack Kent Cooke to find out what was going on.

Years later Francis recalled his conversation with the NHL president and the subsequent events. "I didn't know who the Rolling Stones were and neither did Clarence Campbell," he remembered, "but that was beside the point."[1] Campbell thanked Francis for the important news, saying that there would have been no on-ice officials for an afternoon game at the Forum. The NHL's officials' schedule still had the game listed as an 8 p.m. start. They too had no inkling that there had been a time switch.

Francis was understandably furious at the situation. The significant time change was made without his knowledge, let alone his consent. He would have never agreed for the Rangers to play in Oakland on a Friday night and then play an afternoon game in Los Angeles the very next day. Campbell sided with the Rangers since Kings owner Cooke had never gone through the proper protocols to ask the NHL for a time change—much less gotten one. Cooke, a lawyer by trade, should have realized the problems his arbitrary time switch might create. Campbell ruled that Cooke was wholly at fault and was thus responsible for the scheduling mess. Accordingly, he would have to do something to persuade the Rangers to okay the time switch on very short notice to Saturday afternoon. If he could not do so, Campbell was prepared to forfeit the game to the Rangers. It would have been only the third forfeit in NHL history—and the first resulting from a scheduling snafu.

According to Francis, Cooke called him soon afterward with a somewhat impassioned and frantic plea. "Emile, I desperately have to move that game," he said. "By moving that game to the afternoon, I can get two performances from the Rolling Stones." As an aside, Cooke mentioned he would gross six figures on each rock concert.

Francis was utterly unmoved. "I don't give a damn about your performances," the Rangers' general manager bluntly told him.

Cooke became desperate. He tried again. "Emile, I've made a horrible mistake, but you're a man of compassion," Cooke began. "You'll do the compassionate thing. We're already committed [to having two concerts on Saturday night]."[2]

Francis, holding all the leverage, let Cooke stew until the morning of Friday, November 7—the day of the Rangers–Seals game—and then announced a solution had been mutually reached: Francis agreed to have the New York–Los Angeles game moved from the evening to the afternoon. In exchange for Francis' largesse, Cooke agreed to pay for the Rangers to take a first-class charter flight from Oakland to Los Angeles immediately following their game with the Seals on Friday. Onboard steak dinners would also be provided to the Ranger players and staff.

In a related remarkable and highly unusual side arrangement, the three on-ice officials (referee Bruce Hood and linesmen Neil Armstrong and Willard Norris) were permitted to travel aboard the Rangers' charter flight too—or else they would never have gotten to the New York–Los Angeles afternoon game on time. Normally this sort of fraternization between officials and players would have been strictly prohibited.

The change of schedule had no ill effects on the Rangers. New York soundly thrashed Oakland 8–1 on the evening of Friday, November 7, scoring six times in the first period. The Rangers thoroughly enjoyed their delicious steak dinners en route to Los Angeles—and convincingly beat the Kings 4–1 the following afternoon before 7,028 hockey fans to move into first place in the NHL's East Division.

The pair of Rolling Stones concerts that evening at the Inglewood Forum were sellouts, of course, with the highest-priced tickets selling for $12.50 apiece. The promoters badly underestimated the massive task of preparing for the two shows, however. Even with the Rangers–Kings game switched to the afternoon, the first concert did not begin until around midnight because of the excessive amount of time and labor it took to switch the Fabulous Forum from a hockey arena to a music venue equipped with the Stones' vast and complex sound system. Most of the band's fans had been in their seats for nearly five hours before Mick Jagger and his pals finally made their appearance onstage. Despite not being personally responsible for the mix-up, Jagger nevertheless felt the need to apologize to the patient concertgoers for the very late start. "Sorry you had to wait so long," he told them. "We had to wait, too—right?"[3] The second show did not start until 4 a.m. The Stones' last number ended at about 5:15 a.m. Ironically, the band's next tour stop was in Oakland—at the very same venue where the Rangers had played the Seals on Friday, November 7.

Four days later, a large notice, paid for by the concert promoters and the sponsoring radio station, appeared in the *Los Angeles Times*. It read, "Due to difficulties beyond our control, the two performances of the Rolling Stones concerts on Saturday, November 8th were delayed. We wish to apologize to the Rolling Stones' fans and their parents for any inconvenience."[4]

There was no mention of Emile Francis, Clarence Campbell, Jack Kent Cooke, the New York Rangers, the Los Angeles Kings, or the NHL.

8

Organic Matter

*The East Dominates
the All-Star Game*

"Professional hockey's long survival and its recent rise in
cross-continental popularity has been due to the game
itself—the skating, passing, shooting, body contact, goaltending, and competitive team spirit all wrapped up in
one package. The 23rd annual All-Star Game at St. Louis,
although one-sided in its outcome, had most assets of the
world's fastest sport."[1]

—Pat Curran, *Montreal Gazette*

On Tuesday, January 20, 1970, the best players from the East and West
Divisions gathered at the St. Louis Arena for the NHL's annual All-Star
Game. It was the 23rd edition of the game.

For most of its history, the NHL All-Star Game had matched the
defending Stanley Cup champions versus a group of star players from the
other five NHL teams. Usually it was contested before the regular season
began, with the defending Cup champion normally hosting the event.

The format of the All-Star Game was switched once the league
expanded from six to 12 teams in 1967. The contest now pitted an all-star
team from the East Division versus one comprised of outstanding players
from the West Division—and it now occurred in the middle of the regular
season. The 1970 matchup was the second East-West All-Star clash and the
third time the game was contested at midseason. The 1969 All-Star Game
had been played at the Montreal Forum. To many people's surprise, it had
ended in a tightly contested 3–3 tie.

For many years the All-Star Game was played in a highly competitive atmosphere. The change in format did not alter the participants' men-
tality at all. The game was approached very seriously and played with as
much gusto and professionalism as an average league game—perhaps more
so. There were penalties, body checks, and blocked shots. It contained the

56

passion and the intensity of a typical NHL game, traits that were appreciated by hockey fans everywhere. Alas, in the 21st century, that is no longer the case—but in 1970 it certainly was. Every player wanted to represent his division well. The players from the West strove to prove they were the equals of the older, established teams from the East. The stars from the East, of course, wanted to prove the exact opposite. Broadcaster Dan Kelly noted, "Last year the West declared, more or less, a moral victory from getting a 3–3 tie in Montreal. The East players have been reminded of that. They want to prove … they're superior."[2]

For the first time since 1948, the defending Stanley Cup champions did not host the All-Star Game. St. Louis was chosen as the venue by the NHL well in advance. In fact, on the day of the 1970 All-Star Game, president Clarence Campbell announced the locations for the next three midseason galas: Boston (1971), Minnesota (1972) and New York (1973).

As was traditional, the coaches from the two Stanley Cup finalists the previous season were behind the benches for the All-Star teams: Claude Ruel of the Montreal Canadiens and Scotty Bowman of the St. Louis Blues. The East was the visiting team and wore white uniforms. The West wore dark blue jerseys, presumably as a salute to the host team. The players' last names were on the back of them—something unusual in 1970. Art Skov had the honor of refereeing the game. The two linesmen were Claude Béchard and Matt Pavelich. An enthusiastic full house of 16,587 fans was in attendance. CBS carried the game live—marking the first time an NHL All-Star Game was broadcast nationally on an American television network. Of course, *Hockey Night in Canada* was present with a full crew to describe the game to Canadian viewers on CBC in both English and French.

According to All-Star Game regulations, the teams were permitted to dress 19 players each: two goalies, five defensemen and 12 forwards. The hometown St. Louis Blues were well represented. They had seven players on the West's lineup. Minnesota had five. Philadelphia, Pittsburgh and Oakland had two apiece. Defenseman Bill White was the only Los Angeles King on the squad. (Exactly one month later, White would be traded from the lowly Kings to the ascending Chicago Black Hawks.) The New York Rangers had the greatest representation on the East team with five members. Boston had four. Detroit and Montreal had three apiece. Toronto and Chicago had two each. One of the Black Hawks was Tony Esposito. It was a rarity and quite an honor for any rookie—especially a goaltender—to be chosen for the team. Esposito had already recorded 10 shutouts for the Black Hawks in 1969–70. Tony Esposito was one of only two All-Star Game debutants. The other was Bobby Clarke of Philadelphia—and he was a replacement for St. Louis' Phil Goyette who was injured.

The competitive spirit attached to the 23rd NHL All-Star Game went far afield. A bizarre controversy emerged about the organist at the St. Louis Arena, a man named Norm Kramer. A story circulated amid the St. Louis media that East Division coach Claude Ruel—making his debut as an All-Star game coach—greatly resented how Kramer used his musical talents to rile up the crowd against his Habs during the 1969 Stanley Cup finals! It was seemingly much ado about nothing, but the NHL overreacted tremendously and absurdly. The league performed its version of an organ transplant: Longtime Chicago Stadium organist Al Mengard was dispatched to St. Louis to play for part of the All-Star Game, presumably to placate Ruel and even things up from a musical standpoint.

"I didn't know a thing about it until we [he and the all-stars from the Habs] got to St. Louis from Boston," a perplexed Ruel told Pat Curran of the *Montreal Gazette.* "I was hardly in the hotel lobby before some writers started asking me questions—not about my All-Star Game lineup, but about the organist! I couldn't figure out what they were talking about. What do I care about the organist? He can't skate!"[3]

With the strange organic matter seemingly settled, the focus shifted to the All-Star Game itself. Uncharacteristically, within the first 37 seconds of play each team had scored a goal. An unlikely source got the first tally. Montreal's Jacques Laperrière, a defenseman, scored the game's first goal just 20 seconds after the opening faceoff. (During the course of the 1969–70 regular season, Laperrière would notch just six goals.) It was an unassisted effort. Laperrière intercepted a clearing pass from Minnesota's Danny O'Shea just inside the West's blue line. He fired a long shot that somehow eluded Philadelphia's Bernie Parent in the West goal. Just 17 seconds later, however, Pittsburgh's Dean Prentice leveled the game on an even longer shot—from just inside the red line—that embarrassingly fluttered past Ed Giacomin of the New York Rangers who was guarding the East's cage. The tying goal was assisted by Red Berenson of the St. Louis Blues (who got a big cheer when his name was announced as part of the scoring play) and Bob Woytowich of the Penguins.

It was certainly an inauspicious start for the two excellent netminders. In fairness, Parent later claimed he had been screened on Laperrière's goal by Gordie Howe. Similarly, Prentice's long shot suddenly flew over Giacomin's stick after hitting an unlevel patch of ice. The West's goal had so taken everyone by surprise that Bill Hewitt of *Hockey Night in Canada* twice misidentified the scorer as J.P. Parisé before being told that Dean Prentice was the man whose long shot had tied the game 1–1. Hewitt and Dan Kelly split the play-by-play duties.

After the frantic opening minute of play, the East dominated the game thereafter. At 7:20 of the first period, Detroit's ageless Gordie Howe scored a power-play goal while Frank St. Marseille of the Blues was sitting in the penalty box. Chicago's Bobby Hull and Montreal's Jacques Lemaire picked up assists. The first period ended with the East holding a 2–1 lead. They had also outshot the West 10–6.

The East Division opened up a bigger lead in the second period on goals by Hull and New York's Walt Tkaczuk. Hull's came early, at 1:53. Carl Brewer of Detroit got the only assist. Tkaczuk made the score 4–1 at 9:37. His goal, scored on a rebound, was assisted by two Boston Bruins: Johnny Bucyk and Johnny McKenzie. Before play resumed, both coaches opted to change their goalies. Tony Esposito replaced Giacomin and hometown favorite Jacques Plante took over for Parent. There was no further scoring in the game.

In the West's goal, Plante, who had turned 41 three days earlier, was kept extremely busy as the East continued to carry the bulk of the play. The final statistics for shots on goal showed the East had outgunned the West by a considerable margin: 44–17. Plante faced 20 shots in the third period alone but did not falter. In contrast, Tony Esposito had little to do. He faced just nine shots from the West all-stars in his half of the game.

With the game out of reach in the third period, the West players' objective shifted to ensure Plante kept a clean sheet for his 30-plus minutes of work. He did. Plante was justifiably named the game's second star. He gleefully raised his arms and skated something akin to a victory lap when he was summoned back onto the ice to be acknowledged by the appreciative St. Louis crowd. Afterwards Scotty Bowman made a point of singling out 37-year-old Dean Prentice for being the best player on the ice for the West—excluding Plante, of course.

Bobby Hull was lauded as the game's first star (and thus the official MVP) while Bobby Orr was named its third star despite not getting a goal or an assist. Unlike Plante, Hull and Orr modestly accepted the acknowledgment with traditional brief returns to the ice. A few boos descended from the partisan crowd for the two men—a most unusual noise at an NHL All-Star Game. Not surprisingly, East coach Claude Ruel was the only person who was lustily booed during the pregame introductions.

The highly competitive Ruel had given Orr more than a regular shift on defense, much to the amusement of Gordie Howe. The 41-year-old Howe kidded his temporary 21-year-old teammate, "You'll have to go out and practice tomorrow since you didn't get much work out there tonight."[4] Orr had already set seasonal records for assists and points by an NHL defenseman—and the season was only slightly more than halfway over. A journalist asked Orr if he would ever like to coach such a talented team as the East Division squad once he had retired from hockey as a player. Orr wittily replied, "No, but I'd like to own the team."[5]

Referee Skov enjoyed a relatively uneventful and peaceful night on the ice. He whistled just four minor penalties in the cleanly played contest, three against the West. (Bob Woytowich picked up two of them.)

The disparity in shots and overall play seemed to confirm what most hockey fans already knew in their hearts: The East Division overwhelmingly had the better players in the NHL. "East Stars Prevail with Easy 4–1 Win" accurately trumpeted the headline in the next day's *Calgary Herald*.

East Division coach Claude Ruel drew admiring praise from his players who were not members of the Habs. "That Ruel wouldn't let us coast," marveled Bobby Hull. "It was skate, check, shoot, get three men back. He had every guy on the team into the act."[6] New York goalie Ed Giacomin said it was the most intense atmosphere he had ever been involved in at an All-Star Game. This was his fourth. Ron Ellis of the Toronto Maple Leafs declared, "[Ruel] is a funny little guy, but he must be a whale of a coach."[7] Afterwards, Ruel was praiseful of his players' performance, crediting their 4–1 victory to exceptional team spirit. He also said that the East's players meshed immediately. "They played like they had been practicing for weeks,"[8] he noted.

Opposing coach Scotty Bowman conceded the palpable truth. "The East obviously has the bigger stars," he noted. "There's no way of getting away from it. You couldn't put together a much better team than they had."[9] Bowman also said his West team played as well as they possibly could against the East's overwhelmingly deep lineup of superstars.

Strangely, Bowman seemed miffed that Ruel had not rested his team's most dominant players at any point in the third period and seemed to want to score plenty of insurance goals against the overmatched West Division.

Yes, in 1970, the NHL All-Star Game was that competitive.

9

A Cool Wedding Quashed

In February 1970 the Oakland Seals were experiencing an upsurge of fan interest—at least by that team's modest standards. Ticket sales were up. Paul Thompson and Jo Lane Mickelson were two passionate, regular attendees who loved the Seals and, somewhere along the line, concluded that they loved each other too. According to a story that ran in the sports section the February 26 *Oakland Tribune*, the young couple decided to get married at the Oakland–Alameda County Coliseum Arena—where the Seals' home games were played. That was the plan, anyway.

"Let's get married right here,"[1] Paul suggested while the two were holding hands and watching their favorite hockey team.

"You're crazy!" retorted Jo. "At least it's out of the ordinary. I mean who gets married at the Oakland Arena?"[2]

"Jo Lane Mickelson and Paul Thompson—that's who!"[3] insisted the groom-to-be.

The future bride wanted some clarification. "You mean we'd get married down on the ice—in the middle of the arena?"[4] she asked.

"Why not?" Paul persisted. "It would probably be the first wedding on ice. Maybe we could have the ceremony during one of the games. We'd all be on skates—including the minister! What an unforgettable ceremony that would be!"[5]

The happy couple brought their oddball idea to the door of Seals' publicity man Bob Bestor, who ran it all the way up the chain of command to team president Bill Creasy. Creasy was not especially in favor of the plan, but he was not adamantly opposed to it, either. He was afraid the wedding would be looked upon by many observers as an undignified and tacky sideshow. He took the matter to an even higher authority: Creasy decided to poll the NHL's Board of Governors for their opinions and blessing (so to speak), so he made a telephone call.

In the 53 years the NHL had thus far existed, this was a new request, Creasy was told. The idea had its good and bad points, said the august body. In the end, the NHL's Board of Governors concluded nothing. "It's up to you," they decreed—and swiftly passed the buck back to Creasy. It was his call alone.

The verdict? "I decided not to allow the wedding," Creasy announced. "Our business is hockey—not weddings. I wish the couple well, but they'll have to get married someplace else."[6]

Though disappointed with the outcome, the couple quickly made alternate plans. "We plan to tie the knot in Reno this weekend," said Paul.

"But we'll be back next week to see the Seals play," interjected Jo. "We wouldn't miss them for the world. Besides, Mr. Creasy gave us two tickets as a wedding present."

"Boston's Mighty Orr" Leads the Bruins

"Orr: blond, crewcut Bobby, who could take the puck behind his own net and skate through and past and around the other team. Bobby, who in the days when a young country seemed to be waking up from a long nap, when a minor professional sport began to shake off the cobwebs and look to new horizons, embodied the idea that it didn't have to be as it always had been. A defenseman could take off, could improvise, could be so good that they'd let him defy every bit of conventional coaching wisdom."
—Stephen Brunt, *Searching for Bobby Orr*

"Orr has never basked in being Bobby Orr. Instead, he's been hockey's version of John Lennon, brilliant but purposefully in the shadows, a thoughtful yet unassuming icon."[1]
—Dan Rosen, NHL.com

Modern hockey fans—those under the age of 40—almost always adhere to the notion that Wayne Gretzky is the greatest NHL player of all time. After all, the man who owns every significant scoring record on the books must be at the top of the heap, right?

"That's not true," insist the Baby Boomers (and the rapidly dwindling number of hockey fans who are even older). "You never saw Bobby Orr play."

In 1969–70, Bobby Orr, a defenseman, won the National Hockey league scoring title—and by a fairly comfortable margin. The 22 year old tallied 120 points from 37 goals and 83 assists. (Teammate Phil Esposito finished second with 99.) Such numbers would have been the stuff of far-fetched fiction just a few years earlier.

There is not much NHL film footage taken before the Second World War that still survives. Those small snippets that do exist show a vastly different game than what was played even in 1950. Defensemen played defense. Period. When their team was on offense, they were expected to linger near their own blue line—often standing completely still—in readiness to thwart the opposition's next counterattack. Rushing defensemen were almost unknown in that era, although the NHL had one noteworthy blueliner who occasionally broke the mold. Boston's volatile Eddie Shore sometimes took the initiative to lead a rush into the enemy's zone. Shore remarkably finished tenth in NHL scoring in 1928–29 with a meager sum of 19 points at a time when goals were precious and reckless offensive play was definitely frowned upon by coaches. The introduction of the center red line opened up the game to more passing and greater offensive play, but the stereotypical NHL defenseman remained a lumbering giant who only carried the puck long enough to pass it to a forward. Having a defenseman be the centerpiece of a team's offense was absolutely unheard of until the age of Bobby Orr.

Orr biographer Stephen Brunt said of Boston's brilliant number four, "Bobby Orr was one of those rare [athletes] who was an original; he's a one-off. He arrives [in the NHL] fully formed—really as a kid, almost—and reinvents the game and his position as a defenseman. Orr takes hockey and sees it in a different way. He could express it in a way no one had seen before."[2]

Dink Carroll of the *Montreal Gazette* echoed those same ideas when he wrote in his March 31 column, "Orr is not going to revolutionize the play of defensemen for the basic reason that there has never been another rearguard with his combination of essential skills."

The son of an amateur hockey player of some repute, Robert Gordon Orr was born in Parry Sound, Ontario, on March 20, 1948. Parry Sound is located on Georgian Bay, about 140 miles north of Toronto. Popular with cottagers, it boasts the deepest natural fresh-water port in the world. According to the 2016 Canadian census, Parry Sound has about 6,400 full-time residents—about 1,000 more people than when Orr was born.

As early as the age of 11, Orr was attracting plenty of attention from hockey followers on a local level. Fortunately for the Boston Bruins, they were the first NHL club to notice him. It was at a bantam tournament in Gananoque, Ontario. Longtime Bruins coach and general manager Milt Schmidt easily recalled the details decades later in an interview:

We went up to see two players play that particular night by the names of Eaton and Higgins. They were on our list. They were soon forgotten because we saw this little kid—this towheaded, crew-cut kid—with his pants below his knees on defense. He just took things over by himself. Eaton and Higgins were never part of the Boston Bruins after that. We concentrated on Bobby Orr.[3]

This was still the era before the NHL had an amateur draft. Parry Sound was located beyond the territorial rights of any NHL team. This meant any club could sign Orr, the moment he turned 14, to what was known as a hockey C-form. The "C" stood for commitment. Once a player signed one, he became the property of the NHL club that held the form. The Bruins quickly attempted to win the hearts of Bobby and his parents before any other club caught wind of the future superstar's existence. Wren Blair, then a Bruins scout, would recall he was firmly stationed on the Orrs' front porch every day when Bobby came home from school. Young Bobby did sign a Boston C-form after the Bruins promised to pay for the Orrs to get plastered—literally: The team agreed to finance a stucco job for the family's modest home.

Boston had big plans for Orr and spared no expense to give him the best nurturing. The Bruins revived the dormant Oshawa Generals junior hockey franchise and even created a metropolitan Toronto junior league for the team to play in. Orr joined the Generals at age 14. They played for a season at Maple Leaf Gardens while the Oshawa Arena was being upgraded to handle the adoring and awestruck throngs who wanted to see the modest teenager from Parry Sound in action. Orr was typically playing with and against players between the ages of 17 and 20. Sometimes on the ice the full 60 minutes in each game, Orr still dominated.

Brad Park, who is generally regarded at the NHL's second-best defenseman during the 1970s, was born in 1948—the same year as Bobby Orr. In an interview for a documentary piece about Orr, Park recalled going to watch Orr play junior hockey in Maple Leaf Gardens against young men in 1962 and scarcely believing what he was seeing. Park was playing bantam hockey at the time. "It was amazing,"[4] Park recalled. Orr's opponents often mocked his youthfulness in attempts to needle him. "How was the eighth grade today?" some would derisively ask him. "Are you going to pass the eighth grade?"

Once Orr began playing in larger centers, word about this extraordinary hockey prodigy circulated fast. Chicago's Bobby Hull recalled playing a road game in either Toronto or Montreal. Hull's father had travelled from Belleville, Ontario, to see his son, but another hockey player named Bobby was forefront in his mind. The first thing the elder Hull said to his superstar son was "Robert, you ought to see this blond-haired kid who plays for Oshawa. Is he ever going to be something!"[5]

When Orr did arrive in Boston in 1966 as an 18 year old, he electrified Boston as no other athlete had done before or has done since. David Davis of Deadspin wrote, "Orr revolutionized the position, ignited a city, and carried a black-and-white league into technicolor."[6] Orr's influence was far-reaching and groundbreaking. Numerous players on the gold medal-winning 1980 U.S. Olympic hockey team said they were inspired to take up the sport after watching Bobby Orr and his fellow Bruins on television.

Boston had always been a good hockey town. Despite the Bruins being a perennial doormat in the NHL from 1960 to 1967, they always had decent fan support. The Bruins often outdrew the Boston Celtics in home attendance even though Boston's pro basketball team was winning one NBA championship after another during that same time period. When Orr joined Boston in the autumn of 1966, tickets to Bruins games were suddenly exceedingly precious commodities.

"You couldn't get tickets unless you knew somebody," said Richard Johnson, curator of the Sports Museum, located in the Bruins' present-day home of TD Garden. "It was like getting tickets to a Beatles concert."[7] Others elevated Orr even beyond the fanatical idolatry routinely accorded Liverpool's Fab Four. "He was God," said Stanley Forman, an employee of the *Boston Herald American* who witnessed every game Orr ever played at Boston Garden. "When he was on the ice you just watched him."[8]

Despite being known for his extreme sense of modesty, every so often Orr showed he knew his value to the sport and his team. When he was making $50,000 per year as a rookie—a fabulous amount in 1967—he appeared on *Front Page Challenge*, a long-running Canadian television panel show similar to *What's My Line?* A veteran Toronto journalist, the crusty but lovable Gordon Sinclair, asked Orr if he thought it was right that a mere teenage lad should be earning all that money by playing hockey. Orr responded that it made a lot more sense than when he was filling the arena in Oshawa every game and getting only a measly $10 stipend per week. *Touché!*

Alas, the teenage Orr could not singlehandedly elevate the Bruins out of the NHL basement in his rookie season in Boston. However, help—a lot of it—was soon on the way. After the 1966–67 season—the last year of the old six-team NHL—some key personnel acquisitions came to the Boston lineup from the first-place Chicago Black Hawks. May 15, 1967 is a red-letter day in Bruins history. That fateful Monday, the Bruins dealt Pit Martin, Gilles Marotte and Jack Norris to Chicago. Martin, age 23, was an undersized forward, but he had scored 20 goals for last-place Boston in 1966–67. (He was, in fact, the only 20-goal scorer on the Boston roster that season.) Marotte, 21, was a steady but unspectacular defenseman. Norris, 24, was a goalie who spent most of his professional career languishing in the minor leagues; he would record only 20 NHL victories. In return for the expendable threesome, the Bruins picked up the equivalent of a gold mine: Phil Esposito, Ken Hodge and Fred Stanfield.

It turned out to be one of the most lopsided trades in sports history. Esposito, who had not garnered too much attention outside Chicago despite scoring 27 goals one season, became a prolific goal scorer—the NHL's biggest threat to put the puck in the net for half a decade—notching 459 of them in slightly more than eight seasons in a Bruins uniform, winning the NHL scoring title five times. Hodge was no slouch himself. He collected 289 goals in nine seasons with Boston. Stanfield scored at least 20 goals in each of the six seasons he played with Boston, altogether recording 135 tallies for the Bruins. With one front-office maneuver, the Bruins' fortunes changed dramatically for the better. Esposito, who was not one to withhold his opinions, boldly predicted at his first Boston training camp that his new team would qualify for the playoffs in 1967–68, be strong contenders for the Stanley Cup the following season … and win it in the third year. It turned out to be a remarkably prescient observation.

The Bruins swiftly gelled. After a decade of conspicuously being the NHL's annual doormat, they suddenly were more than competitive. Boston got respectable goaltending from the duo of Gerry Cheevers and Ed Johnston, ample scoring from plenty of players, but Orr was the team's undisputed catalyst. No one could dictate the pace of a game like Orr did. One treat to behold was to watch Orr kill penalties. If he got the puck when the Bruins were shorthanded, he came up with ways to run off the time as no one had done before. He would skate in large sweeping circles toward the opposing blue line, deftly stickhandling, daring someone on the other team to try to dislodge him from the puck. Often he found no takers and retreated to his own blue line—still firmly possessing the puck—to start the same routine all over again. This was something no one had ever seen done in the NHL—or anywhere else, for that matter. Boston goalie Gerry Cheevers, who loved to play the ponies, once kidded that he was tempted to pull out the daily racing form for a leisurely read whenever Orr was killing a penalty because he knew the opposition was unlikely to gain control of the puck.

Orr was likely the biggest beneficiary of the Bruins roster enhancement. He no longer had to worry about trying to win games singlehandedly. Pittsburgh coach Red Kelly noticed the difference, saying that although Orr was still capable of spectacular individual rushes every night, Orr had become a smarter player who used his teammates more wisely during 1969–70 than in his previous three years in the NHL. The amount of attention Orr received in the press dwarfed other noteworthy Bruins. Teammate Phil Esposito scored a league-leading 43 goals and finished second to Orr with 99 points, but few fans talked about Espo's scoring exploits.

The Bruins also noticeably toughened their image around Orr. Their players not only got better—they got bigger and stronger and meaner. Orr himself was no slouch with his fists if someone wanted to test him with rough stuff. "Orr had a temper. They tested him in his first year in the league," remembered renowned hockey writer Red Fisher. "They didn't test him in the second."[9] Not a man to be trifled with, in his tragically truncated career Bobby Orr had more major penalties for fighting than Gordie Howe,

Mario Lemieux and Wayne Gretzky *combined*. In one 1967 game versus the Maple Leafs, Orr put a terrible beating on Toronto's Brian Conacher after Conacher clipped him in the face with his stick and drew blood. He was booed routinely in Toronto for years afterward despite being the most famous, dominant and popular athlete in Canada. Although Orr had shown that he could ably take care of himself in tussles, teammates became dutifully protective of their superstar—especially after the injuries and surgeries to Orr's knees started to mount. Wayne Cashman was especially eager to throttle anyone who messed with Boston's priceless meal ticket.

Veteran goaltender Eddie Johnston, who had suffered through most of Boston's lean years in the first half of the 1960s, had a uniquely different perspective on the team's distinct camaraderie in which pranks and joshing were dressing-room staples. "Let's face it," he told Gary Ronberg of *Sports Illustrated*, "we're just a bunch of kooks and degenerates who happen to get along."[10] (That same *SI* issue featured number four on its cover alongside the pithy but apt caption "Boston's Mighty Orr.") In his 2018 book, *Bobby: My Story in Pictures*, Orr credited the good-natured Johnston and other Bruins for a continuous upbeat attitude that seemed to engulf and unite the entire Boston team. One photo in Orr's book is indicative of this attitude: It was taken in Boston's dressing room on January 7, 1970, shortly after the Bruins had pounded the Seals 6–1 in Oakland. In that game, Johnny Bucyk notched his 300th NHL goal while Orr recorded his 78th career tally. Both men are holding pucks with those numbers taped to them. Johnston is seated between his two teammates comically displaying a puck bearing a zero.

Prior to the 1969–70 season, a panel of 24 experts chosen by *The Hockey News* gazed into their crystal balls and made bold predictions. Twenty of them foresaw Boston winning the regular-season race in the NHL's East Division. (The other four votes went, of course, to Montreal—the two-time defending Stanley Cup champions and always a perennial favorite.) This was an unfamiliar expectation for a Bruins team to face. The last time Boston had a first-place NHL club was 1940–41 when the manpower demands of the Second World War had not yet wrecked the then-powerful Bruins. Bobby Orr's presence had dramatically and positively changed how the Bruins were perceived in the hockey world. They had the swagger of winners for the first time in a generation.

The April 29, 1970, edition of the *Montreal Gazette* had an offbeat photograph atop its sports section. The photo showed Nancy Clifford cheerfully overwhelmed by stacks upon stacks of envelopes from places near and far. The overworked young secretary's task was to collect and sort Bobby Orr's enormous quantity of fan mail. It was most certainly a full-time occupation. In the first four months of 1970, Orr had received about 7,000 pieces of correspondence in care of the Bruins. The photo caption dutifully noted, "All letters are answered." Orr enjoyed receiving letters—especially from youngsters—and he appreciated the efforts his admirers took in writing to him in the days before instant communications. Decades later Orr noted, "The simple act of taking the time to write a letter, putting it in an envelope, finding a stamp and mailing it off—that time has come and gone. And it's too bad. You kept your fingers crossed, and maybe—just maybe [the recipient] would find the time to respond."[11] Orr, with the help of Clifford, almost always did.

No one but Orr himself knows how much anonymous charity and goodwill work he did in Boston and elsewhere—and continues to do as a septuagenarian. He would quietly slip into Boston-area hospitals laden with autographed Bruins paraphernalia to give to bedridden fans who adored him. Stories still circulate each year about Orr personally telephoning lifelong Bruins fans who are on their deathbeds to engage them in long chats.

One day a Boston hockey journalist who was complaining about life's little aches and routine setbacks was urged by Orr to meet him outside the Bruins' practice facility to make a special trip. The man got into Orr's car at the appointed time. Orr, without saying a word, drove to a local children's hospital. The reporter immediately noticed that Orr knew his way around the building; he had obviously been there many times before, alone, without any fanfare or reporters tagging along. Orr tirelessly interacted for hours with children, many who were terminally ill. Upon leaving the hospital, Orr finally spoke to the scribe. He coyly asked, "How do you feel now?"

Frosty Forristal, Boston's longtime assistant trainer, recalled that these hospital visits took a huge emotional toll on Orr. "He goes in and talks with a kid. They have a good conversation. Bobby tells him a story, signs a stick for him, and they become good pals. Then Bobby finds out the kid has cancer and it's only a matter of weeks or days. That kills him. He won't be himself for a couple of days."[12]

"He's a better person than he is a hockey player,"[13] noted one longtime friend.

The Bruins got off to a fast start in 1969–70, amassing six wins and a tie in their first seven games. However, they then surprisingly went five games in a row without a victory. From that point onward, Boston would remarkably not lose two consecutive games for the rest of the regular season. A revitalized Johnny Bucyk was having the best offensive season in his career. Goaltenders Gerry Cheevers and Ed Johnston were playing well enough to give Boston a chance in every game. Both had goals-against averages below three. With the Bruins averaging 3.6 goals per game, the arithmetic meant Boston was winning regularly.

Despite the Bruins playing very well, Boston too was locked in a titanic fight merely to qualify for a playoff spot. The Bruins struggled mightily against East Division teams—especially in games away from Boston Garden. Luckily for the Bruins, they had relentlessly feasted upon the West's clubs all season. Boston just lost twice in 36 meetings in inter-divisional play in 1969–70. It provided an enormous difference in the end. Like every team in the East, the Bruins could not afford to squander points.

While Boston's number four was the epitome of old-school hockey modesty, number 16 on the same club was the polar opposite. Derek Sanderson was anything but the typical self-deprecating puck-chaser. If Sanderson was not his sport's version of Broadway Joe Namath, at least he was trying to be. Outside of Orr, he was the most talked about Bruin. Irrepressible and refreshing, Sanderson was certainly the best interview subject in the NHL. One thing was for certain: Sanderson definitely was enjoying has status as a sports celebrity in Boston. Consider this description of Sanderson's lifestyle from the April 6, 1970, edition of *Sports Illustrated*:

> The loosest player in the National Hockey League's tightest playoff race ever was Derek Sanderson, 23, center of the Boston Bruins. He awoke in a mod, round bed, undreamed of in his street-fighting, high-school dropout days, picked up a phone from the white sheepskin rug and dialed his answering service. Little Joe, as Sanderson is sometimes called, had received no messages in the night from his idol, Big Joe Namath. He ran a brush over his razor-cut hair, got out a pair of flowered bell-bottoms and a shirt the color of orange sherbet and walked outside to his gold 1970 Continental Mark III. The plates read BRUINS 16. "They're welded on," said [Sanderson]. "They'd be stolen every day if they weren't."

The *SI* piece, co-written by Gary Ronberg and Mark Mulvoy, chronicled Sanderson's disappointment when he learned the Bruins' travel arrangements for their final regular-season game in New York City had abruptly been moved up by a day. The change in scheduling had severely harmed his social life. "I had a date with Jackie tonight," he moaned. "No, with Susan. I forgot. Jackie was the backup."

Sanderson was ahead of the curve on a lot of issues. Unlike many of his less worldly peers, Sanderson realized the value attached to publicity and strived to attain it continuously. (One can assume Sanderson was probably irked when it was Chicago's far less worldly Keith Magnuson—conspicuously minus a front tooth—who appeared on *SI*'s April 6 cover instead of him.) He was also the only Bruin who had noticeably long hair along with a mustache—something almost unheard of among the conservative NHL players of 1970. "When I made my NHL debut," Sanderson recalled in his autobiography, "most players were sporting crew cuts and wearing team-issued blazers and gray slacks. Nobody else our age dressed like that. I was just the guy to shake things up."[14] Straight-laced teammate Bill Speer, who was trained as a barber, routinely volunteered to give Sanderson a free sample of his handiwork.

The ladies of Boston and many locales beyond the Hub certainly seemed to be smitten with the playboy image that Sanderson conspicuously oozed. Sanderson was named by *Cosmopolitan* magazine as one of the sexiest men in America. One of Sanderson's roommates was Liv Lindeland, a stunning, voluptuous, blonde Norwegian beauty who became *Playboy*'s 1972 Playmate of the Year. As a publicity stunt, the Bruins once organized a "Win a Date with Derek Sanderson" contest to further enhance his growing notoriety and popularity. The club was overwhelmed by the huge number of entries it received. A septuagenarian grandmother was randomly chosen as the winner.

Apart from his flamboyant persona, Sanderson was a hugely valuable Bruin. Even his bitterest enemies in the NHL—and Sanderson had plenty— had to admit he was one of the NHL's best penalty killers and an excellent center and faceoff man. Sanderson was the centerpiece of Boston's checking line who took extreme pleasure in wrecking the opposition's power plays. Sanderson also specialized in scoring shorthanded goals, notching five in 1969–70. He scored 24 in his nine years with the Bruins. (Entering the 2020–21 season, only Rick Middleton and Brad Marchand have more short-handed tallies in Boston history.) Sanderson was also an aggravating opponent who would do and say practically anything to unnerve his adversaries. Often it was not what Sanderson did but *how* he did things that caused opposing players' blood pressure to rise. Even New York's coach/general manager, Emile Francis, bluntly told *SI*, "I want to punch him in the nose."[15]

Boston did everything well in 1969–70—with the notable exception of playing games against East Division rivals in their buildings. Overall the Bruins were a mediocre 13–14–11 in games not played in Boston. Fortunately for their playoff chances, they more than made up for their poor road record by being nearly unbeatable at home. In their 38 games at Boston Garden, the Bruins were an impressive 27–3–8. Boston also led the NHL in scoring with 277 goals. Critics sometimes labeled the Bruins' goaltending as suspect (they only ranked sixth-best in goals allowed), but their offensive potential could always make up for an occasional defensive lapse or net-minding error. Among the NHL's East Division clubs, Boston was the least volatile throughout the long season—never faltering too badly in the standings to risk falling out of a playoff berth.

The Bruins were an entertaining bunch to watch—and the television networks knew it well. Six of the eight regular-season games Boston played in Montreal and Toronto in 1969–70 were scheduled for Saturdays. That way they would be televised on *Hockey Night in Canada*.

11

The New York Rangers
Revamped and Dangerous

"Beginning in the 1940s, when Fiorello LaGuardia was still
mayor, the Rangers compiled a record of futility unmatched
in major league hockey. For two decades they were incon-
testably the worst team in the NHL. But last weekend,
the new, space-age Rangers were on top in the NHL's
East Division, where they had strutted since way back in
November…"
"The town that gave you the throbbing, real-life stories
of the Knicks, the Jets and the Mets is watching over the
Rangers with a pride that is mingled with astonishment and
some apprehension…"
—Gary Ronberg, *Sports Illustrated*, March 2, 1970.

Back in the late 1920s, when the NHL was full of surprises, the New
York Rangers were one of the league's powerhouse franchises. The Broadway Blueshirts (as some hockey writers liked to refer to them) had entered
the league as one of three new expansion teams in 1926–27. The Rangers
were the second New York City team. The New York Americans, formerly
the Hamilton Tigers, relocated to Manhattan for the 1925–26 season. They
proved to be such a popular and exciting attraction that the NHL promptly
granted an additional NHL franchise to the Big Apple. Famous boxing pro-
moter Tex Rickard owned the team. Using a cute pun, he called his team
"Tex's Rangers." Within a very short time, the New York Rangers quickly
became the more popular and successful of the city's two NHL teams that
each played home games at Madison Square Garden.

Always among the NHL's front-runners before the Second World War,
the New York Rangers won the Stanley Cup in just their second season,
1927–28. Another Stanley Cup came in 1932–33. A third came in 1939–40.
The powerful New Yorkers finished atop the league's standings in 1941–
42—but international affairs well beyond the team's control intervened not

long afterwards. The Rangers swiftly plummeted to the bottom of the table the following season when their roster was decimated by the ever-growing manpower demands of Canada's wartime military. The team never truly recovered from that enormous, franchise-altering setback. Despite being a sub–.500 club during the regular season in 1949–50, the Rangers found new life in the Stanley Cup playoffs that spring and took the Detroit Red Wings to double overtime in the seventh game of the finals before losing. It was a steady descent for New York from that point onward. The only thing that came to hockey fans in the Big Apple in the next two decades was a hefty serving of disappointment—and precious little hope on the horizon. New York City became an NHL wasteland.

The Rangers' revival in 1969–70, the product of a four-year rebuilding campaign, could largely be attributed to one individual. Gary Ronberg wrote in a feature article for *Sports Illustrated* on March 2, 1970, "Beyond dispute [is] the fact that the Rangers have become a very fine team—and that is due entirely to the heart and mind of a single man, Emile Francis, the general manager and coach. Not since Vince Lombardi revived those corpses in Green Bay has one man done so much for one team."

If Emile Percival Francis did not possess the sharpest hockey mind in the NHL in 1969, the list of people who surpassed him was a short one. Certainly, no executive in professional hockey outworked him. At 5'6" and perhaps 145 pounds, Francis did not have much of a physical presence, nor was he a dynamic figure among the city's most glamorous sports personalities. (In the Big Apple, it was the era of Broadway Joe Namath and the Super Bowl champion Jets. The Amazin' Mets rose from the outhouse to the penthouse seemingly overnight to win the World Series in 1969. Even the Knicks were on the cusp of an NBA title in 1970.) Only the city's NHL team lacked panache as the 1960s were coming to an end. In fact, few Rangers had marquee qualities, at least according to Ronberg's assessments. He wrote,

> For a New York sports figure, Francis is strangely inconspicuous. Not much taller than a parking meter, he dresses with no distinction and avoids the hum of Manhattan whenever he can, preferring the anonymous life of a Long Island suburb. He presides over a team almost equally lacking in New York glitter. The closest thing the Rangers have to a swinger is Rod Gilbert, a deeply sideburned forward who makes the discotheque scene but is not exactly a Rocket Richard on the ice. The leading scorer is a mouthful of Czech consonants, Walter Tkaczuk, who doesn't have enough clout to get the Madison Square Garden P.A. man to pronounce his name right. He is "ka-chook" at home but "tay-chuck" on Seventh Avenue.

Francis spent a nomadic 14 years in various levels of professional hockey as a stereotypical small but wiry goaltender. His quick reflexes earned him the nickname "The Cat" early in his pro career, but he only got into 95 NHL games. Francis was a tough customer despite his diminutive stature. In one stint with the Chicago Black Hawks, Francis suited up for a game with a dislocated left shoulder. Unable to lift his injured arm to protect his noggin, Francis took a puck flush in the face. The painful mishap broke his nose and cost him five teeth. Following his retirement as a player, Francis got a job in the New York Rangers organization in 1961 as the coach and general manager of the Guelph, Ontario, junior team. (This was during the era when NHL clubs owned numerous under-21 squads throughout Canada and used them as developmental teams.) He did well there. Francis had found his true calling in life.

Something of a tough taskmaster, Francis insisted always that things be done his way. But there was method and logic to it all. The players who followed his orders—and they all did—saw positive results almost immediately. Francis clearly knew what he was talking about.

By 1964 the lowly Rangers had hired Francis to hold the general manager position with the parent club in New York City. He quickly discovered that the Rangers were an undersized bunch who routinely were pushed around by the NHL's powerhouse teams. Francis set out to rectify matters in a hurry. He brought in some muscle in the persons of Orland Kurtenbach, Reggie Fleming and Wayne Hillman. What the three men lacked in grace, they more than made up for in sheer toughness. Francis also risked the wrath of Ranger fans by trading away aging Andy Bathgate—the man who was the franchise's all-time scoring leader. By 1970, Bathgate was playing in the minor professional Western Hockey League. In the Bathgate trade, the Rangers got some excellent young players from Toronto who were paying dividends in 1969–70: Rod Seiling, Arnie Brown, and Bob Nevin. Francis also saw to it that his team's scouting staff was increased dramatically.

In December 1965, Rangers coach George (Red) Sullivan was fired. Francis took over his job. As he had done in Guelph, Francis wore dual hats as both the team's coach and general manager. Bill Jennings, the Rangers' free-spending owner, persuaded Francis that the team would be better if he would relinquish the coaching duties to someone else. Ex-Montreal great Bernie Geoffrion held the Rangers' coaching post for a while but had to quit for health reasons when he was diagnosed with a dangerously serious case of ulcers. Francis quickly returned to his old job with alacrity.

Jennings had a change of perspective and was happy to have Francis back behind the Rangers' bench. "It took me a while to appreciate Emile as a coach," he said. "For the longest time I had him figured strictly as a GM type. But he really wants to coach, and he's proved there isn't a better coach anywhere. As far as I'm concerned, he can have both jobs for the rest of his life."[1]

If the Rangers wanted to be inspired by work ethic, they had to look no further than their coach as a fine example. Ronberg described the indefatigable Francis as someone who toils "like a Georgia mule." When the Rangers were not on the road, Francis typically left his home at 8 a.m. and often did not return until midnight "depending on the whims of the whimsical Long Island Railroad." Occasionally he put in 18-hour days. Francis' motto was "There never is enough time." Accordingly, he always quaintly brown-bagged his lunch so he could eat quickly at his desk and not waste precious hours in restaurants. Recalling Francis' knack for micromanagement, Rod Gilbert recalled, "If he could have sharpened skates or taped sticks, he would have done it."[2]

Francis was keenly aware of the mental aspects of hockey and was something of an amateur psychologist. "An inveterate worrier," wrote Ranger historian Reg Lansberry, "Francis was always acutely aware that, in his role as coach of the team, he could never allow himself to get too high or too low depending on circumstances, lest his players pick up on it."[3] Therefore, Francis strove to make sure his players did not get too moody over losses nor too cocky after wins. Maintaining a degree of equipoise throughout the long season was Francis' objective.

By his own estimation, Francis typically accrued 75,000 miles in the air each year juggling both his GM and coaching jobs. Francis' thorough commitment to the Rangers even impressed his adversaries. Scotty Bowman, the coach and general manager of the St. Louis Blues, commented, "If New York is here for a game on Thursday night, you can bet Emile will be in Omaha on Wednesday watching his farm club. Emile has everything at his fingertips."[4]

He also had the equivalent of a hockey encyclopedia mounted on his office walls. In the days before computers, Francis had enormous magnetic boards installed. They covered the entirety of his personal enclave at Madison Square Garden. Those invaluable boards contained not only the rosters of every NHL team, but the rosters of all their minor league affiliates too! If a player was traded, retired or released, his magnet could easily be moved or removed as necessary. New players could always be added too. Thus, Francis often knew his opponents' farm system better than its parent team did.

The Ranger players who experienced the down years in Manhattan were quick to point out the difference Francis' presence had made in terms of overall confidence. One such veteran was 29-year-old forward Vic Hadfield, who had been with the team since 1961–62. He told Ronberg,

You really can't appreciate what [Francis has] done unless you played here before he came. You have no idea how hard it is to play, night after night, just knowing you're going to lose. Once in a while maybe we'd play great for one or two periods; we might even be ahead going into the third period. But the other club would come out and play well for 10 or 12 minutes and cancel out everything good we'd done for 40. Lose a few like that and you start to get discouraged.[5]

Francis quickly addressed the negative mindset of the Rangers when he was put in charge. It was a big challenge, but Francis made it quite clear from the get-go that alibis for failure would no longer tolerated. He recalled,

The first thing we had to do was knock all of the excuses out of the hat. There were so many excuses for losing in New York: The city. The commute. The anonymity. Anonymity? Hell, who wants to be recognized if he's a loser, anyhow? I sure as hell don't. If I'm a loser I don't want anybody to know who I am. We told [all the players] to start winning and they'd be recognized soon enough.[6]

"It was great playing for Emile," Rod Gilbert remembered with admiration. "He was the most organized coach and very disciplined. He had it just one way—his way." Gilbert also noted that Francis always treated all his players equally regardless of their importance to the team. "He was afraid the other players would disrespect him [if he didn't]."[7]

Another veteran acquisition, Don Marshall, was horrified when the Montreal Canadiens traded him to New York in 1963. Marshall had played on a superb Habs team that had won five successive Stanley Cups from 1956 through 1960. He had a perception of the Rangers—shared by many NHL players—that the franchise was poorly run both on and off the ice. His first impressions of his new team only reinforced his initial beliefs as an outsider. Marshall bluntly stated,

Nobody wanted to play in New York. Everything used to be all helter-skelter with guys skating all over and nobody knowing where anybody else was. When Montreal traded me to New York I was sick because I knew it would be like that. Under Francis, though, things have changed. He brought in a system—and it's not much different than what they do in Montreal. Now when you get the puck you usually have an idea where everybody else is; you don't have to go around looking for them. You can still play your particular style—just as long as you stay within the system.[8]

Francis' system was not especially complicated. He got the Rangers to play sound, positional hockey—and he acquired the skilled players to do it. Its main focus was to eliminate costly errors in the defensive zone by reinforcing fundamentals. "When I took over, the Rangers were losing because they were making too many mistakes in their own end," he said. "They were giving up as many as 250 or 260 goals in a year. The secret to making the playoff is keeping that number around 200."[9] With Francis in charge, the Rangers' goals-against totals in the previous three seasons were on target: 189, 183 and 196. New York qualified for the playoffs each spring, finishing fourth, second and third respectively. Although they never advanced beyond the opening round, it was the Rangers' longest stretch of postseason appearances since the mid–1950s.

Francis also addressed a problem that had been plaguing Ranger teams for years—the commute to Madison Square Garden for midweek home games. Most of the Rangers lived on Long Island. Many carpooled to the arena. Driving to home games at rush hour was an unpleasant and often stressful experience. Francis simply ordered his players arrive several hours early, thus they made the drive when traffic was considerably lighter. They then met for a noon skate, a team meal, and a mandatory nap at a hotel across the street. The players entered the games well rested and stress-free—and their home record was greatly improved.

One of Francis' key acquisitions was a player who would become a fan favorite at Madison Square Garden for many years: goaltender Ed Giacomin. He saw the 25-year-old Giacomin playing minor league hockey and immediately recognized a quality netminder who had somehow been overlooked by every NHL team. Francis raised a few eyebrows when he traded approximately $100,000 worth of player contracts to acquire the rights to the obscure goalie who toiled for the Providence Reds. At that point in his career, Giacomin had never played a single second in the NHL. Ranger historian Reg Lansberry believes Francis' deal to acquire Giacomin was "not just the most significant he ever made … but the one that proved to be the turning point. Giacomin became the team's backbone as well as a leader and a cultural 'folk hero' over the following decade with the team's fan base."[10]

It did not start out that way. Giacomin's first stint in the Big Apple, during the 1965–66 season, was less than stellar. One night the easily disgruntled patrons at Madison Square Garden cruelly showered him with a barrage of garbage. He was demoted to the minor league Baltimore Clippers shortly thereafter, but Francis did not come close to losing faith in Giacomin's abilities to play NHL hockey at a high level. After seven games with the Clippers, Francis brought Giacomin back to New York. "You're my goaltender," Francis informed Giacomin, "and nobody is going to stop you from being a good one." Francis' words came true. Giacomin was pictured on the cover of *Sports Illustrated* on March 2, 1970, beneath the caption "New York's Rangers on a Rampage"—a rare honor for a hockey player.

The expected kingpins of the Rangers' offense in 1969–70 were a threesome comprised of Vic Hadfield, Jean Ratelle, and Rod Gilbert—a potent combination that would come to be known in hockey circles as the GAG Line. GAG was an acronym that stood for "goal a game." Describing Hadfield as "a big, cheerful blond who possesses a heavy slapshot," Ronberg called him "a solid 20-goal man on the left side." In the middle was the classy and elegant Jean Ratelle. Ronberg opined that Ratelle "had become perhaps the league's smoothest center." Completing the trio on the right side was the handsome Rod Gilbert, who was known to make the female patrons at Madison Square Garden swoon. "Because of his exceptional

French-Canadian good looks, mod dark hair and [side]burns, Rodrique Gabriel Gilbert has been the team's number-one lady-killer, but now he is engaged to a Thai brunette and plans to be married in the spring," Ronberg dutifully reported. Ratelle and Gilbert had been playing with each other since their youth hockey days in Quebec. Somehow this talented pair—who both grew up in Montreal—had escaped the attention of the Canadiens. It was a rare scouting oversight by the Habs. Despite being with the Rangers since 1961 and having five seasons in which he scored at least 24 goals, at age 28 Gilbert had not quite panned out to be the superstar player the team had hoped he would become. To many NHL fans, the Rangers' forward was not truly a household name. Amusingly, he often received fan mail addressed to "Roger Bear" or "Joe Bear."

To most everyone's surprise, in 1969–70 the Hadfield-Ratelle-Gilbert line had been usurped in both offensive production and public acclaim by the second-string line of Walter Tkaczuk, Dave Balon and Bill Fairbairn. Detroit's Gordie Howe admiringly described the hard-working threesome as "so determined." It was a quality noticed by hockey writers too. The combination was dubbed "the Bulldog Line" by team statistician Arthur Friedmann for their general tenacity. The name stuck. Tkaczuk was only in his second NHL season, but his style of play was already being optimistically compared to that of Montreal's Jean Béliveau. Tkaczuk was also displaying an invaluable source of quiet but tacitly understood team leadership in the Rangers' dressing room.

Tkaczuk's linemates were a somewhat unfashionable twosome who together somehow combined to produce magic on the ice. Ronberg wrote,

Tkaczuk's partners, Balon and Fairbairn, could not be more different from one another. Bushy-haired, brown-eyes, and tough as a $1 steak, Fairbairn seems a cinch for Rookie of the Year, while until this season Balon was considered no more than a journeyman player. In 10 years playing for New York, Montreal, Minnesota, and New York again, Balon was basically a 10- to 15-goal man. He always was a worker, however, and this year he has found linemates with whom he fits perfectly.

Fairbairn was not supposed to be a regular member of the Bulldog Line; he joined Tkaczuk and Balon as a temporary measure when usual linemate Bob Nevin was injured. After the threesome combined for 10 points in a game versus Boston, Francis wisely decided to keep Fairbairn on it. Francis employed the Bulldog Line as an all-purpose unit. He had the threesome kill penalties and work the power play as well as take regular shifts during even-strength situations.

The 1968–69 season concluded with a huge disappointment for the Rangers. They again were ousted in a quarterfinal sweep versus Montreal. New York had established a club scoring record during the regular season (231 goals), but they could only muster seven measly scores in four playoff games versus the Habs. Three of them came in the last game. Still, morale was high in the Rangers' camp when the season opened in 1969–70. The Rangers—with Francis capably at the helm—were starting to believe themselves to be Stanley Cup contenders. Few prognosticators thought so. In a preseason poll conducted by *The Hockey News*, the general consensus among 24 experts was that the Rangers would be a third-place club.

Despite dropping their season opener in Boston—where the Rangers lost Bob Nevin to a knee injury—New York got off to a terrific start in 1969–70, losing just five of their first 28 contests. At the end of February, they were 34–13–13 after 60 games and one point ahead of Boston atop the NHL's East Division standings. For the first three and a half months of the regular season, the Rangers had been firmly perched there. Then a series of unfortunate injuries and a general slump severely struck the club. New York slumped badly in March and won just one of its next 12 games. (The downward spiral began shortly after Ed Giacomin appeared on the cover of *Sports Illustrated*—giving more ammo to those who believe in the *SI* cover jinx.) With just four games left in the team's 76-game regular-season schedule, far more than a first-place finish for New York was imperiled. Suddenly a mere playoff spot was unexpectedly in jeopardy too.

12

Chicago Black Hawks
Rising … with Shutouts

At the beginning of the 1969–70 NHL season, the overwhelming favorite as the coach most likely to be fired before the end of the schedule would have been 51-year-old Billy Reay of the Chicago Black Hawks. Reay's team was coming off a terribly disappointing season in 1968–69—and continued with a string of poor results to start the new campaign. Chicago lost their first six games, three of them to West Division clubs. Superstar scorer Bobby Hull conspicuously sitting out due to a contract dispute certainly did not help matters. (Hull would miss Chicago's first 14 games and play in just 61 of the Black Hawks' 76 regular-season contests.) Things looked grim indeed for the Black Hawks—and Reay in particular. Angry patrons at Chicago Stadium began serenading the Hawks' embattled coach with this blunt tune:

> *Goodbye, Billy!*
> *Goodbye, Billy!*
> *Goodbye, Billy!*
> *We'll be glad to see you go!*

Billy Reay had played 10 unspectacular years in the NHL as a center. All but four of his 479 career games (in which he scored 105 goals) were with the Montreal Canadiens. His one picayune claim to fame was that he may have been the first NHL player to raise his stick above his head to celebrate his team scoring a goal. By the 1953–54 season he was the playing-coach of the minor league Victoria Cougars. He had a knack for guiding winners. After leading the Buffalo Bisons to the American Hockey League championship in 1962–63, Reay was hired by the Chicago Black Hawks to do similar magic in the NHL. In each of his first five seasons behind the Hawks' bench, Reay's team qualified for the playoffs. In the spring of 1965, Chicago advanced to the Stanley Cup finals where they lost to Montreal in seven games.

However, in 1968–69, the Chicago Black Hawks somehow managed to finish at the bottom of the NHL's East Division standings despite scoring 280 goals—the second-highest total in the league—and having superstars Hull and Stan Mikita in their lineup. (Furthermore, feisty Pit Martin openly chastised his Hawk teammates, claiming that only three of them showed any desire to win.) In the seventh game of their 1969–70 regular season, on October 22, the 0–6 Hawks tied the New York Rangers 1–1 at Madison Square Garden to finally get a point in the standings. Three nights later, the Hawks upended the Montreal Canadiens 5–0 at the Forum. In retrospect, it was the most important game of the season for Chicago. It turned the team around, perhaps saving Reay's job in the process. It also introduced the hockey world to Tony Esposito, the Black Hawks' rookie netminder who blanked the Canadiens on their home ice. With a renewed focus on tighter defensive play, the Black Hawks lost just once in November and were soon battling for first place in the very tightly contested East Division.

The main reason for the Black Hawks' dramatic upswing in fortune was obvious: new first-string goaltender Tony Esposito and his remarkable total of 15 shutouts in 1969–70. It was a number of whitewashes not seen in the NHL since the days before the Second World War when there was no red line at center ice and the game was played much differently and far more cautiously. (George Hainsworth of the Montreal Canadiens recorded 22 shutouts in just a 44-game season back in 1928–29. Unapproached in nine decades, it is an NHL record that is likely to stand the test of time.) Esposito was truly traipsing in virgin territory for modern NHL goalies.

Tony was the younger brother of Boston's high-scoring center Phil. The Esposito brother wearing the goaltender's equipment was only in his second season in the NHL, but he had played so sparingly in his first stint that he was, by rule, still considered a rookie for the 1969–70 campaign. Nearing the age of 27, Esposito was the surprise star of the season, impressing everyone—including fellow members of the goaltending fraternity from around the league. "I've only been in the league for two seasons," Chicago backup goalie Gerry Desjardins told Ted Blackman of the *Montreal Gazette* during the playoffs, "but I've played a lot of minor [pro] and amateur hockey—and I've never seen a goalie do the things he can do." Desjardins continued,

[Esposito] has a way of dropping to his knees and spreading his pads out to either side on certain kinds of shots, mostly from the point. That way he's in better shape to take care of rebounds than I am after I've done the splits on the same kind of shot.

Another great thing he does is give the shooter a target between his pads, then drop down at the last second to close it off. It requires great timing and he has it down perfectly. His timing is terrific. He always seems to know exactly where the puck is, even with his back turned.[1]

**Bobby Hull, shown in a 1961 photograph, the possessor of hockey's hardest slap-
shot, sat out the start of the 1969–70 season in a contract dispute. Nevertheless, Hull scored 38 goals in 61 regular-season games (courtesy of Library and
Archives Canada; MIKAN inventory #3608193).**

Montreal goaltender Lorne (Gump) Worsley chimed in with plaudits
too—and one criticism. "[Esposito] is a solid goaltender. His only weak-
ness is long shots. He can't see. He wears contact lenses and he still can't see
those long, outside shots. But he's dynamite in close. When you're on top of
him, you haven't much chance."[2]

Esposito had been part of the Montreal system and played in just a handful of games for the Canadiens in 1968–69. (The first NHL game Esposito started for the Habs was against Boston. Brother Phil scored both Bruin goals in a 2–2 tie. Apparently, the Esposito boys' mother was not happy that Phil had done all of Boston's scoring that day.) With Montreal rich in goaltending with Gump Worsley and Rogie Vachon doing the bulk of the work, Esposito was left unprotected and claimed on waivers (then known as "the intraleague draft") by the Black Hawks before the 1969–70 season. It was one of the few major mistakes that Canadiens general manager Sam Pollock made in assessing players.

Pollock tried to downplay the Habs and Esposito's stats—figures that would earn the Chicago netminder a deserved Calder Trophy as the NHL's rookie of the year—by noting, "He wouldn't have had 15 shutouts playing behind the Canadiens this year."[3] It was a reference to the Canadiens' uncharacteristically sloppy defensive play that cost them critical wins on several key occasions during the season.

Esposito was quick to agree that any goaltender's shutout record heavily depends on his teammates and their philosophy of the game. He compared the Hawks of 1968–69 (when he was a Hab) to his 1969–70 crew. "Either I didn't see the Hawks properly from the other end of the rink or it was a different team this year," he surmised. "No one—I don't care who it is—could have that many shutouts without a team like [this year's Chicago team] in front. Hockey had become so wide open that the first team that turned it around had a good chance of winning. We were the first, I guess."[4]

Indeed, the Hawks were a far better defensive team in 1969–70 than they had been the previous season. They would significantly reduce their goals-against total by nearly 31 percent from 246 to 170. Even Bobby Hull—who often let the defensive aspects of hockey not get in the way of his quest to score goals—was markedly improved in that aspect. Teammate Pit Martin was quick to identify Hull's newly found defensive work as a key to the Hawks' turnaround. Hull scored "only" 38 goals in 1969–70, a pedestrian total for him, but his team excelled, nevertheless. Hull also became a cheerleader who advocated that his goalie ought to be the Hart Trophy winner as the NHL's MVP. "There's no question Tony is the most valuable man—next to me and Chico Maki, of course,"[5] Hull joked.

Tony was quick to credit his brother Phil for giving him some sage advice about goaltending. "Phil got me to stand up more and that has helped me," he said. "He told me, 'You've got to make them pick the corners' and that is what I've been trying to do. I've been trying to stay up and only go to the ice as a last resort. If anyone should know, Phil should. However, I've developed most of my skills on my own. I've watched goalies, especially the older ones, on TV and watched where they played and their styles. I tried to pick up a few pointers from all of them."[6]

In late March as the Hawks were battling for the top spot in the East Division, Esposito modestly downplayed his own contributions to his team's success. He said, "It wouldn't have made much difference who was in goal for most of the season. These guys work so hard in front of the goalie that the job has been pretty easy most of the way."[7]

Veteran Doug Mohns saw the Hawks' surprising season as a team achievement with great emphasis on a youth movement. "It's turning out to be the best season we've had since I've been here," the 36-year-old former Bruin said in an Associated Press interview. "Things got off to a really bad start, but that's all in the past now. In my 17 years of [NHL] hockey, I've never seen as many good kids come up on a team at the same time."[8]

Another big plus for Chicago was the excellent play of rookie defenseman Keith Magnuson. The red-headed blueliner from Saskatchewan, who had been part of the University of Denver team that twice won NCAA championships, was making his mark on the NHL. He was not a scoring threat in the slightest—Magnuson scored zero times during the 1969–70 regular season despite playing in all 76 of Chicago's games—but he was a tough customer whose 213 penalty minutes indicated that he was willing to engage anyone at any time. In the April 6, 1970, edition, *Sports Illustrated* said Magnuson "was playing spirited, flawless hockey."[9]

The Black Hawks immensely helped their own cause with a six-player deal they made with the hapless Los Angeles Kings on February 20. To bolster their injury-depleted defensive corps, Chicago acquired Bill White. They also picked up backup goalie Gerry Desjardins and forward Bryan Campbell. (In return the Kings got Gilles Marotte, Denis DeJordy and Jim Stanfield.) White made the biggest impact. More than 45 years later, White confessed that what he thought was a harmless comment to a Los Angeles sportswriter turned out to be the catalyst in his being traded from the Kings to the Black Hawks in 1970.

> One day while I was in the whirlpool getting treatment for a knee injury, a reporter asked me how I liked L.A. I told him I found the hot weather and playing hockey very strange, the two of them going together. [Kings owner] Mr. Cooke took that to mean I didn't like L.A. I said to Mr. Cooke, "Being from the Beaches area of Toronto, you must like the four seasons too." It didn't matter, I was still going, and I went to Chicago.[10]

Known as a thinking-man's defenseman, White was not especially flashy, but he was undeniably superb at his job. Furthermore, the transition from the lowly Kings to the rising Hawks was seamless for the balding 30 year old. White played as if he had been on the Black Hawks' blue line for years. Around the time of the NHL's All-Star Game, scuttlebutt had White being traded to the Boston Bruins to fill the defensive hole created by Ted Green's life-threatening injury. Dink Carroll of the *Montreal Gazette* wrote that the unhappy White was desperate to flee the lowly Kings for a contender—any contender.

When White became a Black Hawk, Chicago had 21 games remaining on their schedule. They lost just three of them. With points being earned in just about every game, the Hawks vaulted from fifth place in the NHL's East Division to lead the pack. Billy Reay's once-vocal critics became noticeably fewer in number and considerably less agitated as the Black Hawks ascended the standings.

13

The Suddenly Soaring
Detroit Red Wings

"For the next 20 minutes, you will sit in silence while I tell
you why the Detroit Red Wings are the greatest franchise in
the history of professional sports…"
                                —Dr. Perry Cox from the TV medical-
                                comedy drama *Scrubs*

When the sun rose on Wednesday, March 1, 1970, the Detroit Red
Wings were sitting in fifth place in the NHL's hotly contested East Division with a 30–18–11 record. Despite having lost only once in their last six
games, had the season ended at the end of February, the Red Wings would
have failed to qualify for the Stanley Cup playoffs for the fourth consecutive season.

Such disappointing campaigns were becoming par for the course
for what used to be the NHL's best American-based franchise. The Red
Wings—who began as the Detroit Cougars as an NHL expansion team in
1926–27—had been a team to reckon with for the second half of the 1930s.
The Red Wings captured consecutive Stanley Cups in 1936 and 1937 and
were finalists in 1934. They had also won Lord Stanley's coveted chalice
in 1943, 1950, 1952, 1954 and 1955. No other NHL franchise based in the
United States had won more than three. Detroit had also finished first in
the standings in the six-team NHL a remarkable seven consecutive seasons
from 1948–49 to 1954–55. It was truly the heyday of hockey in the Motor
City.

The Red Wings featured three of the NHL's most distinguished players. Gordie Howe, approaching age 43, and known as Mr. Hockey, was the
face of the Detroit franchise. He held every significant NHL career offensive mark until Wayne Gretzky came along. Howe had made his debut with
the Red Wings as an 18 year old in 1946. He stayed with the Wings for an
amazing 25 seasons. He was more than productive beyond his 40th birthday. Accruing 71 points, Howe finished ninth in league scoring in 1969–70.

That stat was actually a sign of decline. For 20 consecutive seasons he finished among the NHL's top five scorers. That record will likely stand forever. On October 19, Howe notched his 800th career regular-season goal. He had overtaken Maurice Richard six years earlier to become the NHL's most prolific goal scorer. From that point onward, every time Howe scored another goal, he established a new league mark. He did it frequently.

Modest and friendly, Howe was admired by fans throughout the league for his vast playing skills, but also for his gentlemanly and genial demeanor off the ice. On the ice, however, Detroit's number nine had a renowned mean streak during games. If an opponent displeased Howe, a well-timed subtle elbow to the jaw would often settle matters and render Howe's foe senseless. Few players were foolhardy enough to engage the bull-strong Howe in a fight. (Nevertheless, a "Gordie Howe hat-trick"—a quaint bit of hockey jargon coined well after Howe had retired—means scoring a goal, recording an assist, and getting a fighting penalty in the same game. Statisticians have discovered that Howe himself only achieved this quirky "feat" twice.)

Howe had also recovered from a life-threatening injury near the end of his fourth NHL season. During a Stanley Cup playoff game versus Toronto on March 28, 1950—just three days before Howe's twenty-second birthday—he crashed headlong into the boards at his home arena, Detroit's Olympia Stadium. How it exactly happened has been a matter of debate for years. There is no film of the incident. Some witnesses claimed Toronto's Teeder Kennedy butt-ended Howe while others say Gordie merely lost his footing and awkwardly stumbled. Be that as it may, Howe was unconscious and rushed to Harper Hospital in Detroit in critical condition. His injuries consisted of an apparent hemorrhaging of the brain, a fractured nose and cheekbone, and a badly lacerated eyeball. In a touch-and-go 90-minute operation, a surgeon drilled a small opening in Howe's skull to drain fluid to relieve the pressure on the brain. Howe's health was a major concern for hockey fans across North America. Radio stations—in Canada and Michigan especially—frequently broadcast bulletins about Howe's recovery. A recovery it indeed was: Twenty-six days after being stretchered out of the Detroit Olympia, Howe appeared on the same ice surface (albeit in street clothes) to celebrate the team's Stanley Cup championship victory over the New York Rangers. Howe won the first of his six NHL scoring championships the following season. NHL players were a resilient bunch in those days.

By the 1969–70 season, Howe and his 38-year-old linemate, Alex Delvecchio, were holdovers from the last Detroit team to hoist the Stanley Cup, back in 1954–55. Somewhere along the way in his distinguished career, Delvecchio had acquired the pejorative nickname "Fats." Both Howe and Delvecchio were beloved and iconic figures among Michigan sports fans. Delvecchio, who was the Red Wings' captain, endured an awful scoring slump at the beginning of the 1969–70 season. His first goal did not come until Detroit's 34th game of the year—a New Year's Eve tilt versus Boston. Prior to that night, he had been credited with 85 shots on goal without a single score to show for it. (According to newspaper reports, Delvecchio had been given a crown-shaped pin as a good-luck charm by Pamela Eldred of Detroit, who happened to be the reigning Miss America. She had worn it inside her swimsuit during the beauty pageant. Not having that specific option, Delvecchio attached it to one of his suspenders. One subsequent newspaper headline declared, "Delvecchio charms Bruins.") Despite the embarrassingly poor start, Delvecchio still managed to score 21 times in 1969–70. It was his tenth NHL season where he hit the notable 20-goal mark.

The third player on what was dubbed the "Power Line" was Frank Mahovlich. At age 32, known affectionately as "The Big M," Mahovlich had been the most prominent player on four Toronto Maple Leaf Stanley Cup–winning squads in the 1960s. At one point in his career, Mahovlich was such a star player that the Chicago Black Hawks tried to purchase his rights from the Leafs for $1 million—an unheard-of figure at the time. Mahovlich could be moody and introspective, though. Late in Mahovlich's stint with the Maple Leafs, famed *Toronto Star* sports journalist Milt Dunnell described him as a "sensitive and easily bruised individual" in a feature piece that appeared on the newspaper's front page on March 3, 1968. Such adjectives were generally not what Canadian sports fans associated with their hockey heroes. Toronto coach Punch Imlach—who never could seem to pronounce Mahovlich's surname correctly—frequently clashed with his brooding star, believing it to be the best way to drive the blues from The Big M. It did not work: Twice Mahovlich left the team—once, in 1964, to deal with depression, and again in 1967 for an outright nervous breakdown.

Mahovlich was occasionally booed at Maple Leaf Gardens by the hometown fans for what they perceived as his indifferent play. Mahovlich was dealt to Detroit on March 3, 1968. The change in scenery promptly revitalized The Big M. He scored seven goals and added nine assists for the Red Wings in the 13 games left in Detroit's 1967–68 season. It was an indication of things to come. Playing on the same line as Howe and Delvecchio, Mahovlich scored 49 goals in 1968–69—the best seasonal mark of his Hall-of-Fame career. Yet the Red Wings still missed qualifying for the postseason by seven points. On January 10, 1970—Mahovlich's 32nd birthday—the combined age of Detroit's Howe-Delvecchio-Mahovlich line was 111. Their best years were clearly in the past, yet many hockey observers still thought the trio was the best line in the NHL. When Mahovlich was finishing his career at age 41 with the Birmingham Bulls of the WHA playing on a line with two enforcers, a reporter asked him why he was no longer as productive as he had been. Mahovlich quipped that he seemed to have far better stats when Howe and Delvecchio were his linemates.

Forty-two-year-old Bill Gadsby was the Red Wings' coach when the 1969–70 season began. In one of the more curious developments of the entire NHL campaign, on October 16 Gadsby was fired after only two games—despite Detroit having won both contests, including one the night before in Chicago! (Years later Gadsby quipped that he was the only coach in NHL history who was fired while having an undefeated season.) He had coached the Wings in 1968–69 too and had guided them to a disappointing fifth-place finish in the East Division. Gadsby had played 20 NHL seasons as a defenseman—the final four as a member of the Red Wings—before his retirement in 1966. "We weren't communicating,"[1] was how Wings owner Bruce A. Norris explained Gadsby's swift and head-scratching dismissal to reporters. Whether Gadsby resigned or was fired from the Red Wings is a matter of debate. Nevertheless, Sid Abel replaced Gadsby's behind the Detroit bench—and promptly lost 3–2 to the Minnesota North Stars before a surprised home crowd. Midway through the 1969–70 season, Gadsby was rumored to be the first coach of the expansion Vancouver Canucks for 1970–71. Gadsby absolutely denied the story. He never coached another game in the NHL.

The ticketholders at the October 16 North Stars–Red Wings game only learned of Gadsby's departure once the game began. Upset at the move, the 11,000 fans at the Olympia chanted, "We want Gadsby!" several times during the game. That setback against Minnesota was an aberration. Despite the rocky new beginning, the Red Wings thrived under Abel and were solid playoff contenders throughout the 1969–70 season in the NHL's tough and tight East Division. Abel was returning to a familiar place. He had coached the Red Wings from 1957 to 1968 before giving way to Gadsby. Abel let it be publicly known that he would only be an interim coach. At the end of the season the Red Wings would have to find a new man to replace him.

Although the Red Wings were sitting in fifth place when March began, their 71 points put them only one point out of fourth place—and a playoff berth—and just 10 points out of first place in the up-for-grabs East Division. A strong showing in March could change Detroit's fortunes dramatically. Starting with a 7–1 win over the Oakland Seals at Olympia Stadium on February 26, the Red Wings went on an impressive streak, going 7–0–3 in a ten-game stretch and rocketing up the standings.

Consistency was the hallmark of the 1969–70 Red Wings. Not once during the entire regular season did Detroit lose three consecutive games. Perhaps the team's best performance in that 10-game sequence may have come on Sunday, March 15, 1970, on a CBS *NHL Game of the Week* telecast at Boston Garden. That afternoon they battled the Bruins to a spirited, see-saw, 5–5 tie in a game where Detroit goalie Roger Crozier was bombarded with 48 shots from the home team and Bobby Orr hit the 100-point plateau—previously uncharted territory for a defenseman. (The highlight-reel goal prompted a two-minute standing ovation from the home crowd who further celebrated Orr's milestone by littering the ice with an assortment of debris, delaying play for ten minutes. The hullaballoo prompted Gordie Howe—the NHL's all-time leading scorer—to skate by Boston's bench to comically chide Orr: "That's right, hold up the game!"[2]) Nevertheless, Detroit impressively showed enough moxie to achieve a late game-tying goal from rising star Garry Unger to salvage a critical point in the standings. In 1969–70, Unger would quietly score 42 goals for the Red Wings—only one fewer than NHL leader Phil Esposito.

Thirteen days earlier, on March 2, before an all-time-record crowd at the Detroit Olympia, the hockey gods again favored the Red Wings as they got a last-minute goal to tie the Rangers 2–2 with goalie Roy Edwards pulled for an extra attacker. A long shot deflected off Bruce MacGregor's stick past Ed Giacomin for the important equalizer. MacGregor had replaced Peter Stemkowsi who was feeling unwell with an upset stomach. "It was just a hunch,"[3] coach Abel said of putting MacGregor on the ice in that situation. In the NHL's wild East, every point was extremely precious—and all five playoff contenders knew it.

A 3–2 loss in Oakland on March 20 ended the Red Wings' undefeated skein, but Detroit quickly embarked on another strong series of results to conclude March. Overall, From February 26 to April 2, the Red Wings compiled a terrific 10–2–5 record to put themselves firmly back into the playoff race in the East Division. A cherished playoff position beckoned.

Montreal Canadiens

Unknowingly on Thin Ice

"To you from failing hands we throw the torch. Be yours to
hold it high."
> —an excerpt from John McCrae's First World War
> poem "In Flanders Fields"; it has been the
> Montreal Canadiens' team motto since 1952

"The Canadiens have enjoyed incontestable superiority in
talent all year and haven't made the best use of it. When you
leave it all to the last minute, you run the risk of stumbling
over elements not covered by 'the book.'"
> —Ted Blackman, *Montreal Gazette*, March 9, 1970

Twenty-three games into the 1969–70 season, anyone who suggested
that the Montreal Canadiens would not qualify for the Stanley Cup playoffs would have been mocked. The fabulous Habs—two-time defending
Cup champions—were 12–3–8 after defeating the Chicago Black Hawks 1–0
on December 4 at Chicago Stadium. Montreal was in second place in the
NHL's East Division, just two points behind the inspired and front-running
New York Rangers, but they held a game in hand over the leaders. Certainly, the Canadiens had squandered some points by allowing late goals
that had turned victories into disappointing ties, but the prevailing opinion
was, in the long run, it would not matter all that much. Playoff berths for
the mighty Habs were as annually predictable as a spring thaw.

On New Year's Day, Montreal was residing in third place. They were
not doing as well as expected, but there was absolutely no reason to panic.
Even when the Canadiens sank slowly downward in the standings there
was no wringing of hands nor a palpable sense of urgency in the team or
among the generally supportive Montreal media. The Canadiens would
right their slightly askew ship and do wonderful things in the Stanley Cup
playoffs. Wasn't that always the case?

There was not too much wrong with Montreal's offense. The Habs had four players who scored at least 24 goals in 1969–70—and three who scored exactly 19. Twenty-four-year-old Jacques Lemaire was the most frequent sniper with 32 goals. Yvan Cournoyer and promising 22-year-old Mickey Redmond each notched 24 tallies. Overall, Montreal was fifth in NHL scoring. They were also fifth best in goals allowed.

The Habs were certainly a streaky bunch in the second half of the 1969–70 season. From January 22 to February 11, Montreal lost just one of 11 games—after which they quickly lost three straight contests. This, in turn, led to a three-game winning streak, followed promptly by a skein of four consecutive losses. Next came a nine-game undefeated streak for Montreal that extended to March 28.

On March 9, Ted Blackman of the *Montreal Gazette* opined that the games remaining on the NHL schedule favored Montreal over both Chicago and Detroit solely because of the number of home games the Canadiens had left to play. (Presumably Blackman figured Boston and New York to both be sure things for the postseason.) At the time, the Habs were lingering in fifth place—an unfamiliar outside view of the playoff berths in the East Division. Mixing his metaphors, Blackman noted, "The Montreal Canadiens have had their giant beanstalk chopped. Instead of a first-hand showdown for the big pot, the Habs are having trouble just scratching up the ante." Blackman did caution his readers about putting too much emphasis on Montreal's supposed favorable schedule. "An edge adds up to nothing when you don't take advantage of it," the scribe wrote.

Strange setbacks seemed to happen to the Habs throughout the season. In a 5–2 win over Philadelphia on February 1, Ralph Backstrom suffered a gash on his face that required five stitches to close. The injury occurred seconds after Backstrom had scored a key goal. Teammate Yvan Cournoyer was so excited by the score that he accidentally clipped Backstrom with a high stick.

Six days later rugged John Ferguson was hospitalized after being struck in the face with a puck just 39 seconds into a road game versus the Minnesota North Stars. It was something of a freak occurrence. This time Ralph Backstrom was the catalyst instead of the victim. He whacked at a puck off a faceoff. It caromed off the stick of Minnesota's Grant Erickson and caught the charging Ferguson flush on the face under his right eye. It was the fourth time that an injury had afflicted Ferguson in this, his seventh, NHL season. (Accordingly, Ferguson would play in just 48 of Montreal's 76 games in 1969–70.) X-rays of Ferguson's skull showed no apparent fractures, but after the game, when Ferguson was preparing to board the Canadiens' flight back to Montreal, he complained of lingering and extreme pain. As a precaution, the team ordered him back to Minneapolis' Methodist Hospital for further rest and examination.

A major injury befell the Canadiens at the Forum on Wednesday, March 11. Serge Savard, one of the best young defensemen in the NHL, suffered a broken leg after he crashed awkwardly into his own net while trying to prevent a goal by New York in the Habs' 5–3 victory over the Rangers. (Even worse for Montreal, Bob Nevin scored on the play for the visitors.) The 24-year-old Savard had won the Conn Smythe Trophy as MVP of the 1969 Stanley Cup playoffs. Referee Vern Buffey immediately recognized that Savard had been seriously injured. "I could see he wanted something to hold while in severe pain," the official told Pat Curran of the *Montreal Gazette* after the game. "He said his leg was broken. When I put out my arm, he nearly wrenched it off."[1]

Even peripheral things were going awry for the Canadiens in March. When the team arrived in San Francisco on March 18 to play a Wednesday night game versus Oakland, followed by a Thursday night game in Los Angeles, they discovered their reservations at their usual first-class hotel had not been processed and there were no available rooms. After playing to an uninspired 2–2 tie with the Seals, the Canadiens spent a restless night at what the *Montreal Gazette* described as "a fleabag hotel" before departing for Los Angeles. Despite the hassle, the Habs handily defeated the overmatched Kings 6–1.

The Habs' important March 28 game with New York at the Forum ended in a disappointing 1–1 tie for the home team. The Rangers managed to eke out the draw thanks to a Walt Tkaczuk equalizer with just 2:17 left on the clock. The late-game collapse was becoming all too familiar to the Canadiens. "I don't know how many it is," moaned coach Claude Ruel. "I haven't been able to keep count of them. If we hadn't blown so many, we might be far ahead of everyone else."[2] Gary McCarthy of the *Montreal Gazette* had been keeping track of the Habs' late-game follies. By his reckoning it was the 13th time in 1969–70 the Canadiens had given up key goals late in the game that cost them either wins or ties. Nevertheless, with the draw, Montreal had a solid 37–19–16 record—good enough for 90 points with four games left to play on their schedule. Normally this would have been ample to qualify for the playoffs. But the 1969–70 NHL season was anything but normal.

The next night at Madison Square Garden, before 17,250 fans, the desperate Rangers handed the Canadiens a 4–1 setback. Pat Curran of the *Montreal Gazette* characterized the Habs' Sunday defeat as "an Easter egg" for the Rangers. Indeed, sloppy defensive plays by Bobby Rousseau and minor-league call-up Larry Mickey were directly responsible for two Ranger goals. Despite the loss, Montreal was in third place in the East

Division. But it was a tenuous spot. The Habs were just one point ahead of Detroit and two in front of New York. Detroit also held a game in hand over Montreal.

"Montreal isn't out of the woods yet by any means," insisted Francis. "If we ever had to win a game, it was this one."[3] Displeased Montreal general manager Sam Pollock grumbled about the squandered opportunity to clinch a playoff spot by only managing to acquire one point out of four in the two-game weekend set versus the Rangers. "We should have killed them by the same score on Saturday,"[4] he grumbled.

Three days later, Montreal played well at the Forum in handily beating Boston, 6–3. Jean Béliveau scored two goals for the home team. In the winners' dressing room after the game, ex–Habs coach Toe Blake jokingly told Béliveau and a horde of reporters that congratulations were not in order because the Habs' captain should have scored five times instead of just twice. The dignified Béliveau faked a scowl for a moment and then deadpanned, "He's right, you know."[5] The Canadiens could afford to laugh. The important win gave the Habs 92 points and temporary possession of third place in the East Division. The odds were heavily on their side for making the Stanley Cup playoffs. Bobby Orr figured in on all three Bruin scores with a goal and two assists. Nevertheless, Orr looked bad defensively on a couple of Montreal goals and was summarily criticized in the press for having played less than a stellar game versus the Habs. Boston goalie Ed Johnston was yanked by coach Harry Sinden after Montreal took a 4–2 lead in the second period.

Still nothing about the NHL's East Division was totally certain. There was, in fact, more uncertainty than certainty. The *Montreal Gazette* printed the East Division standings on the morning of April 2 under the headline "What a Finish!" (The *Gazette*'s typesetter erred, listing Boston atop the Black Hawks even though Chicago was ahead based on having accrued more wins than the Bruins.) Here is what the East Division standings truly were on that Thursday morning:

NHL East Division Standings
(after April 1 games)

Team	GP	W	L	T	PTS
Chicago	74	43	22	9	95
Boston	74	38	17	19	95
Montreal	74	38	20	16	92
Detroit	73	38	20	15	91
New York	74	37	21	16	90
Toronto	73	29	31	13	71

Montreal's gentlemanly Jean Béliveau, one of the most popular and respected players in NHL history, only missed the playoffs once in his 18-year NHL career with the Canadiens: the 1969–70 season (courtesy Library and Archives Canada; MIKAN inventory #3608212).

In the team's "game in hand," Detroit upended Toronto 4–2 at the Olympia on Thursday, April 2, to vault ahead of the Habs with 93 points. Alex Delvecchio scored just 16 seconds into the game to lead the way for the home team. His linemates, Gordie Howe and Frank Mahovlich, each scored as well in the Red Wings' comfortable win. It was not a scintillating game by any means, according to the unnamed Associated Press scribe who covered it. He blamed it on "both teams being weary from their games a night earlier and their troubles in traveling through snowstorms and plane delays."[6] A single win on the final weekend for the Red Wings in their home-and-home tilts with New York would put Detroit in the playoffs for the first time since 1966.

Things were becoming quite interesting in the NHL's East Division. Each club had now played 74 of their 76 games. The only two games remaining on Montreal's regular-season schedule were a home-and-home clash with the Chicago Black Hawks, Saturday night at the Forum and Sunday evening at noisy Chicago Stadium. Although they now sat in the unfamiliar position of fourth place, attaining some sort of positive result from either of those two contests would virtually assure the Habs of another Stanley Cup playoff berth. A single Montreal win would definitely do the trick. When it came to performing well when the chips were down, few teams in all of professional sports were more resolute and reliable than the Canadiens. Seldom did Montreal get skunked in a home-and-home weekend—even less often when it really mattered.

Toronto Maple Leafs

Treading Water

"Professional hockey has its chance of a lifetime to make
good in Toronto this season. If the Torontos … deliver the
goods by playing fast, clean hockey, they will earn many
friends who will stick with them in the years to come."
—excerpt from a hockey preview article
in the *Ottawa Journal* published just
prior to the NHL's first season in 1917

When the Toronto Maple Leafs' 1968–69 season concluded, the
end came with a whimper. They had been swept in four games by the
ascending Boston Bruins. The first two contests, played at Boston Garden, were horrific routs. Boston prevailed 10–0 and 7–0 in two laughers.
Games #3 and #4 in Toronto were at least respectable. The Bruins only
won by much closer scores of 4–2 and 3–2. While driving home from
the final game on April 6, Toronto coach and general manager George
(Punch) Imlach apparently was startled to hear a news bulletin on his
car radio that pertained to him: He had been fired. At least that was the
version of the story Imlach often told. According to a Canadian Press
story that appeared in the next day's newspapers, Leafs president Stafford Smythe told his coach two minutes after the game was over, "It's the
end of the Imlach era."[1] Perhaps that comment was not quite specific or
direct enough for the embattled Imlach to comprehend the message. The
radio bulletin, however, made it abundantly clear. Whatever the case,
years later hockey historian Stephen Brunt described Imlach's firing as
"an impulsive, emotional act."[2]

When asked by a reporter why Imlach had been axed, Smythe was
incredulous. "Why?" he began. "We went into the expansion draft as
Stanley Cup champions and two years later we haven't won a game in the
playoffs!"[3] Boston general-manger Milt Schmidt claimed he heard about
Imlach's dismissal almost immediately. "It couldn't have come more than

30 seconds after the teams left the ice," he insisted. "It certainly was swift. But what can you say? I've got problems of my own."[4] Boston's Derek Sanderson, who had a hugely productive series versus Toronto, sympathized with Imlach and openly defended him based on his undeniable past achievements. Sanderson opined that Imlach's firing was a mistake because he had led the club out of the wilderness in the late 1950s to multiple Stanley Cup championships during the 1960s. Bruin coach Harry Sinden sympathetically said, "When I get it, I certainly don't want to get it that way."[5]

Imlach still had a year remaining on his contract and was reputedly earning $38,000 per season with the Maple Leafs. Smythe said he would still honor the deal. "I don't like doing what had to be done in firing a personal friend," he noted, "but it sure hurts to lose four straight." Smythe then added an obvious coda: "This wouldn't have happened if we had won the Stanley Cup."[6]

If Imlach's account of his termination was accurate, it was not exactly a classy way for the Maple Leafs to dismiss the man who had been behind the team's bench for 11 seasons. Under Imlach, the team qualified for the playoffs nine times. Most importantly he brought them four Stanley Cups in the 1960s, as Derek Sanderson accurately noted. The news of his firing was not all that surprising, however. Imlach had clashed with Leafs management earlier in the season. At one point he had been asked by Smythe to step down as coach, but he steadfastly refused. Imlach had his supporters among his veteran players. Two of them, Johnny Bower and Tim Horton, reacted to the sudden and seemingly callous way the 52-year-old Imlach had been discharged by saying they intended to retire instead of play under a new coach the following season. Both eventually reneged on their promises. Replacing Imlach as the coach of the Toronto Maple Leafs for the 1969–70 season would be the unheralded John McLellan. Jim Gregory took over behind the scenes as the team's general manager.

McLellan, ten years younger than his predecessor, was a newcomer to the NHL coaching ranks. The native of South Porcupine, Ontario, had most recently coached the Tulsa Oilers of the Central Hockey League from 1967 to 1969, winning the championship in his first season. Previous to that experience, McLellan had led the Eastern Hockey League's Nashville Dixie Flyers to two consecutive titles in the mid–1960s. McLellan's NHL playing career was very brief; it consisted of just two games with Toronto in the 1951–52 season. He was eventually reinstated as an amateur and played on the Canadian team that thoroughly dominated the IIHF world championship tournament in Czechoslovakia in 1959.

As coach of the Maple Leafs, McLellan was inheriting a popular, storied team that was clearly in a transitional phase. A few holdovers were still lingering from Imlach's championship collection of "old men and older men" from 1966–67, but many players had departed, mostly through trades or the NHL's expansion draft. The most prominent veteran still on the roster was swift-skating center Dave Keon, a fan favorite. He had won the Conn Smythe Trophy as the MVP of the Leafs' most recent Stanley Cup–winning outfit. Reliable George Armstrong was still present, but no longer captaining the squad. Keon had assumed that mantle. The 1969–70 campaign would be the 40-year-old Armstrong's 19th with Toronto. He would only appear in 49 of his team's 76 games, however.

Throughout the season, the Maple Leafs constantly struggled to stay close to the break-even mark. It was a tough task. Halfway through the season Toronto was 15–16–7. Given how strong the NHL's East Division was in 1969–70, it was obvious that just finishing at or around the .500 mark probably would not equate to a playoff berth come springtime. On the morning of February 2, the Leafs' 19–20–8 record put them firmly in last place in their tough division—eight points out of fifth place and 11 points out of fourth place. A similar record would have been good enough for second place in the decidedly weaker West Division on that same date. The glaring inequity between the NHL's two divisions were starting to be noticed more and more.

Ancient Johnny Bower played just one game in goal for Toronto in 1969–70. Injured and demoralized by the Leafs' poor record, he retired before the season ended. Bruce Gamble and Marv Edwards shared almost all of the netminding duties for the other 75 games on the Leafs' schedule. They had their hands constantly full.

Despite having the worst statistics in the East Division in goals scored (222), Toronto had two 30-goal scorers: Ron Ellis (35) and Dave Keon (32). Toronto did, however, have the poorest record for goals allowed (242) in the East Division. Nevertheless, the Maple Leafs, to their credit, never threw in the towel on their 1969–70 season until they were mathematically eliminated from playoff contention. That inevitability came to fruition on March 19 when the Rangers picked up an important point in a tie game versus Philadelphia. Still, the lowly Leafs became objects of pity to some rivals. Chicago's Keith Magnuson readily admitted in a *Sports Illustrated* piece that his team had trouble getting enthusiastic about playing the only team in the East Division that was out of playoff contention, even though the Black Hawks were fighting mightily to finish in first place and every game—regardless of the opponent—meant so much in the standings.

Immediately after they were knocked out of the playoff race, Toronto won their next two games. (One was a 5–2 win at New York which imperiled the Rangers' tenuous playoff aspirations.) However, the Leafs only managed a single tie and six losses in their final seven games to conclude a disappointing season. In the end they finished 21 points out of fourth place. Toronto had a losing record versus every other East Division club. The uniforms were certainly familiar, but the 1969–70 Toronto Maple Leafs looked nothing at all like the team that had won the Stanley Cup just three years earlier.

16

St. Louis Blues
The Biggest of the Small Fish

Of the six West Division teams in the NHL in 1969–70, the St. Louis Blues were easily the most well-known to hockey fans. Two consecutive trips to the Stanley Cup finals had a lot to do with that. In the third post-expansion NHL season, St. Louis was again proving its case to be the best of the new bunch. However, to date they were not quite a big fish in a tiny pond. Instead the Blues were more like the biggest of a school of very small fish.

As the season progressed, the Scotty Bowman–led Blues began to show that the other five West Division teams were clearly a notch or two below the frontrunners. St. Louis coasted to first place by a comfortable and considerable margin—22 points ahead of runner-up Pittsburgh. In fact, the Blues were the only West Division team that won more games than they lost in 1969–70, giving the naysayers and Original Six fans plenty of ammo to argue that only the East Division produced championship-caliber clubs. In 1969–70 teams played six games against each team in the other division. The Blues won 11 games against teams from the East—and beat all of them at least once. By comparison, second-place Pittsburgh won just seven games and Minnesota won nine versus the East.

St. Louis' lineup was replete with numerous veterans. Al Arbour, Phil Goyette, Jean-Guy Talbot, Terry Gray, Camille Henry, Bill McCreary, Ab McDonald and Noel Picard were all over the age of 30. Goalies Jacques Plante and Glenn Hall were 41 and 38 respectively when the Stanley Cup playoffs began. Plante led the Blues' goalies in minutes played. Ernie Wakely, who had been acquired from Montreal, played more minutes than Hall. Experience was, of course, not an issue for the Blues. There comes a point, however, where experience becomes age and age becomes an albatross. That had not happened to the Blues yet. However, it had to be realized that with such a roster, the number of chances St. Louis would get to win the Stanley Cup were dwindling. Perhaps 1969–70 would be the last crack at a Stanley Cup championship for the team's nucleus.

Slow but steady was good enough to lead the West. St. Louis won their first three games of 1969–70—all played at home—by an aggregate score of 15–5. They did not fall into a prolonged slump until late January and early February when they lost six consecutive games. That setback was immediately followed by a stretch where the Blues only lost two of 13 games.

The best game the Blues played all season may have been their surprising 5–0 victory over the Canadiens at the Montreal Forum on December 30. St. Louis led 4–0 after the opening 15 minutes. The result was all the more startling for one notable milestone: Counting the Stanley Cup finals in 1968 and 1969, St. Louis had never beaten Montreal in their 22 previous meetings. Pat Curran of the *Montreal Gazette* wrote, "The historic victory came in a 5–0 rout. St. Louis might have been gloating [about the way they won], but coach Scotty Bowman [and his players] were almost apologetic for the way they humiliated the injury-riddled Canadiens."[1] The seemingly ageless Glenn Hall picked up the shutout that night, the 82nd of his NHL career.

Throughout the season the Blues looked very likely to be the West's team in the Stanley Cup final for the third consecutive spring. But in hockey—especially the NHL—nothing is guaranteed. They still had to win two divisional playoff series to get there.

17

Pittsburgh Penguins

Improving and Anonymous

One of the true success stories of the 1969–70 NHL season was the marked improvement of the Pittsburgh Penguins. In their first two seasons the club that played out of a rink nicknamed "The Igloo" had been frozen out of the playoffs with two uninspired fifth-place finishers. In their inaugural season, the Pens missed the postseason by the slim margin of just one victory. In 1968–69 seven points separated the Penguins from the Stanley Cup playoffs.

A key offseason acquisition had been the signing of Red Kelly to run the club as both the Penguins' coach and general manager. He replaced another Red—George (Red) Sullivan—a former New York Rangers coach, who had been the man behind the Pittsburgh bench for the team's first two unsuccessful seasons. Sullivan was once an offensive juggernaut in the American Hockey League, where he scored 119 points in just 69 games for Hershey in 1953–54. He twice led the Chicago Black Hawks in scoring during his NHL playing days, a career that spanned the years 1949 to 1961. Sullivan scored 107 NHL goals, but he was probably most famous for suffering a near-fatal internal injury at the hands of Montreal's Doug Harvey. Sullivan, a member of the New York Rangers at the time, suffered a ruptured spleen as a result of Harvey spearing him. A Catholic priest was summoned to administer last rites to the severely wounded Sullivan, but he managed to pull through.

Sullivan's dismissal as the Penguins' coach occurred one day after the regular-season finale, on Monday, March 31, 1969. It shocked no one, especially not the Pittsburgh hockey writers who clearly did not like Sullivan. Only a hot spurt at the end of the season—in which Pittsburgh surprisingly went undefeated in six games—elevated the Penguins from the West Division cellar to fifth place. Prior to that too-little-too-late turnaround, Pittsburgh had lost six straight games.

"Penguins Fire Coach After Dismal Season," proclaimed the headline in the April 1 edition of the *Pittsburgh Post-Gazette*. In the accompanying story by Jimmy Jordan, the sports scribe wrote, "George (Red) Sullivan surrendered his coaching portfolio to the Board of Directors for the Penguins yesterday. Actually it was a command performance." Jordan continued, "The fans had become disenchanted, the attendance was off, and the coach became the goat. Now there will be a new start with another bench boss." Bill Heufelder of the *Pittsburgh Press* also pointed out the 39-year-old Sullivan's previous NHL coaching stint was not especially bountiful, either. He wrote, "Sullivan was unable to push the New York Rangers into the Stanley Cup playoffs during his three-year stay as coach from December 1962 to December 1965."[1]

Red Kelly, an eight-time Stanley Cup winner as a player, immediately went to work correcting the low-expectation mindset of the team. On paper he did not have an outstanding collection of players to lead. The best of the bunch was probably 37-year-old Dean Prentice, followed by Ken Schinkel and Jean Pronovost. All three would record at least 20 goals for a team that scored just 182 times in the regular season—an average of not quite 2.4 goals per game. The Penguins did have a promising rookie from Quebec, Michel Brière. He was small in stature, but he had deft puck handling skills. Brière also displayed hockey smarts beyond his years. Pittsburgh management had very high hopes for him.

With a team that did not score often, Pittsburgh needed solid goaltending to be competitive. Allan Smith and Les Binkley did the bulk of the netminding for Pittsburgh, with Thomas Daley also handling the task on some occasions. Smith appeared in 46 games for the Pens. Prior to the 1969–70 season, the 24-year-old Smith had played in just eight NHL games as an occasional goaltender for the Toronto Maple Leafs. Binkley, age 33, was one of many players who benefited tremendously by the 1967 NHL expansion. He had been languishing in the minor professional ranks for years. (Binkley was named the American Hockey League's Rookie of the Year in 1961–62.) He had not seen a single minute of NHL action until he was signed by the Penguins in 1967–68.

Under their new coach, Pittsburgh did not start off especially well in 1969–70. The Penguins were 1–4–3 in October (after beginning the season with three straight tie games!), and 5–6–2 in November. But in the weak West Division of the NHL, even compiling a mediocre record would easily be enough to earn a team one of the four allotted playoff berths. The Penguins' only winning month was February when they went 8–5.

Eventually Pittsburgh finished in second place—22 points behind division leaders St. Louis—but few people witnessed it. The average attendance at Penguins home games in 1969–70 was a wee bit below 7,000. At the Pens' second home game of the season, only 3,010 fans turned out to see the home team play to a 3–3 tie with their intra-state rivals, the Philadelphia Flyers. Even visits by the famous and history-laden Original Six clubs failed to create noteworthy enthusiasm. Twice the New York Rangers drew fewer than 5,000 fans to the Civic Arena. On January 28 only 4,290 fans came out to watch the Toronto Maple Leafs play the Pens.

In February, when the Penguins were vaulting up the West Division standings, the average attendance for games at the Civic Arena was close to 8,000. Even during the Penguins' hot streak, only 4,826 fans turned out to see the home team beat Los Angeles 1–0 on February 26. (Twenty-five-year-old Pittsburgh goalie Al Smith recorded his first NHL shutout that night in front of the sparse gathering. "One-hundred-and-two to go,"[2] quipped Smith afterward—a clear reference to Terry Sawchuk's daunting career shutout record.) Bill Heufelder of the *Pittsburgh Press* blamed the quality of opposition for the disappointing turnstile count. "To be sure," he wrote, "the Kings did not provide stimulating spectator appeal."[3] An action photo that ran in the next day's *Press* showed row upon row of empty seats near ice level. General manager Jack Riley was perplexed by the paltry local support for the Penguins. "If you're playing fairly well and the people aren't coming, you have to wonder about your approach."[4] When another reporter gently proffered the idea that the attendance was weak that night because the lowly Los Angeles Kings were the visitors, Riley asked out of total exasperation, "But why don't they come out to see us?"[5]

The Steel City was still very much a baseball and football town in 1970. The Penguins, in their third year of operation, were generally perceived as something akin to a sideshow attraction. Perhaps a long playoff run might be the panacea needed for hockey to be embraced by Pittsburgh's sports fans.

18

Minnesota North Stars

Drawn and Quartered

"Credit playing-coach Charlie Burns and his new goalie
Gump Worsley for putting the zip into the North Stars,
which may make them the team to beat in the West."[1]
—*Oakland Tribune* hockey writer Spence Conley

The 1969–70 version of the Minnesota North Stars was not especially
memorable. They did set a quirky NHL milestone by becoming the first
team to have more ties than wins in the regular season and still qualify for
the playoffs. Their 19–35–22 record—putting them 16 games under .500—
was still good enough for third place and a quarterfinal playoff spot in the
NHL's weak West Division.

The NHL's schedule in 1969–70 was comprised of 456 regular-season
games. Ninety-one of them—a smidgen shy of 20 percent—ended in ties.
No team benefited more from the single point awarded to each team in a tie
game than the Minnesota North Stars. Tie games were absolutely the difference between a mediocre campaign that earned them a playoff spot and an
utterly disastrous one.

For a team with so many drawn results, the North Stars did not get
their first tie until the 11th game of the 1969–70 season (a 2–2 deadlock at
Montreal on November 5). The Stars, in fact, had just two tie games among
their first 17 results. Starting with the 18th game of the season, however,
Minnesota's ties came in waves. They attained draws in six of their next ten
games.

The North Stars began 1969–70 with Wren Blair serving as both the
team's coach and general manager. Blair admitted he could not handle
both duties capably and installed veteran Charlie Burns as the North Stars'
player-coach 32 games into the season. "I had to pack up [the coach's job] or
probably drop dead,"[2] Wren told Pat Curran of the *Montreal Gazette* about
the pressures of holding both positions simultaneously. Curran also noted

that Wren was "unaffectionately called 'The Bird' by [North Star] players who have been screamed at, fined, and whipped into respectable efforts."[3] (Indeed, when Blair died at age 87 in 2013, former North Stars defenseman Tom Reid told the *Minneapolis Star Ledger*, "[Blair] was a character, he really was. The things he used to do on the bench and in the dressing room were crazy. He was the type of guy who could scream and holler and be your best friend two minutes later."[4]) During the North Stars' inaugural season, Blair criticized the blasé attitude of the team's supporters in an attempt to make them a livelier troupe. Blair humorously recalled in 1991,

> One night, a reporter asked me about the crowd. I said, "Ah, they are nothing but a bunch of phlegmatic Swedes, sitting up there on their hands like pieces of stone." [Jim] Klobuchar wrote a column in the *Minneapolis Star*, saying he was offended because I had ignored all the phlegmatic Norwegians, Italians, Germans and Irishmen.[5]

Over the course of the long season, the North Stars used five different goaltenders: Gump Worsley, Gilles Gilbert, Cesare Maniago, Ken Broderick and Fern Rivard. None had lasting success. Worsley had been acquired from Montreal on February 27 in a move that was unpopular with Habs fans. All the Canadiens received in exchange from the North Stars for the likely Hall-of-Fame netminder was cash.

After their 39th regular-season game—a 1–1 tie versus the Seals in Oakland—the North Stars had four more ties than wins. Immediately thereafter, Minnesota went into an awful slump, going winless in 13 consecutive games from January 17 to February 14. Only one of those games was a tie. Wins were so scarce that the North Stars achieved just one victory over a span of 33 games from December 11 to February 28—including a discouraging run of 20 consecutive games without a single win. Yet, somehow, the North Stars remained in playoff contention in the West Division when February turned to March. After 59 games, Minnesota was just three points out of fourth place.

The North Stars actually came within one game of equaling the all-time NHL record for consecutive winless games. The humiliating skein ended at home with a resounding 8–0 shellacking of the struggling Toronto Maple Leafs on Sunday, March 1. Cesare Maniago got the shutout, stopping 41 Toronto shots in the victory—their first triumph in 45 days. The Leafs were embarrassed by both the loss and the margin of defeat. Defenseman Jim Dorey expressed his frustrations accordingly. According to the Associated Press' game report, at the 3:40 mark of the third period an enraged Dorey "started a fight, swiped at linesman Pet Shetler, and threw a chair onto the ice to after his ejection."[6] That outburst earned Dorey a six-game suspension from NHL president Clarence Campbell. By this point in the season Charlie Burns was the North Stars' playing coach. Burns had some experience in that department. He had been the playing coach of the minor league San Francisco Seals on two occasions. Both times they were midseason maneuvers. Wren Blair, who had begun the season doing double duty as both Minnesota's coach and general manager, handed over the coaching reins to Burns after 32 games.

The turning point in the North Stars' season was when they acquired veteran netminder Gump Worsley who had had a falling out with Montreal Canadiens coach Claude Ruel. Ruel believed in a youth movement for Montreal goaltenders—and the aging Worsley was keenly aware of it. At one point in the season after a win over Toronto, Ruel was lecturing the Canadiens over and over again about skating hard. Worsley grew tired of the oration and muttered—just loudly enough for Ruel to hear—"Does he ever knock it off?"[7] Shortly after the incident, Worsley was released from the team. After a short retirement, Worsley was persuaded to join the North Stars.

In an interview with Ted Blackman of the *Montreal Gazette*, Worsley candidly opened up about being rejuvenated in Minnesota. "Remember how I was telling you back in Montreal that I didn't miss [hockey] at all? Well, when I got here, I found out I had been missing it. I missed playing, hanging out with the guys. Apparently, these guys were really down in the dumps. [Coach] Charlie Burns has been telling me since I've been here there's a whole new attitude."[8]

The proud Worsley was not above enjoying the perverse pleasure of observing the Canadiens struggling to qualify for a playoff spot in the East Division after his abrupt departure from Montreal. "I see they lost two games this past weekend," he pointed out to Blackman. "Hmmm..."[9]

The North Stars featured reliable oldster Leo Boivin on defense. The hard-hitting 37 year old was in his 19th—and final—NHL season and played in 69 of Minnesota's 76 games. Twelve of his seasons had been with the Boston Bruins. For four of those years he was the Bruins' captain. Boivin had also been on the roster of Toronto, Detroit and Pittsburgh during his lengthy career. Boivin was the classic case of someone who had his NHL career elongated by expansion. "After 16 years in the six-team league, expansion added onto my career," he noted. "At that time, there were a lot of players playing in the American Hockey League who were great players who just didn't get a chance."[10] Despite having an NHL career that featured 1,150 regular-season games and began in the 1951–52 season, Boivin never did have his name engraved on the Stanley Cup.

The 1969–70 Minnesota North Stars witnessed Elmer (Moose) Vasco's swansong as an NHL player. The 34-year-old defenseman, who had been in the NHL since 1957, played in three games for the North Stars before being demoted to the Salt Lake Golden Eagles of the Western Hockey League to conclude his pro career. A popular member of the Chicago Black Hawks' 1961 Stanley Cup team, Vasco's imposing size (6'2"; 200 pounds) made him an imposing figure on the ice during the Original Six era. His proudest boast was that he played nearly 800 regular-season games over 13 NHL seasons without losing any teeth—certainly a rarity in those days.

19

Oakland Seals

Struggling to Be Relevant

"Attendance plummeted during the Seals' 1966–67 season,
and the early returns in their first NHL season were hardly
encouraging. San Francisco fans refused to cross the bridge
to Oakland, and Oakland already had very few hockey fans,
therefore attendance was abysmal. After just 25 games, the
team became known as the Oakland Seals in an effort to
attract more local fans, but the Seals still ended up dead last
in attendance, a dubious feat that would be repeated each
and every subsequent season."
—Steve Currier, from goldensealshockey.com,
a website dedicated to preserving the history
of the Oakland/California Seals

The Oakland Seals were a generally unloved lot in their third NHL season, despite having qualified for the playoffs by finishing second in the West
Division in 1969. (The Seals lost to the Los Angeles Kings, their intra-state
rivals, in a tough seven-game quarterfinal series they were favored to win.)
In a region where the NHL struggled to be relevant, the unfashionable Seals
had difficulty attracting patrons to the Oakland–Alameda County Coliseum Arena in sizable quantities. The average home attendance was 6,225
in a building that had 12,500 seats available for hockey. Amazingly, that
small figure was a significant increase over the Seals' first two campaigns
when the club drew an average of just 4,890 and 4,584 fans per game. In
1968–69, the Seals had just 1,100 season-ticket holders. An optimistic new
ownership group, headed by Trans National Communications, bought the
club on June 2, 1969, for $4.5 million. Youthful new team president Bill
Creasy was optimistic heading into the 1969–70 season. "We have the product in a fine young team which finished second last year, the place to play
in the beautiful and comfortable Coliseum Arena, and the organization to
capitalize on both."[1]

Disappointing home attendance—the lowest in the 12-team NHL—was a problem that had to be addressed. The Seals eliminated their Sunday home dates from October through January so they did not have to compete in a decidedly uphill and losing battle with professional football. An overwhelming majority of Oakland home games would be played on weeknights. "This is a tough TV market to break into,"[2] Creasy told William Doyle of the *Oakland Tribune*. (Creasy knew what he was talking about; he had produced some of the *NHL Game of the Week* telecasts for CBS. Those games aired starting in late January—after the football season ended.) There was, in 1969–70, also going to be greater radio coverage of Seals games, both home and away. A marketing agency was hired to promote group ticket sales—a heretofore unknown idea among NHL clubs. More staff was hired to push the sale of Seals ducats wherever and whenever they could. "Programs [for increased group sales] are being developed for groups of every sort," Creasy noted, "from high school students to those from industrial plants."[3]

The on-ice product did not give the locals a whole lot to root for. Over the course of the 1969–70 campaign, the Seals ranked 11th out of 12 teams in goals scored and had the third-worst record for allowing goals to the opposition. Yet, in the watered-down West Division, Oakland remained within striking distance of a playoff spot throughout the year, and, thanks to an outright collapse by the Philadelphia Flyers, attained fourth place on the season's final weekend.

The 1969–70 Oakland Seals were led by second-year coach Fred Glover—the ultimate minor league hockey star. For years Glover held the American Hockey League career records for games played (1,201), goals (520), assists (814), and penalty minutes (2,402). When he retired as an active player following the 1967–68 AHL season, only Gordie Howe and Maurice Richard had scored more goals in professional hockey than Glover had. Three times he was named the AHL's MVP. As a 23 year old, Glover scored 48 goals in 69 games with the Indianapolis Capitals in 1950–51. From a public-relations standpoint, Glover was light-years ahead of his predecessor, the taciturn Bert Olmstead. He was also more than civil with the scribes who regularly covered the Seals. Glover was liked and respected by his players too. Morale on the team improved considerably.

The battle-scarred Glover left a legacy of boisterous play in the AHL—and rival Buffalo fans were mindful of an incident involving Glover that had occurred back in 1965. When the Seals played a preseason game in Buffalo versus the minor league Bisons on October 5, 1969, Glover was attacked by fans between the second and third periods as he strolled down a corridor towards the Seals' dressing room. "The Oakland Seals have had trouble attracting friendly fans to their home games, but they had no trouble attracting unfriendly ones in Buffalo last night,"[4] quipped one scribe. According to one report, as many as 200 people eventually became involved in the fracas. A friend of Glover's who tried to intervene in the melee ended up with a broken jaw for his trouble. Embarrassingly, Oakland fell to the Bisons, 5–1.

In June 1969, the Seals acquired Harry Howell, a terrific, steady veteran defenseman, from the New York Rangers in a cash transaction. The aging Howell was deemed expendable by the Rangers because he had undergone major back surgery leaving his hockey future somewhat up in the air. Howell had won the James Norris Memorial Trophy in 1966–67 as the NHL's top blueliner during Bobby Orr's rookie season. (Upon receiving the award, Howell famously quipped that he was especially glad to have won the Norris Trophy because Orr was going to win it for the next ten years. His estimate was not far off.) Howell would turn 37 during the 1969–70 campaign. With Howell having played 1,160 NHL games, Glover and the Seals' upper management hoped he would provide the team with needed leadership qualities.

Howell was also doing his best to promote hockey in a region where it was largely a foreign curiosity. He told George Ross of the *Oakland Tribune*, "I'm constantly running into people who say they think they'd like to come and see the Oakland Seals play but they don't understand the game. I tell them there isn't much to understand. The idea is to put the puck in the net at one end and keep it out of the net at the other. To me it's much less complicated than football."[5] The team's effort to increase attendance did produce results. The average turnstile count at Seals home games in 1969–70 rose by more than 1,600. That was an increase of about 37 percent.

The Oakland Seals had underperformed (at least according to general expectations) in their first NHL season under unpopular coach Bert Olmstead. In 1968–69, Fred Glover was given the chance to right the floundering Seals' ship. The 40-year-old Glover had experience leading hockey teams as a player-coach for the minor-league Cleveland Barons for six seasons. Only Glover ever led the Seals to postseason berths—and he did it in two consecutive seasons.

Glover did not have an especially strong hand to play in Oakland. Only two Seals managed to score 20 goals in 1969–70: Earl Ingarfield (21) and Carol Vadnais (24). The 17 tallies from Ted Hampson—who had been playing professional hockey since 1957—were good enough for third best on a team that only averaged 2.22 goals per game when the league average was nearly 2.90. The 24-year-old Vadnais, a defenseman, was far and away the team's leader in penalty minutes too, with 212. Yet, as the back of his hockey card stated, Vadnais "scored more points last season than many forwards in the NHL."

Gary Smith was handed the heavy bulk of the Seals' goaltending responsibilities. He would appear in 65 of the team's 76 games and log 3,762 minutes played. He recorded Oakland's only two shutouts of 1969–70 and posted a 3.11 goals-against average. All things considered, Smith's stats were excellent. In his final two seasons as the Seals' first-string goalie, Smith faced more than 4,400 shots. Over the years, Smith played goal for 13 professional hockey teams. His amusing nickname—Suitcase—was wholly appropriate to his many stops he made along the way.

Glover could be brutally harsh on his own team when he deemed it necessary. After the Seals absorbed a thorough 6–1 home loss versus Boston on January 7, Glover told Hugh McDonald of the *San Mateo Times* that his players "don't think"[6] and they could all benefit from a trip to a psychiatrist. This was not Glover's only statement that questioned his players' mindset. Earlier in the season, after the Seals lost a preseason game to their Providence farm team in late September, Glover accused some of his veteran players of being too soft in their approach to hockey. The quotable Seals coach told a reporter from the *Ukiah Daily Journal,* "It's the kids who are doing the fighting—nobody else. The others are afraid to get their face [sic] cut or suffer a fat lip because they're afraid it would make their wife or girlfriend unhappy. Well, I've got 400 stitches in my face and it doesn't look so bad."[7]

Goaltender Gary Smith was having a subpar year—and Glover let him know it. "Smitty is lost in the woods somewhere," his coach told reporters. "We thought progress had been made with him last season, but it all went down the drain."[8] Smith was not a person who reacted well to criticism. He preferred to sulk instead. "All Glover does is bum-rap me," Smith responded. "I'd rather he let me alone." Smith then added an extraordinary and startling afterthought: "I'm not that crazy about the game. If there was something else I could do, I'd rather do it."[9] Smith had good reason to be embittered. Routinely he was overwhelmed in the Seals' net, often facing an avalanche of rubber. (In fact, on 18 different occasions during the 1969–70 season, Smith faced 40 or more shots.) "Smith could have become a test dummy for bulletproof vests and not even flinched,"[10] wrote Steve Currier, a Canadian author who penned a 464-page history of the franchise.

The Seals certainly had no friend in the NHL's schedule-maker in 1969–70. Long stretches on the road were commonplace for Oakland. Given the realities of North American geography and that only two of the 12 NHL teams were located on the Pacific coast, this had to be the case. Still, it did not stop goaltender Smith from being a vocal critic of all the Seals' necessary travel. "We're having our troubles," he admitted, "but some of the reason is the schedule. We had a 17-day road trip and a 19-day road trip.

With the three-hour time difference and the competition, it's really been ridiculous."[11]

Furthermore, the Seals were forced to play seven consecutive road games from December 21 to January 4, ensuring the players would be away from their families over the Christmas and New Year's holidays. Center Earl Ingarfield lamented, "I sent my wife and kids home to Lethbridge [in Alberta] for Christmas and said I'd see them when we got back. It's grim. And when you happen to be in a slump, a trip like this is even worse."[12] The Seals managed just one win and one tie in those seven games. The team's morale, always a fragile commodity, was greatly affected. When the Seals started accepting defeat as routine, Glover was not happy with his players' attitudes. "Even when they been beaten 6–1," he tersely noted, "some of them will go out of this dressing room thinking they've played a good game."[13]

Criticism aimed at the Seals came from all directions. After his Philadelphia Flyers skated to a 2–2 tie at the Coliseum Arena on December 6, coach Vic Stasiuk lambasted the Seals franchise for having a substandard players' bench for the visitors. "It's bush league," Stasiuk declared to reporters. The visiting team's bench was a sway-backed, park-bench-style seat that was situated low to the floor. In contrast, as Spence Conley of the *Oakland Tribune* noted, "The Seals' bench, specially made at the club's request, is a foot higher and topped with a comfortable foam rubber pad."[14]

"It may seem like a small thing, but many of our players had to stand up in order to follow the game. When they did sit down, their knees were in their chests. You can't rest that way," Stasiuk insisted. "That's a direct violation of the rules," Stasiuk continued. "You can bet I'll be filing a protest to [NHL president Clarence] Campbell when I get home."[15] As fate would have it, two years later, Stasiuk would be behind the Seals' luxurious bench as their coach.

With a noticeable paucity of scoring, the Oakland Seals did not put together many long winning streaks. In fact, they never won more than two consecutive games all season. Still, their 22–40–14 record got them into the West Division playoffs—albeit by the narrowest of margins. Oakland's 4–1 loss to the last-place Los Angeles Kings on the regular season's final Saturday nearly cost them a playoff berth. (On the day of the game, one hockey scribe from the *San Mateo Times* foresaw such a calamity unfolding. He wrote, "It's been a long, dreary year for [the Kings]. They have their pride, though, and they'd like to take someone out with them."[16]) However, Philadelphia's 1–0 home loss to Minnesota on the same day dropped the Flyers to fifth place on the basis of having accrued fewer wins than the Seals. It was somewhat appropriate that Oakland qualified for the 1970 Stanley

Cup playoffs by sneaking in through the back door rather than by winning a crucial game.

Thus, the unfashionable, under-supported, unspectacular Bay Area NHL bunch crept weakly into the 1970 Stanley Cup playoffs against the West Division's second-place Pittsburgh Penguins—another team that was struggling to make a lasting impression in the hearts of its local sports fans.

20

The Kings

*Losing and Loathing
in Los Angeles*

When the NHL doubled its membership in 1967, the league's governors decided it was imperative to have a team in Los Angeles. There were, in fact, four different groups hoping to land an NHL franchise in The City of Angels. With American TV money beckoning, the NHL needed to be a continental loop. The folks at CBS pretty much insisted on it. It was generally assumed that having a competitive team in the west coast's most populous city would do wonders for the growth of hockey in the United States. Were the newly minted Los Angeles Kings up to the task?

For the majority of sports fans in Los Angeles, hockey was a quirky, foreign, niche sport. Baseball, basketball and football were the sports of the people in southern California. Thus, over their formative years, the Kings struggled mightily to attract a following to the Great Western Forum (a.k.a. "The Fabulous Forum"), their sparkling new home arena. In their inaugural season, the average attendance at Los Angeles home games was just 8,037. The Kings had been in a battle for first place for most of the 1967–68 season and ended up in second place in the NHL's West Division, so the number of fans passing through the Forum's turnstiles was especially disappointing. Their second season, when the Kings finished in fourth place, home attendance rose by 9.5 percent to an unspectacular 8,802. The 1969–70 Los Angeles Kings would only draw 8,451 spectators per home game—a dip of nearly 4 percent. The decline was understandable. The product on the ice in 1969–70 was not especially an appealing one during the third season of NHL hockey in Hollywood.

Leonard (Red) Kelly had been the Kings' coach for their first two seasons, guiding them in to the playoffs in both years. But Kelly opted to leave after the 1968–69 season to take control of the Pittsburgh Penguins in 1969–70—a team that had not qualified for the Stanley Cup playoffs in either of their first two NHL seasons. Kelly abandoned ship at the right time. Without Kelly, Los Angeles quickly descended into the doldrums—and into the NHL West's cellar in 1969–70. Hal Laycoe, who had a solid 11-year-playing career, was named as Kelly's replacement. He did not last very long; Laycoe was fired 24 games into the season when the Kings were 5–18–1. Johnny Wilson took over the Kings' coaching duties for the rest of the dismal season.

Due to a leg operation that sidelined goaltender Wayne Rutledge, Gerry Desjardins played in goal for every one of the Kings' first 23 games and—had a rotten 5–17–1 record to show for his efforts. "I want to win so much; the pressure really mounts up,"[1] Desjardins told Bill Heufelder of the *Pittsburgh Press* after his team failed to give him any offensive support in a tough 2–0 home loss to the Pittsburgh Penguins on December 10.

Horrible losing stretches were the norm for the Los Angeles lads throughout the dreary and demoralizing 1969–70 campaign. November was a typically awful month. From November 8 through the 29, the Kings managed just a single tie in 10 games. February was a virtual write-off: From January 29 through March 5, the Kings compiled a miserable 17-game winless streak. (They were 0–13–4.) Twice during the 1969–70 season they experienced eight-game losing streaks. Road games were not especially kind to the players in the gaudy purple jerseys. In 11 games away from the Forum from January 11 to February 15, the Kings dropped 11 consecutive decisions. In the team's 38 road games in 1969–70, the Kings won but two—one in Oakland on December 2 and one in Minnesota on January 10. Overall, the Kings were an awful 2–30–6 in road games. They finished 20 points out of fifth place and missed the playoffs for the first time in their brief history.

Pat Curran's column in the February 7 edition of the *Montreal Gazette* summed up the futility of how badly the Kings season was going after 48 games. He wrote, "Hal Laycoe worked 24 games as coach of Los Angeles before being fired after the team only won five games. Since Johnny Wilson took over the Kings they have only won four their last 24. So what's the value of an NHL coach?"[2]

The best of the 1969–70 Kings—in terms of scoring and general showmanship—was the illiterate Eddie (The Entertainer) Shack. Shack was a beloved, goofy, well-traveled character in pro hockey circles. When he wanted to do so, Shack could certainly be a capable offensive player, but he was also just as likely to get himself involved in pointless tussles with opponents and end up sitting in the penalty box. Never to be confused with the elegant Jean Béliveau, what Shack lacked in grace and finesse he more than made up for in raw, boyish enthusiasm. He was indeed a memorable hockey character.

His Wikipedia biography describes Shack as "a colorful third-line agitator who was popular with the fans despite a lack of scoring prowess." That description is not totally fair. Twice before 1970, Shack had recorded 20-goal seasons, one for Toronto and one for Boston. Perhaps a better description of Shack's on-ice persona came from hockey writer Stephen Cole who declared Shack's unique playing style to be reminiscent of "a big puppy being let loose in a wide field."[3]

Shack enjoyed his greatest popularity with the Toronto Maple Leafs from 1960 to 1966 where his shortcomings were overlooked and even celebrated. In 1966, Shack was the subject of a novelty song by Douglas Rankine and the Secrets: "Clear the Track, Here Comes Shack." The tune charted for three months on the Canadian pop charts and eventually ascended to the number-one spot for two weeks in the rankings compiled by CHUM-AM in Toronto. The song was penned by Brian McFarlane of *Hockey Night in Canada*. Shack was always miffed that he was not entitled to any of the royalties the recording generated.

Los Angeles was the fourth NHL club for the energetic, happy-go-lucky 33 year old. In 1969–70 Shack scored 22 goals, two more than Ross Lonsberry, to lead the woebegone Kings in that category. Los Angeles scored just 168 goals all season—the lowest total in the NHL. They allowed 290—the highest total in the NHL.

However, not even the boisterous antics of Eddie the Entertainer could bring people in sizable numbers to the Great Western Forum to watch the pitiful Kings as they struggled and stumbled hopelessly to the wire. Los Angeles lost 52 games in 1969–70. Those 52 setbacks were a new NHL record for futility in a single season.

21

Philadelphia Flyers

24 Ties ... But Still One Short

The 1969–70 Philadelphia Flyers won just 17 of their 76 games—the lowest total in their history. However, they were reasonably certain they would qualify for the playoffs after 70 games. At that point in their schedule, the Flyers held a six-point lead over the Oakland Seals for the fourth and final playoff spot in the NHL's closely contested West Division. A betting man would have liked Philadelphia's chances of finishing fourth or perhaps higher in the weak West when the final batch of regular-season games concluded on the first weekend of April.

Another, more positive record the 1969–70 Flyers established was playing tie games. With 24 games ending in draws (a remarkable 31.58 percent), the Flyers topped the old record of 23 formerly held by the 1962–63 Montreal Canadiens. In fairness to that Habs squad from nearly 60 years ago, the team only played a 70-game schedule that season, so they still hold the record by percentage (32.85 percent). Amazingly, six of those ties came in the six games Philadelphia played New York! Going 0–0–6 versus one team in a single season was unprecedented in NHL history.

Of course, one can look at tie hockey games in two ways: Each draw is undeniably a point earned, but at the same time it is a potential point squandered. In an interview with *The Hockey News*, first-year Flyer coach Vic Stasiuk definitely looked at the glut of ties with an optimist's eye. "The way I look at it, they're 24 beautiful points," he said. "Sure, we'd like to have 24 victories, but, sure as heck, we'd hate to have 24 losses instead."[1] Stasiuk insisted all those deadlocks had virtually guaranteed his team a playoff spot. He was wrong. Apart from the St. Louis Blues who were running away with the West Division, and the languishing Los Angeles Kings, who were destined for the cellar, what the other four teams' final placements might be at the end of the schedule were truly anyone's guess. "The West standings were so close in the final few weeks of the season," noted Seals historian Steve Currier, "that any of the clubs seeded second to fifth had a chance of making the playoffs or falling completely out of the running."[2] Thus, if the Flyers had turned even one of those two dozen ties into a win, they would have finished one point ahead of the Oakland Seals and qualified for the Stanley Cup playoffs. If Philadelphia had managed a 25th tie, the result would have been the same: a coveted postseason berth—the third in the team's first three NHL seasons.

Stasiuk was certainly unafraid to voice his strong opinions when things went awry. After his Flyers lost 5–2 to Montreal on February 1, Stasiuk lambasted linesman Ed Butler whom he blamed for missing an obvious offside pass that led to the Habs' decisive third goal, scored by Ralph Backstrom. "That linesman is either blind or incompetent," the hot-tempered coach declared to reporters after the game. "[Backstrom] was a yard and a half over the blue line."[3]

The Flyers certainly had their chances to wrap up one of the top four spots in the West. However, they instead sputtered, staggered and generally bungled their way to an ignoble finish. The first of their six consecutive losses occurred on Wednesday, March 25, in Oakland. Three days earlier the same two teams met at the Philadelphia Spectrum with the home team winning 3–2. This time the result was reversed: Oakland won 3–2 before a tiny gathering of 5,246 spectators at Coliseum Arena. Philadelphia held a 2–1 lead with four minutes to play, but Oakland rallied. The Seals scored two late goals on goaltender Bernie Parent—one by Don O'Donoghue at 16:42 and another by Joe Hardy with just 12 seconds left on the clock. Thus, a Flyer win suddenly turned into a Flyer loss in less than four catastrophic minutes. It was a harbinger of cruel things to come Philadelphia's way.

The following night, Thursday, March 26, Philadelphia dropped another 3–2 decision, this time at the Inglewood Forum to the last-place Los Angeles Kings. Again, the Flyers held a lead—but this time it was short-lived. Simon Nolet opened the scoring at 11:04 of the first period for the visitors. About a minute and a half later Ed Joyal tied the game for Los Angeles. By the end of the first period the Kings were ahead, 2–1. They upped their lead to 3–1 on a second-period goal by Réal Lemieux. Philadelphia cut their disadvantage in half in the third period on a goal by Andre Lacroix, but they could not manage an equalizer on Los Angeles goalie Denis DeJordy who had a strong game. The Flyers fired 13 shots at him in the final 20 minutes. Overall, Philadelphia outshot the Kings 32–30 and had nothing but a second consecutive one-goal loss to show for their efforts.

The Flyers returned to Philadelphia two nights later to face their intra-state rival, the Pittsburgh Penguins, on Saturday, March 28. This time Philadelphia lost 2–1 with all three goals coming in the first two periods.

Philadelphia never led in the game. The Flyers' lone goal was tallied by Gary Dornhoefer at 4:55 of the second period. The shots on goal were almost a carbon copy of the game two nights previous; the Flyers launched 32 at Penguins goaltender Les Binkley. Bernie Parent had 30 shots come his way. Philadelphia had now lost three consecutive one-goal games. The overworked Parent had been the netminder for each one.

Pittsburgh and Philadelphia met for a second consecutive time four nights later at the Pittsburgh Civic Center before a disappointing turnout of slightly fewer than 8,000 paying customers. The April Fools' Day game ended with Philadelphia on the short end of a 4–1 decision. However, the score was misleading. Pittsburgh tallied two empty-net goals in the final minute of play to put the game out of reach. Again, Bernie Parent absorbed the loss. He could not be faulted for his efforts, though; he made 40 saves in the game. No one knew it at the time, but Andre Lacroix's goal for Philadelphia at 15:43 of the second period was the last one the Flyers would notch in their disappointing 1969–70 season. With just two games left on the schedule, their late-season downfall was now imperiling a once-secure West Division playoff position for Philadelphia if game results beyond the Flyers' control—and those they did control—worked against them.

On Thursday, April 2 the Flyers hosted the division-leading St. Louis Blues before the usual sellout crowd of 14,606 partisan fans at the Spectrum. Their enthusiastic cheering did not muster any offense for the home team. St. Louis won 1–0. The game's lone goal came in the first period. With Barclay Plager of the Blues sitting out a tripping penalty at the 8:09 mark, Jim Roberts got his 13th goal of the year—an unassisted, shorthanded tally—that silenced the Spectrum faithful. Ernie Wakely got the shutout for the Blues, stopping 34 home team shots. He was named the game's first star. Hard-luck loser Bernie Parent—who stopped 33 St. Louis shots in defeat—was the game's second star. The result was somewhat surprising because St. Louis had had first place in the NHL West clinched long ago and had no reason to put forth any sort of extraordinary effort. Philadelphia, on the other hand, was slowly sinking into irreversible and irreparable trouble.

Things were getting complicated for every West team excluding St. Louis (comfortably locked into first place) and Los Angeles (hopelessly destined for a finish in the cellar). Even though they were in third place, a degree of panic was now setting in among the Flyers and their fans as Minnesota and Oakland could still overtake them. In the worst-case scenario, both the North Stars and Seals (who both had two games remaining on their respective schedules) could finish ahead of Philadelphia and knock the Flyers into fifth place. The NHL's West Division standings looked like this on the morning of Friday, April 3:

Team	GP	W	L	T	PTS
STL	75	36	27	12	84
PIT	74	26	36	12	64
PHI	75	17	34	24	58
MIN	74	17	35	22	56
OAK	74	21	39	14	56
LA	74	13	51	10	36

There was one important game on the NHL schedule on Friday, April 3. Philadelphia was not involved it in, but its result on the Flyers' playoff future was potentially huge. The Oakland Seals defeated the Los Angeles Kings 4–1 at home. With the victory, the Seals vaulted from fifth place to third place. That happening pushed the Flyers down to fourth place and the North Stars down to fifth. Minnesota was only two points behind the Flyers with two games left to play compared to Philadelphia's one. If the North Stars and Flyers ended the season level in points, the tiebreaker would favor Minnesota. Philadelphia's last regular-season game was a home date versus the charging Minnesota North Stars on Saturday, April 4. The North Stars would finish their schedule on Sunday, April 5 in Pittsburgh—a team that was locked into second place and therefore had no reason to be overly motivated for the game.

For 47 minutes the North Stars and Flyers battled to a tightly contested scoreless tie with each team getting 20 shots on goal. At the 7:38 mark of the third period, 21-year-old defenseman Barry Gibbs scored a goal that has gone down in infamy in Flyers lore: He fired a puck past Bernie Parent from well outside the blue line—estimates put the distance at about 80 feet—to give the visitors a 1–0 lead. It was just Gibbs' third goal of the season. The Flyers could not muster a response despite having a man advantage with 2:35 to go.

Gump Worsley, who had been purchased from the Montreal Canadiens on February 27 to bolster the North Stars' shaky goaltending, got the shutout for the visitors. It was the 22nd whitewash of Worsley's superb NHL career that dated back to the 1952–53 season.

The Flyers' catastrophic slide out of a playoff position—which had seemed so unlikely just two weeks before—had materialized with a thud. Philadelphia did not score a goal in their last seven periods of play, which, of course, included two frustrating 1–0 shutout losses at home. In their last six games, Philadelphia scored a meager total of just six goals. It was hardly the performance worthy of a playoff contender.

With Philadelphia's fate sealed, Minnesota convincingly beat

Pittsburgh on Sunday, April 5, by a 5–1 score to finish in third place in the West Division. It was just their 19th win of the season. In the year of the tie, the North Stars had accrued 22 valuable draws. The result dropped the Oakland Seals to fourth place.

Despite the disappointing conclusion, Philadelphia fans did get their first look at two new novelty items during 1969–70. One was Bobby Clarke, the team's second-round pick from the 1969 amateur draft. Clarke, who hailed from Flin Flon, Manitoba, a mining town, was considered a risky proposition because he was a diabetic. His affliction was a non-issue. He proved to be the best player during the Flyers' preseason camp—and became an instant fan favorite in Philadelphia. His presence on the team would pay huge dividends in a few short years. Also, on December 19, the Flyers began the occasional tradition of playing Kate Smith's recording of "God Bless America" before games instead of "The Star-Spangled Banner." With America still heavily bogged down in the Vietnam War, the Irving Berlin tune was thought to be less divisive than the national anthem. When Flyer fans began to notice that Philadelphia often won when Kate Smith sang, the song would later evolve into the team's good-luck charm.

NHL's 1969–70
West Division–Final Standings

Team	GP	W	L	T	PTS
STL	76	37	27	12	86
PIT	76	26	38	12	64
MIN	76	19	35	22	60
OAK	76	22	40	14	58
PHI	76	17	35	24	58
LA	76	14	52	10	38

22

The Plummeting
New Yorkers

"For if ever there was a club capable of pulling an *el foldo* in
the spring of the year, it has been the Rangers."
—Gary Ronberg, *Sports Illustrated*,
March 2, 1970

In 1969–70 the New York Rangers found themselves in first place in
the NHL's East Division by the middle of November. They held that lofty
position for three and a half months until the beginning of March. This was
something unfamiliar to most New York hockey fans. It was the first time
since 1940—the year of the Rangers' most recent Stanley Cup triumph—
that the team had been in first place after New Year's Day. Then the injuries began.

The worst setback to New York occurred in Detroit on February 19
when 21-year-old defenseman Brad Park was felled with an ankle injury
while battling Carl Brewer for a loose puck. Park's right skate became
wedged at the base of the boards. He toppled to the ice in obvious pain. Initially it was thought to be tendon damage, but x-rays showed Park had suffered a vertical break in his right ankle. Park had been a terrific force on
the Rangers' blue line all season. So loaded with potential was the youthful Park that some of his teammates kiddingly but affectionately referred to
him as "Baby Jesus."

Perhaps it was the *Sports Illustrated* cover jinx that was hexing New
York. After Ed Giacomin's photo appeared on the front of the magazine's
March 2 issue, the Rangers won just two of 13 games that month.

Twenty-eight-year-old Rod Gilbert was having a hugely disappointing regular season. At what should have been the peak of his career, his goal
production had instead declined sharply. The previous three seasons Gilbert had averaged better than 28 goals per campaign. In 1969–70 he scored
just 16 times. All season long Gilbert seemed to have a knack for rattling

pucks off goal posts and crossbars, but those shots, of course, did not result in Ranger goals. Out of curiosity Gilbert began keeping track of how often he clanged shots off the iron—but he stopped doing it when he realized it was emphasizing that he was not being successful as a scorer. For Gilbert, the stat was also turning into something akin to a self-fulfilling prophesy.

With startling rapidity, the Rangers dropped from first place to fifth in the tight East Division. Prior to their disastrous March, the Rangers had not lost two games in a row all season. The setbacks were especially galling to Ranger fans because of the teams New York was faltering against. On Sunday, March 8, the Rangers could only manage a disappointing 0–0 tie at home versus the Pittsburgh Penguins in which Pens goalie Al Smith stole the show with 33 saves. (According to the report in the next day's *Pittsburgh Post-Gazette*, "The partisan crowd of 17,250 alternately cheered and booed the action of their own Rangers in the error-ridden, ofttimes desultory game."[1] The Rangers had walloped Pittsburgh, 6–0, the last time the teams had played in New York City five weeks before.) A week later, on March 15, the Minnesota North Stars sent the patrons at Madison Square Garden home unhappy. The Stars' Ray Cullen broke a 2–2 tie with 1:15 left on the clock. Bill Collins then added an empty-net goal in the dying seconds for a 4–2 Minnesota victory. Reg Lansberry, the author of *9 Goals*, a terrific book about the 1969–70 New York Rangers, accurately noted, "What had become a mad scramble for playoff positions in the East Division over the past month had now metastasized into a nightmare for Francis & Co. The Ides of March were upon them."[2]

Absolutely nothing was going right for the Rangers. They seemed beset by misfortune in every possible way. Case in point: Beloved team physician Dr. Kazuo Yanagisawa died suddenly of a heart attack at age 55 not long after resetting the cast on Brad Park's right foot. In 1968 Yanagisawa saved the imperiled hockey career of Rod Gilbert with delicate spinal-fusion surgery. Years later Emile Francis praised Yanagisawa as undoubtedly the best physician he had ever encountered in all his years in hockey.

On March 22, the lowly Toronto Maple Leafs convincingly thumped the Rangers 5–2 before another stunned home crowd at Madison Square Garden. That result was especially costly to the New Yorkers. "Rangers Drop Back to Fifth" proclaimed the headline in the next day's *Montreal Gazette*. If the handwringing had not already begun in New York City, it began in earnest that Sunday night. All the promise shown early in the season by the then-rampaging Rangers was in imminent danger of being frittered away in one awful, disastrous month.

It Happened One Night

The Rangers' Long Bus Ride

"Plain and simple, riding the bus improves team unity."
—quote from Positive Coaching
Alliance literature

With the New York Rangers slumping badly in March—having just one win in 11 games—and their excellent season rapidly falling apart, the Rangers found unusual difficulties heading their way late in the troublesome month: a major transportation crisis.

Air travel in the United States suddenly became more complicated with a significant labor disruption. Air traffic controllers began calling in sick in overwhelming numbers. With airports suddenly short-staffed, plenty of flights entering and going out of New York City were delayed or canceled. Ranger coach and general manager Emile Francis took proactive measures, which turned out to be wise—at least in theory. The Rangers had an important road game against the Canadiens on Saturday night, March 28. Francis chartered a bus to transport his team the 430 miles from New York City to Montreal on March 27. The bus picked up the team at JFK Airport at about 4 p.m. where they had been told their scheduled flight would indeed not be departing. As Ranger historian Reg Lansberry noted, it was the start of "their very own Magical Mystery Tour."

In 1970, traversing long distances by bus was still a fairly commonplace occurrence for NHL clubs when traveling to and from preseason games in communities that did not have airports. Seldom were they used to go from one NHL city to another, however. The Rangers had a specific bus-boarding ritual designed by their detail-obsessed coach. The players loaded their equipment and filed into the vehicle first. Francis, as was his custom, was always the last man to board. Francis always sat in a front-row seat; he liked to see everything ahead of him. However, on this day his seat was occupied—by an unknown woman!

The bus driver informed Francis that the woman was his wife. He explained that she wanted to go to Montreal to visit relatives, so he decided to bring her along! Not surprisingly, Francis abruptly nixed that plan. The driver apparently accepted Francis' succinct edict but got his permission to drop her off along the way. Accordingly, not long after leaving JFK, the driver pulled off to the side of a road in Woodside, in the borough of Queens. He and his wife left the vehicle. The driver informed Francis he was going to make a phone call to get a taxi for his wife. With the vehicle's motor running, the driver and his spouse left the bus—and promptly vanished.

After a time, Francis came to the realization that the man who was supposed to chauffeur the Rangers to Montreal had instead abandoned them. Trainer Frank Paice left the bus on a mission to find the wayward driver but came back empty-handed. Francis went to a nearby public telephone and angrily called the bus company. He was told that the driver was not an especially reliable fellow. Francis tersely replied that he had come to that obvious conclusion all by himself. An hour later, a replacement driver was dispatched to the scene, but that was merely a temporary measure. He was just about to end his shift, so he could only drive the Rangers back to the company's garage where a third driver then took charge of the bus.

By happenstance, Francis and Paice both recognized the newest driver; he had capably driven the Rangers when they had played a preseason game in Lake Placid, New York. Driver number three promptly pointed the bus toward Montreal and drove headlong into a snowstorm. He was extra careful behind the wheel—far too cautious for the impatient general manager's liking. The vehicle rarely traveled faster than 35 miles per hour despite Francis' constant pleas for the driver to accelerate. By the time the Rangers arrived at Montreal's Mount Royal Hotel, it was 2 a.m. When the driver asked Francis what time he should pick up the Rangers for the return ride by to New York City, Francis told him to forget it. There was no chance Francis was going to let the man take him and his Rangers on another long, leisurely spin.

Despite their travel woes, New York somehow played a high-quality game later that day and battled the Canadiens to a 1–1 tie. The Rangers got a late goal from Walt Tkaczuk to salvage a hugely important point in the standings.

Following the game at the Forum, flying back to New York was still not an option for the Rangers. This time it was the weather creating havoc. A snowstorm had halted flights departing from Montreal. With no other viable option, the Rangers chartered another bus—this time from a Montreal company—to transport them back to New York City for a return match versus the Canadiens the next night. It proceeded speedily and without incident.

All things considered, the Rangers may have played their finest game of the 1969–70 season that Sunday night, upending the Habs 4–1 with a solid team effort. (Very late in the third period, Ed Giacomin deprived himself of what should have been a deserved shutout—and a $100 bonus—by wandering from his net and making a reckless pass that was intercepted by Henri Richard. Richard fired the puck into the vacated New York net with just nine seconds left on the Madison Square Garden clock.) To a man the Rangers claimed their strange bus odyssey to and from Montreal had been a positive, binding experience. "Maybe all we needed was a little togetherness,"[1] Francis suggested to reporters afterward.

24

Surging Popularity

The Numbers Speak for Themselves

Few times could Clarence Campbell, the strait-laced president of the National Hockey League, be described as giddy. But that would have been an accurate adjective to affix to the 64 year old as the final weekend of the NHL's 53rd regular season approached. Pat Curran of the *Montreal Gazette* interviewed Campbell for his April 4 column. Campbell's comments showed he was delightfully basking in the tightness of the two divisional races plus very encouraging news about overall interest in his league based on attendance and television ratings. The statistics clearly indicated the NHL was on a terrific upswing in popularity.

"There's no question about it being our best season ever," gushed Campbell. "The tightness of the races has been in a large part responsible." He continued,

> It is most gratifying, especially when so much has been made of talk that the league is unbalanced. The race in the East is so close because West Division clubs have influenced the outcome. It is very easy to knock the caliber of the West Division, but the answer is simple.
>
> In the normal process of competition, the new teams have generated improved balance in the East. They have put great pressure on Eastern teams to take as many points as possible in the interlocking games. Some have been more successful than others, hence the close races in the East Division.[1]

Curran noted that there had been a 7.5 percent increase in the league's overall attendance from the same time a year earlier. It had gone up a full 16 percent, Curran wrote, in West Division arenas "with hardly a way of attracting more fans to Eastern rinks due to limited capacity."[2]

As for the NHL's television ratings—which were always strong in Canada—figures showed American viewership of CBS' *NHL Game of the Week* Sunday broadcasts had jumped by 22 percent since the previous season. In 30 key American cities, those numbers were even higher—up by a significant 27.5 percent.

Curran stated in his column, "However, [Campbell] must be wondering what major pro hockey can do for an encore in the annual Stanley Cup playoffs which get underway next Wednesday."[3]

Few people—including Campbell—were likely thinking that far ahead. There were still 48 frantic hours of regulation play left on the NHL schedule. But everyone who followed hockey was pondering which eight teams would qualify for the 1970 Stanley Cup playoffs—and how.

25

Saturday, April 4:
Clearly Clarifying Nothing

"These two games this weekend [for the Bruins] will mean the difference between spending the summer on Cape Cod [or] on the Italian Riviera. And I'd go big on the Italian Riviera."[1]
— Boston forward Derek Sanderson's assessment of the importance of his team's final two games of the 1969–70 regular season

"All I can offer is a medal to the schedule-maker and to some of the players and teams who are responsible."[2]
— NHL president Clarence S. Campbell, in the April 4, 1970 edition of the *Montreal Gazette*, commenting on the tightness if the league's divisional races

Entering the final weekend of the NHL's regular season, a computer—a novelty item at the time—calculated 125 possible outcomes for the standings in the NHL's East Division alone. The six teams that comprised that pool seemed determined to prove that every last one of them was possible. With each team having played 74 of their scheduled 76 games, here is how the East Division standings looked heading into the key games scheduled for Saturday, April 4:

NHL East Division Standings
(on Friday, April 3, 1970)

Team	W	L	T	GF	GA	PTS
Chicago	43	22	9	236	167	95
Boston	38	17	19	270	213	95
Detroit	39	20	15	235	188	93
Montreal	38	20	16	241	187	92
New York	37	21	16	235	178	90
Toronto	29	32	13	219	235	71

Virtually nothing was settled—except that Toronto was doomed to finish at the bottom of the standings—a harsh reality the Maple Leafs and their fans had accepted for quite a while. Adding further intrigue to the matter was this gem of scheduling: the six East Division teams were scheduled to play back-to-back games on Saturday and Sunday, one at home and one on the road, versus the same opponent. Boston and Toronto would play at Maple Leaf Gardens on Saturday night and face off again in Boston Garden the next evening. The Chicago Black Hawks would play the Canadiens at the Montreal Forum on Saturday night and then host the Habs on Sunday evening at Chicago Stadium. New York would play the Red Wings in Detroit on Saturday and again on Sunday afternoon at Madison Square Garden for the weekly CBS telecast. The one-hour time difference separating Chicago from the rest of the East team's venues ensured that the return match between the Canadiens and Black Hawks would be the season's finale.

Chicago and Boston had playoff spots secured, so both of those teams could relax somewhat compared with the other playoff contenders. Still both teams were gunning for the Prince of Wales Trophy—the bauble awarded to the East Division champions and the cash prize associated with it. Amazingly, both Montreal and Detroit could finish anywhere from first to fifth in the standings.

The two Boston–Toronto games were the ones that most people figured as foregone conclusions. The Maple Leafs had gone five consecutive games without a victory and appeared to be a team just playing out the string as March turned to April. However, Boston had not won a regular-season game at Maple Leaf Gardens since November 27, 1965—a remarkable streak of 24 games—so a Bruins win in Toronto on Saturday, April 4 was hardly a sure thing if the recent past was to serve as a gauge. Furthermore, Phil Esposito, who was trailing only teammate Bobby Orr in the NHL scoring race, was nursing a bad back and was listed as doubtful for Saturday's game. Esposito was having none of it. He would play. Boston coach Harry Sinden made light of the situation. He joked with reporters, saying when the Bruins' charter bus was heading to the arena for the game, the driver could detour into Toronto's enormous Italian community and pick up a couple of replacements—as long as they could shoot from the left side as Esposito did.

Not only did Phil Esposito play in the important game, he got the first of four Bruins goals in the opening period. Boston ended up winning the game 4–2.

New York's Saturday night visit to Olympia Stadium in Detroit was again made by bus. The Rangers departed from Brantford, Ontario (the city where Wayne Gretzky was born in 1961)—which had become their headquarters while the air traffic controllers' labor action continued to affect America's airports. The trip was approximately 150 miles.

Detroit was the better team on April 4. New York rookie Jack Egers got his first NHL goal as the two teams ended the first period tied at 1–1. The Red Wings then dominated the final two periods and rolled their way to a fairly comfortable win over the surprisingly lackluster Rangers. With New York losing 5–2 late in the game, Emile Francis tried to pull out all stops. With Detroit a man short late in the game, he pulled Ed Giacomin to try to add at least one more goal to the Rangers' ledger. Instead, it was the Red Wings' Peter Stemkowski who notched an empty-net marker with 50 seconds left in the game to salt away a 6–2 triumph for the home team. It was the first time in four tries that Detroit had beaten the Rangers at the Olympia in 1969–70.

It looked like the Rangers' once-promising season would come to a disastrous climax. However, New York got good news from the Montreal Forum. The Black Hawks had surprised the Canadiens, upending the Habs 4–1. Montreal coach Claude Ruel copied Francis' strategy and pulled his goalie, Rogie Vachon, in a bold attempt to add at least one more goal to Montreal's seasonal total. Neither the Habs nor the Black Hawks managed to score again, although Chicago probably should have. Bobby Hull oddly opted not to shoot the puck into the gaping Canadiens' net from close range. Instead he held onto the disc and ran out the clock. The Rangers were still alive—barely. Sunday's game at Madison Square Garden would have meaning to New York. As far as the never-say-die Francis was concerned, where there was the slightest glimmer of life, there was still hope.

The champagne was flowing in the Red Wings' dressing room. Team owner Bruce Norris gladly provided it so his team could stylishly celebrate clinching a well-earned berth in the Stanley Cup playoffs for the first time since the 1965–66 season. Gordie Howe, one of the joyous imbibers, figured the Rangers were kaput. "It doesn't look good for them," he told a reporter. "They've been hit by so many injuries. It looks like they've just run out of gas."[3]

Both the Red Wings and Rangers had chartered separate flights to take them to New York for the game the following afternoon. As it turned out, the two teams were lingering close to each other at the Detroit Municipal Airport simultaneously to finalize their reservations. Detroit coach Sid Abel approached Emile Francis to exchange pleasantries. Despite their coaching rival NHL teams, the two lifelong hockey men were on friendly terms. When Abel commented that it was a shame the Rangers were not going to make the playoffs as a result of their loss to Detroit that night, Francis quickly lost his temper. He angrily told Abel nothing had been decided yet and his Rangers were going to battle to the bitter end.

Francis told a reporter, "In this crazy race you can't tell what might happen. We haven't scored big for so long we just might break out for eight, nine or 10 goals."[4] Francis also noted, "This game is slippery. It's played on ice. We're not out yet and we won't stop fighting until the last soldier is dead."[5]

Francis, the good general, was going to do everything he could to prepare his troops for one last desperate battle at Madison Square Garden on April 5.

26

Sunday, April 5 (A):
Theater of the Absurd

"The National Hockey League's most unbelievable [regular] season ended, appropriately enough, in an unbelievable manner."[1]

—Hal Bock, Associated Press

"If there is one thing that remains crystal clear about our game ... is that all of us in the Rangers' dressing room were ready to go out on the ice and do whatever was necessary to win and, somehow, make the playoff for Emile Francis and for each other."[2]

—Ranger forward Bob Nevin recalling the April 5, 1970 Detroit–New York game in 2017

Madison Square Garden was a huge hockey venue by 1970 standards. Full houses in excess of 17,000 fans for Rangers home games were the norm during the exciting 1969–70 campaign. The Rangers would set a new seasonal attendance record that season. But when referee Bill Friday dropped the puck at 2:05 p.m. on the afternoon of Sunday, April 5, 1970, the Rangers' vast home building was remarkably less than half filled for the Detroit–New York clash. In fact, it was not even a quarter full despite every ticket being sold. Only the hardest of the hardcore Ranger fans were present. Many ticketholders likely did not want to be present to see a team that had been in first place for about 100 days fail to even qualify for the postseason.

Most of the Rangers' faithful were not so faithful in the face of long odds. They had seemingly given up on their team's chances to qualify for the Stanley Cup playoffs or they had decided to stay home and watch their team on the CBS *NHL Game of the Week* telecast—which was something of a novelty. Even the upper brass at Madison Square Garden had already thrown in the towel on the 1969–70 NHL season judging by who was not there. Among the absent were every director of Madison Square Garden,

135

including William Jennings, the president of the Rangers; Garden chairman Irving Felt; and vice president Edwin Ost. Francis was enraged when he learned they were not in the building to provide a measure of moral support.

On the final day of the regular season, the Rangers were still alive in the playoff chase in the NHL's East Division—but their collective pulse was weak. The mathematics facing the New Yorkers were truly daunting. It would take two remarkable results to turn the Rangers' very thin postseason hopes into a reality.

That day and night, all six teams in the East Division would be in action at some point, in staggered starts, to conclude their schedules. The Red Wings were at Madison Square Garden to play the Rangers at 2:05 p.m., an afternoon game dictated by American television. (The early start forced the cancellation of a matinee performance by Ringling Brothers Circus.) That evening Toronto was the visiting team at Boston Garden while Montreal would take to the ice at Chicago. When the day began, all three games potentially had playoff implications. Here's what the NHL's crowded East Division standings looked like in that Sunday morning's newspapers:

NHL East Division Standings
(after April 4, 1970, games had been completed)

Team	W	L	T	GF	GA	PTS
Chicago	44	22	9	240	168	97
Boston	39	17	19	274	215	97
Detroit	40	20	15	241	190	95
Montreal	38	21	16	242	191	92
New York	37	22	16	237	184	90
Toronto	29	33	13	221	239	71

Only Toronto, hopelessly mired in sixth place, was officially eliminated. (Maple Leaf fans would grumble—perhaps justifiably so—that their 71 points would have been good enough for second place in the NHL's decidedly weaker West Division.) For the other five East Division teams, the situation was quite complex. Either Chicago or Boston could still finish atop the standings. Detroit could finish as high as second place. Montreal and New York were vying for fourth place—albeit not directly against each other. With the Rangers and Red Wings playing an afternoon game, the other three East Division teams that had an interest in the game (Chicago, Boston and Montreal) would all know well in advance if their games that evening were meaningful—and, most importantly, what they would have to do to achieve their separate goals.

According to the NHL's simplistic tie-breaking rules in 1969–70, the following criteria would be used—in the order listed—to settle any deadlocks in the standings if teams were level on points when the 76-game regular season ended:

- most wins;
- most goals scored;
- fewest goals allowed.

Curiously, head-to-head records between the tied teams carried no weight whatsoever. Neither did their divisional records. *Remarkably, goals allowed would only be part of the equation if the teams were tied in both wins and goals scored.* Goal difference (goals scored minus goals allowed) was not a criterion. The Rangers had a better record than the Habs in the goals-scored department. As long as they did not allow seven goals to the Red Wings, New York, would retain that lead over Montreal. It was a quirky oversight that the Rangers were prepared to exploit to the fullest in their game versus Detroit.

Here is what each of the five playoff contenders already knew before the first puck was dropped on Sunday, April 5:

- Chicago would finish first by beating Montreal regardless of the outcome of the other two games. However, if Boston lost or played to a tie versus Toronto, the Black Hawks would need just a tie against the Habs to claim first place. The Black Hawks were guaranteed second place, at least.
- Boston could finish first with a win versus Toronto and anything less than a win by Chicago. However, the Bruins could finish as low as third place if they lost to Toronto and Detroit won their afternoon game in New York.
- Detroit could finish in second place if they beat New York and if Boston lost to Toronto. The Red Wings were guaranteed no worse than third place.
- Montreal would finish fourth with a tie or a win versus Chicago.
- New York could finish fourth only by beating Detroit—and Montreal had to lose to Chicago as well. Not only that, the Rangers had to erase the five-goal edge Montreal held over them (242–237) in the goals-scored department.

Thus, the task was somewhat murky for the New York Rangers, but one thing was obvious: They had to win and score plenty of goals versus the Red Wings to give themselves even a glimmer of hope of making the playoffs.

The absolute bare minimum they needed was five tallies. Coach Emile Francis, the master of minutiae, had convinced himself that nine was the magic number of goals his team required. It would be a rare feat: Only three NHL teams had scored nine goals in a game all season. The Rangers were not one of them, although they had notched eight goals in a game twice in 1969–70.

On paper, at least, it seemed to be a very tough task. Over the first 75 games of the 1969–70 regular season, the Rangers had averaged 3.16 goals per game. The last time the New Yorkers had scored five times in a game was on February 22 in a 6–5 win at Toronto in their 57th game of the season. Thus, it had been 18 games since the Rangers had last notched five goals. A week earlier, coach Emile Francis openly fretted about his team's lack of offense, but figured the Rangers were overdue for a high-scoring game. He optimistically told Dink Carroll of the *Montreal Gazette*, somewhat prophetically, "If we ever break loose, we'll score so many goals we won't know what to do with them all."[3] Nevertheless, if the Rangers could beat Detroit—and score at least five times in the process—pressure would be firmly placed upon Montreal to come up with some sort of positive result that night at Chicago Stadium. Of course, the Habs were hoping Detroit would play well enough against the Rangers so their game versus the Black Hawks would have no playoff implications whatsoever for them.

The Red Wings took a deliberately cautious approach heading into their Sunday afternoon game versus the Rangers. Detroit's management (specifically coach Sid Abel) figured that a second-place finish, though mathematically possible, was highly unlikely to be attained. The Red Wings assumed the Bruins would handily thump Toronto at Boston Garden that night because Boston would have motivation on their side. The Bruins could still finish in first place with a victory (or even a tie if Chicago lost at home to Montreal). In all likelihood, it was assumed the Maple Leafs would not show too much zeal in Boston in what was an utterly meaningless game for them. Convinced that their pursuit of Boston was almost futile, the Red Wings accordingly opted not to expend too much effort versus New York despite being viewed on a national telecast. When reporters questioned the general lack of professionalism of the Red Wings' performance after the game, Abel responded defensively with a rhetorical question of his own: "We clinched our spot [on] Saturday. Why should I tell my guys to go out and beat their heads against a wall?"[4] he said.

Furthermore, a great many Red Wings had consumed liberal quantities of champagne on the Wings' charter flight to New York City to celebrate their clinching a playoff berth. Abel made mental notes about who had imbibed far too much of the bubbly. One such casualty was goaltender Roy Edwards who was supposed to start the game after Roger Crozier had played in Detroit's win on Saturday. Edwards was officially unable to play because of "headaches and chest pains," a phrase that was probably a euphemism. Having no alternative, Abel again started Crozier for the second time in 18 hours. Another imbiber was Garry Unger, Detroit's youthful scoring sensation who was raised in a household where intoxicating beverages were off limits. In a celebratory mood, Unger tasted champagne—and too much of it—for the first and last time in his life.

Despite persistent myths to the contrary, the only regulars who did not play for the Red Wings that afternoon were the under-the-weather Edwards and defensemen Dale Rolfe. Rolfe was legitimately injured, with two split elbows. All the other Detroit regulars played—albeit sparingly in many cases. Still there would be players wearing Detroit uniforms on Sunday who were mildly or moderately hungover. Detroit's blasé approach to their game in New York combined with the Rangers desperately needing a mountain of goals was a perfect recipe for a rout and a memorable debacle in full view of a continental television audience.

Author Reg Lansberry, whose 2017 book *9 Goals* focuses on the two important games on April 5 that decided the 1970 playoff berths in the NHL's East Division, wrote about the positive mindset in the Rangers' dressing room before they came onto the ice for the first period:

> No one needs to tell them what they have to do. For if they do not win, and score at least five goals, a season that included 3-1/2 exciting months in first place during which they were the talk of the league, will be quickly consigned to the dustbin of Rangers history.

With the sober and semi-sober Red Wings interested in little more than a leisurely afternoon skate, the Rangers took the offensive early and often. During the first period, Francis positioned his defensemen several feet inside the Wings' blue line to generate as much offense as possible. He would later move one defenseman back to his regular position to prevent easy Detroit breakaways. Francis did warn goalie Ed Giacomin that he would not be getting as much defensive help as usual—and he could expect to be pulled late in the third period even if the Rangers were leading the game.

It took all of 36 seconds for New York to open the scoring. The slumping Rod Gilbert deftly tipped in an Arnie Brown slapshot. When Lansberry interviewed him 47 years later, Gilbert distinctly remembered being booed when he was announced as the Rangers' goal-scorer. The fans were that critical of his disappointing season.

With New York sacrificing defense for greater offense, Detroit was going to get their fair share of chances to score—and then some. Gary Berman evened the score at 1–1 with a fine individual effort. He deked Rod

Seiling, causing the Ranger defenseman to stumble. Bergman then went in alone on Ed Giacomin and put the puck between his pads. The time of the Red Wing goal was 3:08. The small but vocal crowd was silent again.

The Rangers took to the offensive again. Detroit's Peter Stemkowski was whistled for a penalty at 6:26. With just one second left in the man advantage, the Rangers scored their second goal. Rookie Jack Egers, who possessed a powerful slapshot, blew one past the startled Crozier from 40 feet out at 8:25. It was his second career NHL goal. Egers' first score had come the night before in Detroit. Dan Kelly in the CBS broadcast booth was suitably impressed by the velocity Egers had generated on his slapshot and said so. The Rangers regained the lead, 2–1.

The crowd sensed blood. With the knowledgeable Ranger fans fully aware that the only chance their team had to qualify for the 1970 Stanley Cup playoffs was to win and score as many goals as possible, a greedy chant of "More! More! More!" echoed across Madison Square Garden after each Ranger score was added.

New York followed instructions and merrily continued the onslaught. The Wings tried to get into the game by sending out their top line of Gordie Howe, Alex Delvecchio and Frank Mahovlich for the first time. They did not have much of an impact. Detroit's Al Karlander was penalized. The Rangers went on a power play. Only 24 seconds elapsed before Dave Balon scored for New York at 12:31 with assists going to Walt Tkaczuk and Arnie Brown. The home team now led 3–1. Everything was going as Emile Francis had hoped.

The Rangers kept pressuring the lethargic Red Wings who could not seem to get anything positive going after the Bergman goal. The New Yorkers scored their fourth goal of the first period. Again, it came from young Egers who was easily having the best game of his nascent NHL career. He scored on a rebound off a Tim Horton shot that Crozier could not corral. The time of the goal was 17:48. The small gathering at the Garden went wild knowing that with the Rangers holding a 4–1 lead, one major criterion for the team's playoff hopes—scoring five goals—was well within reach with more than two periods still to be played.

Egers recalled lining up against Gordie Howe for the next faceoff. Howe politely commented, "You're having a good game, eh, kid?" Egers grunted, "Yeah." Within seconds of the puck dropping, Egers was introduced to the subtle but effective stick work of Mr. Hockey who sneakily stuck him in the ribs. "It hurt like hell,"[5] Egers remembered. After the game, Egers discovered a prominent, large welt on his torso. He took it as a badge of honor that Howe had welcomed him to the NHL in such a rough manner.

During the first intermission two remarkable incidents occurred. The first one was a live television interview conducted by Bill Mazer of CBS. His two subjects, one from each team, were 22-year-old Garry Unger of the Red Wings and New York's 21-year-old Jack Egers. The latter was the star of the game so far. Egers got the kid-glove treatment from Mazer—a series of easy, non-confrontational questions. However, with Detroit losing 4–1 and not putting up much of a struggle, Mazer asked Unger a tougher query: "What's the matter with your team?" The naive but truthful Unger gave an honest answer: "Well, the guys are all hammered."[6]

Unger's remark was heard by numerous members of the Montreal contingent who had tuned to CBS' *NHL Game of the Week* telecast in to see how the Red Wings–Rangers game would impact what the Habs needed to do—if anything—in Chicago that night to overtake the Rangers for the final playoff berth. They were not pleased. Montreal general manager Sam Pollock had already suspected the Red Wings were not quite themselves. Now there was no doubt. He took the extraordinary measure of calling Madison Square Garden. Somehow Pollock got connected to the office in the visiting team's dressing room and chewed out Sid Abel, accusing the Red Wings of lying down. Abel passed along the message to his troops in the hope of inspiring them to pick up their game. Meanwhile the atmosphere in the New York dressing room was decidedly upbeat. The Rangers were champing at the bit; they could hardly wait to get back onto the ice to score more goals.

New York began the second period as they began the first period—by scoring inside the first minute. This time the goal came even faster. It was Rod Gilbert again, this time just 20 seconds into the middle period. He beat two Red Wings to a loose puck and blasted a shot past the sprawling Roger Crozier. Assists went to Jean Ratelle and Brad Park. Attendance at Madison Square Garden had improved considerably during the intermission. It was now about half full. The crowd exploded when the red goal light behind the embattled Crozier was turned on. The Rangers had attained the minimum five goals required to stay in the playoff race—with almost two full periods to spare. (This time the fickle patrons cheered loudly this time when Gilbert was announced as the Ranger goal scorer.) New York's task was a little simpler now. They still had to win the game, but every goal scored from this point onward would increase their cushion over Montreal if the Habs failed to attain a win or a tie at Chicago Stadium later that night.

Detroit got a goal back a little more than four minutes later. With New York largely neglecting their checking, Frank Mahovlich was able to collect a pass in front of Ed Giacomin and, while stumbling, awkwardly lifted the puck into the top of the net at 4:21. It was Mahovlich's 38th goal of 1969–70. Alex Delvecchio and Carl Brewer picked up assists. The score was now 5–2. Mahovlich would not return to action in the third period; he had twisted his knee on the scoring play.

The Red Wings were showing a little bit of life—just a little—but not for too long. Three minutes and 17 seconds later the Rangers regained their four-goal edge. Orland Kurtenbach and Bob Nevin combined to relieve Red Wings defenseman Bob Baun of the puck in the Detroit zone in the faceoff circle to Crozier's right. Kurtenbach fed Nevin a short drop pass. Nevin noticed Ron Stewart positioned near the Detroit goal crease. A diagonal pass to him was perfect. Nevin easily redirected the puck past a helpless Crozier. The score was now 6–2 for New York. The rapidly filling arena roared again. All things considered, with 7:38 gone in the second period, the outcome of the game was already a certainty: New York will win. How many goals the Rangers score in doing so was the only thing left to decide—and all that really mattered in the grand scheme of things.

Nearly 11 minutes went by before the next goal was scored. Again it was New York that scored. Again it was Ron Stewart. He connected at 18:35 on a one-timer after receiving another excellent pass from Arnie Brown. It was Brown's fourth assist of the game—a total he will never again duplicate in his NHL career. New York now led 7–2. In Chicago, the startled Canadiens were sitting around televisions. They were worrying and fuming simultaneously.

Detroit mustered a reply just 26 seconds later due to some sloppy play in the New York zone. Giacomin, Gilbert and Nevin all failed to control a loose puck. Detroit's Bruce MacGregor fared better. He got to it and found Peter Stemkowski with a quick pass. Stemkowski beat Giacomin with a wrist shot to the stick side with 59 seconds left in the second period. The Rangers and Red Wings scored no more goals in the final minute. The Rangers outshot Detroit 22–8 in the second period. Despite surrendering a late goal to the visitors, the Rangers headed to their dressing room to thunderous applause with a 7–3 lead. When they returned to the ice for the third period, Madison Square Garden had been transformed to a full house of Ranger supporters. Realizing that something extraordinary was happening, the no-shows had finally arrived en masse to witness a bit of NHL history.

Again, the Rangers excited their fans with an early goal to start the period. This time it took more than a minute to achieve the feat—81 seconds, to be exact. Dave Balon scored his 32nd goal of the season when, from a scramble in front of Crozier, he got his own rebound and beat the Red Wings' netminder with a high shot. It was an unassisted goal. New York led 8–3.

Both teams ran into penalties in the first 10 minutes of the third period, but they were mostly successful in killing them off. Even while shorthanded, the Rangers keep attacking Crozier. With captain Bob Nevin in the penalty box, the Rangers scored a shorthanded goal. The scorer was Dave Balon, who made it a hat trick on the afternoon by finishing off a two-on-one against Crozier. The goal came at 9:48. Seiling and Stewart collected assists. It was the seventh time the Rangers had notched a short-handed goal in the 1969–70 season. The score was now 9–3. With the goal, Balon overtook Jean Ratelle in Rangers goal scoring with his 33rd tally of the season. Remarkably, Emile Francis had attained the nine goals he was aiming for when the game began. All nine had been scored by forwards. Mission accomplished. But Francis was insatiable. He wanted more goals. So did the Rangers and their fans. Every goal tacked on by New York potentially made Montreal's task in Chicago more difficult.

Ten minutes remained on Madison Square Garden's clock. Why not try to run up the score? Detroit now stubbornly turned to defense, trying desperately not to surrender double digits. When the Red Wings' Peter Stemkowski was penalized, Francis, as promised, pulled Giacomin with 3:38 to play to have a six-on-four power play. The knowing crowd loudly roared its approval of the offense-at-all-costs maneuver by the Ranger coach. To the best of anyone's knowledge, it was the first time in NHL history that a team leading a game had pulled its goaltender late in a game in an attempt to increase the score.

The ploy did not work as intended. Gordie Howe—whose line played just six shifts in the entire game—accepted a pass from Carl Brewer. He crossed the red line and backhanded the puck accurately. It slowly but inexorably trickled into the unguarded New York net at 17:29. It was, officially, a shorthanded empty-net goal. It was the 17th time Howe had scored into a vacated net in his long NHL career. The Rangers' sizable lead was whittled down to 9–4.

Giacomin was lifted from the net three more times in the final 2-1/2 minutes whenever the Rangers gained control of the puck and moved it into Detroit's end of the ice. They failed to attain ten goals, but the Red Wings did add one more shorthanded empty-net tally to the scoresheet. Nick Libett got the goal, unassisted, on a 20-foot shot with 55 seconds to play. The score, which will be the final, was now 9–5 in favor of New York. The fifth Detroit goal was more than trivial to the 24-year-old Libett. He had achieved a special milestone. It was Libett's 20th tally of the 1969–70 season. According to a clause in his contract, being a 20-goal scorer earned him a cash bonus from the Red Wings. It meant nothing, but Detroit's fifth goal also gave them 246 for the season—precisely the same total the New York Rangers accrued.

For Ranger fans who saw it on television or in person at Madison Square Garden, their team's victory that afternoon over the Detroit Red Wings would forever fondly be referred to as "the 9–5 game."

Roger Crozier, a pitiable figure, was peppered with 65 Ranger shots—a mark that still stands as a New York record half a century later.

The Rangers also recorded 26 shots in the third period to establish another team record for the most shots in any period. Crozier was both exhausted and shell-shocked when the game mercifully ended. Decades later Crozier's teammate Peter Stemkowski opined, "Roger was one more shot away from [being put] in a body cast and [being sent] to an institution."[7]

Years later, the injured Dale Rolfe, who watched the game in street clothes from ice level, likened the Red Wings–Rangers contest to something one might see in an adult recreational league where there was indeed a hockey game being contested with two teams and officials, but no one was playing with enough intensity to be hurt.

A month later, Crozier, while not specifically referring to the final weekend of the most recent regular season, publicly chastised the NHL for kowtowing to the dictums of American network television. In an after-dinner banquet speech in Barrie, Ontario, Crozier stated, "When a team plays on a Saturday night out of town and has to be ready for a home game on Sunday afternoon, it is hard on the players. Players do not get to bed until 4 a.m. following a tiring trip. To be ready for a game at 1 p.m. is a bit much. Such scheduling did not exist before CBS began carrying its *Game of the Week*."[8] Earlier in the season Pat Curran of the *Montreal Gazette* echoed similar feelings. He humorously declared that CBS had so much influence over the NHL that it would not surprise him to see Carol Burnett, the network's popular comedienne, refereeing a league game sometime soon.

Dan Kelly concluded his *NHL Game of the Week* commentary on Sunday, April 5, by telling CBS' viewers, "The Rangers are still in the playoff picture of the East Division depending upon what happens tonight in a game in Chicago between the Montreal Canadiens and the Chicago Black Hawks."[9] Exactly.

Of course, the media pounced on Detroit coach Sid Abel and his team after the game for their substandard showing. Abel was thoroughly unapologetic, explaining that his tired team was playing its fourth game in five days and had earned the right to coast through the regular-season finale. Abel went as far as to openly express regret for playing his veterans as much as he did. He punctuated his point by noting that the Red Wings had won their playoff spot. It was now up to the Montreal Canadiens to win theirs.

All eyes turned toward Chicago.

Sunday, April 5 (B):
Five Empty-Net Goals

With Detroit's disgraceful and controversial loss to the Rangers entered into the books, the Red Wings were solidly locked into third place. This meant they would play the East Division winner in a Stanley Cup quarterfinal. The result also meant the Boston Bruins were now guaranteed no worse than a second-place finish.

The Toronto–Boston game at Boston Garden on Sunday night would, perhaps, determine if the hometown Bruins could end the 1969–70 campaign in first place and thus capture the Price of Wales Trophy. Top spot was a position where they had not finished an NHL season since the 1940–41 season during the heyday of the team's celebrated Kraut Line of Milt Schmidt, Woody Dumart and Bobby Bauer—three players of German-Canadian descent who had started playing together as youths in Kitchener, Ontario. That 1940–41 campaign was also the most recent Stanley Cup triumph for Boston. Due to the time difference, the Bruins–Maple Leafs game at Boston Garden started an hour before the Montreal–Chicago game.

Few hockey fans expected the Maple Leafs to put up much of a fight in Boston. Why should they exert themselves? Their playoff hopes were completely dashed in the middle of March. Unlike the Red Wings, however, the Leafs showed a healthy degree of both professionalism and pride to finish out their disappointing 1969–70 season. Before a raucous sellout crowd of 14,835 patrons at Boston Garden, Dave Keon surprisingly gave the visitors a 1–0 edge at 17:01 of the first period, clearly against the run of play, with a 50-foot shot that Boston goalie Gerry Cheevers clumsily misplayed. An irked Cheevers would be unbeatable from that point onward.

However, it was Toronto goaltender Marv Edwards—no relation to Roy Edwards of the Red Wings—who was far and away the game's overall star. The unnamed Associated Press correspondent covering the contest described Edwards' play in the Leafs' net as "unbelievable." Edwards faced

54 shots from "the fired-up Bruins"—including 24 in the second period alone. "Edwards held off the Bruins time and again," the AP Scribe marveled. He also commented, "The Bruins staged a virtually continuous bombardment during the last four minutes of the [second] period, holding a manpower advantage most of the time, including a two-man edge for 51 seconds, but were unable to break through."[1]

Edwards did not know it at the time, but he was playing his last game for Toronto. A journeyman goaltender, Edwards would shortly be released by the Maple Leafs and not resurface again in the NHL until 1972–73 when the California Golden Seals (formerly the Oakland Seals) picked him up. The 1969–70 campaign was Edwards' best. He finished the year with a laudable 10–9–4 record and a 3.26 goals-against average for a Toronto team that struggled all season to be competitive against the dominating teams from the NHL's East Division.

Defensemen Rick Ley and Mike Pelyk were also doing stalwart work for Toronto all night in repelling the potent Boston offense, giving Edwards temporarily relief many times. At 1:56 of the second period, however, Boston's Johnny McKenzie finally found a chink in Edwards' armor and leveled the contest with a goal on a 15-foot shot that beat Edwards just inside the far goalpost. Bobby Orr, who fed McKenzie a lovely pass, got an assist on the play—his 87th of the season. It was also Orr's 120th point. No one else in the NHL had attained triple figures. The game remained tied at 1–1 until Derek Sanderson's goal from a wild scramble in front of Edwards' goal crease with under six minutes remaining in the third period put Boston up 2–1 just seconds after a Toronto penalty had expired. About a minute later, Ken Hodge tallied an insurance marker for the home team—a goal that took the remaining pep out of the valiant visitors. Boston ran out the clock to win 3–1. For the moment, Boston was in first place with 99 points, two points ahead of Chicago. However, the Black Hawks could regain the NHL's top spot with a win over Montreal, since the Hawks held the upper hand over Boston in total wins.

All eyes in the hockey world turned to Chicago. At least it was accurate in a metaphorical sense; one could not see anything unless one possessed a ticket to the game. The Black Hawks routinely blacked out their home games—even those that were sellouts. They made no exception for this key contest. The game, oddly, was not even being televised in Montreal. Fans of both teams would have to make do with radio descriptions. Even the radio coverage was less than perfect. As was the custom in many locales, *only a portion of the game* would be broadcast on WGN in Chicago. Its coverage of the game would begin in the second period; the first 20 minutes would be omitted—something utterly incomprehensible today. It was a different world in 1970. Fans who wanted to hear the complete game would have to try to pick up Danny Gallivan's call over the CBC radio network from Canada. The Rangers' radio announcer, Marv Albert, who owned a short-wave radio receiver, was doing just that. (All the while he was also regularly receiving telephone inquiries from friends wondering how the game was progressing.) Hal Bock, an Associated Press hockey writer stationed in New York City, chose another option not available to the masses: He went to his office and read the bulletins that were coming in print form over the AP's ticker tape machine.

Of course, thousands of supporters of both the Rangers and the Bruins—and curious fans in general—tried to pick up a radio description of the contest from Chicago Stadium too. Among them was Rangers coach Emile Francis who, at his home, nervously paced and chain-smoked his way through a wavering broadcast signal emanating some 700 miles away in Chicago. Most of the time he was too charged up to sit and listen. Francis walked steadily around the neighborhood—even during intermissions. He instructed Em, his wife, to alert him after every goal, however. Having had almost zero sleep since the Rangers–Red Wings game on Saturday night, Francis would refer to April 5, 1970, as his longest day in hockey. Most of the Ranger players congregated at their favorite Italian eatery, Il Vagabondo, where the proprietor provided his specialty—veal parmigiana—and a radio broadcast of the Montreal–Chicago game.

The situation was now clear: To qualify for a playoff berth, Montreal had to do one of three things: defeat the Black Hawks, tie them, or score five goals in a losing effort. Montreal coach Claude Ruel was as willing to do the same unorthodox things as Emile Francis to get one of those results. Unlike the Red Wings–Rangers game, both teams would be doing the utmost to win. A Chicago win would tie them atop the East Division with Boston at 99 points. However, Chicago would hold the edge over the Bruins, based on greater number of wins, and be awarded first place. Finishing in first place meant a monetary prize and home-ice advantage in the playoffs. It would be quite an accomplishment for the Black Hawks to finish atop the standings, considering they were a last-place club the previous season and did not record a win in 1969–70 until their seventh game. Every hockey fan understood the Black Hawks would accordingly be motivated to play well. Game time was 7:35 p.m. Central time—8:35 p.m. for anyone in New York or nearby trying to find the broadcast on the radio.

One intangible was the Canadiens' mindset entering the game. They had watched the Red Wings–Rangers game on television earlier from their hotel in Chicago. As they boarded their bus to take them to the game, instead of being totally focused on their own task, many were still seething about Detroit's less than zealous play versus New York. Some of the Habs angrily denounced the afternoon game as a farce. John Ferguson stated one positive reality to everyone within earshot: the Canadiens still had total control of their own destiny. He reminded his teammates that even a tie would get them into the playoffs. From a psychological standpoint, that was an interesting comment. When a hockey team plays for a tie, they typically play differently—more cautiously—than if they are playing for a win. In retrospect, had the Canadiens gone all-out offensively in pursuit of five goals—even if they surrendered a dozen goals themselves—it probably would have served their interests better. They would be facing a Chicago team that had lost just seven of their previous 41 games and were determined to win to finish ahead of Boston in the East Division. Cautious play from a Montreal team seeking only a draw would be welcomed by the Black Hawks.

Montreal started the critical game well. Yvan Cournoyer scored with a man advantage while Doug Jarrett of the Black Hawks was serving a minor penalty. The time of the goal was 9:12. The visitors led 1–0. Later in the first period, Jim Pappin equalized with a power play goal for Chicago while Ted Harris of the Canadiens was sitting in the penalty box. Pappin's goal came at 15:49. Still in the first period, Chicago assumed a 2–1 lead on Pit Martin's goal. It was another power play tally. Seven penalties were called in the first period. It ended with the home team holding a slim, one-goal advantage. Nothing at all had been settled yet.

Only one penalty was called in the middle period. The checking became tighter too. Nevertheless, Bobby Hull gave the Black Hawks a 3–1 lead with a goal at 1:24. The Habs fought back. Captain Jean Béliveau narrowed the Chicago lead to 3–2 with a goal at 3:27. The remaining 16 and a half minutes of the second period produced no goals.

About the time the second period concluded in Chicago, the game in Boston ended, with the Bruins topping the Maple Leafs 3–1. The news from Boston Garden was quickly relayed to all concerned parties—which was virtually everyone. It was the result the Rangers wanted, but the Black Hawks did not. For the moment, the Bruins sat atop the East Division with 99 points. The Hawks now had to win against Montreal rather than just tie to earn first place. On the other hand, back in New York City, the Rangers were pleased as the Bruins' win now forced Chicago to play their best hockey against Montreal to win the divisional championship. For the Habs, the score from Boston was almost trivial. It would only be meaningful in the long term if they could do what they needed to do in the final period versus Chicago. Boston might be a potential first-round playoff opponent for Montreal—if the Canadiens qualified for the playoffs. With 20 minutes left to play in Chicago and the Habs trailing 3–2, the "if" was enormous.

No one in the Rangers' camp was relaxing quite yet. Still too much could happen that would deprive New York of fourth place. Three Montreal goals would certainly do it. Even one might suffice if it resulted in a tie game. Furthermore, the mystique of the Canadiens carried some weight. They were the two-time defending Stanley Cup champions and the most successful franchise in NHL history. Didn't they always qualify for the playoffs? A third-period rally by the illustrious Habs, be it one goal or three, was hardly out of the question.

Hubert Jacques (Pit) Martin, the small-in-stature French-Canadian forward who had been traded to Chicago from Boston in 1967 as part of the famous Phil Esposito deal, provided two more critical goals for the Black Hawks that proved to be the death knell of the Habs. They came about three and a half minutes apart. The first was at 7:15 of the third period. The next at 10:44. Those two tallies gave Martin three for the game. The hat-trick lifted his goal total for the 1969–70 season to 30. (Like Nick Libett of Detroit earlier that day, Martin got a bonus for attaining a goal-scoring milestone.) The noise at Chicago Stadium became deafening and hardly subsided until the final buzzer.

The situation for the Canadiens became extremely grim but very clear. Winning the game was now a long shot. They needed five goals, either to attain a 5–5 tie or just to overtake New York in the seasonal goals-for column. The desperate times called for desperate measures. Montreal coach Claude Ruel showed how desperate he was. He lifted goalie Rogie Vachon for an extra attacker with 7:45 left in the third period. He really had nothing to lose.

Unused to playing in frantic survival mode, the Habs never once had a good opportunity to score on Tony Esposito, despite having six skaters in Chicago's offensive zone for nearly eight minutes. Instead, it was the Black Hawks who gleefully poured goal after goal into the empty Montreal net. Eric Nesterenko struck first into Montreal's gaping goal, scoring at 12:27. Ninety seconds Later Cliff Koroll did the same thing. Bobby Hull got one too at 14:44. His brother, Dennis found the target at 17:08. Gerry Pinder finished matters with Chicago's tenth goal—and their fifth empty-netter—with just three seconds left showing on Chicago Stadium's antiquated analog clock.

The clock ran out and the strange, two-headed debacle of Sunday, April 5, 1970, had ended. Montreal had gone down to ignominious defeat, 10–2. No other NHL team had surrendered 10 goals in a game during the 1969–70 season. It had certainly been a topsy-turvy six months of hockey. Chicago had risen from a last-place team to a divisional winner in one season. Black Hawk fans who had been calling for coach Billy Reay's head in the middle of October were now lauding him as a savior and a genius. A time zone away, the usually stolid Emile Francis celebrated his team's playoff berth at home where he could freely express his joy at the positive turn of events for his Rangers. His 11-year-old son, Bobby Francis, who would be named the NHL's Coach of the Year 32 years later, recalled seeing his father being overtly emotional at the result of a hockey game for the first time.

Most people connected with the Montreal Canadiens could scarcely believe what had transpired. General manager Sam Pollock was one of them. He griped, "Before the season, if someone had told me we'd get 92 points, I'd have said, 'I'll take it. Let's start the playoffs right now.'"[2] Indeed, Montreal's 92 points was the highest total in NHL history ever attained by a team that failed to qualify for the postseason.

Le Devoir, a French-language Montreal daily newspaper, declared on April 6, "Because of a system not very well developed to break one or more equalities between two or three clubs, the game ended like a bad comedy." The headline on the story—with its precise translation into English—read, "A Chicago champion and the Canadiens swallowed 10–2!"[3]

The Canadiens had failed to qualify for the Stanley Cup playoffs for the first time since the 1947–48 season! (That year the Habs, a sub-.500 team, finished four points out of a playoff spot behind … the New York Rangers!) Not only that, the absence of the Toronto Maple Leafs from post-season hockey meant that the NHL playoffs—which would start three days hence—would feature zero Canadian-based teams. That was a first. At a time when Canada's government was drafting legislation to mandate greater Canadian content in the country's radio and television programming, having neither the Leafs nor the Canadiens in the playoffs was a sore spot for many hockey fans and sports journalists above the 49th parallel. Of course, comedians jokingly called for federal legislation to ensure greater Canadian content in the Stanley Cup playoffs.

Although Montreal coach Claude Ruel was absolutely correct in saying the Canadiens had complete control of their own destiny and only had themselves to blame for their failure to finish the season somewhere in the top four spots of the NHL's East Division, many downtrodden and embittered Habs still dwelled on the Detroit Red Wings and their substandard effort in Madison Square Garden earlier in the day. A headline in the next day's *Chicago Tribune* above Bob Verdi's report blared, "Quiet Echoes the Disbelief of Canadiens." For the only time in his terrific 20-year NHL career, Montreal captain Jean Béliveau would miss the Stanley Cup playoffs. Yvan Cournoyer bitterly broke the silence to sum up his feelings about the Red Wings in one terse, five-word statement: "Those guys have no pride."[4]

Hockey fans around the world—literally—were shocked that the Habs would be uncharacteristically absent from the 1970 Stanley playoffs. The April 9 *Montreal Gazette* featured a quirky human-interest story about a young touring pianist from the Soviet Union, Alexander Slobodyanik, who was utterly crestfallen by this tragic development. "My biggest disappointment since coming to Montreal was learning that the Canadiens did not make the Stanley Cup playoffs," he sadly said. "I had been looking forward to [seeing] a playoff hockey game for months. All my friends who had seen professional hockey here had told me I just had to see a game!"[5] A sympathetic *Gazette* columnist invited Slobodyanik to accompany him to a junior hockey playoff game at the Forum. At least Slobodyanik got to witness future NHL superstar Gilbert Perreault, the standout player for the Montreal Jr. Canadiens.

An editorial in the April 10 edition of the *Oakland Tribune* found the development rather amusing. It said, in part,

> Whether the Oakland Seals are a superior hockey team to the Montreal Canadiens or Toronto Maple Leafs is not a question that will be further adjudicated this year.
>
> Suffice to say that in a development that must have caused more than a few anguished tears throughout much of Canada, the final standings of the National Hockey League revealed our own dear Seals laying a firm claim to a Stanley Cup playoff spot. The Canadiens and their neighbors to the west, however, were frozen out of the playoffs for the first time since shinny became a respectable sport.
>
> Such may be the ultimate embarrassment to the perennial well-spring of championship hockey…[6]

While Montreal fans and players stewed, the backers of the Rangers were giddy. New York was in the Stanley Cup playoffs for the fourth season in a row. Remarkably, the Rangers were the only NHL team that could make that claim. (Of course, the six expansion teams had only been in existence for three seasons.)

Emile Francis called Montreal "a bunch of soreheads" in an interview that author Reg Lansberry conducted when Francis was in his nineties. "Montreal never blamed themselves for anything," Francis claimed. "The fact is in our last five games we [the Rangers] earned seven points." Montreal, conversely, picked up just three points in their final five contests. "They had a lot of injuries during the year," Francis continued, "but so did we. You never heard us whining about it."[7]

At those years later, Francis also remained convinced that the Habs had been psychologically damaged by watching the Rangers–Red Wings game on television at their hotel before heading to Chicago Stadium to play their night game versus the Black Hawks. What had initially seemed highly implausible had suddenly become very possible—and the unexpected change had a lingering and negative effect on the minds of the Canadiens before they even took the ice.

Generally forgotten as the drama in the East Division playoff race came to a climax in New York City and Chicago was the one West Division game remaining on the schedule on April 5. It paled to the goings-on in New York and Chicago, but it did have its importance too. Thanks to three power play goals, the Minnesota North Stars won their season finale in

Pittsburgh by a convincing 5–1 margin, thus leapfrogging into third place over the Oakland Seals. Bill Goldsworthy scored one of the visitors' goals to reach 36 for the season. That was a new franchise record. The victory meant the North Stars would face the St. Louis Blues in the opening round of the playoffs while Pittsburgh would face Oakland.

The remarkable and absurd happenings on Saturday, April 4 and Sunday, April 5 were succinctly summed up by Mark Mulvoy of *Sports Illustrated*: "Tranquilizers were useful as the close of the NHL's frantic last weekend."[8] Hal Bock (the Associated Press scribe who had holed up in his office next to a ticker tape machine) concluded his report on the weekend's remarkable goings-on by noting, "The Stanley Cup playoffs open Wednesday with New York at Boston and Detroit at Chicago in the East Division, and Minnesota and St. Louis and Oakland at Pittsburgh in the West. They'll have to be something special to top the last regular-season weekend."[9]

1969–70 Final Standings: NHL's East Division

Team	W	L	T	GF	GA	PTS
CHI	45	22	9	250	170	99
BOS	40	17	19	277	216	99
DET	40	21	15	246	199	95
NY	38	22	16	246	189	92
MTL	38	22	16	244	201	92
TOR	29	34	13	222	242	71

The All-American 1970 Stanley Cup Playoffs

28

The Stanley Cup …
Canada's Trophy?

"Skulls were cracked and blood flowed with shocking regularity. Games were played in drafty, barn-like arenas on ice that was rock-hard, putty-soft, or salted to sabotage a fast team. The fans loved it."[1]
—hockey historian Brian McFarlane

"The Stanley Cup is one of the oldest and most treasured trophies in all sports. It is the ultimate goal and prized reward of the most exciting team game of them all."[2]
—Brian McFarlane

Frederick Arthur Stanley, Lord Stanley of Preston, the Earl of Derby, was the fifth governor-general of a young new nation. In layman's terms, he was the representative of the British Crown in the Dominion of Canada. No legislation that was passed in Canada's parliament could formally become the law of the land without the signature of the governor-general being affixed to it. Lord Stanley was appointed to the largely ceremonial but constitutionally important position by Queen Victoria in 1888.

While attending a winter carnival, Lord Stanley witnessed an ice hockey game between two amateur Montreal teams: the Victorias and the Amateur Athletic Association. He very much liked what he saw and decided Canada needed some sort of national trophy that its many amateur teams could pursue. Near the end of Stanley's five-year assignment in Canada, he was the guest of honor at a banquet at Ottawa's Russell House hosted by that city's Amateur Athletic Association. During a speech that night, Lord Stanley outlined his idea:

"I have for some time been thinking that it would be a good thing if there were a challenge cup which should be held from year to year by the champion hockey team in the Dominion of Canada. There does not appear to be any such outward sign of a championship at present, and considering the general interest which matches now elicit, and the importance of having the game played fairly and under rules generally recognized,

I am willing to give a cup which shall be held from year to year by the winning team."³

Shortly thereafter Stanley purchased a silver bowl for 10 guineas (about $50 Canadian) to serve his purpose. He appointed two trustees in Ottawa to handle all matters pertaining to his trophy. It was first awarded in 1893. The recipients were the Montreal Amateur Athletic Association hockey club for having the best record in their league. There were no playoffs. None were needed. A few months later Lord Stanley, his term as Canada's governor-general over, sailed home to England where he died in 1908. He could hardly have foreseen that his gift to amateur hockey would grow in stature to become the oldest major trophy in North American team sports and would be among the most coveted and recognizable prizes in all athletic competition. In 1945 Lord

Lord Stanley of Preston, Canada's fifth governor-general, donated the famous trophy that bears his name. Beginning with its first presentation in 1893, the Stanley Cup was intended to be awarded to the championship hockey club of Canada. The NHL took sole possession of the trophy beginning with the 1926–27 season (courtesy Library and Archives Canada; MIKAN inventory #3194700).

Stanley was posthumously inducted into the Hockey Hall of Fame as an "honored builder."

Stanley's legacy became a prize for teams comprised of both amateurs and professionals as early as 1907. (The Allan Cup was established for national amateur competition in Canada in 1909.) Championship teams from the eastern National Hockey Association (the forerunner of the NHL) began competing against the champions from various western leagues each spring starting in 1911. After 1926, with the National Hockey League now being the sole major professional hockey circuit in North America, the Stanley Cup fell into its permanent possession.

Nine years earlier, on March 26, 1917, the Seattle Metropolitans of the Pacific Coast Hockey Association handily thumped the Montreal

Canadiens of the National Hockey Association 9–1 at the Seattle Ice Arena to win the best-of-five Stanley Cup final three games to one. They became the first American-based team to win the trophy that Lord Stanley had intended to go to the "championship hockey club of Canada." The triumphant Metropolitans did not get their hands on the coveted trophy right away. The Canadiens were the defending Stanley Cup champions from 1915 to 1916. They were so confident of retaining the Cup that they did not bother to bring it along with them on the long trip to Seattle.

On the hundredth anniversary of the Seattle Metropolitans' historic victory, a local commemoration of the notable feat was observed. "This first U.S. Stanley Cup was potentially a turning point for American hockey," said Ralph Morton, the executive director of the Seattle Sports Commission. "It showed the Pacific Northwest—and the nation—that hockey belonged in America."[4]

In many locales in hockey-mad Canada, news that the country's most famous hockey symbol was now in the possession of a team based in the United States was not particularly well received. Fifty-three years later, the 1969–70 NHL season took American participation in the Stanley Cup playoffs to another level entirely.

With the debacles of April 5, 1970, two days in the past, veteran sports columnist Austin (Dink) Carroll, in the April 7 edition of the *Montreal Gazette,* lamented what the absence of both the Montreal Canadiens and Toronto Maple Leafs from postseason play meant to a great many nationalistic Canadian hockey followers. The 70-year-old former collegiate athlete had been covering sports for his newspaper since 1941, but Carroll was now commenting on a scenario he and no other hockey journalist had ever seen:

What's new? Just this: for the first time in the history of hockey, the entire Stanley Cup playoff series, which starts tomorrow, will be played in the United States.

You always associate spring in this country with the NHL playoffs, and it comes as something of a shock to realize that not a single game will be staged in Canada this year. There's always a first time for everything, but this one is a little painful. The games will be carried on the CBC network, but the atmosphere and the excitement that accompany the playoffs will be missing in the city.

For the first time in 22 years, the Canadiens failed to make it to the playoffs. Over that long stretch they dominated the professional hockey scene, winning far more than their share of league championships and Stanley Cups. They had become such a power that Scotty Bowman, coach of the St. Louis Blues, couldn't imagine the playoffs without them.

"They've got to be the Stanley Cup favorites," he said as recently as last week. "The playoffs are a whole new game, and they play it well."

Bowman will now have to reorient his approach to the playoffs and so will some others. The teams that finished in the playoffs will be happy that they don't have to contend with the Canadiens, figuring that their own chances of winning the Cup will be enhanced by their absence.

The Canadiens had an almost unprecedented number of injuries this season, but that isn't the real reason for their failure. Prolonged success may have made them a little fat. They lost too many games they could have won if they had all worked and played together as a team. They were waiting for George to do it, but George wasn't around.[5]

29

The Quarterfinals

Blowouts, Brawls and a Bounty

As had been the case since the NHL dwindled from a seven-team out-fit to a six-team loop in 1942–43, the top four teams in the regular-season qualified for the Stanley Cup playoffs. Since the landmark 1967 expansion had doubled the size of the league, it was the top four teams in each division that qualified for the postseason and a chance to hoist Lord Stanley's gener-ous gift to hockey.

The playoff format per division was unchanged since 1943. The first-place team played the third-place squad. The second-place club vied against the fourth-place finisher. Theoretically it was better for a team to finish second than first or to finish fourth instead of third. The National Basketball Association also used the same curious post-season format. Hardly anyone questioned the logic of the pairings—at least not yet.

In order to please television interests in both Canada and the United States, the four best-of-seven quarterfinals were played at a breakneck pace. In every series, the first four games were played over just five days, with the lone day off coming between the second and third games to allow for travel. This tight schedule was not especially unusual for either the playoffs or the regular season. No one questioned it at the time. However, in today's NHL a team cannot play four games in five days according to the league's agree-ment with the National Hockey League Players' Association.

The Detroit Red Wings were back in the Stanley Cup playoffs for the first time since they were Cup finalists in 1966, but they were not around for very long. Their quarterfinal series versus the first-place Chicago Black Hawks—officially called "Series A" by the NHL—was the least competitive of the four. It resulted in a nifty and efficient sweep by the regular-season champions. Remarkably, the game scores were 4–2, 4–2, 4–2 … and 4–2! Never before in NHL history had a four-game playoff sweep featured iden-tical scores in each game—and, not too surprisingly, it has not happened again. Tony Esposito played especially well in goal for the Hawks in all four games. The Red Wings held leads in both Game #1 and #2 at Chicago Stadium but could not maintain either of them.

The potent duo of Bobby Hull and Stan Mikita were responsible for most of Chicago's offense in the series; each notched three goals. Forty-two-year-old Gordie Howe—in what would be his final playoff series with Detroit—scored two of the eight Red Wing goals to raise his career total to 66 playoff markers. (A decade later, at the very advanced age of 52, Howe would add one more as a member of the Hartford Whalers. His 67th playoff goal came 32 years after his first one.) Nick Libett got two others. Detroit's poor showing versus Chicago surprised many observers. During the course of the regular season, the Wings and Hawks had evenly split their eight games. The quick sweep gave the Black Hawks the luxury of extra time to rest in preparation for their semifinal round against either the Bruins or the Rangers. The Hawks presumably would have an advantage over whichever team emerged as their next opponents.

Game #1 of the Red Wings–Black Hawks quarterfinal was played at Chicago Stadium before the usual announced attendance of 16,666 fans. The Black Hawks' Eric Nesterenko was a major force in the home team's 4–2 victory. He set up a shorthanded goal for teammate Chico Maki and scored the clincher into an empty net with just 29 seconds left on the clock. Two other Chicago goals came on the power play, one from Pit Martin and the other from Stan Mikita. Those scorers gave the Hawks a 2–1 lead. Penalties were the main factor in how the game developed. Detroit had grabbed a fast 1–0 edge on Wayne Connelly's goal that came a few seconds after the Black Hawks had killed off the first of two penalties that befell them early in the first period. Maki's goal, with teammate Bill White sitting in the penalty box, gave the home team a 3–1 advantage late in the second period. Gordie Howe got one goal back in the third period, but they could get no closer. The game featured a combined total of 81 shots— 44 of them from Chicago.

The next night the series resumed at Chicago Stadium. Detroit opened the scoring on a shorthanded goal. Peter Stemkowski stole the puck from Lou Angotti in the home team's zone and beat Tony Esposito. Jim Pappin scored less than two minutes later for the Black Hawks to tie the game 1–1. Bobby Hull scored on a slapshot in the second period—the only goal of the stanza—to propel Chicago into a 2–1 lead. Bruce MacGregor of the Red Wings leveled the score at 2–2 early in the third period. Pit Martin, still basking in the glory of his hat-trick in the regular-season finale, got the winner for Chicago on the power play with only 4:20 left on the clock in the third period. Dennis Hull salted the game away with a goal with 1:18 remaining. Detroit now trailed in the quarterfinal series 2–0. Counting their dubious 9–5 loss to the New York Rangers on the last Sunday of the regular season, it was the first time the Red Wings had dropped three consecutive games all season.

The Red Wings fared no better when the series moved to the Detroit Olympia for the next two contests. The Canadian Press declared Bobby Hull to be a "one-man show" in Game #3 on Saturday, April 11 as the Chicago star scored two of his team's goals and assisted on the other two Black Hawk tallies.

Game #4 in Detroit the next afternoon was the CBS *NHL Game of the Week* telecast. In it, the Black Hawks led 2–1 after the first period on goals by Jim Pappin and Stan Mikita. Between those tallies was a Detroit goal by Gordie Howe, his second of the playoffs. Dennis Hull gave Chicago a 3–1 advantage 4:43 into the second period, but ten minutes later Nick Libett narrowed the visitors' lead to a single goal to give the 15,300 fans at the Olympia a measure of hope. The home team got no closer, however. Chico Maki added an insurance goal for Chicago at 11:26 of the third period. To a great many people's surprise, the Red Wings were ousted in the minimum four games. A photo of a bloodied but content Bobby Hull appeared in the next day's *Montreal Gazette*. He had taken a nasty gash on his chin in an encounter with Gordie Howe. The picture's caption called Hull a "happy bleeder."

After Game #4, an unnamed Associated Press reporter suggested, "The Red Wings had lost only three of their last 19 regular-season games and may have burned themselves out in their late-season surge."[1] Gordie Howe underwent wrist surgery shortly after the Red Wings' season ended, so he was clearly not in perfect health for the playoffs. Undoubtedly plenty of Montreal Canadiens fans, irked by the Red Wings' non-effort on the regular season's final Sunday, experienced schadenfreude in watching Detroit's swift ouster from postseason play.

Some Red Wings believed, in retrospect, that their 9–5 loss to the Rangers on April 5 inadvertently set the Red Wings up for failure in the playoffs. One was Bruce MacGregor. He commented decades later, "I think Sid's resting us backfired. We lost momentum by losing. You don't think it was a big thing at the time, but it was. It was also tough on Roger Crozier. That loss was very deflating. He was very upset and I don't think he ever recovered."[2] [Author's note: Crozier only played part of one game in the Red Wings' quarterfinal loss to Chicago, allowing three goals on 14 shots in Game #4. Roy Edwards carried the bulk of the goaltending chores, playing more than 200 minutes in the series.] Crozier, the NHL's Rookie of the Year in 1964–65 and the playoff MVP the following season, never played another minute for Detroit. He was picked up in a trade by the expansion Buffalo Sabres prior to the 1970–71 season.

The Boston–New York "Series B" quarterfinal series was a spirited, rough affair—to say the least. In the regular season they had evenly split their eight meetings with four wins apiece (with New York outscoring Boston 28–20), so no one was expecting anything less than a hard-fought series. It happened in every sense of the word. The two teams combined for a whopping 375 penalty minutes over six nasty games to establish a new NHL record for infractions. The Rangers were looking to win their first playoff series since they were Stanley Cup finalists in 1950. Meanwhile, Boston was trying to advance to the semifinals for the second consecutive spring.

The Bruins blew out the Rangers 8–2 in a terribly one-sided Game #1. Phil Esposito had a hat trick. With Boston's Don Marcotte penalized for tripping, Bobby Orr and Derek Sanderson each scored shorthanded goals 44 seconds apart midway through the second period to demoralize the Rangers. Orr's tally was an especially pretty one. He interrupted a rush at center ice, spun around, and fired a long slapshot from just inside the New York blueline. New York goalie Ed Giacomin seemed mesmerized on the play as the puck whistled by him for a goal.

Commenting on the related mayhem, a correspondent from the Associated Press declared, "The wild bruising encounter was marred by five fights, including three in the closing minutes, with the Rangers hopelessly outclassed."[3] With Boston comfortably ahead 7–1 after two periods, coach Harry Sinden rested Bobby Orr for the entire third stanza to rest him for Game #2. Ranger coach Emile Francis mercifully pulled Ed Giacomin after the second period, replacing him in the New York net with veteran Terry Sawchuk. The well-traveled Sawchuk, in the twilight of a brilliant career, had played just eight games for the Rangers all season.

With Sawchuk surprisingly starting the rematch in goal for the Rangers—his 105th career playoff appearance—New York put up a noticeably better effort one night later, but Boston still followed up their opening victory with a workmanlike triumph in Game #2. Dave O'Hara of the Associated Press commented, "The Bruins, bidding for their first Stanley Cup since 1941 … found the going much tougher in the second encounter in steamy Boston Garden." They did indeed. The Rangers held a 2–1 advantage after the first period, much to the consternation of the capacity crowd. Little-used Jim Lorentz got Boston on the scoreboard first at 7:06 of the first period when he deftly redirected a pass from Ed Westfall into the New York net past Sawchuk. Six minutes later, however, the Rangers tied the contest when rookie Jack Egers deflected a shot from Tim Horton past Gerry Cheevers. Four minutes later, Rod Gilbert knocked home his own rebound while Boston's Don Awrey was penalized to put New York in front.

The gritty Bruins responded strongly, however, with four unanswered goals. The first came at 5:39 of the second period when John McKenzie fired a quick, 15-foot shot that eluded Sawchuk. The turning point of the contest came in the final minute of the second period. At the 19:14 mark, Boston veteran Johnny Bucyk scored a goal from a seemingly impossible angle to Sawchuk's left to give the Bruins their second lead of the game. That marker seemed to discourage the visitors. Ken Hodge and Ed Westfall each added goals for Boston before four minutes had elapsed in the third period to take command. Hodge's goal came on a breakaway at 1:24. Westfall's score was on a nifty backhand. Forty-year-old defenseman Tim Horton, a late-season acquisition from Toronto, whittled the Bruins' lead to just two goals with a slapshot tally that whizzed by Cheevers at 6:38, but the Rangers could get no closer in the remaining 13 minutes. The Bruins triumphed 5–3 to win the game fairly handily despite being outshot by New York by a 32–29 margin.

It was a much more serene game than the opener. Referee Bruce Hood just whistled eight minor penalties. Cheevers was steadier than Sawchuk in the battle of the goaltenders. It was pointed out by hockey writers that the Rangers, who had been swept out of the first round of the postseason in each of the previous two springs, had now embarrassingly dropped 10 consecutive Stanley Cup playoff games dating back to the 1968 quarterfinals. (New York's postseason losing streak was actually 12 if one went all the way back to their quarterfinal loss to Toronto in a 1962 Stanley Cup semifinal.)

Faced with being ousted from the playoffs in short order for the third straight season, New York resiliently fought back (in every sense of the word) with two victories at Madison Square Garden by scores of 4–3 and 4–2. Game #3 was a sequence of brawls almost from the get-go as tempers boiled over. The tone was set early when Madison Square Garden organist Eddie Layton humorously played "Talk to the Animals" when the Bruins stepped onto the ice. It took 19 minutes to play the first 91 seconds of the game and an hour to play the first period. In his autobiography, *Hockey in My Blood*, Boston's Johnny Bucyk recalled how it began:

> The turning point in that series actually came in New York where we lost the third and fourth games. In the third game the Rangers ganged up on Derek Sanderson right at the start.
>
> It was one of the worst displays of poor sportsmanship I ever saw in my life. The Ranger players ganged up on him in one corner. There was only a little more than 30 seconds gone in [Game #3]. It was just a big black spot on the entire playoff series. The New York fans were just as bad. It's too bad that the small minority creates a poor image for the vast majority of respectable hockey fans.
>
> When the fans got wild, we played better. We wanted to show them how much class they lacked and how much class we had. Some of the signs they had hung up on the walls of Madison Square Garden were shameful, totally disgraceful. Again, it was just a minority of the Ranger fans, but…[4]

Game #3 was also the contest that went down quite incorrectly in Rangers and Bruins lore as the "Bounty Game." When it was over, Boston's

Derek Sanderson told reporters an absolute whopper: According to Sanderson, Ed Giacomin had told him the Rangers had put a price on his head! The charge was vigorously denied by Emile Francis, who said if the Rangers were going to target anyone—and they certainly had not—it would be Bobby Orr and not agitator Derek Sanderson. Years later, Sanderson, who loved to toy with the media, admitted in his autobiography that the "bounty" tale was utter hogwash. "It was a complete fabrication, a total and farcical lie," he wrote, "but the press ate it up and ran with it like crazy."[5]

Overwhelmed referee, 40-year-old John Ashley, had his hands more than full directly from the opening faceoff trying to control an uncontrollable game. The beleaguered official—who was widely considered the NHL's best in 1970—assessed 80 minutes of penalties within those first 91 seconds. Sanderson and Dave Balon were each given game misconducts. Overall, the Rangers and Bruins combined for an NHL playoff record 174 penalty minutes in Game #1. During the lengthy tussles, the Bruins were pelted by a curious and highly dangerous assortment of unusual debris from the upper reaches of Madison Square Garden, including apple cores, carrots, batteries and shaving-cream cans. Emile Francis had put Giacomin back in the Ranger goal. He responded by playing well.

Forty-two-year-old referee Vern Buffey was supposed to work Game #4 of the Bruins–Rangers series on Sunday, April 12, but instead he was hospitalized in St. Paul, Minnesota. Buffey was feeling unwell after officiating Game #3 of the St. Louis–Minnesota series on Saturday night. As well as being slated for Game #4 at Madison Square Garden, Buffey had been assigned Game #5 of the Blues–North Stars tilt in St. Louis. He was replaced in New York by Bill Friday and by John Ashley in St. Louis. It was thought that Buffey may have suffered a mild heart attack, but cardiac tests proved otherwise, according to supervising physician Dr. Gerald Lee. Scotty Morrison, the NHL's referee-in-chief, said Buffey was expected to be back in his Toronto home by Saturday, April 18. He would, however, be sidelined for the remainder of the 1970 Stanley Cup playoffs.

Referee Friday was handed a difficult task when he was abruptly handed the volatile Boston–New York tussle. Game #4 at Madison Square Garden between the Bruins and Rangers was yet another testy affair. It was decided fairly early, though, as New York's Rod Gilbert scored twice, 71 seconds apart, to give the hometown Rangers a quick 2–0 lead within the first five minutes of play to give him four goals for the series. It was a welcome and overdue offensive spurt for the slumping Gilbert who had failed to score a goal in the last five weeks of the regular season. Ed Johnston was in net for Boston. (It would be his only appearance in the 1970 Stanley Cup playoffs.) Gilbert rammed a rebound past Johnston for his first goal while New York was enjoying a man advantage. His second goal came on a nifty passing play. Assists on the score went to both Jean Ratelle and Ted Irvine.

New York's surprising Bulldog Line was also responsible for the other two goals for the home team with Dave Balon and Walt Tkaczuk doing the honors. Phil Esposito and Bobby Orr provided the Bruins' offense in a game thoroughly dominated by New York. After Esposito had narrowed New York's lead to 2–1, the Rangers regained their two-goal edge just 22 seconds later when Balon intercepted an errant pass from Derek Sanderson and scored an unassisted tally. A Bobby Orr goal at 8:41 of the third period again brought the Bruins to within a goal of the Rangers, but Tkaczuk replied for the home team at 11:16 to provide the unnecessary insurance marker. New York outshot Boston 39–25. It was the first two-game losing streak the Bruins had suffered since October 29 and November 1—the eighth and ninth games of the regular season.

Ed Giacomin played well in goal for New York on the occasions when he had to be sharp—including stopping Derek Sanderson on a short-handed breakaway. With each team having won its pair of home games, the Bruins–Rangers quarterfinal series was now level at two games apiece. Boston goaltender Ed Johnston was benched; Bruins coach Harry Sinden opted henceforth to use Gerry Cheevers exclusively. The shift in the series' momentum was not a totally unexpected development. Boston had trouble winning road games against East Division teams throughout the regular season. In fact, they had won just two of 20 games away from Boston Garden against divisional opponents. Both those rare wins came in the crucial final two weeks of the schedule. One occurred at Madison Square Garden on March 25.

Dink Carroll of the *Montreal Gazette* wondered what had changed the momentum of the series. He wrote in his April 14 column, "Can it be that the Boston Bruins aren't as tough as they think they are? Or is it that the New York Rangers are a lot tougher than anyone thought they were? These thoughts occurred after watching the Rangers beat the Bruins twice in Madison Square Garden over the weekend to tie up their quarterfinal playoff series at two games apiece."

Earlier that same day, the Chicago Black Hawks booked their ticket to the NHL semifinals by completing a tidy four-game sweep over Detroit. It was an afternoon game shown as the CBS *NHL Game of the Week*. The Hawks, with nothing else to occupy them on Sunday evening, watched the Rangers–Bruins conflict. An unnamed correspondent form the Associated Press reported, "Now Chicago will wait for the survivor—if anybody survives—of the small war being staged between New York and Boston in the other East Division series."[6] When asked which of the two possible opponents he would prefer to face in the next round of the playoffs, Hawks coach Billy Reay thoughtfully and humorously replied, "After looking at that game last night on TV, I'd like to stay at home."[7]

Game #5 in Boston, of course, was pivotal. As things unfolded, it turned out to be the critical point of the entire 1969–70 season for the Bruins—and they responded like champions. Boston squeaked out a tough 3–2 home win with all the offense coming from the sticks of the two most prominent Bruins: Phil Esposito scored twice and Bobby Orr once. Dave O'Hara wrote in his report for the Associated Press, "The Boston Bruins, frustrated much of the way, struck from behind on a pair of third-period goals from Phil Esposito and edged the New York Rangers 3–2 Tuesday night to move within one win of winning their NHL quarterfinal playoff series."[8]

Bobby Orr gave the Bruins a 1–0 lead just 2:44 into the first period on a solo rush. Not long afterwards, Jack Egers got his third goal of the series for New York, a power-play marker at 5:18, to level the game at 1–1. The Rangers outplayed Boston in the Bruins' home building for most of the game and held a slight 2–1 edge heading into the third period. New York assumed a lead in the second period on a goal from an unlikely source. Bruising Orland Kurtenbach scored on a fine wrist shot that beat Gerry Cheevers at 9:49 to worry the home team's supporters.

The key point in the game—perhaps the entire series—occurred with New York holding a 2–1 lead in the second period and starting to dominate the action. Phil Esposito drew a five-minute high sticking penalty when he inadvertently clipped Jean Ratelle. Ratelle, normally a mainstay on the Rangers' power play, needed to have his cut patched up and missed the chance to put the game away. The Rangers failed to score; a precious opportunity was wasted.

Esposito made amends for his penalty by scoring twice in the third period. Boston's dominant center tied the game by knocking home a pass from Wayne Cashman at the 2:20 mark. (Seconds earlier, Esposito had redirected a shot from Bobby Orr that clanged off the goal post.) The second Esposito goal was an especially picturesque game-winner. Orr fed Esposito a perfect pass to send him alone on Ranger goalie Ed Giacomin for a breakaway goal at 7:59.

The change in momentum was discernable. As the Bruins pressed strongly for an insurance goal, cagy Ranger coach Emile Francis, always looking for an edge, tried to stem the rising Bruin tide with an obvious delaying tactic: He sent in 40-year-old Terry Sawchuk to replace Giacomin. Under NHL rules at the time, the game was halted as Sawchuk was entitled to warm-up shots. (The flawed rule stayed on the books until 1978.) However, Sawchuk was on the ice for less than a minute—a mere 17 seconds to be exact. That was the duration between whistles. At that point Francis lifted him and put Giacomin back into the game. The ploy, of course, was greeted by loud boos by the Bruin faithful at Boston Garden. "The strategy failed as the Bruins continued their sharp play and hung on for the victory,"[9] according to the Canadian Press report. No one knew it at the time, but the stunt was Sawchuk's final NHL appearance. The brilliant but troubled goaltender would be dead within seven weeks.

The rough play in the Bruins–Rangers series continued unabated. After Game #5, with the series still undecided, Dave O'Hara reported the numbers accompanying the mayhem thus far:

> A couple of Stanley Cup records for the most penalty minutes were set in the series. In five games the two teams have piled up 357 minutes in penalties, breaking the former mark of 340 set by St. Louis and Philadelphia in a seven-game series in 1968. With 198 [minutes in penalties thus far], the Bruins became the most penalized team in playoff history for one series. The former record was 190 set by St. Louis in that same series two years ago.[10]

Boston's comeback triumph in Game #5 seemed to take the starch out of New York. Two nights later, the lynchpin of Boston's attack seemed unfazed by a disparaging banner unfurled by Ranger fans in Game #6: "Bobby Orr wears training blades." He responded by scoring two more goals in the decisive contest to lead Boston to a convincing 4–1 win that wrapped up the series in six games. Hal Bock of the Associated Press knew who the game's star was. He wrote,

> Boston's sensational Bobby Orr scored two goals and carried the Bruins to a 4–1 victory over New York on Wednesday night, finishing the Rangers four games to two in the quarterfinals of the NHL's Stanley Cup playoffs.
>
> Orr, who scored 120 points during the regular season to become the first defenseman ever to win an NHL scoring title, was all over the ice. His goals were studies in contrast—one from in close, the other a 50-foot slapshot.[11]

The Rangers held a 1–0 lead for a time on Brad Park's first-period goal. It was the only scoring of the opening period. "Then Orr started Boston's comeback," wrote Bock. The Bruins were on a power play when Orr, uncharacteristically stationed near the net, deflected a John McKenzie shot past Ed Giacomin to tie the game at 2:48 of the second period. Boston captured the advantage when the Rangers had trouble getting the puck from their own zone. Wayne Cashman intercepted a poor New York clearing attempt and beat Giacomin from the left side. Orr added some insurance when he blew a long slapshot past Giacomin at 3:07 of the third period. It was Orr's seventh goal of the series. If there was any doubt as to the game's eventual outcome, Derek Sanderson, playing on Boston's checking line, removed it with a goal at 7:22 with assists from Ed Westfall and Wayne Carleton. After allowing Park's goal, Cheevers was impenetrable in the Boston net. He would be the Bruins' sole netminder for the rest of the Stanley Cup playoffs.

Battling to the bitter end, Rangers coach Emile Francis refused to concede defeat. In an unusual move for the era, he pulled Giacomin with four minutes to go for a sixth attacker in a vain attempt to make up the three-goal deficit. The Rangers failed to score while the Bruins missed New York's empty net several times. Orr, however, found the net regardless of the situation on the ice. His seven goals in the series were truly a mixed bag: three came on the Boston power play, three were scored when the teams were at even strength, and one came in a shorthanded situation. He also added three assists in the six games for good measure. When Game #6 looked to be out of reach for the Rangers after the despised Derek Sanderson's goal, their passionate fans were not pleased and responded accordingly: They attempted to set Madison Square Garden's mezzanine afire. Eggs and ball bearings were thrown at the Bruins as the game ended. It was not the finest moment in New York Rangers history.

Game #6 had been the most pacific of the turbulent series. Too much was at stake for the teams to play recklessly. (In his autobiography, Johnny Bucyk specifically recalled cautioning Derek Sanderson to tone down his aggressive play for the sake of the team.) Referee Art Skov experienced a light night. He whistled just a combined nine minor penalties against the two teams—and no major fouls whatsoever. The 18 minutes in penalties, however, did up the series total to a record 375. The six-game defeat meant that New York's embarrassing futility streak of not having won a Stanley Cup playoff series since the 1950 semifinals was still intact. The 1969–70 season had come full circle for the Rangers. Their opening-night game six months and four days earlier had come in Boston against the Bruins. They lost that evening too, 2–1.

For the second straight year, the Bruins advanced to the Stanley Cup semifinals. They would play the Chicago Black Hawks who had an extra four days of rest thanks to their unexpected feat of dispatching the Detroit Red Wings in a surprising four-game quarterfinal sweep. Thus, the two teams that had been involved in the 9–5 fiasco on the last day of the regular season—Detroit and New York—did not survive past the first round of the 1970 playoffs. Perhaps there was a smidgen of justice in that development. Montreal fans probably thought so.

Because the Black Hawks had attained first place in the East Division based on having a greater win total than Boston, home-ice advantage went to Chicago for their semifinal clash. The series would begin on Sunday afternoon, April 19, at Chicago Stadium, as the CBS *NHL Game of the Week*, of course.

The West Division playoff matchups, like those in the East were comprised of one sweep and one series that was considerably more challenging for the victors. In the latter, St. Louis ousted Minnesota in six surprisingly tough games in "Series C." During the regular season, St. Louis had accrued a 4–2–2 record versus the North Stars.

The series gave no indication it would be a close one when Game #1 ended. "Blues Wallop Stars, 6–2" roared a headline in the next day's *Montreal Gazette*. They certainly did. Playing before the usual supportive throng at the St. Louis Arena, the Blues romped to a 3–0 lead in the first period and were up 4–1 after 40 minutes of play. St. Louis goalie Jacques Plante faced just four Minnesota shots in the first period. By the time it was over, Terry Crisp and Ab McDonald had scored two goals apiece for the victors. Gary Sabourin and Red Berenson got the others for St. Louis. It was, remarkably, the 10th consecutive playoff victory by the Blues against West Division opposition—a streak that dated back to 1968.

The Blues upped their intra-divisional playoff winning streak to 11 the very next night in Game #2 in a much closer affair. At least it was closer by score. The game's shots on goal told a wholly different story: The Blues badly outshot the North Stars 40–18. St. Louis won, 2–1, but did not score after the first period. Gary Sabourin and Phil Goyette got the tallies for the home team. Minnesota's lone goal, which worried the partisan home crowd, came at 14:20 of the third period when Bob Barlow caught Jacques Plante off guard with a quick shot, capitalizing on a pass from Ray Cullen. Before Barlow connected for the North Stars' goal, their best chance had come in the second period when Jean-Paul Parisé's shot went through the webbing of Plante's catching glove and clanged off the goal post. St. Louis headed to Minnesota for games on Saturday and Sunday up two games to nil, expecting to finish off the reeling North Stars.

The North Stars, however, found their home building very much to their liking and responded with a strong 4–2 win in Game #3. Gump Worsley played especially well in the Minnesota goal. Bill Goldsworthy scored twice in the final 12 minutes of the third period to provide the home team with its winning margin. Danny O'Shea and Tom Polonic also got goals for the North Stars who had jumped out to a 2–0 lead before squandering it. St. Louis's offense came from the sticks of Ab McDonald in the second period and Red Berenson in the third. The Blues fired 34 shots at the sharp Worsley. Minnesota had 31 shots.

Game #4, also at the Met Center in Minnesota, saw Cesare Maniago record an impressive 4–0 shutout win that evened the quarterfinal series at two games apiece. As in the Boston–New York series, the home team had won each of the first four games. Maniago was often tested, facing 34 St. Louis shots. Bill Goldsworthy of the North Stars continued his hot offensive play. The first North Stars goal did not come until the 7:38 mark of the second period when Goldsworthy took a pass from Bob Barlow and beat Glenn Hall from point-blank range. Claude Larose added a second goal for the home team when he collected a loose puck moments after stepping out of the penalty box and beating Hall on a breakaway at 16:54 of the second period. Larose crashed heavily into Hall after the puck was in the net, but neither man was hurt. The North Stars put the game out of reach with two more goals in the third period. The first tally came just 58 seconds after play resumed as Tommy Williams converted a Goldsworthy pass. Minnesota concluded the game's scoring about a minute later when Barlow fired a quick shot past Hall from the faceoff circle. The North Stars left the ice to a rousing ovation from their delighted supporters. Even their most ardent fans were surprised that the series was level after four games.

In Game #5 back at the jammed St. Louis Arena, the Blues broke open a close game with three third-period goals in a span of four and a half minutes to win 6–3 and take a 3–2 lead in the series. One of the goals came when the home team was a man short. Terry Gray, Red Berenson and Jim Roberts scored the goals in the final period that provided the cushion for the Blues' win to the delight of the standing-room-only gathering. Roberts' tally was the shorthanded marker, occurring while St. Louis captain Al Arbour was sitting out a tripping penalty. It came off a Bill Goldsworthy giveaway. The North Stars' player-coach Charlie Burns ended the game's scoring at 9:06. Minnesota had gotten out to a strong start. Jean-Paul Parisé scored twice in the first period, opening the scoring at 1:38 and then giving the visitors a 2–1 lead after Tim Ecclestone had equalized for St. Louis. The second period belonged to the home team decisively. The Blues outshot the North Stars 18–6 in the middle frame and took the lead, 3–2, on goals by Larry Keenan and Gary Sabourin. Sabourin's goal came off a fortuitous deflection. The momentum shift carried into the third period as St. Louis proceeded to blow the game wide open. The solid win left St. Louis one game shy of the Stanley Cup semifinals.

Two nights later, Game #6 in Minnesota saw the favored Blues top the North Stars 4–2 to wrap up the series. Ab McDonald was the offensive hero for the visitors, scoring twice and assisting on a third St. Louis goal. The critical moment of the game occurred in the second period when Minnesota was playing two men short. McDonald and Red Berenson scored twice within 47 second to change a 1–1 tie into a 3–1 St. Louis lead. Minnesota's two best penalty-killers (Charlie Burns and Billy Collins) were the ones who were serving the penalties. The victory earned the Blues their third consecutive trip to the second round of the playoffs. Their next opponent would be the Pittsburgh Penguins.

Series D, according to Ed Levitt of the *Oakland Tribune*, was an unfashionable battle between two expansion teams desperately struggling to gain fan bases. The Pittsburgh Penguins, making their first appearance in the Stanley Cup playoffs in franchise history, dispatched the fourth place Oakland Seals in four straight games, but three of the four battles were quite competitive. During the regular season Oakland had won three games versus the Penguins, Pittsburgh had won two, while the other three games ended in ties. Thus, Pittsburgh's playoff sweep of the Seals was moderately surprising.

Game #1 in Pittsburgh saw the home team emerge as 2–1 victors in the first-ever Stanley Cup playoff game contested at the Civic Arena. The novelty was not a big enticement, however. Only a meager turnout of 8,051 fans took in the action despite new mayor Peter F. Flaherty proclaiming April 8 to be "Pittsburgh Penguins Day" in his city. "Penguins Nip Seals, 2–1, on Disputed Goal" was the headline in the following day's *Pittsburgh Post-Gazette*. Spence Conley of the *Oakland Tribune* described it "as controversial a goal as has ever been scored on the Seals."[12] That was probably a fair assessment.

Jean Pronovost got the home team on the board early, scoring a power play goal just 65 seconds into the first period. Gary Ehman of the Seals tied the game for Oakland with another power goal eight minutes later. "And that's the way it stood," wrote Jimmy Jordan of the *Post-Gazette*, "until Glen Sather, Wally Boyer and Nick Harbaruk combined to score the winning goal and stir up a hornets' nest along the Seals' bench and around referee Bruce Hood at 12:47 of the final period." Jordan detailed what had occurred to cause the controversy:

> Sather started things moving when he took the puck and skated through and around most of the Seals' defense. As he drove towards the goal he flipped the puck to Boyer and then skated to the goal crease, apparently expecting his center to send the disc back to him.
> Boyer passed it to Harbaruk at about the same time Bert Marshall hit Sather. Glen landed almost on goal Gary Smith's lap. Harbaruk triggered a 10-footer at an angle from the left, and that was the ball game.
> Smith flung his stick onto the ice, dropped his gloves, and dashed after the referee. All the Seals on the ice got into the act and those on the bench got in their verbal licks.
> When everything had settled down, Hood admitted that Sather was in the crease, but he had been pushed there by the opposition. That was that.[13]

With 55 seconds left on the clock, Oakland coach Fred Glover pulled goalie Gary Smith in favor of a sixth attacker. "Those closing seconds," wrote Jordan, "were about as hectic as any ever witnessed in the Big Igloo."[14] Pittsburgh thwarted the Oakland threat and left the ice with a 2–1 win that the Seals were still strongly questioning after the final buzzer.

The visitors, not surprisingly, dwelled on Harbaruk's controversial game-winning tally. "You could have cut the air of bitterness, disgust and pure anger with a knife in the Oakland dressing room,"[15] wrote Spence Conley. "That was an illegal goal," declared Glover in a matter-of-fact tone.

"That man [Sather] had all the time in the world to get out [of the crease]. Nobody was holding him. He must have had at least five seconds, anyway. The referee blew it—and he knows he blew it. That's a tough way to lose a hockey game. Damn tough."[16] Of course, Gary Smith passionately concurred with Glover. "I didn't even see the winning shot. How could I? The man [Sather] was on top of me."[17]

The second game of the Oakland–Pittsburgh series was held the very next night. The hometown Penguins were the better team by far, although the scoreboard at the end of 60 minutes only had them ahead 3–1. There was no controversy following this win. Gary Jarrett had put the visiting Oakland Seals in front with a power play goal at 7:13 of the first period. That was all the offense mustered in the game's first 20 minutes. The second period saw Pittsburgh tie the game and take the lead on goals 34 seconds apart by Nick Harbaruk and Wally Boyer. Dunc McCallum got an insurance tally at the 11:41 mark of the third period to secure the home team's win. The Penguins embarked on a cross-country journey for Game #3 and #4 with a 2–0 series lead. Red Kelly said afterwards, "After we went ahead with those two goals within 34 seconds, the Seals were through for the night. They just caved in…"[18]

The Penguins outshot the Seals 39–25, but credit was due to Pens goalie Les Binkley who was stellar when he needed to be. "He's playing great!" declared Pittsburgh coach Red Kelly. "That's just what I've been looking for."[19] Binkley, who stopped 52 of 54 Oakland shots in the first two games, had a personal connection to Oakland coach Fred Glover. Binkley was once the goalie on the minor league Cleveland Barons team coached by Glover. In an interview with Ed Levitt of the *Oakland Tribune*, Binkley generously stated that Glover's coaching and advice were greatly responsible for resurrecting his career. "I guess I should feel sorry for Glover, what with his team down 0–2 in the series. If I have had any success in this sport I owe it to Freddie. Now I'm trying to beat his team in the playoffs."[20]

Jimmy Jordan of the *Pittsburgh Post-Gazette* was thoroughly optimistic about the Penguins' chances in Oakland—even though they had failed to win a single game there in their four visits during the 1969–70 regular season, going 0–3–1. "If the Penguins play as they did last night," he wrote, "there's a better than even chance they'll get a bit closer to the semifinal round of the playoffs before they return home."[21] In contrast to those sentiments, Oakland's Carol Vadnais publicly guaranteed the Seals would come back in the series despite being in a daunting 0–2 hole.

As things turned out, home ice proved to be no advantage at all to Oakland. Game #3, played on Saturday, April 11, was the most one-sided contest of the brief quarterfinal series. Although the Seals held the edge in shots on goal 29–25, Pittsburgh won the game handily, 5–2, before more than 8,800 disappointed spectators. The Seals' Earl Ingarfield opened the scoring in the first period at 3:39 with a shorthanded goal. Pittsburgh finally got rolling offensively in the second period with replies from Nick Harbaruk, Ken Schinkel and Jean Pronovost. Ted Hampson got one back for Oakland from a 30-foot shot in the third period that had a comical aspect to it. According to Michael Watson of the *Fremont Argus*, "Hampson was checked so hard on the follow-up action that he skidded into the net right after the puck."[22] It was not enough for Oakland. The 37-year-old Schinkel scored twice more for the Penguins, giving him a rare playoff hattrick and the visitors an insurmountable lead. After the game, Oakland coach Fred Glover subtly questioned his team's effort the players' drive heading into Game #4. "It has to come from within them," he stated. "Otherwise it's all for nothing."[23]

Game #4, also played in Oakland, was contested the following night before fewer than 5,300 paying customers. (A story in the *San Mateo Times* noted that the disappointing attendance at the Coliseum Arena "undoubtedly could be attributed to a great degree by the poor effort put forth by the Seals on Saturday night."[24]) It required 8:28 of sudden-death overtime before matters were settled. Pittsburgh rookie Michel Brière scored the winner on a pretty passing sequence from two teammates. Jean Pronovost began the decisive play by stealing the puck near the Oakland net from Seals defenseman Bert Marshall. Pronovost dished a pass to Val Fonteyne. Oakland goalie Gary Smith moved out to challenge Fonteyne, who deftly relayed a second pass to Brière. Brière swiftly drove home the series-clinching goal from a sharp angle. The Penguins won the game 3–2 to join the Chicago Black Hawks as the first two teams to advance to the second round of the 1970 Stanley Cup playoffs.

Bert Marshall was aghast at how the Penguins got control of the puck that led to their series-winning tally. "I went to clear the puck," he said, "and hoped to get our player away on a breakaway. My feet slipped out from under me. The puck went free and there wasn't a damn thing I could do about it."[25]

Oakland had opened a 1–0 lead early in the first period on a power play goal by Carol Vadnais while Pittsburgh's Bryan Watson was sitting out a minor penalty for interference. Vadnais' 50-foot blast, which followed a flurry of chances by the home team, eluded Les Binkley in the Penguins' net. Five minutes later, Pittsburgh's Dean Prentice scored his first goal of the 1970 playoffs to level the score. Smith had stopped Jim Morrison's shot, but Prentice knocked home a juicy rebound.

In the second period Vadnais—an offensive-minded defenseman who had scored 24 times during the regular season—tallied again on a power play, this time while Prentice was serving a minor penalty. (Jimmy Jordan of the *Pittsburgh Post-Gazette* called it "a somewhat debatable hooking charge."[26]) He scored from directly in front of Binkley after accepting a splendid pass from Bill Hicke at center ice. Less than two minutes later, however, Brière created the tying goal by wrestling the puck away from two Seals and skillfully feeding a pass to defenseman Bob Woytowich. His long shot, from just inside the Oakland blue line, eluded Smith. There was no further scoring until Brière notched the series winner in extra time.

An Associated Press story that ran in the *Milwaukee Journal* called Brière—whose first name it amusingly misspelled as Michele—"a most unlikely hero." The young Pittsburgh star modestly agreed. "I didn't even think I'd make the team this season," Brière noted. "I had to learn a lot about playing defense and winning faceoffs. But my coach [Red Kelly] kept with me and I came along pretty well."[27]

At one point in the spirited contest, the game was delayed for 18 minutes because of a power failure at the Oakland–Alameda County Coliseum Arena. No one could have foreseen that the overtime loss to Pittsburgh in Game #4 was the last postseason game the Seals would ever play.

Back in Pittsburgh, *Post-Gazette* columnist Al Abrams slyly commented,

> Hockey fans here are ecstatic over their Stanley Cup-chasing Penguins.
> We can tell by the number of letter-writers. Until the recent flood of mail (all letters the same and photocopied) wondering why Pittsburgh newspapers do not devote much more space to high school wrestling, Penguin followers held the trophy for grabbing the most ballpoint pens and typewriters in behalf of their beloved skaters.
> Certainly the Penguins, as winners, deserve space. This is their first winning year in three, and if anyone would bother to check the amount of ink in both newspapers here this season, they will be more than satisfied.
> If enough of the letter-writers would attend the games instead of griping, the club owners wouldn't have to worry about filling the arena.[28]

Spence Conley of the *Oakland Tribune* did not see much hope for optimism on the horizon for the team he covered. For the April 16 edition of his newspaper he wrote, "The Oakland Seals, given the hook after four dreary performances in the Stanley Cup playoffs, may have nearly the same cast of characters next season. Since this is an expansion year in the NHL, and since they don't have a first-round pick in the important amateur draft (they gave it up for Carol Vadnais), the Seals will be lucky if they can add two faces from outside sources for next year."[29]

Seals general manager Frank Selke, Jr., did not pull any punches about his team's 1969–70 season and its quick dismissal from the Stanley Cup playoffs. "It was a terribly disappointing year," he told Conley. "We played for the most part like a no-talent hockey team. But we have more talent than was exposed." Selke did praise the work of goaltender Gary Smith, however. "Without him we wouldn't even have come close to the playoffs,"[30] Selke noted.

Hugh McDonald, a scribe from the *San Mateo Times*, directed his harshest criticism of the Seals' disappointing season quick exit from the Stanley Cup playoffs squarely at coach Fred Glover. He wrote, "In truth the Seals were a fairly tame lot of pussycats in the NHL jungle…. While possibly Glover's own tenacious personality dragged the Seals into the playoffs, he at the same time should be held responsible for failing to teach them any team play worth mentioning."[31]

Boston–Chicago Semifinal

A Surprising Sweep

"[The Black Hawks] would greet a confrontation with Boston in confidence. The Bruins, it is said, do not have dependable goaltending and may be the most exciting but undisciplined team in the race."[1]
—Ted Blackman, *Montreal Gazette*

For two teams that had been NHL rivals since 1926, the Chicago Black Hawks and Boston Bruins surprisingly did not jointly share much postseason history prior to their 1970 clash. In their 43 seasons vying against one another in the NHL, the two Original Six clubs had met exactly twice in Stanley Cup play. Only the most scholarly of fans could recall much about either of those two series.

Their first postseason matchup was in Chicago's inaugural NHL season, 1926–27, when neither team was yet playing in its most famous home. It was an opening-round series between the second- and third-place teams in the NHL's nascent American Division. In a two-game, total-goals series, Boston won rather handily by a 10–5 aggregate. (The Hawks were at a bit of a disadvantage because their home rink, the Chicago Coliseum, was not available. Thus, Chicago was forced to play a "home game" in New York City at Madison Square Garden. The Bruins rolled to a decisive 6–1 win in Game #1 there. Two nights later Boston battled the Black Hawks to a 4–4 deadlock at Boston Arena in Game #2.) Boston, in their third year of existence, would eventually advance to the Stanley Cup finals in 1927— which the Boston press dubbed "the World Series of Hockey." The original Ottawa Senators, however, proved too experienced and strong for the plucky Bruins who had finished the regular season just one game over .500 with a 21–20–3 record. The favored Senators mathematically clinched the best-of-five series with two wins and two ties in the first four contests. It was the seventh—and last—Stanley Cup for the team that proudly represented Canada's capital city.

Fifteen years later, in 1942, the Bruins and Black Hawks met early in the playoffs in the last season of the short-lived seven-team NHL. Six of the seven clubs qualified for the playoffs. (The unfashionable Brooklyn Americans finished in the basement. The NHL dissolved the money-losing franchise in the offseason.) Again, it was an opening-round matchup, pitting the third-place Bruins versus the fourth-place Hawks. In the best-of-three series, Boston prevailed in the maximum number of games. The Bruins took Game #1, 2–1, played in Chicago, on an overtime goal by Des Smith. The Black Hawks rebounded for a solid 4–0 win at Boston Garden in Game #2 to level the series. Game #3 was also played in Boston. The Bruins took it 3–2 to advance to the semifinals where they promptly lost two straight games in an upset to the fifth-place Detroit Red Wings.

Entering their much-anticipated 1970 semifinal, there was not much to choose from between the Bruins and Black Hawks. In their eight regular-season meetings, Boston and Chicago had battled each other to the equivalent of a stalemate. The Bruins and Hawks each won three times, with two other games ending in ties. Boston had outscored Chicago 21–19 in those games. Of course, both had ended the regular season with 99 points. Tony Esposito had recorded two of his 15 shutouts versus Boston, but the Bruins had also shut out the Black Hawks twice. As in the previous two years in the post-expansion era, many fans and hockey writers considered the series to decide the East Division champion to be the de facto Stanley Cup final regardless of which team emerged as the West's winner. Everything pointed to an evenly matched Bruins–Black series. Instead, it was shockingly one-sided.

"If you had told me before the series started that we would take [Chicago] in four straight games, I would have laughed in your face," Boston assistant captain Johnny Bucyk later recalled in his autobiography. "When it was all over, I was shocked—but not as much as the Black Hawks."[2] Chicago came into the series riding a six-game winning streak that dated back to the hectic and crazy final weekend of the regular season.

Game #1 occurred on Sunday, April 19 at Chicago Stadium. It was scheduled for the afternoon to accommodate the CBS *NHL Game of the Week* time slot. Boston won comfortably, 6–3. Bobby Orr, who contributed two assists, put on a show defensively. On three separate occasions he blocked shots that seemed headed for an unguarded Bruins net. However, the offensive damage was mostly done by Phil Esposito who delighted in scoring three times on his younger sibling. The feat was recognized in bold letters atop the *Montreal Gazette*'s sports page: "Boston's Phil Wins Esposito Battle."

Pat Curran of the *Gazette* was thoroughly impressed by the visitors' performance. "Neither brotherly love, nor respect for the [regular-season] champions, nor appreciation for the fans who paid for the show deterred the Boston Bruins in their convincing 6–3 upset of the Black Hawks," he wrote. "Boston simply took the play away from Chicago from the start. Before it was over, Phil Esposito had scored this third playoff hat-trick, with other goals going to Johnny Bucyk, Ken Hodge, and John (Cowboy) McKenzie."[3]

The elder Esposito brother showed little compassion for Tony. "It's hardly a family matter when there's five-grand on the line,"[4] Phil noted, citing the difference in playoff money awarded to players on a Stanley Cup–winning team and a losing divisional finalist. He seemed annoyed at the very idea of taking it easy on his brother.

John McKenzie got into a scuffle with a couple of belligerent Black Hawk fans near the end of the game who had called the Bruins "a bunch of stupid bums." McKenzie fired back, "Any guy who pays $25 for two seats in this dump can't be too smart, either."[5]

Despite Chicago carrying the play for much of the first period, Boston had a 2–0 lead after 20 minutes. The Bruins upped it to a 3–0 advantage 5:11 into the second period. Chicago never got closer than a two-goal deficit. Both teams scored twice on the power play. Boston coach Harry Sinden noted, "We had a good first period and didn't get behind the eight-ball. We had some great goalkeeping [from Gerry Cheevers] and no team can win a Stanley Cup without it."[6] Cheevers handled 32 of the 35 Black Hawk shots that came his way, but even he acknowledged he had received some timely and conspicuous extra help, calling Bobby Orr's block of a Bobby Hull blast with his chest "the save of the day."[7]

Every Bruin seemed to have a big afternoon. Pesky Derek Sanderson, a faceoff specialist and amateur statistician, lost just two draws the entire game and won 16—by his reckoning, at least.

When asked if he thought the Black Hawks were "stale" because they had not played a game in a week, Boston coach Harry Sinden guffawed. "Stale? If we had lost could I say they were stale? Yeah, I guess they were stale."[8]

Chicago coach Billy Reay denied that the Hawks' long respite had any impact on the game. "It's hard to blame the layoff considering the way we started out," he told the press. "We were bombing them for the first 12 minutes but couldn't put the puck in the net." Reay added that overconfidence may have entered the team's psyche. "The trouble wasn't the layoff, just that we were around home for seven days with everyone telling the guys how great they were. This was our lousiest game defensively all season. At the same time, I hardly expected to win five straight games when the playoffs started, let alone knock off Detroit in four."[9]

Game #2 two nights later was an even more dominant performance by Boston. Bobby Orr scored what was described as "a picture-prefect goal" to open the scoring early in the first period on one of his speedy charges. The Black Hawks were strangely listless and gave up two more Bruin goals in the second period to fall behind 3–0. Boston outshot Chicago 15–5 in the period. The Bruins' checkers, especially Ed Westfall and Derek Sanderson, did stalwart duty in stifling the Black Hawks' top scorers. In fact, Chicago coach Billy Reay severely juggled his lines in an attempt to free Bobby Hull from the Bruins' intense attention. The strategy failed. Hull managed just two shots on the Boston goal all game.

"We wanted to play on a low key after getting the first goal and stop their big guys," Harry Sinden explained afterward. "When you cover Bobby Hull and Stan Mikita, it doesn't mean sure victory, but you can make it close."[10]

Bill White beat Gerry Cheevers on a rebound early in the third period to give the Chicago fans a glimmer of hope, but Phil Esposito replied with a goal shortly thereafter to restore the Bruins' three-goal lead. That ended the evening's scoring. The 4–1 win put the Bruins up 2–0 in the series heading home to the cozy confines of Boston Garden where they were extremely tough to beat.

Chicago started well in Game #3 on April 23, jumping out to a 2–1 first period lead. However, 40 minutes later, a 5–2 Boston win gave the Bruins a clear stranglehold in the series. They were just one game away from advancing to the Stanley Cup final for the first time since 1958.

"It's just wonderful,"[11] said a beaming Johnny Bucyk in the victors' dressing room. Boston's 35-year-old leader had uniquely suffered through the lowest period in Bruins history where they missed the playoffs for eight consecutive seasons. He was thoroughly enjoying the thrill of being on a winner for a change.

Bucyk had scored two of Boston's five goals that Thursday evening. The second of them was the essence of simplicity for the man who put the puck over the goal line—but it was still of the highlight-reel variety. With Keith Magnuson in the penalty box, Bobby Orr, on the power play, rushed the puck into the Chicago zone along the right boards. Orr attracted a considerable crowd of pursuers in Black Hawk jerseys. He was fruitlessly chased by all four Black Hawk defenders, three of whom followed him behind the Chicago net. Orr fed a pretty pass to an unguarded Phil Esposito in the slot. After Tony Esposito committed to facing his brother, Phil slid a beautiful pass to wide-open Bucyk who had a gaping net as a target. Bucyk did not miss. The goal, at 13:07 of the second period, made the score 4–2. "That was about the sweetest goal I've ever seen,"[12] declared Harry Sinden afterward. Gary Ronberg of *Sports Illustrated* agreed, marveling at the attention Orr garnered on the play. Ronberg called Bucyk's final touch "the easiest of goals."[13] In typical fashion, Orr did not celebrate the goal he created; he put his head down and congratulated Bucyk in a low-key manner for scoring the easy tally.

Tony Esposito could hardly be faulted for allowing that goal as he was literally left to fend for himself. He had shone in the first period and made a remarkable save off Bobby Orr in the third period when the Bruins threatened to turn the game into a rout. In an unexpected gesture, the Bruin fans spontaneously sang "Happy Birthday" to the Chicago netminder when they learned he had turned 27 that day. It may have been warbled with a tinge of sarcasm.

"Once again it was a case of the Bruins working together and the Hawks having only a few players [being] effective," wrote Pat Curran in the *Montreal Gazette*. "Bobby Hull never got untracked against the checking of Eddie Westfall."[14]

Game #4 was the best match by far of the Boston–Chicago series. It was, perhaps, the most exciting game played during the 1970 Stanley Cup playoffs. Again, it was a CBS *NHL Game of the Week* Sunday afternoon telecast. The Bruins badly outshot the Black Hawks 54–24 but needed a dramatic comeback effort in the third period to win a riveting 5–4 thriller.

It should have been an easy clinching victory for Boston, but Chicago refused to capitulate without a fight. "The Black Hawks, behind the sensational goaltending of Tony Esposito, came up with their best effort of the series and some of the togetherness that carried them to the [regular-season] East Division title,"[15] wrote Pat Curran of the *Montreal Gazette*. An unnamed Associate Press reporter also praised the stellar work of the losing goalie. "Frustrated most of the way by the brilliant goaltending of Vezina Trophy winner Tony Esposito, the Bruins refused to quit and fought back for the victory."[16]

Boston got out to a quick 2–0 first-period lead on goals by Don Marcotte and John Bucyk. In the second period, against the run of play, the Black Hawks fired three goals past Gerry Cheevers in a little more than eight minutes to assume a surprising 3–2 lead. Keith Magnuson, who had played poorly in Game #3, started the Chicago rally with a rare goal at 5:07. (It was the first time all season that Magnuson had scored.) Dennis Hull, Bobby's younger brother, got the next two markers in short order. Fred Stanfield got the Bruins level at 15:40.

Shortly thereafter Boston squandered a golden opportunity to regain the lead. They failed to capitalize on a five-minute power play with Chicago's Cliff Koroll serving a major penalty for high-sticking Rick Smith. During part of Koroll's penalty, Boston had a two-man advantage for two minutes when Bobby Hull was sent off for tripping Phil Esposito. The second period ended with the teams deadlocked at 3–3.

Boston thoroughly dominated the action in the final period, heavily outshooting the Black Hawks 18–6. Nevertheless, Chicago got the first goal of the third period from an unlikely source. Unheralded Bryan Campbell, who had scored just one goal in the regular season, put the Hawks into a 4–3 lead at the 4:10 mark. Chicago held the lead for nine minutes as the noisy patrons at sold-out Boston Garden grew concerned.

The Bruins began an unceasing onslaught against the Black Hawks. Tony Esposito kept them at bay for as long as he could. Several times during the third period, the Chicago goalie skated to his bench during TV time-outs, dead tired, for encouragement and sustenance. On one other occasion, he simply laid his head on the crossbar in fatigue. Afterward, a reporter told the beleaguered Chicago netminder that he had played one of his best games of the entire season. Esposito frankly replied, "I don't think I've played good [sic] any time during this series. You never play good [sic] when you lose."[17]

Something had to give—and it did when Ken Hodge got the equalizing tally for Boston with 6:41 left in the third period. With the game tied 4–4, the Bruins' pressure continued unabated. John McKenzie got the dramatic go-ahead goal exactly five minutes later. McKenzie had been implored to do something by teammate Ed Westfall. The Bruins' checking specialist said to McKenzie late in the game, "You better score a goal; I can't stay with this guy much longer."[18] Westfall was referring to Chicago's Bobby Hull, whom he was assigned to neutralize.

"The game appeared to be headed to sudden-death overtime," said the AP scribe, "when McKenzie intercepted a [Stan Mikita] clearing pass just inside the blue line. He fed linemate Fred Stanfield and then burst in on the right to take a return pass. The hustling winger scored on a high flip shot taken while under full steam."[19] Boston Garden erupted. It was McKenzie's fourth goal of the 1970 playoffs and the biggest tally of the 32-year-old's fine career. McKenzie had played two seasons with Chicago in the early 1960s. The Bruins were his fourth NHL team.

According to Pat Curran, McKenzie's dramatic goal "sent the throng of 14,835 into delirium." The Bruins ran out the clock for the hard-fought 5–4 victory. Even though Boston's opponent in the final had yet to be determined, Curran boldly proclaimed Boston "had virtually clinched its first Stanley Cup in 29 years."[20] In the joyful Bruins' dressing room, McKenzie concurred. "Now we've got either St. Louis or Pittsburgh," he said. "It won't make any difference because this team is hungry."[21]

Harry Sinden complimented the Black Hawks' gritty effort in Game #4 even though they went down to defeat. "We're glad to get rid of them the way they played today," the Boston coach stated. He then pinpointed the turning point of the game. "The one thing that paid off was that we didn't break up after failing to score on the [five-minute] power play. That's what happened to New York against us."[22]

At the final buzzer Phil Esposito did something out of the ordinary: Instead of making the traditional beeline to congratulate his team's goalie, the Boston sniper lingered at the Chicago goal crease ice for a few moments to console and praise brother Tony before joining the Bruins' on-ice celebration. Phil notched two assists in Game #4 but did not manage a goal. He had scored five times against his sibling during the first three games, however. "I told Tony congratulations for a great game and a great series," Phil explained. "He did [have a great game] today, keeping them in there, just like he did all season. He didn't say nothing [sic], but I'll phone him tomorrow. Anyway, we're going away together when the season's over."[23]

"Boston was full value for winning the series," conceded Black Hawks coach Billy Reay. "I hope they can uphold the prestige of the East Division in the finals." The sportsmanlike Reay even managed to inject some unexpected levity into his postgame comments. Knowing that the NHL had already announced the Black Hawks would be shifted to the league's West Division for the 1970–71 season, Reay quipped, "This is probably the last year the East will do well against the West."[24]

Bobby Hull was noticeably dejected in the visitors' dressing room. He had managed a disappointing four shots on goal in Game #4, but it was still twice the total he had launched during Game #3. None had beaten Gerry Cheevers. In fact, Hull had failed to score in the entire four-games series. (He had managed three goals versus Detroit in Chicago's masterful quarterfinal sweep.) In response to criticism in the Chicago print media that the Black Hawks had been lethargic in the first three games of the series, Hull made a point of defending his team and himself. "No matter what some newspapermen have said, we gave it all we had in every game."[25]

Dink Carroll disagreed with Hull. The *Montreal Gazette* reporter penned, "Various reasons were offered for the Hawks' dismal showing. Some pointed at Tony Esposito, their rookie goaltender, who was jittery in the nets. Others claimed their centers let them down. But, come to think of it, you can't name a position at which they weren't outplayed by the Bruins."[26]

Boston general manager Milt Schmidt, who had been a star player on Boston's last Stanley Cup championship team in 1940–41, was beaming with delight at the semifinal series sweep. When told by a reporter that the Bruins were a cinch to beat whomever emerged from the West Division and win Lord Stanley's coveted trophy, Schmidt just smiled and diplomatically noted, "It isn't here yet, but I'd say it's nice to have a pretty good shot at it."[27]

31

St. Louis–Pittsburgh
Semifinal
The Blues Are Tested

"We didn't get to the Stanley Cup finals, but we got to the West Division finals. They [the Blues] had to fight like hang [sic] to knock us out of there. We didn't go down easily. I'm proud of those guys, every one of them. We got here by being a team and we went down as a team."[1]
—Red Kelly, Pittsburgh Penguins coach, after Game #6

In the semifinal featuring the West Division teams, the St. Louis Blues were trying to advance to the Stanley Cup finals for the third successive spring. Their opponents were the unfashionable Pittsburgh Penguins. Many prognosticators at the beginning of the 1969–70 had predicted a last-place finish for the Penguins. The pundits were wrong. Pittsburgh had finished the regular season with a less than stellar record of 26–38–12. Nevertheless, it was still good enough for second place in the West Division. (The 1970 Stanley Cup playoffs marked the first time since the NHL split into two divisions that the top two teams in each pool had all safely advanced past the first round.) The Blues had a respectable mark of 37–27–12. St. Louis prevailed, but not without a mighty struggle.

The first two games, played at the boisterous St. Louis Arena, produced a pair of expected victories for the favored home team. Game #1, played on Sunday, April 19, saw the Blues triumph 3–1 in a nasty affair. "Referee Art Skov was busy calling penalties," wrote Jimmy Jordan of the *Pittsburgh Post-Gazette*, "and the two linesmen, John D'Amico and Pat Shetler, spent more time prying apart various combatants than they spent calling offsides."[2]

Including the final two meetings of the regular season, it was the third consecutive game on St. Louis ice that the Blues had beaten Pittsburgh by a 3–1 score—an oddity for statistical-minded fans who enjoyed

182

such esoterica. Gary Sabourin, Phil Goyette and Red Berenson provided St. Louis with the necessary offense. Ken Schinkel tallied the only Pittsburgh goal. Glenn Hall was especially good throughout the rugged tilt in the St. Louis goal. Jordan further commented, "[The game] was a rough, penalty-ridden brawl. The brawling started 10 seconds after the first puck was dropped. It continued for 10 minutes after the final puck had fallen." Jimmy Jordan continued in his game report,

> There were some [observers] who felt the Penguins came out ahead in the brawling. There could have been an argument on that point, but there was no debate concerning the Blues' superiority for a least a period of five minutes and 46 seconds in the second stanza. That was when Gary Sabourin, Phil Goyette and Red Berenson each scored to put the game out of reach.[3]

One good thing happened to the Penguins the day after Game #1: Red Kelly was formally notified that he had been named the NHL's Coach of the Year by *The Hockey News*. Few people quarreled with that decision as the Penguins were not expected to be much of a threat during the 1969–70 season—and the Coach of The Year award frequently goes to the bench boss of a team perceived to have overachieved. When the season began in October, few hockey followers would have expected the Penguins to be playing hockey in late April, just four wins away from a berth in the Stanley Cup final.

Game #2, played on Tuesday, April 21, was less competitive, with St. Louis winning comfortably. "Blues Bury Penguins Early, Win 4–1" blared the headline atop the *Pittsburgh Post-Gazette*'s sports section the following day. Phil Goyette sored another goal for the Blues. Jean-Guy Talbot, Larry Keenan, and Frank St. Marseille got the other St. Louis tallies. Pittsburgh's promising and exciting rookie star, the diminutive 20-year-old Michel Brière, got the only goal for the visitors.

"The Penguins were flat, their forechecking was far below par, their passing was erratic, and their skating lacked finesse,"[4] declared a disappointed Jimmy Jordan of the *Post-Gazette*.

One of the game's outstanding performers for the Blues was Ab McDonald, who assisted on the first three of the home team's four goals. McDonald had been the Penguins' captain during Pittsburgh's first NHL season in 1967–68. (He had been traded for Lou Angotti in June 1968. Angotti was dealt to the Chicago Black Hawks after one season in Pittsburgh.) McDonald had also played in 61 minor league games for the Pittsburgh Hornets the last season before the NHL expanded to 12 teams. Jordan opined, "The Penguins will have to devise some method of stopping their ex-captain short of the blue line if they hope to remain in the Stanley Cup playoffs."[5]

When the series shifted to the Civic Arena in Pittsburgh for the next two contests, the Penguins' fortunes perceptibly changed. The fans were certainly excited about being in the Stanley Cup semifinals, despite the home team facing a daunting two-game deficit. The *Pittsburgh Post-Gazette* reported that very few of the choice $7 seats at The Igloo remained unsold. The Penguins responded to the favorable crowd enthusiasm. On Thursday, April 23 the Penguins eked out a 3–2 victory in Game #3 after jumping out to a 3–0 lead. A scribe for the Canadian Press reported, "The Pittsburgh Penguins scored the first three goals last night and their strong checking carried them to a 3–2 victory over St. Louis, reducing the Blues lead in the Stanley Cup semifinal playoff to 2–1."[6]

Dean Prentice got the only goal of the first period to give Pittsburgh a 1–0 edge. Two more Penguin goals in the second period, by Jean Pronovost and Michel Brière, upped the home team's edge to 3–0. St. Louis attempted a rally in the third period. The Blues scored their 13th power play goal of the 1970 playoffs, by Larry Keenan at 1:40, who beat Pens goaltender Les Binkley cleanly from the right side. Slightly more than four minutes later, Keenan made the game very interesting with his second goal of the period (and fifth of the playoffs) when he fired a loose puck past Binkley from a scramble in front of the Pittsburgh net. After that goal, Pittsburgh, to their credit, did not waver. They continued to pressure the Blues, seldom letting the visitors mount any sort of offensive threat. Veteran St. Louis goalie Jacques Plante was pulled for an extra attacker with 80 seconds left in the period, but St. Louis could not find an equalizing tally. The Penguins, now trailing the semifinal 2–1, were back in the series with a victory that was well deserved.

Even more well deserved was Pittsburgh's 2–1 triumph three nights later in Game #4. The score was not at all indicative of the flow of play. Pittsburgh dominated the game, outshooting and outplaying the visiting Blues decisively, much to the delight of the sellout crowd at the Civic Arena. The home team had won the first four games of the series. Jimmy Jordan's game report in the *Pittsburgh Post-Gazette* exuded great confidence that the underdog Penguins could muster an upset and advance to the Stanley Cup finals. He wrote,

> If the Penguins can continue to play the type of hockey they have played the last two outings, things are going to be pretty blue around the fans' watering places in St. Louis.
>
> The Pens nipped the Blues 2–1 last night in the Civic Arena before another record crowd, this one 12,962.
>
> But the score tells little of the manner in which the Penguins handled the champions of the National Hockey League West. Nor does it reveal the continuous battle they carried into St. Louis territory—and kept there for much of the night.
>
> The Penguins took 51 shots at the St. Louis net. They stopped the St. Louis attack with just 24 shots at goalie Al Smith. Most of these caused the ex–Maple Leaf goalie little trouble, but when he was called upon to make a big save, he met the challenge.

Duane Rupp, the big defenseman who has played some of his best hockey in this series after being sidelined with a charley horse and a knee injury, scored the first Penguin goal with a bit of alertness.

And Michel Brière, the 20-year-old rookie who has become the darling of the fans since they started jamming the Big Igloo, scored the other on a piece of individual stickhandling which left the Blues' defense goggle-eyed.

The crowd was not only the largest to ever see a hockey game in Pittsburgh, it was also the most vocal. Several times it stood to give the Penguins standing ovations, particularly the penalty-killing units which kept the Blues back up the ice continuously.

The crowd … was just 39 more than the record turnout that saw the Penguins win the first home game of the series, 3–2, on Thursday night after losing the first two games in St. Louis earlier in the week.

Sometimes it appeared the Blues were trying to find a gate in a picket fence as they approached their blue line only to find blue-shirted Penguins who appeared to be everywhere.[7]

Apart from Pittsburgh's excellent forechecking, the home team's offense was doing stalwart work as well, firing 37 shots at St. Louis goaltender Ernie Wakely in the first two periods, with two of them beating him for scores. Pittsburgh's first goal was a product of the hard effort the home team displayed throughout the game. Michel Brière forced a turnover in the St. Louis zone. He flipped a pass to Jean Pronovost. Pronovost's drive bounced off a skate to a Penguin teammate, Duane Rupp. Rupp pounced on it and whacked a 40-foot backhander behind Wakely to give the home side a deserved 1–0 lead.

The St. Louis–Pittsburgh semifinal, like the Boston–Chicago series, featured brothers opposing each other. In the West it was the McCreary lads squaring off. Keith was a Penguin; Bill was a Blue. Each man played a role in the game's scoring. Like Pittsburgh's opening goal, the lone St. Louis tally came off a broken play and a carom. Jean-Guy Talbot had tossed the puck to Bill McCreary, the older of the two McCreary siblings. His shot toward the Pittsburgh goal hit a stick and became airborne. André Boudrias knocked it back down onto the ice with his glove and quickly fired a 15-foot shot past Al Smith to get the Blues level at 3:05 of the second period.

Less than four minutes later, Keith McCreary picked up an assist on Michel Brière's picturesque goal that gave the Penguins a 2–1 advantage. On the play, McCreary fed Brière a pass. The flashy Brière advanced to the St. Louis blue line. He skated parallel to it for a few strides before charging toward the Blues' net. Brière's shot from the left side sizzled between Wakely's pads for what turned out to be the game-winning goal.

The third period was lively but produced no further scoring. Referee Lloyd Gilmour got a standing ovation from the Pittsburgh supporters, however, when he handed Jim Roberts of the Blues a 10-minute misconduct at the 13:53 mark after the St. Louis forward was a trifle too persistent in his complaints about Gilmour's officiating. That penalty effectively kept Roberts off the ice for the remainder of the game.

The Blues pulled Wakely in favor of a sixth attacker with slightly more than a minute remaining on the clock, but it was the Penguins who had the better scoring chances. Three times they fired at long range for the gaping St. Louis net—and three times they missed the target. With the win in the books, Pittsburgh coach Red Kelly could afford to chuckle about his team's faulty marksmanship on the unguarded St. Louis net. He facetiously remarked to the press, "We can make any team's goalie look good—even if he isn't in goal."[8]

Kelly preferred to discuss where the series now stood. "We have the momentum now and I hope we can keep it going," he said to reporters after the game. "But we have to win one game on their ice. It's as simple as that. Maybe we can do it Thursday night."[9]

Game #5, in St. Louis on April 28, was the turning point of the series—and it was no contest. The hometown Blues romped to an easy 5–0 triumph, hardly looking like the team that seemed so out of synch in Game #4 two nights earlier in Pittsburgh. This time it was the Penguins who looked tentative and unsure in all aspects of their play. "The victory, cheered lustily by a throng of 16,872 [St. Louis supporters], gave the Blues a 3–2 lead in the best-of-seven series,"[10] wrote an Associated Press scribe. Frank St. Marseille was the outstanding player on the night. He scored a hattrick to power St. Louis.

St. Marseille had come alive offensively in the semifinal after enduring a prolonged scoring drought. Before his overdue breakthrough, St. Marseille had gone 35 consecutive games without scoring a goal. He got the Blues' first tally of the night at 11:56 of the opening period by lifting a shot over the left shoulder of Penguins goalie Al Smith. Still in the first period, André Boudrias increased the Blues lead to 2–0 on the powerplay. (The terminology had not been coined in 1970, but Boudrias' goal was scored on what would now be called a wraparound.) It came at 15:59. As a result of strong forechecking by Gary Sabourin, at the 5:26 mark of the second period St. Marseille notched his second goal of the game. Twelve minutes later Tim Ecclestone scored on a rebound to up the home team's advantage to 4–0. St. Marseille concluded St. Louis' offense for the evening at 5:17 of the third period. This time he converted a pretty pass from Bill McCreary for the goal.

With the Blues five goals ahead and the game's outcome no longer in doubt, all that remained was to preserve the shutout for ageless Jacques Plante who was appearing in his 105th Stanley Cup playoff game. (His first postseason NHL game was with Montreal in 1953.) Pittsburgh did not score, but they certainly made it interesting. Three times Glen Sather was foiled by Plante on breakaway attempts. The whitewash was the 14th in

Plante's storied career to come in postseason play. He only faced 21 Pittsburgh shots while the far busier Al Smith had 35 St. Louis shots directed at his net. Clearly the momentum had shifted back in the Blues' favor. Pittsburgh now faced elimination in their home building on Thursday, April 30.

It took a comeback, but the St. Louis Blues earned a trip to the Stanley Cup finals for the third consecutive year by edging the Pittsburgh Penguins 4–3 on Pittsburgh ice in Game #6. Nothing was decided until Larry Keenan broke a 3–3 deadlock with just under six minutes remaining in the third period.

By the 4:24 mark of the second period, Pittsburgh had jumped out to a solid 2–0 lead on goals by Duane Rupp and Ron Schock before 12,403 happy, partisan fans at the Big Igloo—as the locals liked to call their arena. At the 7:37 mark of the period, Red Berenson scored his sixth goal of the playoffs to cut the Penguins' lead in half. Goals came in a flurry for both teams in the third period as a tight-checking game suddenly opened up without any warning.

St. Louis tied the game 2–2 on Bill McCreary's tally at 5:26. The goal came on an error by rookie Michel Brière who carelessly gave the puck away in his own zone. Just 51 seconds later, however, Brière atoned for his gaffe and restored the home team's lead by knocking a rebound past Glenn Hall. It was his fifth goal of the Stanley Cup playoffs—and the last time the youthful Brière's name would ever appear on an NHL scoring summary. Just 40 seconds after Brière's go-ahead marker, St. Louis' Tim Ecclestone tied the game again, at three goals apiece, with his third goal of the playoffs. It was a strange goal. The Penguins were expecting the play to be stopped for a St. Louis offside and seemed to freeze in anticipation of a linesman's whistle. It never came, though. Ecclestone paid no mind to the apparent offside and beat Al Smith with a 15-foot shot. It took Keenen's goal at 14:25 to settle matters for good. Pittsburgh had outshot St. Louis 32–30 and were valiant in defeat. Glenn Hall was the winning goalie for the visitors. He outplayed his counterpart, Al Smith of the Penguins.

When there were just two seconds left on the clock and the Penguins had run out of all hope, the sellout crowd at the Civic Arena rose and applauded their team's gallant effort in the series. They also loudly cheered the traditional postgame handshake between the two teams, which *Pittsburgh Post-Gazette* hockey journalist Dennis O'Neil called "a unique custom in sports." O'Neil further noted, "They cheered loudest for Red Kelly, the Penguins' coach and the NHL's Coach of the Year, as he shuffled off the ice in a dress suit and street shoes."[11] Someone in the big crowd must have anticipated the Penguins loss. He unfurled a banner—obviously made before the game—that read, "Thanks Pens for a great hockey season."

Bob Goldham, doing color commentary for the CBC's English-language television broadcast, was impressed by the capacity crowd supporting the Penguins—which had not been the norm during any of the three regular seasons the team had been in existence. He exclaimed, "It looks like hockey has arrived in Pittsburgh. Maybe it will carry over to next season."[12]

O'Neil noted, "The red-haired coach was talking about a team that was the consensus pick to finish last in the West Division. They had the Blues on the run last night until a rash of mistakes blew their chances clear out of the huge dome of the Big Igloo."[13]

When asked about the standing ovation he received when we walked onto the ice for the postgame handshakes, Kelly suddenly became a bit bashful. "It was nice," he stammered. "Pretty nice."[14] Shortly afterward, Kelly, whose future in Pittsburgh had been greatly in doubt, signed a five-year, $250,000 contract to remain with the Penguins. It was a rich deal by 1970 standards. Kelly would also assume the duties as the team's general manager. Kelly had won eight Stanley Cups as a player in a career that spanned 21 NHL seasons—a number of championships unmatched by any player who never skated with the Montreal Canadiens.

"Yes, we were picked to finish last," concurred Pittsburgh defenseman Bryan Watson, "but I never played on a team with so much heart, so much guts. It was just a great team effort."[15]

St. Louis would next meet the high-scoring and well rested Boston Bruins, who, according to the prognosticators, were the odds-on favorite to win the Stanley Cup. However, St. Louis had one advantage on their side: Although Boston had accrued more points than St. Louis in the regular season, the Blues were given the extra home game since they had finished atop the West Division while the Bruins had only finished second in the East Division—albeit on a tiebreaker. Thus, the first two games would be played at the St. Louis Arena. Game #5 and Game #7 would also be held in St. Louis, if necessary. "The Blues are confident and the schedule favors them," noted a Canadian Press story that ran without a byline in the *Montreal Gazette*. "The confidence was expressed Thursday night at Pittsburgh in a noisy St. Louis dressing room after the Blues beat the Penguins to take the West Division final in six games."[16]

On paper, the 1970 Stanley Cup final seemed like a mismatch with Boston having seven players among the top 50 NHL scorers during the 1969–70 regular season. The Blues had just three. After backstopping his team to the clinching victory in Game #6, St. Louis goalie Glenn Hall cockily announced, "They [the Bruins] don't scare us."[17]

Game #1 of the 1970 Stanley Cup finals would be held three days hence. It would be a Sunday afternoon contest at the rowdy St. Louis Arena—and in front of a North American television audience.

PART IV

The Finals—From Shadow Treatment to Classic Finish

32

Game #1:
Plante Goes Down;
Bruins Go Up

"Plante was knocked unconscious and out of the series. The
impact was felt by the entire St. Louis team and its fans."
—Dan Kelly's narration of the NHL's official
highlight film of the 1970 Stanley Cup finals

The 1970 Stanley Cup finals began on Sunday, May 3, 1970, at the St. Louis Arena. As was becoming the routine, Game #1 was an afternoon start, 1 p.m. Central time, at the request of CBS so it could be shown in the usual time slot for its *NHL Game of the Week* broadcast. Whatever CBS wanted from the NHL in 1970, CBS got.

For the hometown Blues, this was their third consecutive crack at being just four games away from capturing the Stanley Cup. In the two previous years, they had failed to win even a game versus the vaunted Montreal Canadiens in eight attempts. The Bruins promised to be at least as difficult an opponent for St. Louis as the Habs had been in 1968 and 1969. The last thing the Blues wanted was to be on the wrong end of another sweep in the Stanley Cup finals. Such a calamity would diminish the collective respect that the six expansion teams desperately sought and thought they deserved.

For the Boston Bruins, winners of three Stanley Cups in their 46-year history, this was the first time they had advanced to the final series since 1958, back when the NHL still had its small, exclusive membership of just six clubs. There was one holdover from that team that lost to Montreal in six games 12 years earlier—assistant captain Johnny (Chief) Bucyk. Approaching his 35th birthday, Bucyk was a distinguished symbol of perseverance, having suffered the frustration of being on the woebegone Bruin teams that missed qualifying for the Stanley Cup playoffs for eight consecutive years from 1959–60 to 1966–67.

Born in Edmonton on May 12, 1935, Bucyk acquired the nickname

"Chief" from teammate Bronco Horvath sometime in the late 1950s. Bucyk recalled he somehow got it because of his unrivaled skill at digging the puck out of the corners and feeding it to Horvath in the slot. Because of the moniker, many fans wrongly assumed Bucyk was at least part native. "For some strange reason, more people are disappointed when I tell them I'm not an Indian," he said in his autobiography. "There's not one drop of Indian blood in my veins, as far as I know. I'm a Ukrainian."[1]

Bucyk played the game ruggedly but he generally played it cleanly. (He would be awarded the Lady Byng Trophy as the NHL's most gentlemanly player in 1970–71.) During the 1968–69 season Bucyk had become the Bruins' all-time leader in games played. He still holds the career goals record for Boston with 545. (Phil Esposito is in second spot, 86 scores behind the Chief.) Sports journalist Russ Conway wrote in 1972, "Johnny Bucyk has more friends in Boston, and the hockey-crazy cities and towns around the home of the Bruins, than any politician."[2] Accordingly, quite a few neutral fans were quietly rooting for Boston for sentimental reasons just because they wanted to see the long-suffering Bucyk get his name engraved on the Stanley Cup.

St. Louis coach Scotty Bowman was upset that his team—not to mention the entire NHL's West Division—was not being accorded much respect by hockey writers and television networks. "I'm really rankled," he told the media. "They keep treating us like second-class citizens. CBC didn't cover the West Division playoffs until there was nothing else left. They try out their new announcers on us. They leave Danny Gallivan at home. They don't treat us like equals. There's only one answer for that—beat 'em!"[3]

In assessing the Bruins compared to the 1968 and 1969 Habs, Bowman concluded, "They're not as fast as Montreal, which is good because we're not a fast club. They like to beat you with muscle, but their defense isn't as good as the Canadiens.' Last year we couldn't get through to the Montreal net."[4]

In the six regular-season meetings between the two teams, Boston won three games, St. Louis won one, and two ended in ties. St. Louis won the last meeting, at home, on March 4 by a 3–1 score. Only one game had a lopsided score (Boston's 7–1 win at Boston Garden on February 8). Thus, five of the six regular-season meetings between the Bruins and Blues had been very competitive. St. Louis fans and players alike could at least cite that statistic as a reason for optimism.

The underdog Blues, of course, had greater experience playing in the championship round than the Bruins. Not one Boston player had ever participated in the Stanley Cup finals. In contrast, most of the Blues had been members of one, if not two, of the St. Louis teams who had appeared in last two Cup finals. Both, of course, were losing efforts to Montreal. St. Louis defenseman Jean-Guy Talbot, a 38-year-old veteran of 16 NHL seasons, was remarkably making his 12th appearance in the Stanley Cup finals!

Bowman was obsessed with Boston's Bobby Orr—not an unreasonable worry for an opposing NHL coach to have. He was convinced the only way the Blues had a chance to upend the Bruins was to totally neutralize Orr. Bowman had seen what Orr had done to the New York Rangers in the quarterfinals and especially the Chicago Black Hawks in the semifinals. Even if he did not score or directly create a goal with an assist, Orr routinely dictated the pace of any game in which he played. If Orr had control of the puck, bad things would often happen to the Bruins' opponents. There was only one thing to do, Bowman concluded: assign a player to "shadow" Boston's #4 whenever and wherever he was on the ice.

Major scoring threats being shadowed was nothing new in hockey. It had been going on since the days of Howie Morenz in the 1920s and 1930s, and likelier even earlier than that. Don Marcotte and Ed Westfall were two superb checkers on the Bruins who were often assigned the sole duty of preventing a superstar opponent from even touching the puck. Westfall had gotten rave reviews for his work that kept Bobby Hull off the scoresheet in Boston's four-game sweep of the Black Hawks. However, assigning someone to *shadow a defenseman* was something utterly new. As the Blues were heavy underdogs, Bowman figured he would give his novel strategy a try in Game #1, handing the bulk of the containment duties to veteran forward Jim Roberts.

Bowman told a handful reporters in advance of the game that he was going to focus on derailing Orr. "We've got to stop Bobby Orr … as you know," Bowman said. "I'm going to put one guy on him all the way. Maybe two guys. You know, Chicago would have had a better chance putting Bobby Hull on Orr instead of letting Eddie Westfall tie him up."[5]

Dick Beddoes, the colorful writer for the Toronto *Globe & Mail*, dutifully reported the high price of tickets to see Game #1 of the Stanley Cup finals at the St. Louis Arena. He was aghast when he learned the best ducats in the house had an exorbitant face value of $9 apiece.

As North America watched, Orr skated out for the opening faceoff. So did Roberts. As soon as the puck was dropped, Roberts immediately was on Orr's tail. Even when St. Louis launched an offensive thrust in the Boston zone, Roberts stayed close—very close—to Orr.

At first, Orr did not know what to make of this constant and oppressive attention. Having a forward following him about the ice was utterly new to him. After realizing that Roberts would be a persistent pest, Orr simply concentrated on playing defensive hockey. He let the other Bruins worry about scoring. The constant pursuit seemed to tire Roberts more than Orr. Occasionally, Bowman replaced Roberts with another forward, but the containment strategy remained the same at all times: neutralize Boston's number four.

Although Roberts had virtually forfeited his offensive role, he did manage to score a goal in the second period. While keeping close tabs on Orr, Roberts found himself part of a two-on-one rush into the Boston zone. Tim Ecclestone fed Roberts an excellent pass. He knocked a backhand shot past Bruin goalie Gerry Cheevers to tie the game 1–1. It was the high point of Bowman's strategy. The rest of the Bruins responded with an easy 6–1 win. Orr was on the ice for five of Boston's six goals. Johnny Bucyk scored three of them.

Bucyk was no fool. He fully realized why he had been so successful in Game #1. "I've got to admit that I had more chances today than I've had in a long time," he said. "What did I get, nine shots? That's a lot. I think the way they were checking Bobby had a lot to do with it."[6]

Happy with the outcome of the game, Orr was amused by St. Louis' unorthodox tactics. "If they watch me like that in the next game, I won't even have to take a shower afterwards," he joked. "I could have gone out for lunch for all the chances I had to get in the play, so I just stayed out of things."[7]

Boston coach Harry Sinden thought Bowman's strategy was not especially a sound one. "[The Blues] think this team is Bobby Orr," he said. "Bobby is not the whole Boston Bruins. By them watching Orr, we sprung Johnny Bucyk loose."[8]

Game #1 also featured a truly scary incident: With the game tied 1–1 in the second period and St. Louis playing a man short, goaltender Jacques Plante was felled by a Fred Stanfield slapshot that was tipped by Phil Esposito. The deflection caused the puck to suddenly rise sharply. The puck struck Plante squarely on his face mask above the left eye at the 3:57 mark. Plante, age 41, dropped slowly to ice. His collapse was reminiscent of a boxer who had just taken a knockout punch. "He was out cold," reported Blues trainer Tom Woodcock. "I think it's a concussion."[9]

Plante was senseless for three minutes before he awoke from his stupor. A stretcher was brought onto the ice, but Plante declined to use it. Instead, he skated off the ice on his own power, all the while being supported by worried teammates. Nobody knew it at the time, but Plante had played his last game as a member of the Blues. Two weeks later St. Louis would deal him to the Toronto Maple Leafs in a cash transaction.

It was Plante, of course, who had ushered in modern goalie masks 11 years earlier after getting smacked in the face by an Andy Bathgate backhand on November 1, 1959, at Madison Square Garden. On this afternoon Plante was wearing a tight, molded, form-fitting mask that was quite snug—quite common for goalies in all levels of hockey in 1970. The design protected the goalie's face from cuts, but the impact of a puck striking it could still be enormous. Stanfield's drive had considerable force behind it. It cracked Plante's mask. He was taken to St. Louis Jewish Hospital for x-rays and observation. Early reports had Plante listed in satisfactory condition. Nevertheless, Plante would stay in the hospital for a week before being released. Luckily, he suffered no serious or long-term injury. Plante did, however, issue a statement while en route for medical treatment in which he credited his mask for saving his life. (Bill Mazer quoted it during the CBS telecast.) Plante also cavalierly dismissed his injury, claiming it to be "a little bump on the head."[10]

Johnny Bucyk had opened the scoring at 19:45 of the first period. His shot from about 25 feet beat Plante, who was screened on the play by two defenders. In the second period Jim Roberts got his game-tying goal for the Blues at 1:52. Shortly thereafter, Plante was kayoed by Stanfield's rising shot. Journeyman goaltender Ernie Wakely replaced him in the St. Louis net. Wakely had never played in the Stanley Cup finals before. "The Bruins, sensing they were on the trail of a championship, wasted no time in putting Wakely to the test," declared one report.[11] Seventy-nine seconds after Wakely entered the game, Bucyk got his second goal of the afternoon. Phil Esposito had picked up a loose puck in the corner to Wakely's left. He passed to Johnny McKenzie in the slot. McKenzie saw Bucyk uncovered at the side of the net and sent him a sharp pass which Boston's number nine put behind Wakely. Boston led 2–1.

The floodgates opened the third period as the Bruins' quality overwhelmed the home team with four goals. Twenty-three-year-old Wayne (Swoop) Carleton scored his second goal of the playoffs at 4:59 when he beat Wakely low on the short side from about 15 feet away. Carleton had been acquired by the Bruins from Toronto in a midseason trade that sent 22-year-old Jim Harrison to the Maple Leafs. Bucyk got his hattrick 38 seconds later to up the Boston lead to 4–1 by deftly banging a rebound past Wakely. The momentum of the game had clearly and irreversibly tilted Boston's way.

Plante wasn't the only Blue to be transported to a hospital during the game. Barclay Plager passed out suddenly while sitting on the St. Louis bench during the third period. An examination showed that he had separated some ribs.

With St. Louis on a power play late in the game, Derek Sanderson scored a pretty shorthanded goal—his specialty—for the visitors on a breakaway created by Bobby Orr's superb pass. (Orr's assist was his 16th of the 1970 playoffs, equaling an NHL record set by Tim Horton of the Toronto Maple Leafs in 1961–62.) Sanderson did a little post-goal celebration dance—somewhat unusual for the era. Ninety-eight seconds after

Sanderson's back-breaking goal, Phil Esposito made it 6–1 for the Bruins on a terrific individual effort. Esposito, showing fine dexterity, picked up a loose puck in the neutral zone and carried it over the St. Louis blueline. He then maneuvered around defenseman Noel Picard, and, while slightly off balance, beat Wakely who was pulled out of position. Esposito tied two Stanley Cup playoff records with that highlight-reel marker: 12 goals in one postseason (matching the standard held jointly by Jean Béliveau and Maurice Richard) and 21 total points (held by Stan Mikita).

In speaking to the media afterwards, Harry Sinden referred to Plante's injury as the game's turning point. "We got a big break when Plante got hurt," he stated. "He had made some pretty good stops."[12] There was also the emotional aspect of the incident that favored the Bruins. Bill Heufelder of the Pittsburgh Press wrote, "The sight of a fallen hero … destroyed the enthusiasm of a standing-room crowd of 16,715 in the muggy St. Louis Arena."[13]

Another key point in the game came when Boston successfully killed off a two-man disadvantage in the first period. The second penalized player was goalie Gerry Cheevers who was given two minutes for delay of game. Cheevers' minor penalty was served by Bill Lesuk who had been elevated from the minors as an injury replacement. He probably enjoyed his moment in the sun—and on national television—sitting in the penalty box. During the Blues' subsequent power play, Cheevers made a couple of spectacular and acrobatic saves. He also thwarted St. Louis late in the second period, preserving Boston's 2–1 lead after 40 minutes when the game's outcome was still in doubt. In his seventh consecutive start for the Bruins, Cheevers was solid in the Boston net all afternoon and was sharp when he needed to be.

Referee Art Skov drew some ire from the Bruins for what they thought were a few chintzy penalty calls. The game was surprisingly nasty at times and featured some rough play. Wayne Cashman and Noel Picard squared off in a couple of brief battles. Police officers had to be summoned to the Bruins' penalty box to prevent trouble between heckling fans and Boston players after Cashman nearly got into an altercation with a St. Louis rooter in the first period. The gendarmes remained there for the duration of the game just to be on the safe side. (In the CBS broadcast of the game, Cashman can clearly be heard yelling at his tormenter, "What the hell do you know?") At the St. Louis Arena, there was nothing separating spectators from the penalized players. Surrounding the penalty boxes with barriers of high glass had not yet occurred to anyone in 1970.

In the previous two Stanley Cup finals, the worst defeat St. Louis suffered was a 4–0 loss versus Montreal in Game #3 in 1969. Surrendering six goals at home to Boston to open the 1970 Cup finals did not bode well for the Blues. After watching Game #1, Dink Carroll of the *Montreal Gazette* did not expect St. Louis to be much more than a slight nuisance to Boston the rest of the way. He wrote,

> It's true that only one game has been played in the current series between the Blues and the Bruins, but the latter won it so easily that taking the next three games just seems a formality. Even before the series started, the big debate was whether or not the Blues could win one game. That's how much of a disparity exists between teams in the two divisions.[14]

When a reporter suggested to Scotty Bowman that his team might be tired after having played six tough games in their semifinal versus Pittsburgh, the St. Louis coach quickly dismissed that notion. "It's all psychological," he said. "It's the easiest excuse in the world. When you're in the Stanley Cup finals there aren't any excuses."[15]

Sitting in his office after the one-sided loss, Bowman did exhibit a wry sense of humor in his postgame comments. When asked by a scribe, "Do you plan to shadow Bobby Orr for the rest of the series?" Bowman responded, "Not me, personally."[16]

The Boston sports journalists covering the Stanley Cup final—at least those old enough to remember radio dramas—quickly bestowed a humorous and fitting nickname upon Jim Roberts: They dubbed him "Lamont Cranston." That was the alter ego of "The Shadow."

33

Game #2:
Another Half Dozen Goals

> "We just couldn't compete offensively with Montreal or
> Boston."[1]
> —St. Louis forward Tim Ecclestone on his
> team's three losses in the Stanley Cup finals

With Jacques Plante medically disqualified for the foreseeable future, on Tuesday Bowman, who often played hunches, surprised everyone by starting 29-year-old Ernie Wakely in the Blues' net for Game #2; most hockey experts figured the more experienced Glenn Hall would be summoned to try his luck against the formidable Bruins. Wakely did not look particularly good.

The Bruins merrily rolled to another decisive win on St. Louis ice on May 5 before a record crowd of 17,506 at the St. Louis Arena. "Any hopes this year's Stanley Cup final would go past the minimum four games took a beating last night as the Boston Bruins skated to an easy 6–2 win to take a two-game edge in the series,"[2] wrote a "special correspondent" for the *Montreal Gazette* who did not receive a byline above his comments. The story was accurately headlined "Bruins Continue Cup Rush."

The situation facing St. Louis was not at all promising. The *Gazette* story continued, "Now they have to go back to Boston for the next two games. The Bruins, who lost only three games on home ice all year, have yet to lose a playoff game at home. Nor have they lost in the Boston Garden this year to any West Division club."[3] Barclay Plager was also deemed medically unfit for the contest, further hurting the Blues' chances in Game #2.

Bobby Orr's presence on the ice was still causing Scotty Bowman fits. "The Blues had hopes to stop Bobby Orr and thus stop the Bruins' attack in the series," continued the report in the *Gazette*, "But they couldn't do it Sunday and they couldn't do it last night either."[4]

Indeed, before Game #2 Jim Roberts was once again ordered by

Bowman to closely follow Orr, but when Boston broke out to a 3–0 first-period lead, the ineffective strategy was abandoned. Orr had not scored, but he did assist on two of the three Boston tallies. Afterwards Bowman said he had tried his best to curtail Orr's offensive prowess. "It wasn't as effective as I'd hoped," Bowman confessed, "because the other guys didn't accept the drudgery of checking Orr the way Roberts did. But really, how do you practice something like that? We worked on it for six hours, but we didn't have Bobby Orr to practice against."[5]

Commenting on Bowman's unexpected choice of goaltender for the second game, the *Gazette* scribe noted, "It was soon obvious that it wasn't going to make much difference [who was in net for St. Louis]. The Bruins put on relentless pressure against the Blues almost from the start and had rushed to a 3–0 lead by the end of the first period."[6]

Fred Stanfield opened the scoring for Boston at 9:10 of the first period while Noel Picard was in the penalty box serving a holding penalty. Orr had started the play by rushing down the right wing before feeding a pass to Phil Esposito at the St. Louis blue line. Esposito moved the puck close enough to fire a shot at Wakely. Wakely failed to corral the rebound, however. Esposito beat him to it and passed the puck to Stanfield who was smartly trailing the play in the slot. "Stanfield had a lot of net to shoot at and he didn't miss," according to the *Gazette*. "The assist gave Esposito his 22nd point of the playoffs, a league record surpassing the 21-point output of Stan Mikita in the 1962 playoffs."[7]

Just over four minutes later, the Bruins upped their lead to 2–0. Defenseman Rick Smith was the catalyst this time. He drew the St. Louis defense to the left of Wakely, firing a shot between two Blues. Again, Wakely stopped the first shot. This time Ed Westfall got to it first and flipped it over the sprawling netminder. Bulky St. Louis defenseman Noel Picard actually helped Westfall by falling on top of Wakely, immobilizing him.

Late in the first period the Bruins were penalized by referee Bill Friday for too many men on the ice—a transgression they hotly disputed. The two-minute bench penalty was served by the seldom used Bill Lesuk who had played most of the season with the minor-league Hershey Bears. The aggrieved visitors from Boston responded by scoring a spectacular short-handed goal authored by Bobby Orr. "Orr grabbed a loose puck to the right of Gerry Cheevers and took off," reported the *Gazette*, "racing the full length of the ice before passing [the puck] to Westfall at the last moment."[8] Westfall one-timed Orr's pass behind Wakely. With 45 seconds left in the first period, Boston had extended their lead to 3–0. The rout was on—again.

Both teams got a power play goal in the second period. At 9:12 Bob Plager was penalized for checking Ed Westfall heavily into the boards behind Wakely. Westfall, who crashed heavily, appeared to injure his shoulder on the play. Derek Sanderson scored 25 seconds into the man advantage by tipping a perfect pass from Phil Esposito through heavy traffic in front of the St. Louis net past the helpless Wakely. St. Louis got a goal back when Sanderson was sitting out an elbowing infraction. Terry Gray deflected a Noel Picard shot from the point past Gerry Cheevers at 17:26. The second period ended with Boston holding a huge and secure 4–1 lead.

Not content with conservatively nursing their three-goal edge, Boston came out strongly in the third period. Sanderson, who was becoming a focal point in the game, got his second goal of the night 58 seconds into the period. Wakely's inability to control rebounds was again a factor as Sanderson knocked home a loose puck following a long shot from defenseman Dallas Smith. At 4:15, St. Louis got their second goal of the night—another power play effort—on a screen shot from Frank St. Marseille to narrow Boston's advantage to 5–2. The Blues hopes of a comeback, slim as they were, fizzled completely away when Johnny Bucyk made the score 6–2 with exactly five minutes left on the clock. Bucyk's goal was similar to the sixth goal of Game #1 scored by Phil Esposito. Starting from behind is own goal, Bucyk plowed his way through two St. Louis defenders to beat Wakely with a backhand on a terrific individual effort. There was no further scoring. Boston had outshot St. Louis 35–19 in the one-sided affair. The Bruins were heading back to Boston Garden with a 2–0 series lead. The Bruins and their fans could now smell the Stanley Cup.

34

Game #3:
"We Are Looking Forward
to Sunday"

"The victory [in Game #3] was a record-breaking ninth
straight in the playoffs for the Bruins, and again, as in
the first two games of the series, they weren't particularly
hard-pressed to get it."[1]

—Associated Press

He was stating the obvious, but it did not matter. "One more to go!"
bellowed Wayne Cashman in the Boston Bruins' upbeat dressing room following the home team's solid 4–1 victory over St. Louis in Game #3 of the
1970 Stanley Cup final on Thursday, May 7. "One more to go!"[2] he repeated
for emphasis.

Cashman had every right to be jubilant. His two third-period goals
had been the major factor as to why Boston had taken a commanding 3–0
series lead over the Blues before a highly partisan and enthusiastic full
house at Boston Garden. The score could have been much more one-sided
if not for the excellent goaltending of Glenn Hall—the third different goalie
the Blues had started in the three games thus far contested in the Stanley
Cup finals. It was the veteran Hall's 106th career Stanley Cup playoff game.

It was initially surprising that the 38-year-old Hall had not played in
Game #2 after Jacques Plante had been knocked senseless by a Fred Stanfield drive 24 minutes into Game #1. However, it was later learned that Hall
was suffering from an infected catching hand. According to Blues coach
Scotty Bowman, the infection was the result of Hall adversely reacting to
the dye in his goalie glove. Hall was not supposed to play in Game #3, but
the desperate times the Blues found themselves in called for desperate measures. Ernie Wakely seemed overwhelmed by the Bruins' offensive juggernaut during the first two games of the finals, so Hall volunteered to guard
the pipes in the third game—sore glove hand or no sore glove hand.

By its flow of play, the game was a one-sided contest, but it was not decided until the Bruins broke things open in the third period. St. Louis did not possess anything close to the weapons needed for mounting a comeback.

Still, St. Louis jumped out to a fluky 1–0 advantage 6:32 into the opening period. It was the first lead they had enjoyed in the series thus far. Frank St. Marseille was credited with an unassisted goal for the visitors while Don Awrey was serving a Bruins minor penalty for boarding. It was not a pretty tally by any means, but it counted just the same. St. Marseille, during the Blues' power play, rushed the puck into the Boston zone. St. Marseille attempted to make a pass into the slot. However, the play was broken up by Boston goaltender Gerry Cheevers who had played every second of the semifinals and the finals in the Bruins' goal. Dallas Smith tried to control the rebound, but he accidentally redirected the puck into the Boston net. Afterwards Smith could afford to chuckle about his egregious boo-boo. "I wouldn't mind scoring in the Stanley Cup finals—but not this way," he told reporters. "I was trying to clear the puck into the corner. I thought I had a lot more room than I did."[3]

The Blues retained their edge on the scoreboard for just seven minutes. Johnny Bucyk notched his 10th goal of the Stanley Cup playoffs to level matters at 13:23. His goal, also on a power play, came on a rebound after Glenn Hall had robbed Phil Esposito from close range. Bucyk reacted quickly and lifted a high shot over a sprawling Hall and into the net for his sixth goal of the finals. The goal was the 14th that the Bruins had scored in the 1970 playoffs while enjoying a man advantage. Both the Bruins and Blues were dangerous with an opponent seated in the penalty box. They had finished first and second respectively in the NHL in power-play goals during the regular season.

Precisely five minutes after Boston tied the score, they took the lead on a shot by Johnny McKenzie at the 18:23 mark. It came on a nifty three-way passing play that also included Bobby Orr and Fred Stanfield. McKenzie modestly declared his goal to be lucky, but then added, "It made up for the ones that don't go in."[4] The two teams headed into the first intermission with Boston ahead by a goal, 2–1.

There was no scoring in the second period—it was the first scoreless frame in the 1970 Cup finals—but the zeroes were only on the scoresheet because of the strong play of Glenn Hall in the St. Louis net. He faced 17 Boston shots in the middle period. Cheevers, on the other hand, was a lonely figure. He faced just five St. Louis shots. "Hall was bouncing all over the ice to make saves, getting help on a couple of occasions from his goalposts,"[5] declared the AP scribe. Cheevers was undoubtedly in a good mood entering the game. Cenacle's Image, a four-year-old gelding the goaltender owned, had won a six-furlong claiming race at Suffolk Downs a day earlier. "It only paid $4.60 to win," according to Bill Heufelder of the *Pittsburgh Press* who was clearly enamored with peripheral minutiae. "But if the Bruins are winners here on Sunday afternoon," the scribe continued, "Cheevers can bank on collecting $7,500 for his share for his share of the playoff money."[6]

Nineteen more shots were fired at Hall in the third period. The unnamed AP reporter continued, "Hall … kept the Blues in the game with a number of remarkable saves. His goaltending gave St. Louis its best chance of the series, but the Blues' forwards rarely bothered Boston netminder Gerry Cheevers. [Wayne] Cashman's two third-period goals put the game out of doubt."[7]

"[St. Louis] should have been out of it in the second period, but they weren't,"[8] Harry Sinden generously said after the game. Heufelder noted in his report that a Bruins win, despite Hall's ongoing heroics in the Blues' net, seemed almost inevitable. "The usually snarly Garden fans," he noted, "who have been known to be equally as harsh on their own heroes as opposing players, were patient and tranquil while the Bruins pressured Hall."[9]

In the third period, Wayne Cashman's first goal of the game was a beauty, set up wonderfully by Phil Esposito. It came 3:20 into the period. Two Blues defensemen converged on Esposito as he entered the St. Louis zone. He was taken out of the play but not before he managed to neutralize both defenders. He left the puck for Ken Hodge who was trailing the play. Hodge fed an unguarded Cashman with a perfect pass. Cashman moved in alone on Hall from the left side and slipped the puck between the goaltender's legs putting Boston ahead by two goals. With the few offensive chances the Blues were getting, it was a significant lead. Cashman made it an absolutely insurmountable advantage at 14:46 with another goal on a scramble after Hall had already made two fine saves on the play. It was Cashman's fifth goal of the playoffs. Boston comfortably cruised home 4–1 victors. The Bruins had only lost seven games at home—including playoffs—in the past two NHL seasons.

A bit of levity occurred near the end of the game. When the outcome was no longer in doubt, the hometown fans chanted, "We want Speer!"— an allusion to seldom-used, journeyman defenseman Bill Speer who had notched one goal and three assists in 27 regular-season games for Boston in 1969–70. Harry Sinden graciously obliged. He put Speer on the ice for one shift. Speer had scored once in Boston's quarterfinal series versus New York. It was the only point Speer would ever tally in an NHL playoff game.

The most linguistically creative banner displayed in Boston Garden that night was one that parodied the well-known Budweiser beer slogan. The sign said, "ORR IS THE KING OF BEARS."

Despite the decisive defeat, after the game St. Louis coach Scotty Bowman heaped praise on his veteran netminder who had been inundated with 46 Boston shots. "I've never seen him better. He made the game," Bowman insisted. When Bowman was asked why the score was not quite as lopsided as in the first two games of the finals, Bowman said, "We played a lot better defensively. There were no breakaways on us." When asked if Hall would be St. Louis' goalie for Game #4, Bowman basically assured the media that would indeed be the case. "I don't want to play an injured man, but I need his experience. If Glenn is okay, he'll play."[10]

Hall was not the only Blue not at 100 percent. Defenseman Al Arbour was absent from Game #3 with a nagging shoulder problem—diagnosed as a damaged muscle—that had initially badly afflicted him in the Blues' quarterfinal series versus Minnesota. "He wanted to have [the shoulder] frozen," Bowman noted, "but it was pretty painful."[11] Arbour, however, was expected to be available for Game #4 in three days' time.

Phil Esposito did not score any of Boston's four goals, but he did add three more assists to his ever-growing tally. He now had 26 total points in the 1970 playoffs. Each point he accrued was establishing a new record for Stanley Cup play in a single season.

Jack Dulmage of the *Windsor Star* reported, "The fans were fairly well behaved, not always the case in Boston, throwing only one frozen fish and one balloon on the ice. The linesmen took care of the fish. The Blues punctured the balloon—nothing else." The droll Dulmage further noted, "Game #4 in this last of three years of Cup final mismatches between divisions of unequal talent is scheduled at Boston Garden on Sunday afternoon."[12]

Boston's Ken Hodge adroitly sidestepped a reporter's query as to whether the Cup final was something of an anticlimax compared to the East final versus the Black Hawks. "I think we played our finest hockey against Chicago," he replied, "but we're playing well now too. We're checking well; we've contained the Blues."

Hodge continued, "None of us [Bruins] have ever won the Stanley Cup. We won't let up until we get it. It's the prestige, not the money." When asked if he expected the series to end in the four-game minimum, Hodge smiled and responded, "Let's just say we are looking forward to Sunday."[13]

35

"First Annual Bobby Orr Awards Luncheon"

Because of the additional day off between the third and fourth games of the Stanley Cup final, the NHL used the extra 24 hours of rest to hand out most of its major individual awards at a special noontime bash in Boston on Friday, May 8. Bobby Orr picked up three of the major trophies. When Orr went to collect them, he received a standing ovation from his Bruin teammates. A headline in the *Montreal Gazette* comically referred to the event as the "First Annual Bobby Orr Awards Luncheon." The hyperbole was only slight.

A Canadian Press correspondent wrote, "The shy, Parry Sound native, a veteran of four NHL seasons at the age of 22, won the Hart Memorial Trophy as the league's most valuable player, the James Norris Memorial Trophy as best defenseman, and the Art Ross Trophy as the first defenseman ever to win the regular-season scoring title."[1] Orr, to no one's surprise, was a unanimous choice for the Norris Trophy. It was his third consecutive Norris win.

"Orr was kept busy parading to the presentation table,"[2] an Associated Press reporter accurately noted. Only Stan Mikita of the Chicago Black Hawks had ever before won three of the NHL's major awards in one season.

Orr was only the fifth defenseman to win the MVP award, matching the feat of Eddie Shore, Babe Pratt, Babe Siebert and Tommy Anderson. Shore, a former Bruin known for his short temper and reckless offensive rushes, won the Hart Trophy four times in his career which predated the Second World War.

Typical of his modesty, Orr seemed embarrassed by the special, individual attention that he could not avoid. He seemed at a loss for words, especially when his fellow Bruins stood and applauded his trophy-winning feats. "I am very thrilled," he said quietly. "I must thank my teammates. It's unbelievable how well they play."[3] Orr picked up $10,750 in cash prizes that went along with winning the three trophies.

In a nice touch, Boston general manager Milt Schmidt personally presented the Hart Trophy to Orr. Schmidt had won the award in 1950–51. When Schmidt was asked what he thought of Orr, his praise was enormous. Schmidt gushed, "He's the greatest thing I've seen in the past, the greatest thing in the present, and if anything greater comes along in the future, I hope the good Lord will let me stay around to see it."[4]

Orr told reporters he had never dreamed of ever winning the Hart Trophy when he was a boy growing up and hoping he would make it to the NHL some day in the distant future. "It's the highlight of my life—until Sunday," said Orr. "The Stanley Cup means more to me than anything. I don't think there will be a problem," he said confidently. "We have our home rink and we're up 3–0."[5]

Tony Esposito was voted the NHL's Calder Trophy winner (for Rookie of the Year) by a substantial margin. New York's Bill Fairbairn came in second place. The goaltending Esposito also finished second in the MVP voting—well in arrears of Orr. Orr graciously pointed out to the media that he had not scored a single goal against Tony Esposito in Boston's eight regular-season games versus Chicago. (Orr politely declined to mention that he had beaten Esposito in spectacular fashion during the second game of the Boston–Chicago semifinal.)

The St. Louis Blues did not go unrepresented at the NHL awards ceremony. Thirty-six-year-old Phil Goyette, who was having a poor series versus Boston, was honored as the Lady Byng Trophy winner for gentlemanly conduct combined with skillful play. During the regular-season, Goyette had scored 29 goals and added 49 assists, all the while accruing only 16 minutes in penalties.

Chicago's small but mighty Pit Martin won the Bill Masterton Memorial Trophy, an award presented annually "to the National Hockey League player who best exemplifies the qualities of perseverance, sportsmanship, and dedication to ice hockey." The 5'8" Martin used the occasion to push for mandatory helmet usage in the NHL. He said in his acceptance speech, "I think helmets should be compulsory in this day and age. Guys like Bill Masterton or Ted Green would never have been injured if they wore helmets."[6]

One major individual NHL trophy could not yet be awarded: the Conn Smythe Trophy. Since 1965 it had been annually presented to the MVP of the Stanley Cup playoffs. Its first five recipients were Jean Béliveau, Roger Crozier, Dave Keon, Glenn Hall and Serge Savard. As Bobby Orr noted, with the Bruins holding a commanding 3–0 in the finals—and Game #4 set for Boston Garden—the odds were likely that the Conn Smythe Trophy winner would be determined two days hence.

36

Anticipation

"It appears the only possible bar to a Boston triumph tomorrow—other than the heroic efforts of Glenn Hall—is overconfidence"[1]
—Canadian Press story, May 9, 1970

On Saturday, May 9 a Canadian Press story from Boston featured an interview with Bruin center Phil Esposito who characteristically stated in no uncertain terms that his team would win Game #4 at home the following afternoon to complete a four-game sweep of the 1970 Stanley Cup finals. In Esposito's opinion, there was no doubt about it whatsoever.

"We all thought [the series] would be a contest," Esposito bluntly declared about the one-sided final after the Bruins assumed a daunting 3–0 series lead. "I'm not taking anything away from [the Blues], but I guess it's just that we're too good a hockey club. The way we are playing, no team in the NHL could handle us. It's the momentum we have as a team."[2]

Esposito stated what many longtime hockey fans felt about the post–1967 NHL: the three Stanley Cup finals since the league expanded from six to 12 teams had all been disappointing affairs because of the disparity in talent between the East and West Division clubs. "I watched two games of the [Montreal–St. Louis] finals on television last year—and I couldn't take it anymore,"[3] Esposito stated.

Esposito continued, "I think it's the truth that the reason they are changing the [playoff] format for next year is because what has happened in the finals the past three years."[4] Esposito was referring to the NHL's recent decision, that would take effect in 1970–71, to have the two semifinals be interdivisional matchups. This would mean that two teams from the same division could advance to the Stanley Cup final, which would make it more likely to be a far more competitive and compelling climax to the NHL season than had been the case in recent years. Chicago would also be moving to the West Division while two further expansion teams would be slotted in the East.

Goaltender Gerry Cheevers was a little less bombastic in his public comments on the topic, but his message was basically the same as Esposito's: Boston was simply too good for St. Louis. He said, "If they [the Blues] could play Red Berenson and three or four others for 60 minutes, it would be a tough hockey game."[5]

Still, Cheevers expressed a degree of caution. "But I am worried about Sunday's game," Cheevers insisted. "Anytime you are anticipating something big, it's always a tough situation. It's a mental thing."[6]

Derek Sanderson concurred with teammates Esposito and Cheevers. He said the series was over after the second game. "I thought this [series] was going to be a lot tougher," Sanderson told reporters after Boston's easy 6–2 triumph. "[St. Louis] didn't throw a check all night. They're known for checking only in the Western Division."[7]

Montreal Gazette columnist Dink Carroll wholeheartedly echoed the Bruins' confident statements the day before Game #4. He wrote, "The Boston–St. Louis series should be over tomorrow afternoon, but it was really over before it started. There are all sorts of new playoff records being set, but they are a little ersatz because a whole new series has been added to the playoffs following expansion. Baseball had a somewhat similar experience [in 1961] when Roger Maris broke Babe Ruth's home run record. The schedule had been lengthened and the pitching diluted."[8]

One Boston scribe strongly chastised the NHL for devaluing the Stanley Cup final. Larry Claflin of the *Boston Record-American* wrote, "The National Hockey League's system of guaranteeing an expansion club a spot in the finals was absurd when it was conceived, and its absurdity has never been more evident than now."[9]

Minnesota general manager Wren Blair, displaying an utter lack of optimism, concurred. "Parity?" he chuckled. "It may take forever as far as I'm concerned."[10]

One article in the *Boston Globe* was devoted to reminding the Hub's hockey fans to behave themselves when the inevitable Cup triumph came. Boston's mayor Kevin White certainly thought a home team win on Sunday, May 10—and the awarding of the Stanley Cup—was a foregone conclusion. He already had made all the necessary arrangements for the Bruins' victory parade to roll through the city on Monday morning.

All the Bruins had to do now was win Game #4 on Sunday afternoon to keep the celebration plans on schedule.

Game #4:
"And What Could Be
Better Than That?"

"When Bobby scored, the yell that I gave, you would have
thought that I was getting killed."[1]
                                        —Phil Esposito

"If there's such a thing as a poetic goal, that was it by young
number four."[2]
                                        —CBS hockey analyst Bill Mazer

At the beginning of the 1970 Stanley Cup finals, hockey journalists
wondered aloud if the underdog St. Louis Blues could extend the Boston
Bruins as they had not extended the Montreal Canadiens in either 1968
or 1969. The Blues did indeed extend the series—by 40 seconds. That was
the length of the sudden-death overtime period in the fourth and deciding game at Boston Garden on Sunday, May 10, 1970. What Game #4's extra
stanza lacked in length it made up for in iconic imagery. No NHL playoff
overtime goal is as famous. None comes close. "You couldn't have written
a better finish,"[3] insisted Derek Sanderson who assisted on Bobby Orr's climactic tally.

By far Game #4 was the best game of a thoroughly one-sided Stanley
Cup final. The Bruins had won the first three games rather handily and were
expected to crush St. Louis for the fourth consecutive time. No one seriously expected a St. Louis comeback. Thus, the television viewers across
North America who tuned in on that Mother's Day afternoon in anticipation of another Boston rout were surprised by the valiant effort put forth
by the outgunned and overmatched Blues. "The mouse roared," wrote
Jimmy Jordan of the *Pittsburgh Post-Gazette*, "but not loud enough or long
enough."[4]

For the Bruins, they knew after the first three games that their triumph was virtually a certainty. Their goal that Sunday was to win the Stanley Cup at home in front of their home fans. That now became the primary motivator for the Bruins in Game #4. "The last thing I wanted to do was go back to St. Louis for the fifth game," Harry Sinden recalled, "because we were going to win that series."[5]

Apart from the famous way the game ended, the most common thing that the players on both teams and the officials seem to remember about that historic afternoon was the scorching temperature. Boston was experiencing unseasonably warm 90-degree temperatures for the second week of May—and old Boston Garden had no air conditioning. "It was hot, hot, hot," recalled St. Louis' Noel Picard. "I lost 13 pounds that game."[6] Referee Bruce Hood said in a 2003 interview, "I remember walking around Boston in the afternoon, and it was so warm, so hot, and there I was getting ready for my first Stanley Cup finals game."[7] Hood had been an NHL referee since 1966.

A festive atmosphere permeated the aging Boston Garden. Every ticketholder expected another convincing Boston win. As it was the second Sunday in May, one thoughtful fan posted a large banner with the message, "Happy Mother's Day, Mrs. Orr." It would be.

All seemed well to the Boston supporters when the Bruins opened the scoring in Game #4 at 5:28 of the first period on a goal from an unlikely source: 22-year-old defenseman Rick Smith, who had scored just twice in 69 regular-season games in the 1969–70 regular season. He beat Glenn Hall with a low drive from between the faceoff circles after Derek Sanderson, who was in an awkward position behind the St. Louis net, had creatively put his stick along the ice and swept the puck to Smith in front of the goal. At the time of Smith's rare tally, both teams had two players seated in the penalty box. It was the only lead Boston would enjoy through regulation time.

It looked like Boston would head to the second period holding a lead, but St. Louis scored an equalizing goal with less than a minute left in the first period. Red Berenson connected at 19:17 with assists going to Bob Plager and Tim Ecclestone. Boston Garden became a little less rowdy heading into the first intermission.

Just 3:22 into the second period, the Blues assumed a lead for just the second time in the series when Gary Sabourin beat Cheevers with a low shot to the stick side from the faceoff circle to Cheevers' left. Frank St. Marseille picked up the only assist on the play. Suddenly St. Louis was in front 2–1 and a Stanley Cup presentation that Sunday was no longer a certainty. Just moments later, Larry Keenan failed to connect on a perfect pass from Terry Crisp with an open Boston net staring him in the face. The Bruins had dodged a bullet.

Referee Bruce Hood's judgment became a factor at the 7:30 mark of the second period. He disallowed an apparent equalizer from Phil Esposito, ruling that the Boston center had hit the puck into the St. Louis net illegally with a high stick. Had the game not ended with a Boston win, Hood's call would have been a major talking point. Today, very few people recall it even happened.

Aggrieved but undaunted, precisely 11 minutes after Sabourin's goal, Phil Esposito got one that counted. He won a faceoff and knocked the puck to Ken Hodge at his right. Hodge returned the favor with a quick return pass. Esposito beat Hall with a waist-high wrist shot to tie the score 2–2. It was his 13th goal of the 1970 playoffs. Boston at least headed into their dressing room after 40 minutes no longer trailing the Blues.

Dallas Smith was penalized for interference at 18:52 of the second period. Boston successfully killed off the first 1:08 of the infraction, but the remaining 52 seconds of Smith's penalty would carry into the third period. The Blues required fewer than 20 of those seconds to retake the lead. Larry Keenan notched his seventh goal of the playoffs after just 19 seconds of play, converting a pass from Jim Roberts. Phil Goyette also picked up an assist. Keenan actually banked the puck into the net off Gerry Cheevers' mask as the Boston goalie slid across the goal crease in a vain attempt to make a spectacular save.

The Bruins put continuous pressure on St. Louis throughout the third period. For a while it appeared that Glenn Hall, who made quite a few sparkling saves, and his defensemen might just thwart a Boston comeback. The Blues even killed off a penalty to Bob Plager in the middle of the period. However, Johnny Bucyk deftly redirected a Johnny McKenzie pass into the top corner of the St. Louis net to level the game 3–3 with 6:32 left on the clock. Overtime beckoned. Boston's line of Bucyk, Fred Stanfield and McKenzie had combined to score 52 points in the Stanley Cup playoffs.

As the final seconds of the third period wound down, Orr picked up the puck in his own zone and embarked on one of his trademark speedy solo dashes into the St. Louis zone to try to decide matters within the regulation 60 minutes. He ended up circling around the St. Louis net looking for a teammate in front of the goal to feed with a pass. None was available. Orr's wraparound attempt was stopped as the buzzer sounded. To this point, the game was about as evenly contested as possible: Each team had scored one goal in every period. Over the three periods of regulation time, both the Blues and the Bruins had managed 31 shots on goal.

When the overtime period was about to begin, Harry Sinden sent his checking line of Ed Westfall, Derek Sanderson and Wayne Carleton onto the ice. There was some strategy behind the curious selection. Sinden figured the longer the overtime lasted, the more likely the Bruins would prevail since they had the stronger and deeper lineup. Therefore, since Sinden assumed Scotty Bowman would put his strongest line on the ice, he reasoned he ought to neutralize it with his defensive specialists and play for time. Backing up his checkers, Sinden put Don Awrey and Bobby Orr on defense. Carleton recalled asking Sinden afterwards why his line had started the overtime period. "He told me it was easy for him to do because we had been the best line on our team for the last three games."[8]

For St. Louis, Scotty Bowman decided to send out the line of Red Berenson, Larry Keenan and Tim Ecclestone with Jean-Guy Talbot and the soon-to-be famous Noel Picard as the defensemen. "Play underway," said Dan Kelly in the CBS broadcasting booth, omitting a verb. "The first team to score wins."[9]

St. Louis won the faceoff to start the fourth period, but the Blues did not possess the puck for very long. Just in front of his own blue line, Bobby Orr intercepted Jean-Guy Talbot's clearing pass along the boards. Orr made a quick pass to Derek Sanderson at center ice. Sanderson propelled the puck into the St. Louis zone. Boston's Wayne Carleton was the first man to get to it.

Dan Kelly then described an iconic moment in hockey history:

> Now Sanderson … a drive … and that one whistled wide. Awrey for the Bruins … tied up by Ecclestone and Berenson. Westfall rolled it in front. Sanderson tried a shot that was wide, and Keenan cleared it but not out. Bobby Orr … behind the net to Sanderson … to Orr! Bobby Orr scores and the Boston Bruins have won the Stanley Cup![10]

Orr had taken a chance on the goal. When Larry Keenan attempted to clear the puck along the boards out of the St. Louis zone, Orr had moved dangerously far inside the blue line to block it and keep it inside the Blues' zone. Ed Westfall sensed the potential danger and was retreating into a defensive position. Nevertheless, had the puck gotten past Orr, the Blues may have been able to move up the ice on a two-on-one or perhaps a three-on-one counterattack.

But the hockey gods were having none of it. The game would end here and now with the appropriate result and climax. Orr stopped Keenan's clearing pass along the boards, and the Bruins swiftly regained the initiative. Orr fed a pass to Sanderson who was stationed behind the goal to Glenn Hall's left. Sanderson recognized what Orr was likely to do—receive a pass on a give-and-go play they had practiced numerous times. Sanderson was correct. After Orr passed the puck to Sanderson, he made a beeline to the front of the St. Louis net. Sanderson passed it back to Orr. Orr knocked it toward the middle of the net. Orr has always maintained that he did not aim his shot; he just wanted to get it somewhere on the net. Hall happened to open his legs as he moved across the goal crease. The puck went between them and hit the center of the net about a foot off the ice. It was Orr's first goal of the final series but his ninth overall during the 1970 Stanley Cup playoffs.

When Orr realized he had scored, he was about to begin a rare celebration. Noel Picard, number four on St. Louis, decided to trip Orr well after the fact. Orr became airborne and sailed for several feet—almost descending beyond the width of the television picture. He crash-landed on the ice where he was quickly engulfed by his excited teammates who came racing off the bench. It was the first time Boston had won a playoff game in overtime since Jerry Toppazzini's goal in Game #2 of the 1958 Stanley Cup semifinals beat the New York Rangers by the same 4–3 score.

Referee Bruce Hood got caught up in the moment too. Although he signaled the Boston goal, in the chaos that followed he neglected a slight technicality in protocol. He recalled,

> We [the officials] went off the ice pretty quickly. Our job was over. The game was over. I was in the dressing room and I realized I never did go to the penalty box to give the score! The truth of the matter is that the referees don't need to announce the goals, but it's just part of the tradition of the game.[11]

Even without Hood's say-so, the goal officially went into the record books as Orr from Sanderson at 40 seconds of overtime. In nearly a century of Bruins hockey, no one has scored a faster overtime goal for Boston in Stanley Cup play than Bobby Orr did on that steamy Sunday afternoon.

Although Dan Kelly's call of Orr's Stanley Cup–winning goal is by far the most familiar play-by-play description of the iconic hockey moment, Fred Cusick's call, made on Boston's WBZ radio broadcast, survives too. (It was thought to have been lost, but surprisingly a recording of it turned up in the station's archives when, decades later, someone was searching for appropriate material to compile a tribute to Orr.) Cusick's description ends with a wonderful rhetorical question:

> Orr fights to keep it in…. Does…. Has it in the corner…. To Sanderson…. Back in front to Orr. Shot! Scores! Bobby Orr from Sanderson! And what could be better than that?[12]

Danny Gallivan's call of Orr's goal for *Hockey Night in Canada* is believed to be lost forever. Preserving sports or television history was not a high priority for networks in either Canada or the United States in 1970—and it would not be for some time. Videotapes of sports events were routinely reused—taped over, that is—as a cost-cutting measure. Retaining old videotapes was also thought to be a pointless waste of valuable storage space.

Dan Kelly's famous call of the deciding goal for CBS survives only due to the actions of WSBK-TV. In 1970 WSBK was an independent Boston television station. It had CBS' permission to simulcast Game #4 live and to rebroadcast the overtime period as part of a Bruins highlight show that aired exactly one week later. Orr's goal was preserved in its archives.

Although other parts of Game #4 exist as part of the NHL's official highlight films, there is no complete version of the CBS *NHL Game of the Week* broadcast from May 10, 1970, known to exist. What a pity.

Years later coach Harry Sinden thoughtfully commented on the spectacular storybook finish to the 1969–70 NHL season:

> I would never have thought of this during the game, but after the fact I thought about how appropriate it was that Bobby scored the goal. It was such a spectacular goal for a defenseman, but in the previous four years he had ushered in a way to play the game that no one had ever played before (or since, for that matter). From the time we entered the league together in 1966 to the time he scored the goal, he changed the way the game was played. No one has ever played like that since. No one.[13]

All sense of order disappeared at Boston Garden when the game ended. "Fans climbed over the plexiglass barriers onto the ice," wrote Pittsburgh hockey journalist Jimmy Jordan. "All manner of debris was showered out of the balconies. The players could hardly get together for the traditional handshake that marks the end of any playoff series."[14] An orderly procession never did truly materialize. The players from both teams gathered in clusters in the St. Louis zone and tried to find each other among the growing mob as best they could to complete the expected sportsmanlike ritual.

Amidst the chaotic scenes unfolding on the ice, Dan Kelly mused, "It must be great to be 22 years of age, and wear the colors of the Boston Bruins, and be the man who scored the overtime goal to bring the Bruins their first Stanley Cup in 29 years."[15] Although employed by CBS for its *NHL Game of the Week* broadcasts, the 33-year-old Kelly was the St. Louis Blues' announcer throughout the regular season. He exuded so much professionalism in his play-by-play of the games that few viewers outside of St. Louis realized one of the teams participating in the Stanley Cup final was Kelly's primary employer. So highly regarded was Kelly for his impartiality (and his magnificent voice) that he worked 16 consecutive Stanley Cup finals for various American and Canadian television networks. All this was accomplished in a truncated life. Kelly died far too young, a victim of lung cancer, on February 10, 1989, at just 52 years of age.

The Blues quietly departed the ice, having now lost 12 consecutive games in the Stanley Cup finals spread over three successive seasons. On the other hand, the Bruins had now won 10 playoff games in a row in the same season. Their last loss was Game #4 of the quarterfinals versus the New York Rangers at Madison Square Garden four weeks earlier on April 12. No other NHL team had achieved that feat before. Of course, an asterisk was necessary. Such a winning streak within one playoff year had only been possible since the league had expanded to two divisions in 1967–68 and increased the number of best-of-seven Stanley Cup playoff rounds from two to three.

Aging NHL president Clarence Campbell needed a police escort to enter the congested ice surface with the table holding the Stanley Cup. He was surrounded by youths when he handed the famed silver trophy over to the Bruins' four assistant captains: Johnny Bucyk, Don Awrey, Ed Westfall and Phil Esposito. (No one on Boston wore the "C" in 1969–70.) The team's most senior player, Bucyk, began a new tradition by skating around the ice with the Stanley Cup raised high above his head, so everyone who had lawfully remained in the stands could get a good look at it. No one had yet come up with the idea of passing the chalice around to each individual player on the winning club.

A touching moment occurred when injured Bruin Ted Green, who had not played a single moment of hockey for Boston since being clubbed by Wayne Maki in the infamous preseason game in Ottawa on September 21, walked onto the ice in street clothes to be part of the Stanley Cup festivities. Several times Green, who was clearly overcome by the emotion of the occasion, wiped tears from his face. For sentimental reasons, Green had his name engraved on the Cup despite having played zero minutes in the 1969–70 regular season and playoffs. (The NHL tightened its rules over such matters the following seasons.) Green would return to the Bruins' roster for the 1970–71 season—wearing a helmet—and not miss a game during the entire 78-game schedule.

Eventually the Bruins retreated from the gleeful disorder on the Boston Garden ice to the expected full-scale mayhem of their dressing room with Bucyk hauling the Stanley Cup with him for safekeeping. Police and Boston Garden ushers jointly prevented jubilant fans from following the team there. Nevertheless, Jimmy Jordan also reported, "Long after most of the fans had left the building, the police had to escort an exuberant fan in Bermuda shorts, possibly a frustrated cheerleader, off the ice."[16]

Leaning against a wall in the Bruins' dressing room, coach Harry Sinden proclaimed, "My God, what a day!" several times to all and sundry. Later, when the tumult died down, Sinden thoughtfully placed a thank-you telephone call to Minnesota North Stars general manager Wren Blair. A decade earlier Blair was the scout who was largely responsible for steering 12-year-old Bobby Orr in the direction of the Boston Bruins.

When asked about the Boston overall dominance of the finals, Sinden noted, "Most of the Bruins' games against the Blues during the past three years had been close, but playing St. Louis [in] a four-of-seven series was easier than playing St. Louis once a month."[17]

The Toronto *Globe & Mail* reported an amusing verbal exchange between a Boston police officer and his dispatcher shortly after the arena started to empty. The policeman phoned in to make a routine report that a large, boisterous crowd was gathering outside Boston Garden. Just six days had passed since the Ohio National Guard had controversially opened fire on demonstrators at Kent State University, so the dispatcher feared something awful was about to unfold in Boston's streets. When she asked the officer if reinforcements were urgently needed, the cop quickly replied, "No, they're not protesting anything. They're celebrating."[18]

Even Noel Picard—whose full name was Joseph Jean-Noel Yves Picard—came to appreciate his trivial niche in Stanley Cup history as the man who sent Bobby Orr sailing into the ether. He was amused by the notoriety of it all. For the 31-year-old Picard, it was the most noteworthy incident in a rather unremarkable seven-year career as an NHL defenseman that ended with the expansion Atlanta Flames in 1972–73. "[Orr's goal] was scored by number four against number four," Picard liked to point out. "If [I'm] going to get scored on, I don't mind as long as it's Bobby Orr. To my mind he was the greatest hockey player in the world."[19] Before Game #4, Picard's most prominent action in the 1970 Stanley Cup finals was twice engaging Wayne Cashman in scuffles in Game #1. Regarding the pointless post-goal trip he applied to Orr, Picard commented, "Those things happen so quickly. My God, he went six feet in the air!"[20] Upon retiring from hockey, Picard worked as a broadcaster for the Blues, and, for a time, operated a restaurant in the small town of Cuba, Missouri. Proving there is a unique kinship among hockey players, years later Orr helped Picard's daughter find lodgings in Boston when she was attending school there. Picard passed away on September 6, 2017, in Montreal at the age of 78.

A day after the clamor, it was announced on Monday, May 11 that Bobby Orr, by vote of the NHL's Board of Governors, had won the Conn Smythe Trophy as the MVP of the 1970 Stanley Cup playoffs. "I wish there were about 19 other guys right here with me,"[21] Orr modestly stated.

The announcement was met with near universal approval. Some hockey writers and broadcasters had suggested Johnny Bucyk or Phil Esposito or even Gerry Cheevers were legitimate contenders for the award too, but 1969–70 was indisputably the year of Bobby Orr. His Bruins had won the Stanley Cup. Individually Orr had harvested the Conn Smythe Trophy, Norris Trophy, Hart Trophy, and Art Ross Trophy. All in all, it was a nice little collection of shiny hardware for the NHL's golden boy. By the end of 1970, Orr had also been named *Sports Illustrated*'s Sportsman of the Year (the first hockey player to be so honored) and Canada's Athlete of the Year. "There is no question," proudly stated Bruins coach Harry Sinden. "Bobby is the best hockey player I have ever seen. He can do more things than anyone who ever put on skates. [He's] just fantastic."[22]

Wrote Bud Collins in the *Boston Globe*, "It is generally agreed that Bobby Orr is the greatest thing since The Pill."[23]

38

A Photo for the Ages

"One image looms above the rest: Ray Lussier's photograph of Bobby Orr immediately after he scored the Stanley Cup–winning goal for the Boston Bruins in Game 4 of the 1970 Finals. The black-and-white image shows Orr in mid-air, hovering above the ice, as all of Boston Garden—all of New England—erupts."

—David Davis, Deadspin.com

"That picture, it's probably one of the top five photographs in sports journalism—not just hockey. It's amazing. It captures the whole thing. It's Bobby Orr's commitment. He's horizontal to the ice. It's the winning goal. It's the whole thing."[1]

—actor Jon Hamm, a longtime fan of the St. Louis Blues

If it had not been for a parched rival photographer who craved a cold beer, one of the most famous photographs in all sports history would not have been captured by Ray Lussier on the humid afternoon of Sunday, May 10, 1970. Numerous hockey photographs have captured airborne players for posterity. What makes Lussier's prize image so special is that it shows a wonderfully joyous, airborne Stanley Cup–winning goal celebration.

Lussier and his trusty camera really had no business being where they were in Boston Garden when Bobby Orr scored his "flying goal" 40 seconds into overtime to clinch the 1970 Stanley Cup for his Bruins. Hockey historian Andrew Podnieks—who wrote an entire book on this one goal and its images—declared Lussier's familiar photo was the result of "serendipitous circumstances."[2] Perhaps, but his positioning was also a quirky combination of selfish moxie, journalistic instincts, street smarts, and the absence of air conditioning in the steamy old arena.

In 1970 Lussier was a capable, 38-year-old photographer employed by the *Boston Record American* who was not particularly well known outside his own newspaper's office. For Game #4 of the Stanley Cup finals, Boston

216

Garden was jammed with media. Lussier was just another member of the fifth estate. News photographers, who generally had free run of the arena at Bruin games, were, on May 10, 1970, instead assigned special stools that had been stationed every few feet along the glass. It was a confining arrangement, but also a very sensible one under the crowded circumstances that day.

Lussier's personal stool was located at the east end of the Garden, where Boston was attacking during the first and third periods. At the beginning of the game, Lussier figured that was the absolute best area of the Garden to be stationed—just in case the Bruins notched a dramatic goal in the third period. When the third period ended with the game level at 3–3, however, Lussier knew he at least had to try to switch his vantage point to the west ends for the overtime period. Lussier and several other wily photographers headed to the other end of the arena while the Zamboni resurfaced the Barden Garden ice surface for period number four—rules and niceties be damned.

With the temperature outside Boston Garden hovering near 90 degrees Fahrenheit, beverage sales were brisk inside Boston Garden that afternoon. By chance, when Lussier changed ends of the arena against the protocols of the day, he came across an empty stool. Its occupant had gone in search of a beer vendor. Lussier decided to temporarily occupy the rightful owner's stool until he made his way back to claim it. He would relinquish it to its rightful occupant upon request, of course. By the time the luckless man (whom Lussier knew but always declined to identify) returned with a refreshing beer in his hands, Orr had already scored the game-winning goal—and Lussier had been positioned perfectly to preserve the dramatic moment on film forever.

"It's all yours," a grinning Lussier coolly told his horribly unlucky colleague. "I've got what I need!"[3] What Lussier got was a sequence of three terrific action photographs. One of them would become the most famous National Hockey League photo ever taken. It captured Boston's number four a fraction of a second after Noel Picard had senselessly sent him airborne after Orr had raised his stick to uncharacteristically celebrate a goal. The photograph appeared in hundreds of daily newspapers the following day. In many of them it graced the front page.

In the subsequent decades, Bobby Orr has signed tens of thousands of autographs. Undoubtedly, the image he has most often affixed his autograph to is Lussier's photograph of his "flying finish." Orr first saw Lussier's photo in the newspaper the next morning when he was having breakfast with his father, Doug, who had traveled from Parry Sound to attend Game #4. Bobby's mother, Arva, remained in Canada. She never watched her son's games in person; she was too nervous. Doug Orr did not see the goal.

He himself had been too antsy to watch the overtime and was lingering in a corridor near the Bruins' dressing room. According to one account, it was CBS' Pat Summerall who told him that his son had scored. When the senior Orr asked the broadcaster why he was so certain his son had been the goal-scorer, Summerall reputedly replied, "Because they wouldn't be yelling this loudly if Esposito had scored!"[4]

"I've told Bobby the game was over long before he landed," said beaten St. Louis goaltender Glenn (Mr. Goalie) Hall, who has also autographed Lussier's photo thousands of times too—sometimes while sitting at the same table as Orr. He happily recalled one financial windfall: "When I played at the [1971] All-Star Game in Boston, every fan had a copy and I got a dollar for every autograph."[5] Hall also is a realist about the daunting, uphill task the Blues faced in 1970 Stanley Cup finals. "We knew if we [St. Louis] played to our potential and [Boston] played to theirs, [Game #4] would have been over in the first period. Geez, [Harry Sinden] must have been saying to them in the dressing room, 'Look at their lineup and look at ours. What are we doing in overtime with these guys?'"[6]

Thirty-seven-year-old Blues defenseman Jean-Guy Talbot was also on the ice when the overtime goal was scored. In Lussier's photo Talbot is the downcast-looking St. Louis player behind his team's net wearing number 17. "We were lucky to make the finals," he declared in an interview years later. "Even if we had won [Game #4], we didn't have the team to beat those guys."[7] By the end of the 1969–70 campaign, Talbot had played in 999 NHL regular-season games. He extended his career one further season—as a member of the expansion Buffalo Sabres—in 1970–71 to surpass the milestone 1,000-game mark. He finished his fine career with 1,056 NHL games on the books.

Noel Picard, who, of course, also prominently appears in all the photographic versions of Orr's goal, concurred with his goalie and defense partner Talbot.

> We had a good family team, but with the team we played against, we were lucky to get into overtime with them. If we could have had one player to score goals, it would have made a difference. But Boston had Esposito, Hodge, Cashman, Bucyk and Sanderson, so eventually they're going to score goals. We had good players, but they were all old.[8]

Interestingly, several other news photographers got similar shots of Orr's goal. In fact, one image taken by Fred Keenan of the *Quincy Patriot Ledger* was deemed the best of the bunch; it was voted best photograph of 1970 by the Boston Press Photographers Association. Most photography buffs would likely give the nod to Keenan's picture as being superior to Lussier's. Keenan's photo, unlike Lussier's, clearly shows the puck slamming into the mesh and Orr just on the rise as Picard lifts him skyward.

Andrew Podnieks noted, "Shooting with a Nikon F and without a flash, Keenan produced a sequence that seems to indicate that he knew a goal was going to be scored and he knew how it would be scored, so perfect are the moments of each frame."[9] Keenan and Lussier were standing beside each other when Orr scored. Lussier's photo was more widely circulated simply because the *Boston Herald American* was a much larger and far more renowned newspaper than the *Quincy Patriot Ledger*. Keenan continued to specialize as a sports photographer for his newspaper until 1984. Keenan passed away in 1997.

Fame is fleeting. Lussier too worked as a sports photographer for the *Herald American* until 1980. (The *Herald American* lives on today as the *Boston Herald*.) Late in Lussier's life he worked with little fanfare as a microfilm camera operator at a document preservation center in Andover, Massachusetts. In 1990, Orr personally invited Lussier and his wife to a 20th anniversary reunion party for the 1969–70 Bruins. He died on March 19, 1991, the victim of a heart attack, at the young age of 59.

One of the few known color photos of Orr's goal was taken by an amateur—a fan named Ernie Cormier who decided to bring his slide camera to Boston Garden that day in hopes of recording something significant. He took only a few pictures during regulation time, but, as Andrew Podnieks wrote, "When overtime started he readied his camera because history seemed so close as to be almost tactile, predictable."[10]

Cormier was seated in the first row of the second balcony with his wife and a friend among the Garden's Gallery Gods. "I saw Bobby Orr keep the puck in the zone. He started skating toward the direction of the net, not in a straight line but in that direction, and I thought, 'Wow! Something might happen.' So I put the camera up to my face and centered it on the net. The instant the red [goal] light came on, I hit the shutter."[11]

When Cormier got home he put his camera on a shelf and forgot about it for a while. "Because [slide] developing was expensive, I had to be selective in how many pictures I took. I didn't get the film developed right away. I was just married and had a kid on the way."[12] When he finally did get his Ektachrome slide film developed, Cormier noticed a remarkable coincidence: His picture had been snapped at precisely the same moment that Ray Lussier's famous news photo had been taken, albeit from considerably farther away and from a different angle.

Still it is Ray Lussier's photograph that remains the iconic one half a century after it was snapped from that purloined stool. In his biography of Bobby Orr, author Stephen Brunt explained its eye-catching quality:

…That image, frozen in one of the greatest sports photographs ever captured, was singular and spectacular and laden with symbolism. Bobby Orr, taking off. And rather than bracing for the moment when gravity would surely reassert itself, rather than panicking at the sudden loss of control, in midair, in mid-flight, he exults, lifting both his arms to the heavens. Life is suspended, physics defied. What you see in that picture, in that illusion, is magic.[13]

In 1999, Orr's overtime goal was deemed the greatest moment in NHL history by a panel of sportswriters who covered the league on a regular basis.

On Monday, May 10, 2010, on the fortieth anniversary of Boston's 1970 Stanley Cup triumph, a huge bronze statue was unveiled in front of TD Garden—the Bruins' home building since 1995. It depicts the airborne Bobby Orr celebrating the most iconic moment of the franchise whose rich history dates back to 1924. Ray Lussier's photo was used as its model. Derek Sanderson was on hand to provide another assist, of sorts. He introduced number four, his old teammate.

Sculpted by artist Harry Weber, the piece is officially called "The Goal." Locals usually refer to it as the Bobby Orr Statue.

PART V

Denouement

39

Celebrations

"We [the on-ice officials] were supposed to catch a 7 o'clock
flight that [Sunday] night. We got home on Tuesday! We
partied with the people in Boston. The town was pretty
happy!"[1]
—Ron Ego, one of the two NHL linesmen who
worked Game #4 of the Stanley Cup final

"A silversmith used a mallet to pound the names [of the
players] into the Stanley Cup, but the players themselves
pounded the memories into our hearts forever."[2]
—Bruins announcer Andy Brickey's remarks during
the club's 40th anniversary tribute to the
1970 Stanley Cup Champions in 2010

"You could tell Boston loved their Bruins, and I can tell you
the Bruin players loved those Boston fans as well."[3]
—Bobby Orr

Having waited 29 long years for the Stanley Cup to return to Boston,
the city's residents—along with thousands of Bruin fans from near and
far—celebrated their team's triumph wildly. Wasting no time, the official
Stanley Cup parade began less than 24 hours after Game #4 had ended—at
10 o'clock in the morning on Monday, May 11. Happy disorder and outright
chaos were the themes of the joyous day for the Bruins and their supporters. Derek Sanderson recalled the raucous scene in his 2012 autobiography,
Crossing the Line:

A parade through downtown Boston was held the next morning ... and concluded at
Government Center Plaza in front of City Hall. It was insane. There were more people in one place than I had ever seen before. Girls were throwing their bras at our cars
during the parade. There were so many fans crowding the platform that they couldn't
do the presentations, so they moved us inside City Hall. Mayor Kevin White presented
all of us with Paul Revere water pitchers. Johnny McKenzie filled one with beer and
dumped it on the mayor's head. Thank goodness Mayor White was a good sport![4]

About two months later, Orr was individually feted back in Parry Sound on July 6. As usual he did not like to be singled out for special attention, but the testimonial dinner was part of a local fund-raising drive to build a new community center, so the modest hockey hero could hardly say no. He reluctantly agreed to be the main attraction. Milt Schmidt and a handful of number four's Boston teammates made the long trip to be part of Bobby Orr Day. So did Terry Crisp and Gary Sabourin of the St. Louis Blues. They also hailed from Parry Sound, and they too were bona fide NHL hockey players. Both were five years older than Orr. Crisp had begun his NHL career in Boston, playing three games for the Bruins in 1965–66. St. Louis had selected the unprotected Crisp from Boston's roster in the 1967 expansion draft.

There was another parade, of course. It was certainly smaller and less boisterous than the May 11 hoopla in Boston, but just as enthusiastic on a lesser scale. An enormous and heavy 40-foot hockey stick, created especially for the occasion, was carried by a group of burly young men at the front of the procession. (Afterwards, unsure what was to become of the large chunk of lumber, the men simply propped it up against a side wall of the Orr home. It remained there for many years as an odd curiosity.) The guest of honor rode in an open convertible and shook hands with just about everyone who reached towards him. A group of excited boys followed the vehicle on foot for the entire parade route. Later, a throng of approximately 500 people gladly paid a princely $10 per plate for a dinner of cold cuts and macaroni, served banquet-style, in the gymnasium of Parry Sound High School. Undoubtedly, for years afterward, many of the attendees would proudly boast that one summer's evening in 1970 they had dined with Bobby Orr on Bobby Orr Day in the hometown of Bobby Orr. Accompanying the guest of honor was Margaret Louise (Peggy) Wood, a Detroit-born speech therapist whom Orr had met in Florida. They would be married in 1973.

Bobby's paternal grandmother Elsie, still actively employed as a nurse, was asked by a reporter if she was proud of her grandson. She had a rehearsed answer at the ready for such a trite and predictable question. "Which one?" she coyly asked. "I have three grandsons."[5]

40

Michel Brière

An Athlete Dying Young

"[Pittsburgh] had a guy, and God rest his soul, this guy, this
kid could have been one of the greatest of all time. This kid
was 20 years old and he played against the Seals in the playoffs, and he killed us."[1]
—Oakland Seals fan Larry Schmidt recalling
Michel Brière's play in the 1970 Pittsburgh–Oakland
quarterfinal nearly five decades later

The time you won your town the race
We chaired you through the market-place;
Man and boy stood cheering by,
And home we brought you shoulder-high.

Today, the road all runners come,
Shoulder-high we bring you home,
And set you at your threshold down,
Townsman of a stiller town.

—From the 1896 A.E Housman poem
"To an Athlete Dying Young"

Five days after Bobby Orr's goal clinched the Stanley Cup for the Boston Bruins, a terrible tragedy occurred on a highway in the province of
Quebec. It involved Pittsburgh's promising young star center Michel Brière.

Brière was the Penguins' second-round pick in the 1969 amateur draft.
In junior hockey he had scored 129 goals for the Shawinigan Bruins in just
100 games. At the Penguins' training camp in September 1969, coach Red
Kelly remembered, "[Brière] was showing me moves you can't put into a
hockey player."[2] Brière had just finished his rookie season with Pittsburgh
but he had an impact larger than his statistics might show. He appeared
in all 76 of his team's regular-season games, scored 12 goals, and recorded
32 assists for 44 points. Brière's assist total was good enough to lead the

Penguins. He added five more goals and three assists during the Stanley Cup playoffs, including the series-clinching overtime goal versus Oakland. Brière, who weighed only about 150 pounds, suffered considerable physical abuse from much larger opponents, but he endured—largely because of his natural talents on the ice that made him tough to stop.

Roy McHugh of the *Pittsburgh Press* noted, "Brière skated easily. He skimmed across the ice like a water bug, not with great speed but with phantom elusiveness, deftly avoiding body checks, probing and questing for the puck. His shot was quick rather than powerful, coming invariably when the goaltender least expected it, preceded, as likely as not, by a feint, by a dip of the shoulder."[3]

McHugh continued, "The heavies of the league, taking him for a pipsqueak, were impatient to lean on Brière. They would chase him right out of the rink, they told themselves with a smirk. But when the moment came to lean, they'd be leaning, quite often, against nothing. Brière would have slithered away. In Philadelphia one night, two Flyers took a run at Brière, collided head on, and knocked each other out."[4] Teammate Jean Pronovost said Brière looked like a little boy, but was impressive on the ice. Coach Red Kelly agreed. "When he picked up that puck, you knew things could happen. You felt he could take it down and it would end up in the other guys' net."[5]

McHugh also recalled an endearing degree of shyness in Brière. When the scribe mentioned to the young Penguin that he would soon be signing as many autographs as Gordie Howe, Brière noticeably blushed at the idea.

Brière was a coach's dream—a player who was always ready to listen and learn. He told Dink Carroll of the *Montreal Gazette*, "I feel very bad about some of the draws I miss [as a center]. But coach Kelly is very patient with me. That is one of the great things about him. He never yells; he just points out your mistakes. And, in the beginning, I made plenty of stupid mistakes."[6]

During the 1970 Stanley Cup playoffs, St. Louis coach Scotty Bowman tried to contain Brière with his burliest defensive twosome: Noel Picard and Bob Plager. They had little success. A common sight during the Blues–Penguins playoff series, McHugh recalled "was Brière skating towards the goal while the two St. Louis bad boys were sprawled on the ice in his wake."[7] Brière scored three game-winning goals for Pittsburgh during the 1970 postseason.

It was hoped in Pittsburgh that Brière would become the face of the young NHL franchise in a city where hockey clearly lagged behind baseball, college football and pro football in fan support. He was well on his way to doing it. "Finally, after three years, the people who do support hockey here had a young star to identify with," noted Bill Heufelder of the *Pittsburgh*

Press. "He gave the building a whole lift. Attendance was picking up. He was becoming their idol."[8]

After the Penguins were eliminated by St. Louis in the Stanley Cup semifinals, the 20-year-old Brière headed back to his small hometown of Malartic, in northwestern Quebec, to marry Michele Beaudoin, his childhood sweetheart. The couple already had a child, a son named Martin. The wedding date was set for Saturday, June 6. It was not to be.

At about 9 p.m. on the evening of Friday, May 15, Brière was riding in his flashy, burnt-orange 1970 Mercury Cougar along Route 117 in Val-d'Or, Quebec, about 70 miles from Malartic. He and two others were returning from a trip to Rivière-Héva, a nearby town. Brière had purchased the vehicle in Pittsburgh shortly after arriving there. There was still daylight at the time of the accident and the road was clear, police would later assert. Brière's vehicle may have been speeding. It also may have hit a frost-covered patch of the road. Be that as it may, the car failed to negotiate a curve. An investigating officer noted the bend in the highway was notoriously bad; a fatal accident had occurred there two years earlier.

Renald Eilodeau and Yvon Fortin were also in the car. (Whether Brière was driving was initially unclear. Red Kelly stated in an interview that Brière was a backseat passenger. Later news reports would claim Brière had been behind the wheel.) Eilodeau, 22, described as Brière's best friend in subsequent news stories, luckily escaped with just a few lacerations to his face and arms. Fortin, a 28-year-old teacher, suffered five broken ribs. Their injuries were considerably less serious than those Brière received. The hockey player was ejected from the wrecked vehicle which rolled over at least once before landing upright on the highway. He seemed nearly unmarked by the crash, but Brière suffered a fractured skull and major internal head trauma. Quebec did not have mandatory seatbelt laws in 1970—and would not for another six years.

The automobile crash was a two-pronged tragedy: On the way to rushing the severely injured Briere to a local hospital in Val d'Or, the ambulance struck and killed Reauld Perreault, a luckless 18-year-old cyclist, who, according to police, lost control of his bicycle and veered into the speeding ambulance's path. Brière was eventually transported to Notre Dame Hospital in Montreal by fighter jet where the province's leading neurosurgeons were available to examine him. The first of four delicate brain surgeries was performed by Dr. Claude Bertrand. Despite the best medical treatment available, doctors told Brière's family his prognosis for survival was, at best, a 50/50 proposition, although the medical team said youth and vigor were Brière's allies. He was comatose. Newspapers, especially those in Pittsburgh, presented an unrealistically optimistic picture. "Brière Listed as Satisfactory," declared a hopeful headline in the *Pittsburgh Post-Gazette* on May 18.

Red Kelly was devastated by the news from Quebec, but he did cite some recent NHL history for optimism. He reminded reporters that Boston's Ted Green was thought to have suffered a fatal head injury in September but, after undergoing brain surgery, was on his way to a full recovery. "All you can do is pray, I guess, and hope for the best,"[9] Kelly said.

News of the accident, of course, shocked sports fans in Pittsburgh. Most affected were the members of the Hodill family. In junior hockey circles in Canada, it is common for players to be billeted with local families when they are playing for teams far away from home. The Hodill family in Pittsburgh extended the courtesy to the young pro player by sharing their home with Brière. Family patriarch Bill Hodill acted as a substitute father figure for Brière who was residing away from Quebec for the first time. Hodill struggled with French names, so he referred to Brière with the anglicized version—"Mike"—rather than Michel. (Typical of the times, the Pittsburgh media often did too.) Brière adapted quickly to his surrogate family. "I remember the very first day we brought him home," Hodill recalled. "After we showed him around, we couldn't find him. He was playing touch football with the kids in a field."[10]

A few weeks prior the crash, Hodill lectured Brière about automobile safety. Hodill knew Brière loved to drive, but he was concerned about Brière's inexperience behind the wheel—especially on major thoroughfares. Hodill informed Ted Blackman of the *Montreal Gazette*, "When Roger Haberg of the Oakland Raiders was killed in a car crash [on April 15], I spent a lot of time talking to Mike. I just wanted him to be so careful. I used to take him out in my car on the turnpike here and check him out with questions about the road."

Hodill continued, "[Brière] is just so dedicated to hockey. I guess everyone figured he was the swinging bachelor, but he didn't go out three times in the seven months he was with us. Most of the time he'd go out with us to dinner and a movie. All he thought about was staying in shape and being ready to play hockey."[11] Brière was especially terrific with Hodill's three young sons. They loved having a prominent athlete in their home.

Whenever the Penguins played in Montreal the following season, Kelly frequently visited the hospital, just to hold Brière's hand. Brière could not talk, but sometimes he would open his eyes and turn his head.

More than ten months after the crash, Brière was transferred to another facility in Montreal, the Marie-Clarac Rehabilitation Hospital. Nearly three weeks later, on April 13, 1971, Brière was pronounced dead at 4:20 p.m. without ever truly regaining his senses. The *Calgary Herald* did note, however, that "during his stay in hospital, Brière regained enough consciousness to be able to recognize certain familiar people, such as Dick Goss, the man who scouted him for the Pittsburgh club. Brière was also able to recognize his parents and his sister."[12] According to a hospital spokesman, Brière "died a fighting death."[13] The Canadian Press story about Brière's passing plainly stated that the hockey player was indeed driving the Cougar when the accident occurred. (It also mentioned, wrongly, that a passenger in Brière's car had died in the mishap.)

Brière had turned 21 on October 21, 1970. He died while the first round of the 1971 Stanley Cup playoffs was underway. Without Brière in the lineup, Pittsburgh did not qualify for the playoffs in the season directly following his car accident. In fact, they would not be part of postseason play again until the 1974–75 campaign.

In Pittsburgh, Red Kelly was saddened but not at all surprised by the news. He had been receiving discouraging bulletins about Brière's declining condition for some time. "It's hard to say it this way, but we have been expecting it," Kelly noted, "so when the end came it was with a feeling of relief. Mike is better off and so is his family. It's so sad. Mike was so young, with a full life ahead of him."[14] Kelly and several members of the Penguins attended Brière's funeral service just outside Montreal. In Pittsburgh, a memorial service was held at St. Paul's Cathedral. It was well attended by Penguin club officials and players.

When the Penguins gathered near Brantford, Ontario for their training camp prior to the 1970–71 season, Brière's future was still uncertain. Tactfully, his number 21 was immediately made unavailable for any other Pittsburgh player by trainer Ken Carson, the man responsible for assigning jerseys to Penguin newcomers. Brière's equipment bag travelled with the Penguins during the entire 1970–71 season as a reminder that he was still part of the team. Carson recalled that over the ten seasons he worked for the hockey club, nobody ever specifically asked to wear #21. Had anyone done so, Carson said he would have explained why it was in limbo. Still, the number was not formally retired by the club until January 5, 2001. As of 2020, only two Penguins have had their jerseys retired: Brière and Mario Lemieux. At the end of each season the club presents an award in Brière's name to the team's top rookie. In 1972, the Quebec Major Junior Hockey League renamed its MVP award the Michel Brière Memorial Trophy.

In 2006, hockey blogger Joe Pelletier discussed Brière's brief and oh-so-promising NHL career: "We are left only to wonder how good Brière could have been, and how he could have changed the landscape of hockey history in Pittsburgh forever," Pelletier ruefully summarized. "The Penguins seemed to toil for years without their French-Canadian star until 1985 when they picked up another French sensation: Mario Lemieux. Had Brière been able to play during all those years in between, perhaps the Penguins might not have been as bad as they were."[15]

41

An Unexpected Resignation

"There's no doubt now that the Bruins will offer Sinden a rich new contract when the playoffs have ended."[1]
—Pat Curran, writing in the April 28, 1970, issue of the *Montreal Gazette*

"It is difficult, really, to believe a guy in Sinden's position would quit. He coached the Boston Bruins to their first Stanley Cup since 1941, his contract was up for renegotiation, the team is a cinch to say at or near the top for a long, long time, and Sinden gave it up."[2]
—Bob Mellor, *Ottawa Citizen* sports columnist

Almost as startling as the sad news about Michel Brière was the shocking announcement out of Boston on Thursday, May 14 that Harry Sinden was resigning as coach of the newly crowned Stanley Cup champions. Declared one startled scribe, "Sinden's announcement, at a hurriedly called news conference, was a shocker to everyone, including the Bruins' brass, who were still savoring the sweetness of the club's first Stanley Cup in 29 years."[3]

Sinden was just 37 years old. He had been the Bruins' coach for four seasons. The 1966–67 campaign was another in a string of disasters for Boston, but the Bruins showed dramatic improvement in the NHL's expansion era. Sinden had control of a team that obviously seemed poised to be very good for a considerable time. Some hockey people simply could not fathom why Sinden was quitting under those circumstances.

Among them was Wren Blair, a onetime Bruins scout who, in 1970, was both the general manager and the coach of the Minnesota North Stars. He publicly said Sinden could have the coaching job with the North Stars—with his blessing—anytime he asked for it. Blair had known and respected Sinden for more than a dozen years, dating back to their amateur hockey days.

In simple terms, Sinden wanted more money; he passionately felt he deserved it. The Bruins were not prepared to offer him what he wanted.

It tuned out that a difference of $5,000 drove Sinden from Boston. (He wanted an $8,000 raise; the Bruins made a counter-offer of $3,000, which Sinden perceived as insulting.) By NHL standards of the time, it was not a minuscule sum. The folks who handled the Bruins' payroll matters during the early 1970s were never known for their profligate ways. "I have never liked coyness," Sinden stated, "and I have never negotiated when I felt I was in a solid position."[4]

Sinden's relationship with Bruins ownership had quietly but steadily deteriorated over the course of the 1969–70 season—and apparently was never exceptionally good at any time. Sinden truly thought his talents were being undervalued and underappreciated. The Bruins were startled by Sinden's surprising hardline response against salary negotiation and quickly put him on the Bruins "voluntarily retired list." This meant that Sinden was forbidden to work for another NHL team for at least a year. With at least 365 days to kill, Sinden accepted a non-hockey job with a Rochester, New York, construction company—the Stirling Homex Corporation. It specialized in building modular homes.

With thousands of hockey fans wondering why he was no longer the coach of the Boston Bruins, Sinden also penned a feature article for the October 19, 1970, issue of *Sports Illustrated* titled "No Room at the Top for Me." In it Sinden outlined his decision to resign his position. It contained some surprising revelations. The piece basically said he had decided to quit the team when he was told he would not be getting the raise he desired for the 1970–71 season. Sinden also expressed his displeasure at being kept totally in the dark about the biggest trade in Bruins history: the deal that brought Phil Esposito, Ken Hodge and Fred Stanfield to Boston from Chicago on May 15, 1967. Surprisingly, Sinden had no inkling such a deal was even in the works. He got the startling news via a telephone call from Milt Schmidt—while presenting awards at an amateur sports banquet—telling him the huge player transaction had been completed. "This was the first time I realized a Bruin coach was not a member of management's inner circle,"[5] he bitterly noted.

Sinden declared that other incidents of "disharmony" irked him during his four seasons behind the Bruins' bench. "For example," he wrote, "I learned that sometimes when I fined a player for some offense, the club did not deduct the amount from his paycheck. This made me look ridiculous to the players, who knew they could violate my rules without losing their money."[6]

The *Sports Illustrated* article concluded with Sinden declaring, "I'll miss hockey. I know that. It was my life for more than 20 years. But I'm leaving a winner—the coach of the Stanley Cup champions—and that is the way to go."[7]

With Sinden gone, speculation ran wild as to who might wind up behind the Boston bench for the 1970–71 season. Few observers thought that 52-year-old Bruins general manager Milt Schmidt would return to handling the team's coaching duties as he had done, with a one-year hiatus, from 1955 to 1966. Murray Davidson, the coach of Boston's Oklahoma City farm team, was suggested as Sinden's replacement, as was former Toronto bench boss Punch Imlach. Injured defenseman Ted Green was nominated as a practical candidate. An Associated Press scribe commented, "Teddy sat out the season after suffering a fractured skull in a stick-swinging duel with Wayne Maki in an exhibition game in September. Green's future as a player is still a question mark. He reportedly has another year remaining on his contract, which pays him about $35,000 per season. It would save the Bruins a lot of loot if Green, unable to play, was named coach."[8]

When it was legally permissible to do so, the Toronto Maple Leafs, St. Louis Blues, and the expansion New York Islanders all offered Sinden a chance to coach in the NHL again. He politely declined all three opportunities. Instead, in June 1972, Sinden was persuaded to take a sabbatical from Stirling Homex and accept the short-term position from Hockey Canada to be the head coach of Team Canada—an outstanding assemblage of NHL all-stars—for their eight-game series versus the Soviet Union's national team in September 1972. (Sinden had experience in international hockey. He had played on a Canadian team—the Whitby Dunlops—that beat the Soviet Union to win the International Ice Hockey Federation world amateur championship 1958.) What occurred in September 1972 was a groundbreaking, epic, riveting encounter, replete with high drama, plot twists and marvelous hockey, that saw the Canadian squad win the final three games in Moscow to emerge victorious by the narrowest of margins. To this day, the Summit Series (as it came to be known) routinely tops polls as the most memorable sports event in Canadian history. Sinden received high praise for skillfully managing a roster of 40 players—many with large egos—brought together for the first time, and turning them into a tight-knit, cohesive, winning team.

Partway through the series, Sinden learned that Stirling Homex Corporation had gone bankrupt. Within days of returning to North America, the newly unemployed Sinden returned to Boston and signed a five-year deal to be the Bruins' new general manager. (Milt Schmidt was moved upward to a senior executive director position with the club.) Sinden would prominently hold that job with the Bruins for the next 28 seasons.

42

The Strange Death
of Terry Sawchuk

"Sawchuk, who was notably a star with the Detroit Red
Wings, was one of hockey's greatest goalies in his prime
despite a life plagued by emotional and drinking problems."[1]
—Ronald Goldstein, *New York Times*

"I played against Terry in the old Central Hockey League
and in the American League. He is the greatest goaltender I've ever seen. And nothing is ever going to change my
mind."[2]
—Emile Francis

On Wednesday, April 29, 1970, Ron Stewart and Terry Sawchuk, teammates on the New York Rangers, were preparing to close the house the twosome had shared on Long Island's East Atlantic Beach during the 1969–70
NHL season. Both men were divorced. Their season had ended on Thursday, April 16 with the Rangers' disappointing and hard-fought quarterfinal
loss in six games to the Boston Bruins.

Before they began the task, Stewart and Sawchuk went to a local bar,
the E&J Pub, separately. Stewart arrived first. Each man was well known
there. Neither had ever caused trouble before. Details of what transpired
between the two New York Rangers are more than a bit sketchy, but with
the libations flowing freely, a heated argument ensued. Bartender Joe
Craine said the confrontation was due to "bad blood." The dispute escalated
from words to actions. The two men started shoving each other. Craine had
to restrain the men twice and finally asked them to leave.

They calmed down long enough to travel back to their Long Island
house together, but round two of the lively confrontation soon began
anew. This time the shoving became more vigorous. According to some
versions, Sawchuk may have been pushed over a barbecue or stumbled
over a barbecue pit. Whatever the case, Sawchuk ended up falling violently
onto Stewart's knee. Sawchuk was seriously hurt. The impact severely

injured the goalie's liver and gall bladder. He was transported to Long Beach Memorial Hospital with severe abdominal injuries where he had his gall bladder removed. The liver damage was even more serious. Sawchuk's misadventure and subsequent hospitalization were kept quiet for a long time. (Apparently Sawchuk's father had been hospitalized in Detroit, and the goaltender did not want to worry him.) When it became known, however, Stewart initially said he had nothing whatsoever to do with Sawchuk's injuries and further claimed Sawchuk being hospitalized was news to him. Later he changed his story when there was a possibility that he could face criminal charges. The Rangers hired a lawyer to assist Stewart if any legal ramifications did arise.

Sawchuk was eventually transferred to Manhattan's New York Hospital. Over the course of the next month, Sawchuk endured three operations to stop internal bleeding in that organ. He succumbed to a pulmonary embolism—a blood clot—on Sunday, May 31. Thus ended the troubled existence of one of professional hockey's most accomplished goalies. Sawchuk was only 40 years old but his years had been strenuous ones. As with any death by misadventure, an official investigation followed. Nassau County district attorney William Cahn called Sawchuk's curious death "tragic, senseless and bizarre."[3]

In Canada, Sawchuk's death was front-page news in most daily newspapers. Many carried this official statement form Emile Francis:

> The death of Terry Sawchuk is a tragic and shocking loss to hockey in general and the Rangers in particular. His record speaks for itself. He was one of the greatest of them all. The entire Rangers family extends its condolences to Terry's family.[4]

Francis was notified of Sawchuk's death. Somehow the ordeal of claiming the body fell to him. It was not a pleasant experience. "They called me at six in the morning to tell me he had died," Francis recalled. "I'll never forget it was Memorial Day weekend in New York and I had to go to get his body from the morgue on Second Avenue. Honest to God, there were 30 people lying on the floor in bags like we carry hockey sticks in. The guy who took me down there, I could tell he'd been drinking; I could smell it. He said, 'Okay, which one is the body you came to claim?' I looked over and I see Terry's head sticking out from one of the bags with a tag around his neck to identify him. God damn, that's where he ended up: on the floor in a morgue in New York City on Memorial Day weekend! And I said to myself, if this guy only knew that's the greatest goalkeeper ever…"[5]

According to a great many of hockey's most respected historians, Sawchuk was indeed the greatest netminder of all time. Today Sawchuk is best known to hockey buffs for his 103 career regular-season shutouts. That impressive figure was an NHL record until Martin Brodeur surpassed it in

2009. Sawchuk had held the record since 1964 when he overtook George Hainsworth's longstanding mark of 94. (Hainsworth's last season was 1936–37.)

Sawchuk ended up playing for five different NHL clubs over 21 seasons. He was elected to the Hockey Hall of Fame in 1971, a year after his death. That same year Sawchuk was posthumously awarded the Lester Patrick Trophy for his contributions to the growth of the sport in the United States. The Red Wings retired his #1 jersey in 1994. In 2010, *The Hockey News* ranked Sawchuk as the number-one NHL goaltender of all time.

On March 17, 2012, Ron Stewart passed away from cancer in British Columbia at the age of 79. His death prompted Ronald Goldstein of the *New York Times* to revisit the strange circumstances of Terry Sawchuk's demise. Goldstein interviewed 85-year-old Emile Francis. He asked the Rangers' ex-coach and general manager what he recalled about the odd Stewart–Sawchuk incident 42 years earlier. Francis said that when he visited Sawchuk in the hospital, "[Sawchuk] said: 'It wasn't Ron Stewart's fault; don't blame him. I was the aggressor in the whole thing.'" Goldstein elaborated:

> By Sawchuk's account, Francis said, the arguing began when Sawchuk told Stewart that he owed him $8 on a phone bill. But Dr. Denis F. Nicholson, a physician for a number of Rangers families, said at the time that Sawchuk had told him that he punched Stewart at the bar because he "had been bugging him all year" and that he jumped Stewart at the house "and I fell on his knee."[6]

A Nassau County grand jury concurred. Sawchuk's death was ruled to have been an accident. Ron Stewart was absolved of all blame. Hockey writers and other journalists began calling Sawchuk's death the tragic result of "horseplay."

Years later hockey journalist Trent Frayne said of Sawchuk, "I think Terry knew he wasn't going to live very long. He had a fatalistic attitude about him. He was always gloomy. He didn't seem to enjoy life."[7]

Francis said Stewart never spoke to him about the incident. It is known, however, that Stewart visited Sawchuk at least twice in the hospital. Stewart was reluctant to attend Sawchuk's funeral in Pontiac, Michigan, but Francis persuaded him to go with other members of the Rangers. "You're coming with us," Francis told Stewart. "You've got nothing to hide from."[8] In the end, Stewart served as an honorary pallbearer during the rites.

Years later Francis admitted he kept the aging Stewart on the Rangers' roster for one more season solely because of the circumstances. He did not wish to release or trade Stewart because the action might be perceived as something akin to an ostracism. Sawchuk's death was a touchy subject for the entire club during the 1970–71 season. Francis remembered one incident outside Maple Leaf Gardens in Toronto when the Rangers were boarding a bus. A heckler called Stewart "a murderer." Vic Hadfield angrily rushed off the vehicle and roughly flung the man into a snowbank.

After retiring as a player following the 1972–73 season, Ron Stewart became a coach. He led Springfield to an American Hockey League title in 1974–75 and was subsequently named head coach of the New York Rangers for 1975–76, replacing Emile Francis who had given up the team's coaching duties. Stewart signed a three-year deal but did not last even half a season behind the New York bench. He was dismissed after just 39 games with the team sporting a disappointing 15–20–4 record. Stewart was given the ax on January 7, 1976—the day after Emile Francis was fired as the Rangers' general manager.

43

Social Notice

Say, Who's That Fellow Dating Bernie Geoffrion's Daughter?

The June 1, 1970, edition of the *Montreal Gazette*'s sports section had an item that was probably best suited for the newspaper's society pages. It was a large photograph of pretty Linda Geoffrion, the blonde-haired daughter of former Montreal Canadiens great Bernie (Boom Boom) Geoffrion.

Linda, dressed elegantly in a formal, eye-catching white gown, was heading to her graduation dance accompanied by a distinguished and prominent young bachelor—Robert Gordon Orr, presently of Boston, Massachusetts, and formerly of Parry Sound, Ontario. Orr, nattily decked out in a tuxedo, was standing to the right of the beaming Linda in the photo. It was taken on "the youngsters' first date," according to the caption. The handsome couple had been introduced when the Boston Bruins played a road game at the Forum in Montreal this past NHL season.

The photo caption also noted that Linda's maternal grandfather was the late Howie Morenz, another all-time hockey great and Hall of Famer.

44

The NHL's Tiebreaker and Divisional Realignment

"Every sporting event implies an offense and a defense. This [tiebreaking] system wasn't previously tested, but it showed no defense was required. It's not the way to play."[1]
—NHL president Clarence S. Campbell, explaining why the league's tiebreaker system needed tweaking.

The champagne in the Boston Bruins' dressing had hardly lost its fizz when changes to the NHL for 1970–71 were being discussed. There were obvious problems that needed to be resolved over the summer.

St. Louis' third trip to the final round of the playoffs without winning a game—they actually did not outscore the Bruins in any of the 13 periods in the series—conclusively proved that the league's postseason format was preventing the two best teams from advancing to the Stanley Cup finals each spring. The climactic end to the NHL season had been once again largely anticlimactic in 1970. Something had to be done to rectify the problem—and it was. Thanks to the addition of two new NHL expansion teams, the process was made a little bit easier.

The Buffalo Sabres and Vancouver Canucks entered the NHL in 1970–71, thus making the league a 14-team circuit. In its wisdom, the NHL decided to put both new teams in the East Division. (Yes, contrary to logic, Vancouver somehow was placed in the East—and had a brutal travel schedule because of it—while the Chicago Black Hawks were shifted to the weaker West. No longer would all the "Original Six" NHL teams ever compete in the same division again. Despite the obvious realities of geography, Philadelphia and Pittsburgh remained in the West Division.) Thus, the NHL's two divisions now had seven members apiece. More importantly, the six 1967 expansion teams now had the Black Hawks as company. Furthermore, the semifinal round of the playoffs would feature inter-divisional matchups. No longer was the Stanley Cup final guaranteed to be a matchup between a team from the East and the West. (As it turned out, the Stanley

237

Cup finals in 1971 went the full seven games, the first time that had happened since 1965.) Even when the NHL expanded to 16 teams for 1972–73 with the addition of the Atlanta Flames and New York Islanders, it kept its format of an East Division and a West Division. For two seasons it was possible to finish a distant eighth place (which the California Golden Seals and New York Islanders did twice). That arrangement lasted until the NHL expanded to 18 teams (with the addition of the Washington Capitals and the short-lived Kansas City Scouts) for the 1974–75 season, at which point the league switched to two conferences and two divisions per conference. As an additional bonus, the NHL All-Star Game became much more competitive too. In 1971's game, the West prevailed 2–1 at Boston Garden.

The most important change was the one that was made glaringly necessary with New York's 9–5 win over Detroit and Chicago's 10–2 triumph over Montreal on Sunday, April 5. As compelling as those two games were, league president Clarence Campbell had a sound point which few people would dispute: The game was not supposed to be played that way. The NHL's tiebreaker system badly needed an overhaul. How drastic it should be was a matter of opinion.

Before applying the necessary fixes to the NHL's rules for 1970–71, Campbell launched an investigation into the Red Wings–Rangers game to determine if Detroit had deliberately thrown the game. This fact-finding task was relatively small potatoes for Campbell who was educated at the University of Alberta. A Rhodes Scholar at Oxford (where he had played on the school's hockey team) and an accomplished lawyer, Campbell had been Canada's prosecuting attorney at the Nuremburg Trials in postwar Germany and was awarded the Order of the British Empire for those services.

After interviewing Sid Abel and Emile Francis at length by telephone, Campbell concluded that the Rangers and Canadiens had not violated any rules in pulling their goalies (albeit for entirely different reasons) for extended periods in their respective April 5 games. They were, in fact, well within their rights to do so. He found no evidence to suggest that the Red Wings had deliberately lost to New York. (The press generally preferred the grammatically incorrect term "laid down.") Nor did Campbell find any evidence of collusion between the two teams to rig the outcome of their season-ending game. No fines or discipline were ever handed out to anyone as everybody had indeed played by the existing rules of the 1969–70 NHL season—a point that Campbell was quick to stress. Now, however, was the time to amend those same rules to prevent another end-of-season fiasco in the future.

Writing in *The Hockey News*, Bill Libby advocated dramatic changes. He preferred the idea that a one-game playoff ought to break any ties in the standings. Failing that, he suggested that a team's goals allowed be subtracted from its goals scored rather than put the emphasis on goal scoring alone. Libby also supported rethinking the 1st-vs.-3rd and 2nd-vs.-4th playoff matchups as they seemed to reward the second-place team ahead of the first-place team and the fourth-place team over the third-place team.

After due deliberation, Campbell presented his proposed amendments to the NHL's Board of Governors for consideration at their next meeting in June 1970. (Interestingly the committee was chaired by New York Rangers president Bill Jennings.) Campbell's suggestions were adopted in October just before the 1970–71 season opened. The new rule for breaking ties between teams that finished a season with identical point totals would be in the following order:

- Greatest number of wins
- Superior head-to-head record between the tied teams
- Superior record versus teams within that division
- Greatest number of goals scored
- Fewest number of goals allowed

Remarkably, the concept of "goal difference" (a team's overall goals-scored total less the number of goals it surrendered) was not included as a criterion. This is a surprising decision considering what Campbell had told the press about defense being as important to the lifeblood of competitive sports as offense. Even though the chances of it happening were reduced, it also meant that there still could be a repeat of the April 5 situations in Chicago and New York if the tied teams had identical head-to-head records and records within their division. Teams would still be as unconcerned about conceding empty-net goals if they were doggedly pursuing the more important goals-scored criterion. (The NHL finally did make that criterion count ahead of goals scored—but not until the mid–1990s.)

Had head-to-head records been the next criterion after most wins in the 1969–70 tiebreaker system, the Canadiens would have finished ahead of the Rangers. In their eight regular-season meetings, Montreal won four games, New York won three, and one game ended in a 1–1 tie.

Apart from the near dead heat between the Rangers and Canadiens, fans often are unaware there were two other ties in the final NHL standings of 1969–70. Boston and Chicago both had 99 points in the East Division. In the West, Oakland and Philadelphia each had 58 points. In each case, superior win total determined who finished ahead of whom. Nobody questioned the wisdom of greater wins being the decisive factor. Almost nobody, that is. The thoughtful Bill Libby was the exception. He put forth an interesting perspective in *The Hockey News*:

> Since the NHL recognizes tie games as positive accomplishments by awarding a point for each, why split positional deadlocks on the basic of victories? The team with the

most victories might also have the most losses, as was the case this season, so why should Chicago have been adjudged more entitled to first place than Boston?[2]

[Author's note: Chicago did have five more losses than Boston during the 1969–70 regular season. Coincidentally, Oakland had five more losses than Philadelphia too.]

45

The Cup, the Bruins and the Rest of the Original Six

The Stanley Cup presentation in 1970 was historic as it was the last time the trophy featuring Lord Stanley's original bowl from 1892 was awarded to the championship team. Fearing it was becoming too brittle with age, the NHL retired it to a display case in the Hockey Hall of Fame and replaced it with a replica following the 1969–70 season. When the Bruins had last won the Stanley Cup in 1941, it did not even have its familiar modern shape, but rather a long and narrow "stovepipe" appearance. In 1941 the Bruins also swept the finals, defeating the Detroit Red Wings in four straight games. That year's clincher came at the Detroit Olympia—not Boston Garden. Milt Schmidt, Boston's general manager in 1970, had assisted on Bobby Bauer's Cup-winning goal 29 years earlier.

The annual engraving on the Stanley Cup sometimes includes errors. This was certainly the case for the 1969–70 champion Boston Bruins. A few curiosities ended up on the Cup. Tom Johnson, Boston's assistant general manager, had his name listed on the Cup alongside the incorrect abbreviation "TR"—meaning "trainer." Ted Green had his name engraved on the Cup despite never having played a game during the regular season or playoffs due to his head injury. Curiously, Ivan Boldirev—who made his NHL debut in 1970–71—somehow got his name etched on the trophy too. So did goalie John Adams—who did not play his first NHL game until 1972–73! He had spent the 1969–70 season with the minor league Oklahoma City Blazers. (In 2010, the Bruins oddly perpetuated this wrongdoing when the team celebrated the 40th anniversary of the 1970 Stanley Cup championship. During a pregame ceremony, both John Adams and Ivan Boldirev were feted as members of the championship team.) Having three "phantom" players' names on Lord Stanley's chalice was a little bit much. Accordingly, the qualification rules were tightened immediately afterward.

Harry Sinden's unexpected departure from the Bruins left a noticeable and highly coveted coaching vacancy in the NHL. It was filled by the aforementioned Tom Johnson. Johnson had been a Norris Trophy–winning defenseman with Montreal who finished his career in Boston in the mid–1960s. In the two and a half seasons he coached Boston, he compiled the greatest winning percentage of any NHL coach with at least 200 games on his résumé: a whopping .738. (Having Bobby Orr and Phil Esposito in their heydays is always an asset to any hockey coach.) Johnson is probably best remembered for leading the utterly dominant 1970–71 Boston Bruins to a record-shattering regular season in which they accumulated 121 points. Those Bruins averaged 5.1 goals per game! However, that team was stunningly upended in seven games against Montreal in the Stanley Cup quarterfinals. Boston regrouped to win the Cup in 1971–72, defeating Emile Francis' New York Rangers in the Cup finals in six tough games, four of which were decided by a single goal. Boston won Game #6 at Madison Square Garden 3–0 to finish off the gallant New Yorkers. Bobby Orr again won the Conn Smythe Trophy as playoff MVP. In a surprising move, partway through the 1972–73 season Johnson opted to move from behind the Bruins' bench to return to an executive position with the club—assistant general manager. The bevy of Stanley Cups that were supposed to come Boston's way in the Orr-Esposito era never materialized—although the Bruins were finalists in 1974. (They were finalists in 1977 and 1978 too, well after Orr and Esposito had departed.) After 1972, the Stanley Cup did not return to Boston until 2011—a lengthy gap of 39 seasons for the Bruins and their passionate fans. It was number six in the team's history.

The Chicago Black Hawks thrived as a result of their move to the NHL's West Division. They were the proverbial big fish in a small pond. In 1970–71, they won 49 games and finished a distant 20 points ahead of their closest chasers—former West Division kingpins the St. Louis Blues. (It was the first of a trifecta of consecutive West Division titles for Chicago.) The Black Hawks advanced all the way to the Cup finals in 1971 but lost at home in the seventh game to Montreal. The Black Hawks were leading 2–0 more than halfway through the deciding game. The turning point was when Jacques Lemaire scored on a slapshot from outside the blue line that somehow eluded Tony Esposito's catching glove. The goal only cut the Hawks' lead in half, but it was a clear harbinger for a collapse. Henri Richard scored two goals for Montreal that led to an eventual 3–2 Canadiens win. The Black Hawks' trip to the playoffs in 1970 was the first of 28 successive postseason berths the team would earn, but no Stanley Cups came to Chicago in that era. Hawk fans would have to wait patiently until the 2010 season to enjoy the team's first Stanley Cup since 1961. Two more followed before the end of the decade. Like the Bruins, the Black Hawks have also accrued six total Stanley Cup championships.

Despite losing in a quarterfinal round to Boston in 1970, the New York

Rangers had a very positive future ahead of them. They had been the only team to beat the Boston Bruins in the 1970 playoffs—and they did it twice. (They also led Game #5 of that series in Boston heading into the third period.) Decades later Phil Esposito told an interviewer that he strongly suspected early on that whichever team won the hard-fought Bruins–Rangers quarterfinal would eventually lift the Stanley Cup in 1970.

In the 1970–71 season, the Rangers did not have to wait until the final day of the season to qualify for the playoffs; they made it by a comfortable margin this time. (Again, the NHL schedule-maker had the Red Wings playing at Madison Square Garden on the final Sunday of the season. New York won in a rout, 6–0.) New York lost just two of their 39 home games—an impressive feat. Yet, even with 109 points, they finished 12 points behind the powerful Boston Bruins in the East Division standings. Ranger goalies Ed Giacomin and newcomer Gilles Villemure combined to win the Vezina Trophy by leading the NHL in fewest goals allowed. By the time of the 1971 Stanley Cup playoffs, Emile Francis had strengthened the Rangers further. He picked up three key players from the Detroit Red Wings: Peter Stemkowski, Dale Rolfe and Bruce MacGregor. The Rangers got past Montreal in a quarterfinal. Stemkowski earned a place in Rangers history by scoring two overtime goals in the Stanley Cup semifinal versus Chicago. Nevertheless, it was not enough: the Black Hawks prevailed in seven games.

In 1971–72 New York advanced to the Stanley Cup finals where they lost to Boston in six games. The following year the Rangers knocked off the Bruins in the quarterfinals. In 1973–74 they ousted Montreal again in the opening round of the playoffs—thus becoming the only team in NHL history to beat the defending Stanley Cup champions in the first round of the playoffs in three consecutive seasons. However, Lord Stanley's trophy remained maddeningly elusive for New York. The Rangers of the early 1970s were arguably the best team never to win the Stanley Cup. Emile Francis was dismissed by the Rangers' management in early January 1976 when his team was faltering badly. In the previous few months Francis had orchestrated major trades involving Jean Ratelle, Brad Park, Ed Giacomin and Gilles Villemure. Those moves—and the threat of more to come—failed to shake the listless team out of its doldrums. In 1975–76, for the first time in a decade, New York did not qualify for the Stanley Cup playoffs. Francis was dismissed by club president Bill Jennings, the same man who had gleefully—but ingenuously—told *Sports Illustrated* in 1970 that Francis could be the Rangers' general manager for life.

Sid Abel kept his promise to merely be the Detroit Red Wings' interim coach. He formally relinquished his coaching duties with the club on May 22, 1970. Abel was replaced by 50-year-old Ned Harkness, a man who had experience coaching both hockey and lacrosse at the NCAA level, but had zero experience with pro sports. In 1969–70, Harkness had coached Cornell University's hockey team to a perfect 29–0 record and an NCAA championship. Finding it difficult to relate to NHL players, Harkness lasted not quite half a season in 1970–71, compiling a poor 12–22–4 record. (He was replaced by Doug Barkley who fared worse than Harkness, accruing just 10 wins and seven ties in the team's final 40 games.) Harkness was moved from the Wings' bench to an upper management position with the team, but he had little success in that role. Detroit became a perennial NHL doormat. In a particularly awful stretch from 1970–71 to 1982–83, the Red Wings failed to qualify for the playoffs 12 times in those 13 seasons. (Wings fans jokingly refer to this bleak period in the club's history as the "Darkness with Harkness" era.) Abel himself later accepted NHL coaching positions in both St. Louis and Kansas City before returning to Detroit to do television color commentary of Red Wing games in the late 1970s and early 1980s. Abel died on February 8, 2000, two weeks before his 82nd birthday. He never wavered when confronted by criticism over how he handled his Red Wings on April 5, 1970. He always believed he had acted in the best interests of his team on that crazy Sunday afternoon in New York.

According to Habs lore, the Montreal Canadiens played with a vengeance for years against the Detroit Red Wings because of what happened on the final regular-season Sunday in 1970. That first year, 1970–71, the Habs went 4–1–1 against a badly declining Detroit team that failed to make the playoffs, but just one of the six games was especially lopsided. (The Habs decisively crushed the Red Wings 9–2 in the teams' final meeting on March 27 after Detroit had been eliminated from the playoff chase.) Montreal rallied to win the Stanley Cup in 1970–71, starting their playoff run with their famous upset over the favored Boston Bruins. The Habs were no slouches that year, having accrued 97 points. One key acquisition was picking up Frank Mahovlich on January 13, 1971, from the rebuilding Red Wings for three players, including rising star Mickey Redmond. (The Big M was happy to leave the faltering Wings by then. Eleven days earlier, the Toronto Maple Leafs mercilessly hammered Detroit 13–0 at Maple Leaf Gardens.) Another Montreal Stanley Cup followed in 1972–73—and four more in succession from 1976 to 1979—to conclude the decade. (Ex–St. Louis coach Scotty Bowman led the Habs to Stanley Cup glory five times. Bowman's greatest rivals when he coached the Canadiens were the Boston Bruins. Unlike in 1970, he won every playoff series versus Boston when he piloted the Habs. He did not have to worry about shadowing Bobby Orr again. Orr last skated for the Bruins in 1975 and, after playing a handful of games for the Chicago Black Hawks on crippled knees, retired at age 30 in 1978.) Starting from 1970 to 1971, the Habs made the playoffs 24 years in a row. Thus, in the 46 NHL seasons from 1948–49 to 1993–94, the mighty

Montreal Canadiens failed to qualify for the Stanley Cup playoffs just once: It was the wild season of 1969–70.

Since the Original Six era ended in 1967, no old-time team has fared worse than the Toronto Maple Leafs. To date, the NHL's expansion era has somehow rendered them impotent. As defending Stanley Cup champions entering the 1967–68 season, the Leafs failed to even make the playoffs—a rarity for a defending titlist. For the next few years they were either knocked out of postseason play in the first round or failed to qualify altogether. After winning the Stanley Cup in 1967, Toronto did not win another playoff series until 1975. In 1970–71, Toronto had two future Hall of Fame goaltenders: aging Jacques Plante and rising Bernie Parent. The Leafs finished fourth in the East Division and lost to the New York Rangers in a six-game quarterfinal—a series that ended the long drought of Ranger postseason futility that dated back to 1950. Although they have often had capable and occasionally very good teams in the half century since the NHL doubled in size, the Leafs have not even made it to a Cup final since 1967 much less hoisted the trophy, much to the exasperation of their large and fanatical fan base. As of 2020, 19 different teams have won the Stanley Cup since Toronto last managed to achieve the feat. Fourteen of those clubs were not in existence in 1966–67.

46

The 1967 Expansion Teams

"The National Hockey League embarks on a new era, fifty
years after its founding. Its Golden Jubilee year has been a
memorable one."[1]
 —Brian McFarlane, from his 1968 NHL history book
The Lively World of Hockey

Of the six teams that entered the NHL in 1967–68 season, the Philadelphia Flyers have been the most consistently supported, even during times
when they were clearly not playoff contenders. They rewarded their loyal
fans by being the first of the 1967 expansion clubs to win Lord Stanley's coveted trophy.

The Flyers finished third in 1970–71 in the West Division but were
swiftly ousted by the Chicago Black Hawks in a quarterfinal. Against all
odds, the Flyers duplicated their calamitous regular-season collapse of
1969–70 in 1971–72. Conclusively proving that history does repeat itself,
this time on the final day of the regular season (April 2), it was the Buffalo
Sabres' Gerry Meehan—a former Flyer—who scored on a long shot that
eluded goalie Doug Favell with just four seconds remaining on the clock
to give the Sabres a totally unexpected 3–2 victory. The Flyers had led the
game 2–0 at its midway point. Thanks to Clarence Campbell's revised tiebreaker, the result meant the Pittsburgh Penguins qualified for the playoffs
instead of the Flyers because of their head-to-head record; Pittsburgh held
a slim 3–2–1 edge. "Flyers Blow It, Penguins In" said a terse but accurate
Montreal Gazette headline the next day.

However, Philadelphia was a team on the rise. Taking their cue from
the successful style of the Boston Bruins and expanding on it exponentially,
the Flyers became decidedly meaner and tougher. Once the most pusillan-
imous team in the West Division, the Flyers reinvented themselves as the
terrifying Broad Street Bullies. In 1974 they became the first of the 1967
expansion teams to reach the Cup finals after one was no longer guaranteed
a spot. They bludgeoned their way two consecutive Stanley Cups, beginning

with their minor upset of the Bruins in that 1974 final. By doing so, the Flyers became the first non–Original Six team since 1935 to win Lord Stanley's coveted trophy. They had plenty of talent: Bobby Clarke, Rick MacLeish, Reggie Leach and others were terrific offensive forces. Bernie Parent—who had spent a couple of years with Toronto—returned to Philadelphia (in a deal for Doug Favell!) and won consecutive Conn Smythe Trophies as playoff MVP in both 1974 and 1975. Montreal, Boston and Philadelphia were the only three NHL teams to win the Stanley Cup during the 1970s.

Philadelphia turned out to be the true jewel of the six NHL expansion clubs from 1967. The other five all struggled at various points in their existence for solid fan support. Two of the teams no longer exist.

The California/Oakland/Bay Area Seals threw in the towel after the 1975–76 season. The 1969–70 season was the last full one where they were called the Oakland Seals. In an attempt to broaden their appeal to a larger geographical area, they were renamed the California Golden Seals two games into the 1970–71 season. One Seals beat writer humorously declared the new name sounded "like a floor wax."[2] Steve Tadevich of the *Fremont Argus* wrote, "Perhaps the best idea came from an Oakland evening newspaper to just refer to them as the Oakland Seals and let [new owner Charlie] Finley call them anything he likes."[3] The paper Tadevich was referring to was the *Oakland Tribune*. One writer, John Porter, perceived the name change as a deliberate insult to his city and flatly refused to go along with it. Out of spite, Porter indeed steadfastly continued to refer to the team in his reports as the "Oakland Seals" or just "the Seals."

A series of dismal campaigns—five last-place finishes in their final six seasons—discouraged a huge chunk of whatever fan base the Seals had left. The Seals averaged just 20 wins per season and had seven coaches in their nine-year history. Five different men guided the team from 1971 to 1975 alone. Still, most Seals alumni look back at their days with the team with a surprising degree of fondness. "I have great memories out there in Oakland, other than we didn't win enough hockey games,"[4] said Walt McKechnie, who spent three seasons playing in the unmistakably garish green-and-gold Seals uniforms. (At least they matched the hideous color scheme of the players' personal luggage—which they were all supposed to use on road trips. It was a club rule that was never fully obeyed or enforced.)

When colorful Charles O. Finley bought the team in 1970, he bluntly stated in his first press conference on July 6, "I know absolutely nothing about hockey." That obvious shortcoming did not stop him from adding a generally noteworthy personal touch to the team: the famously reviled white skates. He also said, "I firmly believe the Seals are here to stay and can become championship contenders."[5] Veteran Seals center Ted Hampson was not at all impressed with the new owner—who also owned the Oakland Athletics of Major League Baseball. Hampson likened him to a fast-talking, disreputable used-car dealer who considered his players to be chattel. Mark Armour wrote this in his biography of Finley for the Society for American Baseball Research: "When his team lost, [Finley] blamed everyone but himself. When they won, he was apt to call the radio booth during the game if his name was not mentioned often enough." Armour's assessment held true of Finley the NHL owner too. Finley was a self-made millionaire who, sportswriter Jim Murray wryly quipped, "worshipped his creator."

Sometimes Finley could be generous with his wealth. The Seals were the first NHL team to regularly fly first-class to all road games. After big wins, Finley sometimes bought the players expensive gifts (Gucci shoes, for example). Other times he was notoriously niggardly. Deeming it a waste of money, Finley abruptly ceased the Seals' popular postgame goodwill gesture of having the players loft two or three dozen pucks into the crowd as souvenirs. He was also famously stingy with player contracts and seldom negotiated with anyone. It was mostly take-it-or-leave-it with Charlie O. Finley's meddling in hockey operations also drove two high-quality hockey men out of the Seals' organization. Both Frank Selke, Jr., and Bill Torrey resigned within a few months of Finley acquiring the team. Neither man was out of work for very long: Selke worked for *Hockey Night in Canada* for 20 years. Torrey became the general manager of the New York Islanders. He smartly and patiently nurtured the expansion team into a Stanley Cup champion within eight years. The first year the Seals were under Finley's control, the team lost 53 games to establish a new NHL record for losses in a season—having accrued one more defeat than the pitiful 1969–70 Los Angeles Kings.

Never short on quirky promotional ideas, Finley thought a live seal would make a terrific mascot for his hockey team. It was tried—once. The creature Finley procured for the occasion lacked sprightliness, however. With appropriate fanfare the seal was presented to the home crowd. It lazily flopped on the ice and did nothing. (Some cynical observers saw a great deal of symbolism there.) The lethargic pinniped did not get a return engagement. In 1973 Finley sold the Seals back to the NHL for $6.5 million and netted himself a tidy profit from the deal. For two seasons the NHL's other clubs assumed responsibility for the team's operating costs—and absorbed huge losses in the process. A chagrined Clarence Campbell vowed the league would never again bail out a financially troubled franchise under his watch.

Over the years the Seals had several players whose names ought to be recognizable to serious contemporary hockey fans because they achieved some degree of stardom in the NHL. (Examples include Reg Leach, Ivan

Boldirev and Charlie Simmer.) Unfortunately for the Seals, those three players—and others like them—became big names for other NHL clubs after being dealt from hockey's worst team in short-sighted trades. Being freed from the woebegone Seals and the team's ingrained defeatist culture commonly spurred them to do great things elsewhere.

There were perhaps about 4,000 hardcore Seals fans—but there were too few casual ticket-buyers to pick up the slack. Crowds could be discouragingly small. A Seals home game versus the Los Angeles Kings on Christmas Eve 1972 drew fewer than 1,000 spectators. The team never averaged 7,000 fans per home game in any of their nine seasons. Every year the Seals were dead last in the NHL in attendance. However, one semi-regular rooter at Seals home games was *Peanuts* cartoonist Charles M. Schulz. Long before he became a major film star, a teenage Tom Hanks was once a Seals employee. He worked for a time as a hot dog vendor at the Coliseum Arena. (Some sources say he sold popcorn and peanuts too.) Talented but eccentric forward Bobby Sheehan, who played for the Seals only in 1971–72 and scored 20 goals that season, was Hanks' favorite player. Long after Hanks became world renowned as an actor, he and Sheehan exchanged autographed photos.

Of the 138 players who played at least one game for the Seals, the last to be an active NHL player was Dennis Maruk, who played for them during his 1975–76 rookie season. Maruk appeared in all 80 games in the team's last year in Oakland and scored 30 goals. He finished third in the voting for the league's Rookie of the Year. Seemingly cursed by being part of weak NHL teams, Maruk had to wait nine seasons just to be on a team that qualified for the Stanley Cup playoffs. Maruk retired in 1989 after a 14-year career in which he played 888 regular-season games.

When plans for a new, modern, downtown arena to be built in San Francisco unexpectedly fell through—after being initially approved—the Seals' days in California were numbered. (They did go out as 5–2 winners in their final game, at home versus Los Angeles, on April 4, 1976. It was a good way to wrap things up as Seals fans had long considered the Kings to be their greatest rivals.) During their tumultuous nine years in California, the Seals played 698 regular-season games and compiled an overall record of 182 wins, 401 losses and 115 ties. Their winning percentage was .343. They scored 1,826 goals and allowed 2,580. In the two seasons they qualified for the Stanley Cup playoffs, the Seals won just three of their 11 postseason games and never advanced past the first round.

The official end of the California Golden Seals came on July 14, 1976. That was the date the NHL approved owner Mel Swig's application to transfer the club to Cleveland for the 1976–77 season. The team was promptly renamed the Barons, an homage to Cleveland's longtime minor league team. More accurately the Seals relocated operations to suburban Richfield, Ohio, midway between Cleveland and Akron. There the biggest arena in the NHL awaited them—the impressive 20,000-seat Richfield Coliseum. The *Oakland Tribune* ran something akin to an obituary for the departing team which stated, in part, "The Seals had been sickly from birth when they joined the NHL nine years ago. They suffered with unstable management and last-place teams…"[6] According to Seals historian Steve Currier, the team left a legacy of "apathetic owners and ridiculous marketing decisions. [The Seals] lost tons of money, cheated death more often than Evel Knievel, and left behind a long trail of broken dreams."[7]

One huge reason for poor attendance at Seals home games over their checkered history was infrequently discussed openly: urban decay. Many well-to-do hockey fans from the region simply did not feel safe going to Oakland to watch an NHL game. Gary Simmons, a Seals goalie from 1974 to 1976, said years later, "All the hockey population was on the peninsula down in San Jose and in San Francisco, but they would not go across that bridge into Oakland. Oakland had a lot of crime, it didn't have a good name, and people just didn't go."[8] Barry Van Gerbig, the principal owner of the Seals during the club's inaugural season, lamented that reality by noting, "People from San Francisco don't cross the bay for anything. If Jesus Christ came on a donkey over [to Oakland], they wouldn't come."[9]

Team owner Mel Swig was optimistic about the franchise's new location. "The Cleveland area is going to be a great opportunity for us. I think the fans have already shown great enthusiasm."[10] Swig badly misread the appetite for the NHL in Ohio. It simply was not there. Not once in their two years did the Barons ever fill "The Palace on the Prairie," as the Richfield Coliseum was billed in its promotional literature. Most nights it was not even half filled; the average attendance in the Barons' first NHL season was just above 6,000. Along with general apathy, there were other reasons why fans did not turn out in droves for Barons home games. A single two-lane highway provided the only access to the arena, thus travel to the Richfield Coliseum was often a slow ordeal. Unluckily, Ohio experienced a horrendously severe winter in 1976–77, making the 26-mile trip even less appealing to Clevelanders. Because the franchise moved from Oakland to Cleveland after the NHL schedule had been made, the Barons only got a handful of weekend home games when the schedule was hastily revised. By early 1977 the Cleveland Barons were dangerously close to insolvency. With a sizable loan from the NHL Players' Association—secretly orchestrated by its director Alan Eagleson—the Barons muddled through their first campaign. Cleveland missed the playoffs—making it seven straight season the franchise was shut out of Stanley Cup play. New ownership took control of the team for the 1977–78 campaign. Attendance did not improve in the

Barons' second season. The club lost approximately $3 million and again was absent from the playoffs. The plug had to be pulled.

Despite promising their season-ticket holders at least a third season of NHL hockey in Cleveland, in June 1978 the Barons were granted permission by the league to merge with the struggling Minnesota North Stars. In effect the Barons folded—making them the last NHL team to do so. The NHL thus was reduced in size from 18 to 17 teams for the 1978–79 season. Sportswriter Jerry Rombach of the *Elyria Chronicle-Telegram* declared the demise of the Barons to be a blow to the prestige of Cleveland, but he noted, "I am particularly upset with the Cleveland people who last year bought the Barons and promised the fans here a trial of at least two [more] years before making a decision. People [here] will support hockey, as well as baseball, football and basketball in this area. It's just that they are so starved for a title contender that they can't stomach anything less…"[11]

Not forgotten in their original Bay Area home, the Seals were recognized in special ceremonies and historic displays by the San Jose Sharks on what would have been the team's 50th anniversary season in 2017. Despite the passage of more than four decades without having an existing team to support, a California Golden Seals booster club remains active. It holds bimonthly meetings at a sports bar.

In 1967, the NHL was thought to be a can't-miss proposition in Minnesota. The locals had always supported both NCAA and high school hockey quite well. Surely the world's top professional hockey league ought to be a major attraction too. However, for some reason, the North Stars seemed to struggle for long-term fan support. It never truly manifested in a long-term basis. By the mid–1970s, attendance had fallen to below 10,000 fans for Minnesota home games.

After merging with the woebegone Cleveland Barons in 1978, the North Stars began a rapid, short-term ascension. Two highlights occurred in the early 1980s. In the 1980 Stanley Cup playoffs, the North Stars eliminated the four-time defending champion Montreal Canadiens, winning three games at the Forum, no less. The following year they made it to the Cup finals—despite finishing ninth overall during the regular season—before losing to the New York Islanders in five games. A decade later, in 1991, the North Stars compiled a sub–.500 regular season but pulled off three huge playoff upsets to reach the finals for the second time in their 24-year existence. They won two of the first three games against the Pittsburgh Penguins, but eventually lost the championship series in six games. To date, the 1991 Stanley Cup final is the only case where two of the 1967 expansion teams have met in the championship round.

Leading up to the 1991 finals, the North Stars attendance was underwhelming and did not improve over the next two years. The 1992–93 season was the last for the North Stars in their original home. They faltered in the last week of the season and missed the playoffs that year, finishing with a record of 36–38–10. They lost their final three games, including their home finale—a 3-2 defeat inflicted on them by the Chicago Black Hawks on April 13, 1993. It was an emotional night for the ticketholders. An Associated Press reporter wrote, "The overflow Met Center crowd of 15,445 gave the North Stars a long, standing ovation before the game, cheered throughout the national anthem, and regularly chanted vulgarities that included team owner Norm Green's name."[12] Interestingly, the North Stars had their best home attendance in almost a decade during their final campaign in Minnesota.

By the 1993–94 season the team's name was truncated and the club relocated to Texas. The Dallas Stars, led by Brett Hull (Bobby's son), won the Stanley Cup in 1999. When the 2019–20 NHL season began, the Stars franchise had been in Dallas longer than it had been located in Minnesota. Seven years after the North Stars departed, the NHL returned to the Gopher State in the form of the Minnesota Wild, an expansion outfit that began play in the 2000–01 season.

Like those of the departed California Seals, diehard North Stars fans still linger despite the inexorable passage of years. One is Dan Cote. He was a teenager when the North Stars played their last game in 1993 and admittedly only saw a handful of the team's games. Cote created a Facebook page for likeminded, nostalgic individuals. He also passionately collects North Stars memorabilia of all types wherever he can find it—sometimes operating outside the boundaries of the law to do so. One day Cote was driving near a Minneapolis alley when an object caught his eye: a barrel. "It was set out with the trash, and it was full of garbage," Cote recalled in a 2016 interview for the *Minneapolis Star Tribune*, "but it was custom-painted, yellow with green banners and [it had] a North Stars logo. It was really shoddy. I made sure no one was watching me, and I grabbed it and threw it in the back of my car."

The once-fashionable St. Louis Blues started to lose their luster not long after their third successive appearance in the Stanley Cup finals. St. Louis still regularly qualified for the playoffs during most of the 1970s before sliding dramatically into irrelevance. Poor attendance and financial mismanagement had the Blues teetering on bankruptcy, having debts approaching $9 million. At one especially low point, the Blues cut their support staff to a mere three employees—one of whom was the esteemed Emile Francis.

In 1977, the team was sold to Ralston Purina—the St. Louis–based pet food company—prompting the inevitable jokes about the Blues going to the dogs. The company, however, only bought the club out of a sense of civic responsibility until a new owner could be found that would keep the Blues in Missouri. (One short-lived rumor had the team relocating to Saskatoon, a Canadian prairie city that only had a population of about 150,000.) By the 1978–79 season the Blues had sunk to a franchise low, winning just 18 of 80 games. That dismal season, in a desperate attempt to attract fans to the renamed Checkerdome, St. Louis became the first NHL outfit to hire a cheerleading troupe—the Blue Angels. Francis Rosa, the stately and veteran *Boston Globe* hockey writer, was disheartened by what he saw when covering a Bruins–Blues game at the Checkerdome in October 1978. He wrote,

> The Blues took four rows of seats out of their stands to give the Blue Angels a platform. They stand there and shake their gold and blue pompoms together, maybe trying to distract the fans from what's going on on the ice. It is also a sad commentary about what has happened to hockey in this city, taking out seats in an arena that once rocked to the cheers of 20,000 people per game.[13]

Within a couple of years, St. Louis' fortunes on the ice had rebounded. They were one of the best teams in the NHL in 1980–81, but they suffered an early and disappointing ouster from the playoffs. The Blues did qualify for the playoffs for 25 straight seasons, but after they shook hands with Bobby Orr and his happy Bruin teammates at Boston garden on May 10, 1970, they were not seen again in a Stanley Cup final until 2019 when their opponents were, by a quirky happenstance, once again the Boston Bruins. Boston won the first game of the series to extend St. Louis' winless record in Cup final play to an embarrassing 13 games, but the Blues won the second contest in overtime and eventually prevailed in seven games to capture the Stanley Cup in the club's 52nd year of existence.

The Pittsburgh Penguins did not gain much momentum from their fine playoff showing in 1970 and upsurge in attendance. Red Kelly, who was perceived as something as a hockey savior in Pittsburgh, signed a five-year contract extension as the team's coach and general manager. But the Pens fell on hard times. With the sudden and tragic loss of Michel Brière, the Penguins dropped to sixth place in the seven-team West Division in 1970–71 and did not qualify for the Stanley Cup playoffs. By the middle of the 1972–73 season, Kelly had been terminated from both his jobs.

After 1970, the Penguins did not return to the Stanley Cup playoffs until 1975. That spring they knocked off St. Louis 2–0 in a best-of-three preliminary round, but the Penguins stunningly failed to win their best-of-seven quarterfinal versus the New York Islanders despite jumping out to a commanding 3–0 series lead. Pittsburgh only scored four goals over the final four games. Islanders rookie goalie Glenn (Chico) Resch was superb. After New York's 1–0 victory in Game #7 in Pittsburgh, Al Abrams, of the *Pittsburgh Post-Gazette*, concluded, "Both the Pens and Islanders are young teams of the future. They aren't far away from Stanley Cup championships."[14] He was half right. The Islanders were indeed on the cusp of forming an NHL dynasty—which would begin in 1979–80—while the Penguins were descending into mediocrity again. In a city where the NFL Steelers and MLB Pirates were constantly contenders in their respective sports, the Penguins were largely an unfashionable and forgotten assemblage of outcasts in the "City of Champions."

Earlier in 1975, the Penguins were on the verge of bankruptcy as creditors brought legal actions to collect overdue debts from the club. At one especially low point, the doors to the team's offices were padlocked. Scuttlebutt had the Penguins shutting down their operations in Pennsylvania and relocating to either Seattle or Denver. Luckily for the dwindling number of diehard hockey fans in Pittsburgh, a group (which included former Minnesota North Stars general manager Wren Blair) intervened and prevented the Penguins from folding. Under new ownership from shopping mall impresario Edward J. DeBartolo, Sr., the team's fortunes went upward rapidly. By the late 1980s, with Mario Lemieux and Jaromir Jagr leading the way, Pittsburgh was suddenly the newest NHL powerhouse team. Five Stanley Cups have been won by the Penguins since 1991.

The Los Angeles Kings struggled to stay relevant in a sports market dominated by successful baseball and basketball teams. Improvement over their thoroughly dismal 1969–70 campaign was a slow procedure. Los Angeles did not make a Stanley Cup playoff appearance until 1974. The 1973–74 Kings were, in fact, the first installment of the club to finish with at least a .500 mark, compiling a 33–33–12 record.

In 1974–75 Los Angeles suddenly became a team to be reckoned with. High-scoring Marcel Dionne, acquired from Detroit, became the face of the Los Angeles franchise for more than a decade. The Kings enjoyed a terrific 105-point season only to waste it in a disappointing first-round playoff loss to Toronto. In the spring of 1982, the seemingly overmatched Kings pulled off one of the truly great upsets in sports history by knocking off the ascending Edmonton Oilers in the first round of the playoffs. Yet, the team struggled to attain a reliable fanbase and came nowhere near capturing hockey's greatest prize in its first 20 years of existence.

On August 9, 1988, new team owner Bruce McNall boldly did two noteworthy things that memorable day: He changed the Kings' logo and uniform color scheme. More importantly McNall pulled off one of the greatest coups in NHL history by acquiring 27-year-old Wayne Gretzky from the formidable Stanley Cup champion Edmonton Oilers. It was part of a five-player transaction that also included $15 million. The shocking news was almost beyond belief in Canada. It was an out-of-the-blue move that completely stunned hockey fans—especially those who resided in hockey's heartland. "Gretzky gone" blared a huge front-page headline on the next day's *Edmonton Journal*. A *Sports Illustrated* feature article on the deal was aptly titled "Woe, Canada." Canadian politicians weighed in on the stunning news. One was 46-year-old Nelson Riis of the New Democratic Party who had more than a passing interest in the game. (As a member of parliament, Riis had successfully introduced legislation to formally declare ice hockey to be Canada's official national winter sport.) Riis thoroughly denounced the trade, saying Gretzky was a living Canadian national symbol who should not be sold. Riis also noted that the Edmonton Oilers without Wayne Gretzky "is like *Wheel of Fortune* without Vanna White."[15]

With Gretzky on the Kings' roster, the NHL suddenly became fashionable and important in southern California. Gretzky would eventually score more than 900 points in his eight seasons in a Kings uniform, but even he could not bring them a championship. The Kings advanced to the Stanley Cup finals in 1993 but lost to Montreal in five games. Stanley Cups would eventually be won by Los Angeles in both 2012 and 2014—putting them on par with the Philadelphia Flyers.

Aftermath: Miscellany

Clarence Campbell continued to capably serve as the president of the NHL until the conclusion of the 1976–77 season. Often working 18-hour days, Campbell was nearing his 72nd birthday when he retired after 31 years of dedicated service to the league.

Campbell was always a somewhat imposing and imperious figure. Not only was Campbell held in respect by a sometimes-dissenting board of governors, he was also held in high esteem by the media. He made himself available to reporters virtually around the clock. "Nobody ever called him anything but 'Mr. Campbell,'" recalled Don Cherry, who coached the Boston Bruins in the final years of Campbell's presidency and nervously had to answer to him on a few occasions. "He had me scared."[1] Campbell was not humorless, however. Rose Cherry (Don's wife) once spotted Campbell sitting nearby at a game at Boston Garden and told her preteen son, Tim, to introduce himself. He did. Not knowing quite what to say to the esteemed NHL president, the boy chose the first thing that popped into his mind: Tim Cherry asked Campbell if he had received the check to pay for a recent fine that had recently been levied on his father. An amused Campbell confirmed that he had—and convulsed with laughter.

The NHL tripled in size from six to 18 teams under Campbell's watch. He was also a driving force behind many league initiatives. Campbell actively assisted in the establishment of a pension plan for retired players. In the early 1950s Campbell was responsible for creating an intra-league draft that allowed the NHL's weak teams to claim players who were under contract to strong teams but languishing in the minor leagues. That move may have saved the struggling Chicago Black Hawks franchise from bankruptcy. Danny Gallivan, the loquacious English-language broadcaster for the Montreal Canadiens, told the *Montreal Gazette*, "[Campbell] was respected, a man of integrity. He took his job very seriously and did it with a very high degree of proficiency. He did so much that the ordinary hockey fan was not aware of—it was just mind-boggling."[2] Even Toronto Maple Leafs owner Harold Ballard, who rarely showered compliments on anybody, declared Campbell to be a heroic figure in NHL history.

Late in his tenure, Campbell ran afoul of Canadian law. In 1976 Campbell was convicted of bribing senator Louis Giguère to use his influence to assist him in an investment deal pertaining to duty-free shops at Canada's airports. Due to his advancing age, Campbell received no prison sentence, but merely a fine—which the NHL paid for him.

However, that sordid, non-hockey incident is mostly forgotten. Instead, Campbell is largely regarded as one of the most important behind-the-scenes people in sports history. His biography on the Hockey Hall of Fame's website lauds him. It states, "Few individuals had as significant an influence on professional hockey as former NHL president Clarence S. Campbell. He demonstrated unshakeable faith in his principles while moving with the times when necessary. Campbell presided over the NHL during its most dramatic period of change while going down in history as one of the key sports administrators of the 20th Century." Campbell was in ill health during his final few years. He died of pneumonia and respiratory troubles in Montreal on June 24, 1984, 15 days shy of his 79th birthday. Upon hearing of his passing, Campbell's successor John Ziegler jointly issued a statement with Bill Wirtz, chairman of the NHL's board of governors:

> Canada and the National Hockey League have truly lost a great citizen and friend. Clarence Campbell and the NHL have been synonymous for over 40 years.
>
> We realize today how inadequate our words seem to be when trying to convey the significance of the person and his impact and contribution upon our game and our league...[3]

In 1968, Campbell predicted the NHL would eventually grow beyond the narrow confines of North America. "I look forward to the day," Campbell said, "when with the growth of hockey in Europe, we'll be spectators to a world playoff for the Stanley Cup."[4] That, of course, has not happened yet. Nevertheless, the three Hall of Famers (so far) who were born during the course of the 1969–70 NHL season represent the rapid and thorough globalization of the present NHL player pool: Nicklas Lidström (Sweden), Sergei Fedorov (Soviet Union) and Rob Blake (Canada).

In honor of the NHL's greatest leader, the Clarence S. Campbell Bowl is annually presented to the playoff champion of the NHL's Western Conference.

CBS continued to broadcast the *NHL Game of the Week* until the end of the 1971–72 season. Its coverage of select games of that year's Boston–New York Stanley Cup finals garnered some of the highest ratings the program ever received. The network had been paying the league less than $2 million per season. NBC offered $5.3 million per season for the American network television rights to the NHL beginning in 1972–73. That figure was far too rich for CBS to match. It was not especially interested in shelling out that much money to cover a league, which despite its presence across the continent and growing popularity, was still very much perceived as a regional passion. CBS did not altogether abandon professional hockey in 1972–73, however. It instead chose to cover the inaugural season of the fledgling World Hockey Association. NBC ended its weekly NHL broadcasts following the 1974–75 season.

It has now been more than 50 years since the 1969–70 NHL season began with games in Pittsburgh, Montreal, Detroit, St. Louis and Minnesota on Saturday, October 11, 1969. The result of every one of those five games greatly affected the final standings in both the East and West divisions nearly six months later. Who could have foreseen that? There has never been another season in the NHL that rivaled 1969–70 for the tightness of its playoff races and sustained drama over the course of the regular season. Will there ever be another hockey season so wild, so topsy-turvy, and so chock full of surprises? It is impossible to know for certain, of course—and a wise person should never say never about such random things—but the confluence of results and peculiar events that were so compelling to hockey fans in the spring of 1970 have not come close to reoccurring on so many levels in all the subsequent NHL campaigns. Let us just accept the obvious: Hockey followers may never witness such sights again.

Chapter Notes

Chapter 1

1. Dink Carroll, "Habs Win 4–0, Fifth Straight Cup," *Montreal Gazette*, April 15, 1960, 16.
2. Dink Carroll, "The Rocket and Retirement," *Montreal Gazette*, April 15, 1960, 16.

Chapter 2

1. Brian McFarlane, *The Lively World of Hockey* (New York City: Signet Books, 1968), 79.
2. Reg Lansberry, *9 Goals* (Scotts Valley, CA: CreateSpace Independent Publishing Platform, 2017), 10.

Chapter 3

1. Andrew Zadarnowski, "50 Years Later: A Look Back at the NHL's First Expansion Draft," habseyeson the prize. com, June 6, 2017.
2. Steve Currier, *The California Golden Seals: A Tale of White Skates, Red Ink and One of the NHL's Most Outlandish Teams* (Lincoln: University of Nebraska Press, 2017), 24.
3. "Maximum TV Coverage Rules Out Vancouver," *Montreal Gazette*, February 10, 1966, 29.
4. Pat Curran, "Draft Day Arrives for NHL Expansion," *Montreal Gazette*, June 6, 1967, 22.
5. *Ibid.*
6. Pat Curran, "Habs Regain Larose in Draft Deal," *Montreal Gazette*, June 7, 1967, 37.
7. Steve Currier, *The California Golden Seals: A Tale of White Skates, Red Ink and One of the NHL's Most Outlandish Teams*

(Lincoln: University of Nebraska Press, 2017), 53.
8. *Ibid.*
9. Al Abrams, "Sidelights on Sports," *Pittsburgh Post-Gazette*, June 7, 1967, 25.

Chapter 4

1. "Bill Masterton Remembered," TSN documentary, January 16, 2008.
2. Arthur Pincus, *The Official Illustrated NHL History* (Montreal: Carlton Books, 2018), 123.
3. Randy Starkman, "Star Investigation: What Really Killed NHL's Bill Masterton," *Toronto Star* online archives, May 28, 2011."
4. "Masterton Tragic Death Raises Helmet Question," *Montreal Gazette*, January 16, 1968, 19.
5. *Ibid.*
6. *Ibid.*
7. *Ibid.*
8. *Ibid.*
9. "Bill Masterton Remembered," TSN documentary, January 16, 2008.
10. Dick Beddoes, Stan Fischler and Ira Gitler. *Hockey!.* (New York: The MacMillan Company, 1970), 109.
11. *Ibid.*
12. Pat Curran, "Draft Day Arrives for NHL Expansion," *Montreal Gazette*, June 6, 1967, 22.
13. Dick Beddoes, Stan Fischler and Ira Gitler. *Hockey!.* (New York: The MacMillan Company, 1970), 109.
14. *Ibid.*
15. *Ibid.*
16. *Ibid.*, 110.
17. *Ibid.*
18. *Ibid.*
19. *Ibid.*

260   Chapter Notes

20. "Jack Kent Cooke," Wikipedia biography.

21. Jimmy Jordan, "Canadiens Spoil Penguins' NHL Debut, 2–1," *Pittsburgh Post-Gazette*, October 12, 1967, 32.

22. Pat Curran, "Penguins Surprise... But Lose 2–1," *Montreal Gazette*, October 12, 1967, 34.

23. Dick Beddoes, Stan Fischler and Ira Gitler. *Hockey!*. (New York: The MacMillan Company, 1970), 132.

24. Pat Curran, "Hall Likely Winner of Smythe Trophy," *Montreal Gazette*, May 13, 1968, 26.

26. Brian McFarlane, *The Lively World of Hockey* (New York City: Signet Books, 1968), 165.

27. Dick Beddoes, Stan Fischler and Ira Gitler. *Hockey!*. (New York: The MacMillan Company, 1970), 87.

28. Tom Fitzgerald, "Future Belongs to the Bruins," *Boston Globe*, April 27, 1969, 83.

30. "Canadiens Capture Stanley Cup Again," *Schenectady Gazette*, May 5, 1969, 28.

Chapter 5

1. Roger I. Abrams, "A Dubious Anniversary," huffpost.com, September 19, 2009.

3. Derek Sanderson, *Crossing the Line* (Toronto, HarperCollins, 2012), 123.

4. "Bruins Play Rough...But Lose Twice," *Windsor Star*, September 22, 1969, 29.

5. Roger I. Abrams, "A Dubious Anniversary," huffpost.com, September 19, 2009.

6. "Wayne Maki and the Terrible Stick-Swinging Incident," greatesthockeylegends.com, January 14, 2003.

7. "Boston's Ted Green Suffers Skull Fracture in Ottawa," *Calgary Herald*, September 22, 1969, 16.

8. "Doctors give Green 'reasonable chance,' *Montreal Gazette*, September 23, 1969, 42.

9. Hal Walker, "Hal Walker," *Calgary Herald*, September 23, 1969, 16.

11. Wayne Botchford, "Wayne Maki a Fighter to the End," canada.com, September 14, 2014.

12. "Clarence Campbell Interview,"

Weekend (CBC Television program), November 22, 1969.

13. "Doctors give Green 'reasonable chance,' *Montreal Gazette*, September 23, 1969, 42.

15. Jim Matheson, "Ted Green Was Tough On The Ice But Kind-Hearted Off It," *Edmonton Journal* (online archives), October 12, 2019.

Chapter 6

1. "Jacques Plante Quotations," quotetab.com.

2. Tomas Hertz "Goaltender Quotations: A Small Collection to Enjoy," *In Goal Magazine* online archives, January 24, 2012.

3. "The Canadians: Jacques Plante," History Television documentary.

4. "Plante Hurt, Finishes Up with Mask," *Montreal Gazette*, November 2, 1959, 21.

5. "The Canadians: Jacques Plante," History Television documentary.

6. "Legends of Hockey: Gump Worsley," YouTube video, November 27, 2010.

7. "Gump Worsley," Wikipedia biography.

8. "Quotes by Gump Worsley," Azquotes.com.

10. "Quotes by Johnny Bower," Azquotes.com

11. Colin Dambrauskas, "The Original Six Goalies—and Their Masks—Part #2: Toronto Maple Leafs," hockeybuzz.com, August 30, 2012.

12. Dick Beddoes, Stan Fischler and Ira Gitler. *Hockey!*. (New York: The MacMillan Company, 1970), 196.

13. "Legends of Hockey: Terry Sawchuk," YouTube video, June 9, 2012.

Chapter 7

1. Reg Lansberry, *9 Goals* (Scotts Valley, CA: CreateSpace Independent Publishing Platform, 2017), 48.

3. Jerry Hopkins, "The Rolling Stones' Fall 1969 Tour," *Rolling Stone* online archives, December 22, 1969.

Chapter 8

1. Pat Curran, "The game's the thing, not the organist," *Montreal Gazette*, January 22, 1970, 17.
2. Dan Kelly, *Hockey Night in Canada* broadcast of the 1970 NHL All-Star Game.
3. Pat Curran, "The game's the thing, not the organist," *Montreal Gazette*, January 22, 1970, 17.
4. "East Stars Prevail with Easy 4–1 Win," *Calgary Herald*, January 21, 1970, 69.
5. *Ibid.*
6. Pat Curran, "The game's the thing, not the organist," *Montreal Gazette*, January 22, 1970, 17.
7. *Ibid.*
8. *Ibid.*
9. "East Stars Prevail with Easy 4–1 Win," *Calgary Herald*, January 21, 1970, 69.

Chapter 9

1. Ed Levitt, "A Cool Romance," *Oakland Tribune*, February 26, 1970, 41.
2. *Ibid.*
3. *Ibid.*
4. *Ibid.*
5. *Ibid.*
6. *Ibid.*

Chapter 10

1. David Davis, "The Story Behind Hockey's Most Famous Photo," Deadspin. com, May 5, 2016.
2. "Stephen Brunt on Bobby Orr," Penguin Random House YouTube channel, January 4, 2007.
3. "Legends of Hockey: Bobby Orr," YouTube video, April 23, 2009.
4. *Ibid.*
5. *Ibid.*
6. David Davis, "The Story Behind Hockey's Most Famous Photo," Deadspin. com, May 5, 2016.
7. *Ibid.*
8. *Ibid.*
9. "Legends of Hockey: Bobby Orr," YouTube video, April 23, 2009.
10. Gary Ronberg, "Tea Party for Boston's Bruins," *Sports Illustrated*, May 4, 1970, 21.
11. Bobby Orr. Bobby: *My Story in Pictures* (China, Viking Books, 2018), 112.

12. Stephen Brunt. *Searching for Bobby Orr* (Toronto: Knopf Canada, 2006), 221.
13. "Best of Bobby Orr," YouTube, May 10, 2017.
14. Derek Sanderson, *Crossing the Line* (Toronto, HarperCollins, 2012), 120.
15. Mark Mulvoy and Gary Ronberg, "The Desperate Hours," *Sports Illustrated*, April 6, 1970, 21.

Chapter 11

1. Gary Ronberg, "Flashing Blades for a Mini Mastermind," *Sports Illustrated*, March 2, 1970, 21.
2. Reg Lansberry, *9 Goals* (Scotts Valley, CA: CreateSpace Independent Publishing Platform, 2017), 28.
3. *Ibid.*, 226.
4. Gary Ronberg, "Flashing Blades for a Mini Mastermind," *Sports Illustrated*, March 2, 1970, 22.
5. *Ibid.*
6. *Ibid.*
7. Reg Lansberry, *9 Goals* (Scotts Valley, CA: CreateSpace Independent Publishing Platform, 2017), 226.
8. Gary Ronberg, "Flashing Blades for a Mini Mastermind," *Sports Illustrated*, March 2, 1970, 22.
9. *Ibid.*
10. Reg Lansberry, *9 Goals* (Scotts Valley, CA: CreateSpace Independent Publishing Platform, 2017), 34.

Chapter 12

1. Ted Blackman, "Tony Esposito credits team with record 15 shutouts," *Montreal Gazette*, April 17, 1970, 25.
2. *Ibid.*
3. *Ibid.*
4. *Ibid.*
5. *Ibid.*
6. Dink Carroll, "Playing the Field," *Montreal Gazette*, February 7, 1970, 14.
7. "Chicago—sixth to first could be record in NHL," *Montreal Gazette*, March 31, 1970, 8.
8. *Ibid.*
9. Mark Mulvoy and Gary Ronberg, "The Desperate Hours," *Sports Illustrated*, April 6, 1970, 21.
10. Rick Cole, "An Evening with Bill White," Thehockeywriters.com, July 30, 2015.

Chapter 13

1. "Wings Lose Coach, Bow to Stars, 3–2," *Schenectady Gazette*, October 17, 1969, 6D.
2. "Orr Sets Record With 100th Point," *Pittsburgh Press*, March 16, 1970, 30.
3. Jim Nelson, "MacGregor tip gains Wings tie," *Windsor Star*, March 3, 1970, 19.

Chapter 14

1. Pat Curran, "Habs win but lose Savard," *Montreal Gazette*, March 12, 1970, 28.
2. Gary McCarthy, "Habs blow it for 13th time," *Montreal Gazette*, March 30, 1970, 18.
3. Pat Curran, "Rangers rekindle, tip Habs," *Montreal Gazette*, March 30, 1970, 17.
4. *Ibid.*
5. Pat Curran, "Big Jean can still dot it—ask Bruins," *Montreal Gazette*, April 2, 1970, 31.
6. "Detroit boosts playoff hopes," *Montreal Gazette*, April 3, 1970, 14.

Chapter 15

1. "Punch fired as Leafs ousted," *Montreal Gazette*, April 7, 1969, 21.
2. Stephen Brunt, *Searching for Bobby Orr* (Toronto: Knopf Canada, 2006), 168.
3. "Punch fired as Leafs ousted," *Montreal Gazette*, April 7, 1969, 21.
4. *Ibid.*
5. *Ibid.*
6. "Imlach fired after 11 years with Leafs," *Calgary Herald*, April 7, 1970, 10.

Chapter 16

1. Pat Curran, "Blues no long blue after victory," *Montreal Gazette*, December 31, 1969, 21.

Chapter 17

1. Bill Heufelder, "Migay Penguin Dark Horse," *Pittsburgh Press*, April 1, 1969, 32.
2. RoyMcHugh, "Happy Warrior," *Pittsburgh Press*, February 27, 1970, 31.
3. Bill Heufelder, "Shutout Puts Penguins in Second," *Pittsburgh Press*, February 27, 1970, 31.
4. *Ibid.*
5. *Ibid.*

Chapter 18

1. Spence Conley, "Seals Start Playoffs Against Penguins," *Oakland Tribune*, April 6, 1970, 29.
2. Pat Curran, "NHL coach's job to motivate not teach—Blair," *Montreal Gazette*, February 7, 1970, 14.
3. *Ibid.*
4. Michael Russo and Chris Miller, "Wren Blair, first North Stars coach, dies at 87," *Minneapolis Star Tribune* online archives, January 4, 2013.
5. *Ibid.*
6. "Leafs Burned," *Montreal Gazette*, March 2, 1970, 17.
7. Ted Blackman, "Gump Worsley fits in well with new Minnesota mates," *Montreal Gazette*, March 12, 1970, 28.
8. *Ibid.*
9. *Ibid.*
10. "One on One with Leo Boivin," *Legends of Hockey Spotlight*, Hockey Hall of Fame website, April 25, 2008.

Chapter 19

1. William Doyle, "Ice Not Only for Long, Cool Drinks," *Oakland Tribune*, July 20, 1969, 35.
2. *Ibid.*
3. *Ibid.*
4. "Buffalo Fans Jump Seal Coach," *Hayward Daily Review*, October 6, 1969, 13.
5. George Ross, "His Pitch is Catching," *Oakland Tribune*, October 10, 1969, 32.
6. Hugh McDonald, "Seals' Problem? They Don't Think," *San Mateo Times*, January 8, 1970, 25.
7. Steve Currier, *The California Golden Seals: A Tale of White Skates, Red Ink and One of the NHL's Most Outlandish Teams* (Lincoln: University of Nebraska Press, 2017), 101.
8. *Ibid.*
9. *Ibid.*
10. *Ibid.*, 105.
11. *Ibid.*, 106.
12. *Ibid.*, 105.
13. *Ibid.*, 108.

14. Spence Conley, "Flyer Coach Blasts Seals," *Oakland Tribune*, December 7, 1969, 60.

15. *Ibid.*

16. "McDonald's Ice Chips," *San Mateo Times*, April 4, 1970, 12.

Chapter 20

1. Bill Heufelder, "Pens have playoffs in their eyes," *Pittsburgh Press*, December 11, 1969, 48.

2. Pat Curran, "NHL coach's job to motivate not teach—Blair," *Montreal Gazette*, February 7, 1970, 14.

3. "Eddie Shack," *The Canadian Encyclopedia* online version.

Chapter 21

1. Ed Conrad, "Flyers Turning Road Record Ties into Big League Playoff Spot," *The Hockey News*, April 3, 1970, 9.

2. Steve Currier, *The California Golden Seals: A Tale of White Skates, Red Ink and One of the NHL's Most Outlandish Teams* (Lincoln: University of Nebraska Press, 2017), 109.

3. Pat Curran, "Backstrom gets three as Habs win 5–2," *Montreal Gazette*, February 2, 1970, 17.

Chapter 22

1. Jimmy Jordan, "Penguins and Rangers in 0–0 Standoff," *Pittsburgh Post-Gazette*, March 9, 1970, 29.

2. Reg Lansberry, *9 Goals* (Scotts Valley, CA: CreateSpace Independent Publishing Platform, 2017), 84.

Chapter 23

1. Pat Curran, "Rangers rekindle, tip Habs," *Montreal Gazette*, March 30, 1970, 17.

Chapter 24

1. Pat Curran, "NHL ratings, crowds rise," *Montreal Gazette*, April 4, 1970, 29.

2. *Ibid.*

3. *Ibid.*

Chapter 25

1. Mark Mulvoy, "Chicago! New York! Miltown!," *Sports Illustrated*, April 13, 1970, 96.

2. Pat Curran, "NHL ratings, crowds rise," *Montreal Gazette*, April 4, 1970, 29.

3. Reg Lansberry, *9 Goals* (Scotts Valley, CA: CreateSpace Independent Publishing Platform, 2017), 84.

4. Marty Knack, "Prophet Francis Calls the Shots," *Windsor Star*, April 6, 1970, 19.

5. Reg Lansberry, *9 Goals* (Scotts Valley, CA: CreateSpace Independent Publishing Platform, 2017), 121.

Chapter 26

1. Hal Bock, "Hawks Complete Surge as NHL Ends Wildest Season," *Portsmouth Times*, April 6, 1970, 14.

2. Reg Lansberry, *9 Goals* (Scotts Valley, CA: CreateSpace Independent Publishing Platform, 2017), xii.

3. Dink Carroll, "Playing the Field," *Montreal Gazette*, April 4, 1970, 30.

4. John Robertson, "NHL Tiebreaker Put to Test in 1970," *Kitchener-Waterloo Record* online archives, April 6, 1995.

5. Reg Lansberry, *9 Goals* (Scotts Valley, CA: CreateSpace Independent Publishing Platform, 2017), 143.

6. *Ibid.*

7. *Ibid.*, 153.

8. "Crozier Dislikes CBS Hockey Schedule," *Montreal Gazette*, May 12, 1970, 19.

9. Hal Bock, "Hawks Complete Surge as NHL Ends Wildest Season," *Portsmouth Times*, April 6, 1970, 14.

Chapter 27

1. "Bruins Nip Leafs, 3–1, But…," *Schenectady Gazette*, April 6, 1970, 23.

2. Reg Lansberry, *9 Goals* (Scotts Valley, CA: CreateSpace Independent Publishing Platform, 2017), 171.

3. "Un Chicago champion et des Canadiens engloutis 10–2!," *Le Devoir*, April 6, 1970, 13.

4. Reg Lansberry, *9 Goals* (Scotts Valley, CA: CreateSpace Independent Publishing Platform, 2017), 173.

5. Jacob Siskind, "Russian pianist sorry to miss hockey playoffs," *Montreal Gazette*, April 9, 1970, 18.

6. "Sock it to 'em, Seals!," *Oakland Tribune*, April 10, 1970, 18E.
7. Reg Lansberry, *9 Goals* (Scotts Valley, CA: CreateSpace Independent Publishing Platform, 2017), 181.
8. Mark Mulvoy, "Chicago! New York! Miltown!," *Sports Illustrated* April 13, 1970, 96.
9. Hal Bock, "Rangers Still Alive After Blitzing Wings," *Daytona Beach Morning Journal*, April 6, 1970, 18.

Chapter 28

1. Brian McFarlane, *The Lively World of Hockey* (New York City: Signet Books, 1968), introduction.
2. *Ibid.*
3. "Backcheck: A Hockey Retrospective," Library and Archives Canada (online), January 28, 2003.
4. Larry Stone, "100 Years ago Seattle won the Stanley Cup and expanded the reach of pro hockey," *Seattle Times* online archive, March 26, 2017.
5. Dink Carroll, "Stanley Cup playoffs minus Habs is a shocker," *Montreal Gazette*, April 7, 1970.

Chapter 29

1. "Chicago Sweeps Detroit in 4," *Pittsburgh Post-Gazette*, April 13, 1970, 23.
2. Reg Lansberry, *9 Goals* (Scotts Valley, CA: CreateSpace Independent Publishing Platform, 2017), 184.
3. "Bruins triumph 8–2 in wild melee," *Montreal Gazette*, April 10, 1970, 23.
4. Johnny Bucyk, *Hockey in My Blood* (Richmond Hill, ON: Scholastic-TAB Publications, Ltd., 1972), 71–72.
5. Derek Sanderson, *Crossing the Line* (Toronto, HarperCollins, 2012), 139.
6. "Black Hawks Beat Detroit, Win Series," *Milwaukee Journal*, April 13, 1970, Section 2, pg. 10.
7. *Ibid.*
8. "Esposito Paces Bruin 3–2 Victory," *Pittsburgh Post-Gazette*, April 15, 1970, 22.
9. "Bruins Late Rally Earns 3–2 Edge Over Rangers," *Schenectady Gazette*, April 15, 1970, 23.
10. "It was Boston's Turn, 3–2," *Montreal Gazette*, April 15, 1970, 14.
11. Hal Bock, "Orr Helps Bruins

Eliminate Rangers," *Schenectady Gazette*, April 17, 1970, 28.
12. Spence Conley, "Freak Goal Beats Seals," *Oakland Tribune*, April 9, 1970, 37.
13. Jimmy Jordan, "Penguins Nip Seals, 2–1, on Disputed Goal," *Pittsburgh Post-Gazette*, April 9, 1970, 19.
14. *Ibid.*
15. Spence Conley, "Freak Goal Beats Seals," *Oakland Tribune*, April 9, 1970, 37.
16. *Ibid.*
17. Steve Currier, *The California Golden Seals: A Tale of White Skates, Red Ink and One of the NHL's Most Outlandish Teams* (Lincoln: University of Nebraska Press, 2017), 111–112.
18. *Ibid.*, 112.
19. Jimmy Jordan, "Pens Go Two Up on Seals with 3–1 Win," *Pittsburgh Post-Gazette*, April 10, 1970, 18.
20. Ed Levitt, "Blame It on Fred," *Oakland Tribune*, April 10, 1970, F45.
21. Jimmy Jordan, "Pens Go Two Up on Seals with 3–1 Win," *Pittsburgh Post-Gazette*, April 10, 1970, 18.
22. Michael Watson, "Penguins Paste Seals for 3–0 Cup Margin," *Fremont Argus*, April 12, 1970, S1.
23. *Ibid.*
24. Hugh McDonald, "Seals Season Ends Badly" *San Mateo Times*, April 13, 1970, 20.
25. Steve Currier, *The California Golden Seals: A Tale of White Skates, Red Ink and One of the NHL's Most Outlandish Teams* (Lincoln: University of Nebraska Press, 2017), 113.
26. Jimmy Jordan, "Penguins Whip Seals, 3–2, Win Series," *Pittsburgh Post-Gazette*, April 13, 1970, 26.
27. "Penguins Win; Rookie Stars," *Milwaukee Journal*, April 13, 1970, Part 2, Pg. 10.
28. Al Abrams, "Sidelights on Sports," *Pittsburgh Post-Gazette*, April 13, 1970, 28.
29. Spence Conley, "New Tune for Old Seals," *Oakland Tribune*, April 16, 1970, 40.
30. *Ibid.*
31. Steve Currier, *The California Golden Seals: A Tale of White Skates, Red Ink and One of the NHL's Most Outlandish Teams* (Lincoln: University of Nebraska Press, 2017), 114–115.

Chapter 30

1. Ted Blackman, "Tony Esposito credits

team with record 15 shutouts," *Montreal Gazette*, April 17, 1970, 25.

2. Johnny Bucyk, *Hockey in My Blood* (Richmond Hill, ON: Scholastic-TAB Publications, Ltd., 1972), 72.

3. Pat Curran, "Boston's Phil wins Esposito battle," *Montreal Gazette*, April 20, 1970, 17.

4. *Ibid.*

5. *Ibid.*

6. *Ibid.*

7. *Ibid.*

8. *Ibid.*

9. *Ibid.*

10. Pat Curran, "Bruins wins 4–1, leading 2–0," *Montreal Gazette*, April 22, 1970, 15.

11. Pat Curran, "Bruins need just one more," *Montreal Gazette*, April 24, 1970, 29.

12. *Ibid.*

13. Gary Ronberg, "Tea Party for Boston's Bruins," *Sports Illustrated*, May 4, 1970, 18.

14. Pat Curran, "Bruins need just one more," *Montreal Gazette*, April 24, 1970, 29.

15. Pat Curran, "McKenzie Scores on Order," *Montreal Gazette*, April 27, 1970, 17.

16. "Boston Sweeps into Cup Finals," *Pittsburgh-Post Gazette*, April 27, 1970, 35.

17. Pat Curran, "McKenzie Scores on Order," *Montreal Gazette*, April 27, 1970, 17.

18. *Ibid.*

19. *Ibid.*

20. *Ibid.*

21. *Ibid.*

22. "Bruins Complete Sweep Past Black Hawks," *Schenectady Gazette*, April 27, 1970, 25.

23. Pat Curran, "McKenzie Scores on Order," *Montreal Gazette*, April 27, 1970, 17.

24. *Ibid.*

25. *Ibid.*

26. Dink Carroll, "Stanley Cup playoffs lack usual excitement," *Montreal Gazette* May 5, 1970, 16.

27. Pat Curran, "McKenzie Scores on Order," *Montreal Gazette*, April 27, 1970, 17.

Chapter 31

1. Dennis O'Neil, "Crowd Cheers Defeated Pens," *Pittsburgh Post-Gazette*, May 1, 1970,

2. Jimmy Jordan, "Blues Rip Penguins, 3–1, in Series Opener," *Pittsburgh Post-Gazette*, April 20, 1970, 24.

3. *Ibid.*

4. Jimmy Jordan, "Blues Bury Penguins Early, Triumph 4–1," *Pittsburgh Post-Gazette*, April 22, 1970, 22.

5. *Ibid.*

6. "Penguins nip Blues, 3–2," *Montreal Gazette*, April 24, 1970, 29.

7. Jimmy Jordan, "Nip Blues 2–1, for 2–2 Set," *Pittsburgh Post-Gazette*, April 27, 1970, 34.

8. *Ibid.*

9. *Ibid.*

10. "Frank's 'Hat' Beats Penguins," *Montreal Gazette*, April 29, 1970, 13.

11. Dennis O'Neil, "Crowd Cheers Defeated Pens," *Pittsburgh Post-Gazette*, May 1, 1970, 22.

12. *Ibid.*

13. *Ibid.*

14. *Ibid.*

15. *Ibid.*

16. "St. Louis hoping third time is lucky," *Montreal Gazette*, May 2, 1970, 41.

17. *Ibid.*

Chapter 32

1. Johnny Bucyk, *Hockey in My Blood* (Richmond Hill, ON: Scholastic-TAB Publications, Ltd., 1972), 33.

2. *Ibid.*, 9.

3. Ted Blackman, "Bowman will have to try something different now," *Montreal Gazette*, May 4, 1970, 18.

4. *Ibid.*

5. *Ibid.*

6. John Robertson, "Bobby Orr was shadowed in '70 Cup finals," *Kitchener-Waterloo Record* online archives, May 9, 1996.

7. *Ibid.*

8. "Plante injury helped Bruins," *Montreal Gazette*, May 4, 1970, 17.

9. *Ibid.*

10. Bill Mazer, *NHL Game of the Week*, CBS Television, May 3, 1970.

11. Bill Heufelder, "Bruins Batter Blues in NHL," *Pittsburgh Press*, May 4, 1970, 36.

12. "Plante injury helped Bruins," *Montreal Gazette*, May 4, 1970, 17.

13. Bill Heufelder, "Bruins Batter Blues in NHL," *Pittsburgh Press*, May 4, 1970, 36.

14. Dink Carroll, "Stanley Cup playoffs

lack usual excitement," *Montreal Gazette,* May 5, 1970, 16.

15. Bill Heufelder, "Bruins Batter Blues in NHL," *Pittsburgh Press,* May 4, 1970, 36.

16. *Ibid.,* 37.

Chapter 33

1. Andrew Podnieks, *The Goal* (Chicago: Triumph Books, 2003), 27.

2. "Bruins continue Cup rush," *Montreal Gazette,* May 6, 1970, 10.

3. *Ibid.*

4. *Ibid.*

5. John Robertson, "Bobby Orr was shadowed in '70 Cup finals," *Kitchener-Waterloo Record* online archives, May 9, 1996.

6. "Bruins continue Cup rush," *Montreal Gazette,* May 6, 1970, 10.

7. *Ibid.*

8. *Ibid.*

Chapter 34

1. "Bruins only one win away," *Montreal Gazette,* May 8, 1970, 17.

2. "Bruins eye playoff cash," *Montreal Gazette,* May 8, 1970, 17.

3. "Time, Bruins Overtake Goalie Hall, Blues, 4–1," *Pittsburgh Press,* May 8, 1970, 36.

4. "Bruins eye playoff cash," *Montreal Gazette,* May 8, 1970, 17.

5. "Bruins only one win away," *Montreal Gazette,* May 8, 1970, 17.

6. "Time, Bruins Overtake Goalie Hall, Blues, 4–1," *Pittsburgh Press,* May 8, 1970, 36.

7. "Bruins only one win away," *Montreal Gazette,* May 8, 1970, 17.

8. "Time, Bruins Overtake Goalie Hall, Blues, 4–1," *Pittsburgh Press,* May 8, 1970, 36.

9. *Ibid.*

10. "Bruins eye playoff cash," *Montreal Gazette,* May 8, 1970, 17.

11. *Ibid.*

12. Jack Dulmage, "Bruins best despite Hall, 4–1," *Windsor Star,* May 8, 1970, 31.

13. *Ibid.*

Chapter 35

1. "Bruins' Orr Wins Three Loop Awards," *Pittsburgh Post-Gazette,* May 9, 1970, 9.

2. "First Annual Bobby Orr Awards Luncheon," *Montreal Gazette,* May 9, 1970, 17.

3. "Bruins' Orr Wins Three Loop Awards," *Pittsburgh Post-Gazette,* May 9, 1970, 9.

4. "First Annual Bobby Orr Awards Luncheon," *Montreal Gazette,* May 9, 1970, 17.

5. "Bruins' Orr Wins Three Loop Awards," *Pittsburgh Post-Gazette,* May 9, 1970, 9.

6. "Pit Martin," *Legends of Hockey,* Hockey Hall of Fame website, 1997.

Chapter 36

1. "Good Grief! It Ends Sunday" *Montreal Gazette,* May 9, 1970, 13.

2. *Ibid.*

3. *Ibid.*

4. *Ibid.*

5. *Ibid.*

6. *Ibid.*

7. Dink Carroll, "Playing the Field," *Montreal Gazette,* May 9, 1970, 15.

8. *Ibid.*

9. *Ibid.*

10. Pat Curran, "NHL coach's job to motivate not teach—Blair," *Montreal Gazette,* February 7, 1970, 14.

Chapter 37

1. "Memories: Orr scores in overtime to win Stanley Cup," NHL YouTube Channel, May 10, 2017.

2. Bill Mazer, *NHL Game of the Week,* CBS Television, May 10, 1970.

3. "Best of Bobby Orr," YouTube, May 10, 2017.

4. Jimmy Jordan, "Bruins Win in Sudden Death," *Pittsburgh Post-Gazette,* May 11, 1970, 24.

5. "Memories: Orr scores in overtime to win Stanley Cup," NHL YouTube Channel, May 10, 2017.

6. Andrew Podnieks, *The Goal* (Chicago: Triumph Books, 2003), 17.

7. *Ibid.,* 35.

8. *Ibid.,* 21.

9. Dan Kelly, *NHL Game of the Week,* CBS Television, May 10, 1970.

10. *Ibid.*

11. Andrew Podnieks, *The Goal* (Chicago: Triumph Books, 2003), 35.

12. Fred Cusick, WSBK radio broadcast of Game #4 of the 1970 Stanley Cup finals, May 10, 1970.

13. Andrew Podnieks, *The Goal* (Chicago: Triumph Books, 2003), 3.

14. Jimmy Jordan, "Bruins Win in Sudden Death," *Pittsburgh Post-Gazette*, May 11, 1970, 24.

15. Dan Kelly, *NHL Game of the Week*, CBS Television, May 10, 1970.

16. Jimmy Jordan, "Bruins Win in Sudden Death," *Pittsburgh Post-Gazette*, May 11, 1970, 24.

17. Harry Sinden, "No Room at the Top for Me," *Sports Illustrated* online archive, October 19, 1970.

18. *Globe & Mail*, May 11, 1970.

19. Andrew Podnieks, *The Goal* (Chicago: Triumph Books, 2003), 17.

20. *Ibid.*

21. "Smythe Trophy Fourth Win for Bobby Orr," *Montreal Gazette*, May 12, 1970, 14.

22. *Ibid.*

23. Bud Collins, "Bruins Lock Out 'Chicago Six,'" *Boston Globe*, April 24, 1970, 29.

Chapter 38

1. "Bobby Orr's Cup-winning goal in 1970 remains top NHL moment," ESPN.com, December 25, 2017.

2. Andrew Podnieks, *The Goal* (Chicago: Triumph Books, 2003), 15.

3. *Ibid.*

4. "Pat Summerall," Wikipedia biography.

5. Andrew Podnieks, *The Goal* (Chicago: Triumph Books, 2003), 13.

6. *Ibid.*

7. *Ibid.*, 37.

8. *Ibid.* 17.

9. *Ibid.*, 7.

10. *Ibid.*, 31.

11. *Ibid.*

12. *Ibid.*

13. Stephen Brunt. *Searching for Bobby Orr* (Toronto: Knopf Canada, 2006), 213–214.

Chapter 39

1. Andrew Podnieks, *The Goal* (Chicago: Triumph Books, 2003), 29.

2. Andy Brickley, "Boston Bruins Honor 1970 Stanley Cup Team—The Ceremony," YouTube video, March 20, 2010.

3. Bobby Orr, *Bobby: My Story in Pictures* (China: Viking Books, 2018), 84.

4. Derek Sanderson, *Crossing the Line* (Toronto, HarperCollins, 2012), 144.

5. Stephen Brunt. *Searching for Bobby Orr* (Toronto: Knopf Canada, 2006), 219.

Chapter 40

1. Steve Currier, *The California Golden Seals: A Tale of White Skates, Red Ink and One of the NHL's Most Outlandish Teams* (Lincoln: University of Nebraska Press, 2017), 113.

2. Roy McHugh, "Briere's Magic," *Pittsburgh Press*, April 14, 1971, 65.

3. *Ibid.*

4. *Ibid.*

5. *Ibid.*

6. Dink Carroll, "Playing the Field," *Montreal Gazette*, February 7, 1970, 14.

7. Roy McHugh, "Briere's Magic," *Pittsburgh Press*, April 14, 1971, 65.

8. Ted Blackman, "Briere's Pittsburgh pal 'shook up' by accident," *Montreal Gazette*, May 18, 1970, 13.

9. *Ibid.*

10. *Ibid.*

11. *Ibid.*

12. "Briere finally loses fight for life," *Calgary Herald*, April 14, 1971, 47.

13. "Death Ends Vigil Over Pens' Briere," *Pittsburgh Press*, April 14, 1971, 65.

14. "Penguin Rookie Star Michel Briere Dies," *Pittsburgh Post-Gazette*, April 14, 1971, 23.

15. Joe Pelletier, "Michel Briere," Greatest Hockey Legends.com, December 19, 2006.

Chapter 41

1. Pat Curran, "More Praise from Sinden," *Montreal Gazette*, April 28, 1970, 19.

2. Bob Mellor, "Those strange motives," *Ottawa Citizen*, May 19, 1970, 19.

3. "Guessing Game Starts on Sinden Successor," *Lewiston Daily Sun*, May 16, 1970, 13

4. Harry Sinden, "No Room at the Top for Me," *Sports Illustrated* online archive, October 19, 1970.

5. *Ibid.*
6. *Ibid.*
7. *Ibid.*
8. "Guessing Game Starts on Sinden Successor," *Lewiston Daily Sun*, May 16, 1970, 13.

Chapter 42

1. Ronald Goldstein, "Ron Stewart, Star of Maple Leaf Champs, Dies at 79," *New York Times* online archives, March 28, 2012.
2. Reg Lansberry, *9 Goals* (Scotts Valley, CA: CreateSpace Independent Publishing Platform, 2017), 35.
3. Ronald Goldstein, "Ron Stewart, Star of Maple Leaf Champs, Dies at 79," *New York Times* online archives, March 28, 2012.
4. "May Charge Stewart in Sawchuk Death," *Montreal Gazette*, June 1, 1970, 17.
5. George Grimm, "Retro Rangers: The Sawchuk Tragedy," Insidehockey.com, February 13, 2013.
6. Ronald Goldstein, "Ron Stewart, Star of Maple Leaf Champs, Dies at 79," *New York Times* online archives, March 28, 2012.
7. "Legends of Hockey: Terry Sawchuk," YouTube video, June 9, 2012.
8. Ronald Goldstein, "Ron Stewart, Star of Maple Leaf Champs, Dies at 79," *New York Times* online archives, March 28, 2012.

Chapter 44

1. Reg Lansberry, *9 Goals* (Scotts Valley, CA: CreateSpace Independent Publishing Platform, 2017), 186.
2. Bill Libby, "Hockey Ad Lib: Thoughts on a Season…," *The Hockey News*, April 24, 1970, 8.

Chapter 46

1. Brian McFarlane, *The Lively World of Hockey*. (New York: Signet Books, 1968), 171.

2. Steve Currier, "Finley's White Skates," goldensealshockey.com.
3. Steve Currier, *The California Golden Seals: A Tale of White Skates, Red Ink and One of the NHL's Most Outlandish Teams* (Lincoln: University of Nebraska Press, 2017), 126.
4. Ross McKeon, "Seals, the Bay Area's first NHL team, had more fun than success," *San Francisco Chronicle* online archives, January 4, 2017.
5. Steve Currier, "Finley's White Skates," goldensealshockey.com.
6. Steve Currier, *The California Golden Seals: A Tale of White Skates, Red Ink and One of the NHL's Most Outlandish Teams* (Lincoln: University of Nebraska Press, 2017), 309.
7. *Ibid.*, book jacket.
8. *Ibid.*, 30.
9. *Ibid.*, 68.
10. *Ibid.*, 309.
11. *Ibid.*, 360.
12. "Stars go south in finale," *Pittsburgh Post-Gazette*, April 14, 1993, D7.
13. Francis Rosa, "Bruins Come Out Smoking, Send Blues Sprawling, 7–2," *Boston Globe*, October 25, 1978, 61.
14. Al Abrams, "Defeat is Sadness, Victory so Sweet," *Pittsburgh Post-Gazette*, April 28, 1975, 20.
15. E.M. Swift, "Woe, Canada," *Sports Illustrated*, August 22, 1988, 22.

Aftermath

1. "Don Cherry's Grapevine" (podcast), Episode #6, December 16, 2019.
2. "Campbell hailed for leadership, dedication to NHL," *Montreal Gazette*, June 26, 1984, C1.
3. *Ibid.*
4. Brian McFarlane, *The Lively World of Hockey*. (New York: Signet Books, 1968), 170.

References

Books

Beddoes, Dick, Stan Fischler, and Ira Gitler. *Hockey! The Story of the World's Fastest Sport.* The MacMillan Company, New York, 1971.

Brunt, Stephen. *Searching for Bobby Orr.* Knopf Canada, Toronto, 2006.

Bucyk, Johnny. *Hockey in My Blood.* Scholastic-TAB Publications, Ltd., Richmond Hill, ON, 1972.

Currier, Steve. *The California Golden Seals: A Tale of White Skates, Red Ink and One of the NHL's Most Outlandish Teams.* University of Nebraska Press, Lincoln, 2017.

Diamond, Dan. *The Ultimate Prize: The Stanley Cup.* Andrews McMeel Publishing, Kansas City, MO, 2003.

Duff, Bob. *The First Season: 1917–18 and the Birth of the NHL.* Biblioasis, Windsor, OR, 2017.

Esposito, Phil, and Peter Golenbock. *Phil Esposito: Thunder and Lightning.* Triumph Books, New York, 2003.

Gilbert, Rod, and Brad Park. *Playing Hockey the Professional Way.* HarperCollins, New York, 1972.

Irvin, Dick. *In the Crease: Goaltenders Look at Life in the NHL.* McLelland & Stewart, Toronto, 1995.

Kalman, Matt. *100 Things Bruins Fans Should Know & Do Before They Die.* Triumph Books, Chicago, 2011.

Keene, Kerry. *Tales from the Boston Bruins Locker Room,* Sports Publishing, New York, 2011.

Kiczek, Gene. *High Sticks and Hat-Tricks: A History of Hockey in Cleveland.* Blue House: Euclid, OH, 1996.

Lansberry, Reg. *9 Goals.* CreateSpace Independent Publishing Platform, Scotts Valley, CA, 2017.

Maguire, Liam. *Next Goal Wins.* Random House Canada, 2012.

Mahovlich, Ted. *The Big M: The Frank Mahovlich Story.* HarperCollins Publishers Ltd., Toronto, 1999.

McFarlane, Brian. *The Lively World of Hockey.* Signet Books, New York, 1968.

Orr, Bobby. *Bobby: My Story in Pictures.* Viking Books, China, 2018.

Park, Brad (with Stan Fischler). *Play the Man.* Dodd, Mead & Co., New York, 1971.

Pincus, Arthur. *The Official Illustrated NHL History.* Carlton Books, Montreal, 2018.

Podnieks, Andrew. *The Goal.* Triumph Books, Chicago, 2003.

Raider, Adam. *Frozen in Time: A Minnesota North Stars History.* University of Nebraska Press, Lincoln, 2014.

Sanderson, Derek. *Crossing the Line.* HarperCollins ebooks, 2012.

Sears, Thom, and Brad Park. *Straight Shooter: The Brad Park Story.* John Wiley & Sons Canada, Ltd., Mississauga, ON, 2012.

Zweig, Eric. *Stanley Cup: The Complete History.* Firefly Books, Richmond Hill, ON, 2018.

Newspapers

Boston Globe
Calgary Herald
Chicago Tribune
Daytona Beach Morning Journal
Le Devoir
Dubuque Telegraph-Herald
Edmonton Journal
Elyria Chronicle-Telegram
Fremont Argus
Hayward Daily Review
Kitchener-Waterloo Record

Lewiston Daily Sun
Los Angeles Times
Milwaukee Journal
Milwaukee Sentinel
Minneapolis Star Tribune
Montreal Gazette
New York Times
Newburgh Evening News
Oakland Tribune
Ottawa Citizen
Ottawa Journal
Pittsburgh Post-Gazette
Pittsburgh Press
Portsmouth Times
Regina Leader-Post
Rochester Sentinel
San Francisco Chronicle
San Jose Mercury News
San Mateo Times
Schenectady Gazette
Seattle Times

The Sporting News
(Toronto) Globe & Mail
Toronto Star
Vancouver Sun
Windsor Star

Online Resources

Bobbyorr.com
Brittanica.com
Goldensealshockey.com
Hhof.com
Hockey-reference.com
Hockeydb.com
NHL.com
NHLofficials.com
Si.com
Thehockeynews.com
Youtube.com

Index

Abel, Sid 89, 133, 138, 139, 141, 144, 238, 243
Abrams, Al 19, 23, 173, 253–254
Abrams, Roger I. 34, 35
Adams, John 241
Albert, Marv 147
Allen, Keith 23
Allen, Sarah Addison 1
American Hockey League 35, 40, 48, 80, 103, 104, 108, 111, 235
Anderson, Tommy 204
Angotti, Lou 25, 159, 183
Arbour, Al 101, 169, 203
Armour, Mark 248
Armstrong, George 99
Armstrong, Neil 54
Ashley, John 163, 201
Atlanta Flames 215, 238
Awrey, Don 161, 201, 211, 214

Backstrom, Ralph 92, 120
Ballard, Harold 40, 256–257
Balon, Dave 18, 78, 140, 142, 149, 163, 164
Barkley, Doug 244
Barlow, Bob 168, 169
Barwell, Thomas 53
Bathgate, Andy 44, 74, 193
Bauer, Bobby 145, 241
Baun, Bob 142
The Beatles 49, 66
Beaudoin, Michele 226
Béchard, Claude 57
Beddoes, Dick 24, 25, 26, 28, 192
Béliveau, Jean 26, 30, 78, 94, 117, 148, 150, 195, 205
Berenson, (Gordon) Red 58, 168, 169, 183, 187, 207, 209, 211
Bergman, Gary 139, 140
Bertrand, Dr. Claude 226
Bestor, Bob 61
Binkley, Les 42, 104, 121, 171, 172, 184
Birmingham Bulls (WHA team) 88
Blackman, Ted 81, 91, 92, 108, 227
Blair, Wren 21, 22, 65, 106–107, 108, 207, 214, 229, 254

Blake, Rob 257
Blue Angels (cheerleading troupe) 253
Bock, Hal 136, 147, 152, 166
Bodendistel, Ken 35, 37
Boe, Douglas 23
Boivin, Leo 108
Boldirev, Ivan 241
Boudrias, André 23, 185, 186
Bower, Johnny 42, 48–49, 98, 99
Bowman, Scotty 57, 59, 60, 75, 101, 102, 156, 191, 192–193, 196, 197, 200, 203, 211, 225, 244
Bowman Morey, Patricia Ann 52
Boyer, Wally 170, 171
Brewer, Carl 59, 124, 141, 143
Brickley, Andy 222
Brière, Michel 104, 172, 173, 183, 184, 185, 187, 224–228, 229, 253
Broderick, Ken 107
Brodeur, Martin 233
Brooklyn Americans (NHL team) 12, 176
Brown, Arnie 74, 139, 140, 142
Brunt, Stephen 63, 64
Bucyk, Johnny 59, 68, 69, 162, 167, 176, 177, 178–179, 190–191, 193, 194, 199, 201, 210, 214, 215, 218
Buffalo Bisons (minor league team) 40, 80
Buffalo Sabres 160, 218, 237, 246
Buffey, Vern 93, 163
Burnett, Carol 144
Burns, Charlie 106, 107–108, 169
Bush, Walter, Jr. 22
Butler, Ed 120

Cahan, Larry 21, 23
Cahn, William 233
Campbell, Bryan 84, 180
Campbell, Clarence 12, 16, 29, 30, 37, 38, 39, 53, 54, 55, 57, 107, 129, 130, 213–214, 237, 238, 239, 246, 248, 256–257
Carleton, Wayne 166, 194, 210, 211
Caron, Alain (Boom Boom) 18
Carroll, Austin (Dink) 6, 64, 84–85, 138, 156–157, 164, 181, 196, 207, 225
Carson, Ken 228

Cashman, Wayne 18, 68, 165, 166, 195, 200, 202, 215
Cenacle's Image (racehorse) 201–202
Central Professional Hockey League 17
Cerf, Bennett 44
Cheevers, Gerry 67, 69, 145, 161, 165, 165, 177, 178, 179, 181, 193, 195, 198, 199, 201, 202, 207, 210, 215
Cherry, Don 256
Cherry, Rose 256
Cherry, Tim 256
CHUM-AM (Toronto radio station) 118
Claflin, Larry 207
Clark, Mike 23
Clarke, Bobby 57, 123, 247
"Clear the Track, Here Comes Shack" (song) 118
Cleveland Barons (minor league team) 13, 112, 171
Cleveland Barons (NHL team) 249–251
Clifford, Nancy 68–69
Cole, Stephen 118
Collins, Billy 169
Collins, Bud 215
Collins, John 7
Compton, Dick 23
Conacher, Brian 68
Conley, Spence 106, 114, 170, 173
Connelly, Wayne 21, 159
Conway, Russ 191
Cooke, Jack Kent 26, 53–55
Cormier, Ernie 219
Cosmopolitan (periodical) 71
Cote, Dan 252
Cournoyer, Yvan 92, 148, 150
Cox, Dr. Perry 86
Craine, Joe 232
Cranston, Lamont 196
Creasy, William (Bill) 61–62, 110
Crisp, Terry 168, 209, 223
Crosby, Bing 13
Crozier, Roger 29, 90, 138–139, 140, 141, 142, 143, 144, 160, 205
Cullen, Ray 125, 168
Curran, Pat 18, 27, 28–29, 56, 58, 93,102, 106–107, 117, 129, 143, 177, 179, 180, 229
Currier, Steve 18, 110, 113, 119–120, 250
Cusick, Fred 212

Daley, Thomas 104
Dallas Black Hawks (minor league team) 35
Dallas Stars 252
Daly, John 44
D'Amico, John 182
Davidson, Murray 231
Davis, David 216
DeBartolo, Edward J. 254
DeJordy, Denis 84, 120
Delvecchio, Alex 51, 88, 95, 140, 141
Denver Spurs (minor league team) 18

Desjardins, Gerry 81, 84, 117
Dionne, Marcel 254
Dorey, Jim 107
Dornhoefer, Gary 121
Douglas Rankine and the Secrets (musical group) 118
Doyle, William 111
Dryden, Ken 42
Dulmage, Jack 203
Dumart, Woody 145
Dunnell, Milt 88

Eastern Hockey League 98
Ecclestone, Tim 18, 169, 186, 187, 193, 197, 209, 211
Edwards, Marv 42, 99, 145–146
Edwards, Roy 90, 138–139, 145, 160
Egers, Jack 133,140, 141, 161, 165
Ego, Ron 222
Ehman, Gary 170
Eilodeau, Renald 226
Eldred, Pamela 88
Ellis, Ron 60, 99
Erickson, Grant 92
Esposito, Phil 37, 63, 66–67, 81, 83, 90, 132, 149, 161, 164, 165, 176, 177, 178, 179, 181, 191, 193, 194, 195, 198, 199, 201, 202, 203, 206, 208, 210, 214, 215, 218, 230, 242, 243
Esposito, Tony 57, 59, 81–83, 149, 158–159, 176, 177, 179, 181, 205, 242

Fairbairn, Bill 78, 205
Favell, Doug 17, 246, 247
Fedorov, Sergei 257
Felt, Irving 136
Ferguson, John 92–93, 147–148
Finley, Charles O. 247–248
Fisher, Red 45, 67
Fitzgerald, Tom 30
Flaherty, Peter F. 170
Fleming, Reggie 74
Fonteyne, Val 172
Forman, Stanley 66
Forristal, John (Frosty) 69
Fortin, Yvon 226
Francis, Bobby 149–150
Francis, Em 147
Francis, Emile 54–55, 71, 73–77, 125, 126–128, 133, 134, 135, 138, 139, 143, 147, 149–150, 151, 161, 163, 165, 167, 232–235, 238, 248, 242, 243, 252
Frayne, Trent 234
Friedmann, Arthur 78
Front Page Challenge (television show) 66

Gadsby, Bill 89
Gallinger, Don 38
Gallivan, Danny 147, 191, 212, 256
Galt Red Wings (junior hockey team) 49
Geoffrion, Bernie 16, 18, 74, 236

Geoffrion, Linda 236
Giacomin, Ed
Gibbs, Barry 122
Giguère, J.S. 29
Giguère, Louis 257
Gilbert, Rod 11, 73, 75, 76, 77, 78, 124–125, 139, 141, 161, 163
Gilmour, Lloyd 185–186
Glover, Fred 111, 112, 113, 170–171, 172, 174
"The Goal" (statue) 220
Goldham, Bob 187–188
Goldstein, Ronald 232, 234
Goldsworthy, Bill 152, 168, 169
Goss, Dick 227
Goyette, Phil 57, 101, 168, 183, 205, 210
Gray, Terry 101, 169, 199
Green, Norm 252
Gregory, Jim 98
Gretzky, Wayne 63, 68, 86, 132, 254–255
"The Gumps" (comic strip) 45

Haberg, Roger 227
Hadfield, Vic 75–76, 77, 235
Hainsworth, George 81, 234
Hall, Glenn 17, 28–29, 42, 51, 101, 102, 168, 183, 187, 188, 197, 200, 201, 202, 203, 205, 206, 209, 210, 211, 218
Hamilton Tigers (NHL team) 72
Hamm, Jon 216
Hampson, Ted 112, 172, 247–248
Hanks, Tom 249
Harbaruk, Nick 170, 171, 172
Hardy, Joe 120
Harkness, Ned 243–244
Harris, Ron 21, 23
Harris, Ted 148
Harris, Wally 21
Hartford Whalers 159
Harvey, Doug 102
Henry, Camille 44, 101
Heufelder, Bill 104, 105, 117, 195, 202, 225–226
Hewitt, Bill 58
Hewitt, Foster 6
Hextall, Ron 29
Hicke, Bill 173
Hicke, Pat 18
Hillman, Wayne 74
History Television 48
The Hockey News (periodical) 19, 68, 79, 119, 183, 234, 238, 239
Hockey Night in Canada (television show) 1, 6, 8, 11, 14, 39, 45, 57, 58, 71, 118, 212, 248
Hodge, Charlie 42
Hodge, Ken 66, 146, 162, 177, 180, 202 203, 210, 230
Hodill, Bill 227
"Honky the Christmas Goose" (song) 49
Hood, Bruce 54, 162, 170–171, 209, 210, 212
Horton, Tim 98, 140, 161, 162, 194
Horvath, Bronco 191

Housman, A.E. 224
Howe, Gordie 58, 59, 67, 78, 86–87, 88, 89, 90, 95, 111, 133, 140, 143, 159, 160, 225
Howe, Syd 15
Howell, Harry 112
Huevos Rancheros (musical group) 47
Hull, Bobby 22, 47, 58, 59, 60, 65, 80, 81, 82, 83, 133, 148, 149, 159,160, 177, 178, 179, 180, 181, 236
Hull, Brett 252
Hull, Dennis 159, 160, 179
Hull-Ottawa Canadiens (minor league team) 20

"In Flanders Fields" (poem) 91
Imlach, George (Punch) 88, 97–99, 231
Indianapolis Capitals (minor league team) 111
Ingarfield, Earl 112, 114, 172
Irvin, Dick (Sr.) 43
Irvine, Ted 164

Jagger, Mick 54–55
Jagr, Jaromir 254
Jarrett, Doug 148
Jarrett, Gary 171
Jennings, Bill 74, 239, 243
Johnson, Richard 66
Johnson, Tom 242
Johnston, Ed 42, 67, 68, 69, 94, 163, 164
Joplin, Janis 53
Jordan, Jimmy 26, 104, 170, 171, 172–73, 182, 183, 184, 208, 213, 214
Juckes, Gordon 40

Kannegiesser, Bob 18
Kansas City Scouts 238
Karlander, Al 140
Keenan, Fred 218–219
Keenan, Larry 169, 183, 184, 187, 209, 210, 211
Kelly, Dan 1, 36, 57, 58, 140, 144, 190, 211, 212, 213
Kelly, Red 67, 103, 104, 171, 173, 182, 183, 186, 187, 188, 224, 225, 226, 227, 228, 253
Kennedy, Teeder 87
Kent State University 215
Keon, Dave 49, 99, 145, 205
Kerr, Dave 45
Klobuchar, Jim 107
Koroll, Cliff 148, 179
Kramer, Norm 58
Kurtenbach, Orland 74, 142, 165

LaGuardia, Fiorello 72
Lansberry, Reg 75, 77, 125, 126, 139, 151
Laperrière, Jacques 58
Larose, Claude 168–169
Laycoe, Hal 117
Layton, Eddie 162
Leach, Reggie 29, 247, 248
Lee, Dr. Gerald 163

Lemaire, Jacques 18, 59, 92, 242
Lemieux, Mario 68, 228, 254
Lemieux, Réal 120
Leonard, Benny 15
Lesuk, Bill 195, 198
Levitt, Ed 169, 171
Ley, Rick 146
Libby, Bill 238–239
Libett, Nick 143, 149, 159, 160
Lidström, Nicklas 257
Life (periodical) 51
Lindeland, Liv 71
Lindsay, Ted 51
Lombardi, Vince 73
Lonsberry, Ross 118
Lorentz, Jim 161
Lumley, Harry 49
Lussier, Ray 216–220

MacGregor, Bruce 90, 142, 159, 160, 243
MacLeish, Rick 247
Magnuson, Keith 70, 84, 99, 178, 179
Mahovlich, Frank 88–89, 95, 140, 141, 244
Maki, Ronald (Chico) 38–39, 41, 83, 159, 160
Maki, Wayne 34–41
Malone, Joe 25
Maniago, Cesare 107, 168
Marchand, Brad 71
Marcotte, Don 161, 179, 192
Maris, Roger 207
Marotte, Gilles 66, 84
Marshall, Bert 170, 172
Marshall, Don 76
Martin, Hubert (Pit) 11, 66, 81, 83, 148, 149, 159, 205
Maruk, Dennis 249
Masterton, Bill 20–23, 205
Masterton, Carol 22
Mattiussi, Dick 23
Mazer, Bill 140–141, 194, 208
McCallum, Dunc 171
McCarthy, Gary 93
McCrae, John 91
McCreary, Bill 101, 185, 186, 187
McCreary, Keith 185
McDevitt, Bob 39
McDonald, Ab 101, 168, 169, 183
McDonald, Hugh 113, 174
McFarlane, Brian 8, 9, 29, 45, 118, 154, 246
McHugh, Roy 225
McKechnie, Walt 247
McKenzie, Johnny 34, 59, 146, 161–162, 166, 167, 177, 180, 194, 201, 210, 222
McLellan, Johnny 98
McNall, Bruce 254
McNeil, Gerry 43
Meehan, Gerry 246
Mellor, Bob 229
Mengard, Al 58
Messier, Mark 41

Mickelson, Jo Lane 61–62
Mickey, Larry 93
Middleton, Rick 71
Mikita, Stan 81, 159, 160, 178, 180, 195, 198, 204
Minnesota Wild 252
Mohns, Doug 84
Moncur, Dr. Ashby 37
Montreal Jr. Canadiens (junior hockey team) 151
Morenz, Howie 192, 236
Morrison, Jim 172
Morrison, Scotty 37, 163
Mulvoy, Mark 70, 152
Murray, Jim 13, 248
Myre, Phil 46

Namath, Joe 70, 73
Nashville Dixie Flyers (minor league team) 98
Nesterenko, Eric 9, 149, 159
Nevin, Bob 74, 78, 79, 93, 135, 142
New York Americans (NHL team) 14–15, 24, 72
New York Islanders 231, 238, 248, 251, 253
NHL Game of the Week (television show) 1, 90, 111, 129, 135, 141, 144, 160, 164, 167, 176, 179, 190, 213, 257
Nolet, Simon 120
Norris, Bruce A. 89
Norris, Jack 66
Norris, Willard 54

O'Donoghue, Don 120
O'Hara, Dave 161, 165, 166
Oklahoma City Blazers (minor league team) 241
Olmstead, Bert 18, 111, 112
O'Neil, Dennis 187–188
O'Shea, Danny 58, 168
Orlando, Jimmy 38
Orr, Arva 217
Orr, Bobby 16, 34, 36–37, 41, 59, 63–70, 90, 94, 112, 132, 146, 161, 164, 165, 166, 167, 176, 177, 178, 179, 192–193, 194, 196, 197–198, 201, 202, 204–205, 208, 210, 211–212, 214, 215, 216–220, 222, 223, 224, 242, 244, 253
Orr, Doug 217–218
Orr, Elsie 223
Oshawa Generals (junior hockey team) 65
Ost, Edwin 136
Ottawa Senators (original NHL team) 15, 175

Pacific Coast Hockey Association 155
Paice, Frank 127
Pappin, Jim 148, 159, 160
Parent, Bernie 17, 58, 120, 121, 122, 245
Parisé, Jean-Paul 58, 168, 169
Park, Brad 65, 124, 125, 141, 166, 243
Pavelich, Matt 57

Pearson, Lester 14
Pelletier, Joe 228
Pelyk, Mike 146
Perreault, Gilbert 151
Perreault, Reauld 226
Philadelphia Quakers (NHL team) 15
Picard, Noel 101, 195, 198, 209, 211, 212, 215, 217, 218, 225
Pilous, Rudy 18
Pinder, Gerry 149
Pittsburgh Hornets (minor league team) 26, 183
Pittsburgh Pirates (NHL team) 14–15
Plager, Barclay 121, 194, 197
Plager, Bob 18, 198, 209, 210, 225
Plante, Jacques 6, 42–45, 58, 168, 184, 186–187, 193–194, 197, 200, 245
Plante, Thérèse 43
Playboy (periodical) 71
Podnieks, Andrew 216, 219
Poile, Bud 25
Pollock, Sam 16, 83, 94, 141, 150
Polonic, Tom 168
Porter, John 247
Positive Coaching Alliance 126
Pratt, Babe 204
Prentice, Dean 58, 59, 104, 172, 184
Pronovost, Jean 104, 170, 172, 184, 185, 225
Pronovost, Marcel 11
Providence Reds (minor league team) 77
Putnam, William (Bill) 16

Quebec Aces (minor league team) 25
Quebec Major Junior Hockey League 228

Ralston Purina 252
Ratelle, Jean 11, 77, 78, 141, 143, 164, 165, 243
Reay, Billy 80–81, 85, 149, 165, 177, 178, 181
Redmond, Mickey 92, 244
Reid, Tom 107
Resch, Glenn (Chico) 253
Richard, Henri 128, 242
Richard, Maurice 7, 87, 111, 195
Rickard, Tex 72
Riis, Nelson 255
Riley, Jack 105
Rivard, Fern 107
Roberts, Jim 121, 169, 185–186, 192–193, 194, 196, 197–198, 210
Rolfe, Dale 139, 144, 243
Rolling Stones (musical group) 53–55
Rombach, Jerry 251
Ronberg, Gary 68, 70, 72, 73, 124, 178
Rosa, Francis 253
Rosen, Dan 63
Ross, George 112
Rousseau, Bobby 93
Ruel, Claude 46, 57, 58, 59, 60, 93, 108, 133, 147, 149, 150
Rupp, Duane 185, 187

Ruth, Babe 207
Rutledge, Wayne 117

Sabourin, Gary 18, 168, 169, 183, 186, 209, 210, 223
St. Louis Braves (minor league team) 35
St. Louis Eagles (NHL team) 15
St. Marseille, Frank 58, 183, 186, 199, 201, 209
Salomon, Stanley 28
Salt Lake Golden Eagles (minor league team) 108
San Francisco Seals (minor league team) 108
San Jose Sharks 251
Sanderson, Derek 35, 70–71, 97, 131, 146, 161, 162, 163, 164, 166, 167, 177, 178, 194, 199, 207, 208, 209, 210, 211, 212, 220, 222
Sarrazin, Dick 49
Sather, Glenn 170, 171, 186
Savard, Serge 18, 28, 93, 205
Sawchuk, Terry 17, 42, 48, 49–52, 105, 161, 165–166, 232–235
Schinkel, Ken 104 172, 183
Schmidt, Milt 37, 64, 97–98, 145, 181, 205, 223, 230, 231, 241
Schulz, Charles M. 249
Seattle Metropolitans (PCHA team) 155, 156
Seiling, Rod 18, 74, 139–140
Selke, Frank, Jr. 173–174, 248
Shack, Eddie 117–118
Shawinigan Bruins (junior hockey team) 224
Sheehan, Bobby 249
Shetler, Pat 107, 182
Shore, Eddie 64, 204
Siebert, Babe 204
Simmer, Charlie 249
Simmons, Gary 250
Sinclair, Gordon 66
Sinden, Harry 94, 98, 132, 161,164, 177, 178, 180–181, 193, 195, 202, 209, 210–211, 213, 214, 215, 218, 229–231, 242
Six-Day War 16
Skov, Art 57
Slobodyanik, Alexander 150–151
Smith, Al 104, 105, 125, 184, 185, 186, 187
Smith, Dallas 199, 201, 210
Smith, Des 176
Smith, Gary 113, 170, 171, 172 173–174
Smith, Kate 121
Smith, Rick 179, 198, 209
Smith, Sidney 45
Smythe, Stafford 97–98
Sons of Freedom (musical group) 47
Speer, Bill 70–71, 202
Sport (periodical) 36
Sports Illustrated (periodical) 68, 70, 72, 73, 77, 79, 84, 99, 124, 152, 178, 215, 230
The Sports Network 23
Stanfield, Fred 66, 179, 180, 193, 198, 200, 201, 210, 230
Stanfield, Jim 85

Stanley (of Preston), Lord 154–155
Stasiuk, Vic 114, 119–120
Stemkowski, Peter 90, 133, 140, 142, 143, 144, 159, 243
Stewart, Gaye 38
Stewart, Ron 142, 232–235
Stirling Homex Corporation 230, 231
Sullivan, George (Red) 74, 103, 104
Summerall, Pat 218
Swig, Mel 249, 250

Tadevich, Steve 247
Talbot, Jean-Guy 101, 183, 185, 192, 211, 218
"Talk to the Animals" (song) 162
Tate, Harold J. 24
Tator, Dr. Charles 21
Taylor, Billy 38
Thompson, Paul 61–62
Tkaczuk, Walter 59, 73, 78, 93, 127, 140, 164
Toppazzini, Jerry 212
Torrey, Bill 248
Tulsa Oilers (minor league team) 98
Tuner, Tina 53

Unger, Garry 90, 139, 141
University of Alberta 238
University of Denver 20, 23, 84

Vachon, Rogatien (Rogie) 29, 46, 82, 133, 149
Vadnais, Carol 112, 171, 172–173
Vancouver Canucks (minor league team) 46
Vancouver Canucks (NHL team) 40, 89, 237
Van Gerbig, Barry 250
Vasco, Elmer (Moose) 108
Verdi, Bob 150
Victoria, Queen 154
Villemure, Gilles 243

Wakely, Ernie 101, 121, 185, 194, 197, 198, 199, 200
Walker, Hal 38
Washington Capitals 238
Watson, Michael 172
WBEN-TV (television station) 1
WBZ (radio station) 212
Weakerthans, The (musical group) 47
Weber, Harry 220
Weekend (CBC television program) 39
Western Hockey League (professional) 13, 17, 18, 46, 74, 108
Westfall, Ed 161, 162, 166, 178, 179, 180, 192, 198–199, 210, 211, 214
What's My Line? (CBS television program) 44, 66
"When the Saints Go Marching In" (song) 28
Whitby Dunlops (amateur team) 231
White, Bill 57, 84, 159, 178
White, Kevin 207, 222
White, Vanna 255
Williams, Tommy 11, 169
Wirtz, William (Bill) 257
Wolman, Jerry 16
Wood, Margaret Louise (Peggy) 223
Woodcock, Tom 193
World Hockey Association 23, 40, 258
World War II 63, 68, 72, 81, 204
Worsley, Lorne (Gump) 42, 45–47, 82, 106, 108, 122, 168
Woytowich, Bob 58, 60, 173
WSBK-TV (television station) 212

Yanagisawa, Dr. Kazuo 125

Zadarnowski, Andrew 12
Ziegler, John 257